DOUGLAS A. KNIGHT is Drucilla Moore Buffington Professor of Hebrew Bible and Professor of Jewish Studies at Vanderbilt University. A leading biblical scholar, he is the general editor of the Library of Ancient Israel.

D1103849

Law, Power, and Justice
in Ancient Israel

LIBRARY OF ANCIENT ISRAEL

Douglas A. Knight, *General Editor*

Other books in the Library of Ancient Israel series

Sage, Priest, Prophet: Religious and Intellectual Leadership in Ancient Israel
Joseph Blenkinsopp

Oral World and Written Word: Ancient Israelite Literature
Susan Niditch

Scribes and Schools: The Canonization of the Hebrew Scriptures
Philip R. Davies

The Israelites in History and Tradition
Niels Peter Lemche

Reconstructing the Society of Ancient Israel
Paula M. McNutt

The Religion of Ancient Israel
Patrick D. Miller

The Politics of Ancient Israel
Norman K. Gottwald

Life in Biblical Israel
Philip J. King and Lawrence E. Stager

Law, Power, and Justice in Ancient Israel

DOUGLAS A. KNIGHT

WESTMINSTER
JOHN KNOX PRESS
LOUISVILLE · KENTUCKY

© 2011 Douglas A. Knight

First edition
Published by Westminster John Knox Press
Louisville, Kentucky

11 12 13 14 15 16 17 18 19 20—10 9 8 7 6 5 4 3 2 1

Translations from the Hebrew Bible are by the author. Any Scripture quotations from the New Revised Standard Version of the Bible are copyright © 1989 by the Division of Christian Education of the National Council of the Churches of Christ in the U.S.A. and are used by permission.

Book design by Publishers' WorkGroup
Cover design by Mark Abrams
Cover illustration © Exactostock/Superstock

Library of Congress Cataloging-in-Publication Data is on file at the Library of Congress, Washington, D.C.

ISBN 978-0-664-22144-7

PRINTED IN THE UNITED STATES OF AMERICA

♾ The paper used in this publication meets the minimum requirements of the American National Standard for Information Sciences—Permanence of Paper for Printed Library Materials, ANSI Z39.48-1992.

Westminster John Knox Press advocates the responsible use of our natural resources. The text paper of this book is made from 30% postconsumer waste.

To Catherine,

my best friend and inspiration

Contents

Foreword

The historical and literary questions preoccupying biblical scholars since the Enlightenment have focused primarily on events and leaders in ancient Israel, the practices and beliefs of Yahwistic religion, and the oral and written stages in the development of the people's literature. Considering how little was known just three centuries ago about early Israel and indeed the whole ancient Near East, the gains achieved to date have been extraordinary, due in no small part to the unanticipated discovery by archaeologists of innumerable texts and artifacts.

Recent years have witnessed a new turn in biblical studies, occasioned largely by a growing lack of confidence in the "assured results" of past generations of scholars. At the same time, an increased openness to the methods and issues of other disciplines such as anthropology, sociology, economics, linguistics, and literary criticism has allowed new questions to be posed regarding the old materials. Social history, a well-established area within the field of historical studies, has proved to be especially fruitful as a means of analyzing specific segments of the society. Instead of concentrating predominantly on national events, leading individuals, political institutions, and "high culture," social historians attend to broader and more basic issues such as social organization, living conditions in cities and villages, life stages, environmental contexts, power distribution according to class and status, and social stability and instability. To inquire into such matters regarding ancient Israel shifts the focus away from those with power and the events they instigated and onto the everyday realities and social subtleties experienced by the vast majority of the population. Such exploration has now gained new force with the application of various forms of ideological criticism and other methods designed to ferret out the political, economic, and social interests concealed in the sources.

This series represents a collaborative effort to investigate several specific topics—societal structure, politics, economics, religion, literature, material culture, law, leadership, ethnic identity, and canon formation—each in terms of its social dimensions and historical processes within ancient Israel. Some of these subjects have not been explored in depth until now; others are familiar areas currently in need of reexamination. While the sociohistorical approach provides the general perspective for most volumes of the series, each author has the latitude to determine the most appropriate means for dealing with the topic at hand. Individually and collectively, the volumes aim to expand our vision of the culture and society of ancient Israel and thereby generate new appreciation for its impact on subsequent history.

The present volume focuses on law—not so much the laws recorded in the Hebrew Bible but more the legal systems at work among the people of ancient Israel. Access to these legal processes involves drawing on archaeological findings about the living situations of various population groups in ancient Israel. This physical evidence provides new opportunities to extend the discussion beyond the scope of written texts, whether from the Hebrew Bible or from neighboring cultures. While these texts reflect and generally promote the views of those close to power, broad sections of the population are not given direct voice in this literature. This study selects three primary social and institutional contexts—villages, cities and states, and cultic settings—for closer examination. In each case the archaeological and historical evidence leads to a reconstruction of potential areas of legal conflict, which in turn suggests the kinds of adjudications needed for the social groups to remain viable. Methods at home in modern legal studies aid this effort to ferret out the plausible legal principles at work in ancient Israelite life. The result is a sociohistorical and political picture of laws not mainly as they were recorded and transmitted in biblical form but as they functioned among the people.

Douglas A. Knight
General Editor

Acknowledgments

I owe many debts from the years spent in planning, researching, and writing this book. The variety of settings in which I have taught courses on Israelite and biblical law enriched the project by offering perspectives beyond what I alone could have provided: Vanderbilt University Divinity School and Graduate Department of Religion; Doshisha University, Kyoto, Japan, where some of the seeds of this project were planted during a course I taught in the spring semester of 1997; the Chinese University of Hong Kong, where I wrote one of the chapters while teaching during the spring semester of 2004; and the Riverbend Maximum Security Prison in Nashville, where I taught the law course during the fall semester of 2006, reading the laws of ancient Southwest Asia and the Hebrew Bible with the inmates and a group of Vanderbilt students. I am especially grateful to my hosts, Professors Akira Echigoya at Doshisha and Archie Lee at CUHK, for their many acts of hospitality during my semester at their universities.

A number of friends with specializations in several areas treated in this study—archaeology, biblical studies, law, sociology, history, and medicine—have been especially helpful. Daniel Cornfield, James Gooch, Niels Peter Lemche, Don Welch, and Taylor Wray read the manuscript, and Norma Franklin, Wanda McNeil, Virginia Scott, and Gay Welch reviewed certain sections. My colleagues in biblical studies at Vanderbilt have provided a stimulating intellectual environment over the years: Annalisa Azzoni, Alice Hunt, Herbert Marbury, and Jack Sasson in Hebrew Bible, as well as Amy-Jill Levine, Daniel Patte, and Fernando Segovia in New Testament. I deeply appreciate our numerous conversations, sometimes about details of the present study. At the same time I readily take responsibility myself for any errors that survived the scrutiny of my friends and colleagues.

Two former Vanderbilt colleagues, both now deceased, have left their marks on this book as well. Howard L. Harrod encouraged my thinking in sociology, ethics, and phenomenology; his expertise in Native American studies gave us many occasions, often over our favorite martinis, to compare that field with the social situations in ancient Israel. James Barr was for me not only a model of incisive, critical thinking but also a gracious friend who took delight in conversing with his younger colleagues.

At a few places in this book the discussion draws on earlier methodological probes I made in the study of ancient Israel's laws. Excerpts from two articles appear here in revised form, and I want to acknowledge, with gratitude, the permission of their publishers or editors to use them in this context. They are "Whose Agony? Whose Ecstasy? The Politics of Deuteronomic Law," in *Shall Not the Judge of All the Earth Do What Is Right? Studies on the Nature of God in Tribute to James L. Crenshaw*, ed. David Penchansky and Paul L. Redditt (Winona Lake, IN: Eisenbrauns, 2000), 97–112, translation and expansion of "Herrens bud—elitens interesser? Lov, makt, og rettferdighet i Det gamle testamente," *Norsk teologisk tidsskrift* 97 (1996): 235–45; and "Village Law and the Book of the Covenant," in *"A Wise and Discerning Mind": Essays in Honor of Burke O. Long*, ed. Saul M. Olyan and Robert C. Culley, Brown Judaic Studies 325 (Providence, RI: Brown Judaic Studies, 2000), 163–79.

All translations from the Hebrew Bible are my own.

Jon Berquist has been as good an editor as he is a scholar, providing suggestions at significant points to strengthen the manuscript. Marianne Blickenstaff succeeded him at Westminster John Knox Press and has been enormously helpful in bringing the publication to a conclusion. I also want to take this opportunity to thank Daniel Braden, S. David Garber, and others at WJK who have helped with this book and with the series, Library of Ancient Israel. I am grateful to Jennifer Williams, graduate student at Vanderbilt University, who compiled the bibliography; and to Steve Cook and Chris Benda, both from Vanderbilt, who carefully read the manuscript.

My two children, now academics in their own right, have been sheer delights to me over the years, and they have also served as resources and sounding boards for a variety of issues in this book. Lisa I. Knight, an anthropologist specializing in South Asia, has clarified a number of anthropological topics and approaches, especially regarding the workings of gender and power in social systems. Jonathan W. Snow, a biologist specializing in genetics and immunology, has helped me to think about the importance of the scientific method for social-scientific and humanistic studies.

Throughout these years of researching and writing this book, my most supportive and most discerning reader has always been my wife, Catherine Snow. To her I owe a debt that extends to the very existence of this book. I am delighted that I can *finally* dedicate it to her.

Douglas A. Knight
Nashville, Tennessee
April 2010

Abbreviations

AASOR	Annual of the American Schools of Oriental Research
AB	Anchor Bible
ABD	*The Anchor Bible Dictionary*. Edited by D. N. Freedman. 6 vols. New York, 1992
ANET	*Ancient Near Eastern Texts Relating to the Old Testament*. Edited by J. B. Pritchard. 3rd ed. Princeton, 1969
AOAT	Alter Orient und Altes Testament
AS	Assyriological Studies
ASOR	American Schools of Oriental Research
BA	*Biblical Archaeologist*
BASOR	*Bulletin of the American Schools of Oriental Research*
BBB	Bonner biblische Beiträge
BHT	Beiträge zur historischen Theologie
BJS	Brown Judaic Studies
BM	British Museum
BMI	The Bible and Its Modern Interpreters
BN	Bibliothèque nationale, Paris
BWANT	Beiträge zur Wissenschaft vom Alten und Neuen Testament
BZAW	Beihefte zur Zeitschrift für die alttestamentliche Wissenschaft
c.	century/centuries
CANE	*Civilizations of the Ancient Near East*. Edited by J. Sasson. 4 vols. New York, 1995
CAD	*The Assyrian Dictionary of the Oriental Institute of the University of Chicago*. Chicago, 1956–
CBQ	*Catholic Biblical Quarterly*
CC	Covenant Code
CHANE	Culture and History of the Ancient Near East
CLS	Critical Legal Studies
COS	*The Context of Scripture*. Edited by W. W. Hallo. 3 vols. Leiden, 1997–2002

D	Deuteronomic source in the Pentateuch
DC	Deuteronomic Code
E	Elohistic source in the Pentateuch
EB	Early Bronze Age
esp.	especially
EvT	*Evangelische Theologie*
HC	Holiness Code
HL	Hittite Laws
IEJ	*Israel Exploration Journal*
IRT	Issues in Religion and Theology
J	Yahwistic source in the Pentateuch
JAOS	*Journal of the American Oriental Society*
JBL	*Journal of Biblical Literature*
JCS	*Journal of Cuneiform Studies*
JE	Redaction of J and E sources in the Pentateuch
JEOL	*Jaarbericht van het Vooraziatisch-Egyptisch Genootschap, Ex oriente lux*
JESHO	*Journal of the Economic and Social History of the Orient*
JNES	*Journal of Near Eastern Studies*
JSOT	*Journal for the Study of the Old Testament*
JSOTSup	Journal for the Study of the Old Testament: Supplement Series
LAI	Library of Ancient Israel
LB	Late Bronze Age
LCL	Loeb Classical Library
LE	Laws of Eshnunna
LH	Laws of Hammurabi
LHBOTS	Library of Hebrew Bible/Old Testament Studies
LL	Laws of Lipit-Ishtar
LU	Laws of Ur-Namma
LXX	The Septuagint
MAL	Middle Assyrian Laws
MB	Middle Bronze Age
MT	Masoretic Text, with versification as in NJPS
NBL	Neo-Babylonian Laws
NJPS	*Tanakh: The Holy Scriptures; The New JPS Translation according to the Traditional Hebrew Text.* Philadelphia, 1999
NRSV	New Revised Standard Version Bible
NTT	*Norsk teologisk tidsskrift*
OBO	Orbis biblicus et orientalis
OLA	Orientalia lovaniensia analecta

OTL	Old Testament Library
P	Priestly source in the Pentateuch
PC	Priestly Code
PN	personal name
PEQ	*Palestine Exploration Quarterly*
RB	*Revue biblique*
RGG	*Religion in Geschichte und Gegenwart*. 4th ed. Edited by Hans Dieter Betz et al. 8 vols. Tübingen, 1998–2007
RLA	*Reallexikon der Assyriologie und vorderasiatischen Archäologie*
SAC	Studies in Antiquity and Christianity
SBLBSNA	Society of Biblical Literature Biblical Scholarship in North America
SBLDS	Society of Biblical Literature Dissertation Series
SBLSBL	Society of Biblical Literature Studies in Biblical Literature
SBLSP	*Society of Biblical Literature Seminar Papers*
SBLSymS	Society of Biblical Literature Symposium Series
SBLWAW	Society of Biblical Literature Writings from the Ancient World
SemeiaSt	Semeia Studies
SHCANE	Studies in the History and Culture of the Ancient Near East
SJOT	*Scandinavian Journal of the Old Testament*
SLEx	Sumerian Laws Exercise Tablet
SPRTS	Scholars Press Reprints and Translations
STDJ	Studies on the Texts of the Desert of Judah
SWBA	Social World of Biblical Antiquity
TDOT	*Theological Dictionary of the Old Testament*. Edited by G. J. Botterweck, H. Ringgren, and H.-J. Fabry. Translated by J. T. Willis, G. W. Bromiley, D. E. Green, and D. W. Stott. 15 vols. Grand Rapids, 1974—
THAT	*Theologischer Handwörterbuch zum Alten Testament*. Edited by E. Jenni, with assistance from C. Westermann. 2 vols. Munich, 1971–1976
ThWAT	*Theologisches Wörterbuch zum Alten Testament*. Edited by G. J. Botterweck and H. Ringgren. Stuttgart, 1970–
TLOT	*Theological Lexicon of the Old Testament*. Edited by E. Jenni, with assistance from C. Westermann. Translated by M. E. Biddle. 3 vols. Peabody, MA, 1997
VT	*Vetus Testamentum*
WMANT	Wissenschaftliche Monographien zum Alten und Neuen Testament
ZABR	*Zeitschrift für altorientalische und biblische Rechtsgeschichte*

Ancient Legal Texts

CC   Covenant Code (Exodus 21:1 [or 20:22]–23:19)
DC   Deuteronomic Code (Deuteronomy 12–26)
HC   Holiness Code (Leviticus 17–26)
HL   Hittite Laws
LE   Laws of Eshnunna
LH   Laws of Hammurabi
LL   Laws of Lipit-Ishtar
LU   Laws of Ur-Namma
MAL   Middle Assyrian Laws
NBL   Neo-Babylonian Laws
PC   Priestly Code
SLEx   Sumerian Laws Exercise Tablet

Chronologies

Archaeological Periods		Empires and Legal Texts	
Early Bronze Age	3500–2000 BCE	Sumerian	ca. 3100–1900 BCE
		Ur-Namma	ca. 2100 BCE
		Lipit-Ishtar	ca. 1930 BCE
		Sumerian Laws Exercise	ca. 1800 BCE
Middle Bronze Age	2000–1550 BCE	Old Babylonian	ca. 2000–1500 BCE
		Eshnunna	ca. 1770 BCE
		Hammurabi	ca. 1750 BCE
		Hittite	ca. 1650–1200 BCE
Late Bronze Age	1550–1200 BCE		
		Middle Assyrian	ca. 1300–1075 BCE
Iron Age I (Iron I)	1200–900 BCE		
Iron Age II (Iron II)	900–586 BCE	Neo-Assyrian	744–612 BCE
Neo-Babylonian	586–539 BCE	Neo-Babylonian	612–539 BCE
Persian	539–331 BCE	Persian	539–331 BCE
		Biblical "Codes"	ca. 500–200 BCE
Hellenistic	331–63 BCE	Hellenistic	331–63 BCE
		Biblical "Codes"	ca. 500–200 BCE

Introduction

What will become of us if we ever stop asking questions?
—André Brink[1]

This book differs in several significant respects from other studies of biblical law. Its starting point is not the biblical text but the social world of ancient Israel. Its analytical methods do not attend primarily to literary forms, history of redaction, or theological interpretation but to ideologies, the functioning of social power, and the political and economic landscape. Its conclusions deal not with the contributions of biblical laws to theology and ethics but with the differences observable within ancient Israel's social makeup and the roles played by law in the interactions among the people. In this project I am much more interested in social, political, and economic history than in literary, intellectual, or religious history.

Anthropological and sociological studies of law in other cultures and societies have emphasized the relation of laws to social norms, societal systems, ideology and ethos, and power groups. The basic argument is that laws, particularly in traditional folk societies, tend to emerge not through formalized legislative action but through a gradual process rooted either in customs or in conflicts between parties. Laws thus reflect social values insofar as they result from negotiations among the group's members. In reality, power in a given social group is rarely shared equally by all but is concentrated in certain subgroups, classes, offices, or charismatic individuals. In a nation-state the power wielders can become even further removed from the larger populace as the governmental system pursues its own interests. Uneven distribution of resources and capital can similarly skew the legal system by effecting laws and judicial procedures that favor certain persons or groups over others. Thus arises a moral issue aptly described in

1. André Brink, *A Dry White Season* (New York: William Morrow, 1980), 291.

the statement "Justice and law . . . could be described as distant cousins, . . . not on speaking terms at all."[2]

The present volume aims to assess the interrelationships among law, power, and justice in ancient Israel. The biblical evidence provides one point of access, and other ancient Southwest Asian legal documents form a second. But the primary task will be to describe the plausible social settings in which laws functioned to maintain order in the community, at times with broad-based support and at times with partiality toward certain powerful interest groups. The latter circumstance will be pursued through examination of the types of Israelites who became disempowered and mar- ginalized—not only the often-mentioned categories of widows, orphans, poor, slaves, and strangers, but also such disadvantaged groups as women vis-à-vis men, children and elderly vis-à-vis adults in their prime, rural vis- à-vis urban, and subjects vis-à-vis royalty. I will direct particular attention not only to the use of law in establishing justice or in redressing injustice, but especially to structures in which the powerful employ laws to dominate people and the powerless are too often without recourse.

Two approaches on the rise since the 1960s are particularly attractive to me. The *hermeneutics of suspicion* counsels us not to take much for granted but to interrogate actions, institutions, and policies for ulterior motives, which typically will be concealed in order to be successful. I employ this approach, frankly, when confronted with any biblical law or any law from surrounding cultures. If we take a written, canonical law at face value, we may miss a hidden agenda that caused it to come into being or that manipulated it through self-interest. Yet inquiring into the sociohistorical background of individual biblical laws, while important, does not adequately reach to the level of systemic political and economic structures undergirding that society. The *hermeneutics of recuperation*, on the other hand, seeks to recover what has been lost to history. As I will argue, the vast majority of ancient Israelites have only minimal traces of themselves in the Hebrew Bible, which was produced and preserved primarily by upper-class male urbanites. The masses, found mostly in the numerous villages scattered throughout the country, must have developed legal systems of their own to guarantee the orderly functioning of their social groups and to remedy disputes and violations that occurred. We today will not be able to recover the actual wording of their customary laws, which existed in oral form, but it should be possible to discern

2. Spoken by Marlon Brando in the film *A Dry White Season* (1989), directed by Euzhan Palcy, novel by André Brink, screenplay by Colin Welland and Euzhan Palcy.

some of their legal conflicts and the principles according to which they settled them.

I readily acknowledge that much of what I am proposing is speculative, but I see no other way forward if the goal is to try to recover the experiences and the voices of those with scant mention in the written records. In this book I develop several constructs to highlight three different social and institutional settings: the villages, the cities and states, and the cultic contexts. The Hebrew Bible does not break down Israelite history and society in this manner, although some of it is implied in the text, often unintentionally. For example, if the books of Samuel and Kings devote most of their space to the doings of kings and elites, one has to wonder about the rest of the populace, the unmentioned and unprivileged peasants and slaves who built the palaces, temples, walls, roads, and other conveniences that they themselves were not destined to enjoy. It is not speculation to assert that the unprivileged masses existed, but we do conjecture in trying to describe their terms of living. Archaeology delivers some material evidence to help with the effort, and comparative studies provide additional information from similar societies.

Hypothesizing or speculating becomes even more necessary and apparent when one then tries to envision the kinds of legal disputes that could have occurred in these Israelite settings. To move forward, though, involves surmise. If, for example, a farmer possesses little in the way of tools and household goods, then theft or damage to any item must certainly have been met not with acquiescence and equanimity nor necessarily with belligerence and vengefulness, but probably with an expectation that the community will ensure that in-kind restitution will replace the loss. For such a case, our speculation begins with the social and economic construct, followed by imagining a realistic loss or conflict, which in turn needs a judicial response. Each step along this path may need to be rethought, beginning with the construct itself. Is it worth the effort to pursue this line of inquiry? My answer is yes, because only in this way can we attempt, and perhaps to some extent succeed, to recover the experiences and expectations of our hidden ancestors in antiquity. And I would add that speculating or hypothesizing should not, in itself, seem objectionable since it happens in all interpretive and historical work—whether in asserting or citing a word's etymology, or in construing the meaning of a sentence, or in suggesting that one text stands in some type of relation to another text, or in dating a text, or in trying to assess a text's theological or ethical import, or in describing historical causation, or in dating and situating an event or a person, or in interpreting many individual acts as a macroevent such as a revolution or a reform, or in any other number of everyday analytical and interpretive acts carried out by humanists and social scientists. The current project is one of them.

Not all hypotheses are created equal. The test is twofold: plausibility and evidence. Plausibility often resides in the eye of the beholder; or to state it differently, it depends heavily on a person's presuppositions, perspectives, critical acumen, knowledge, and imagination. Evidence is also debatable in most cases, material evidence (such as archaeological findings) seemingly weightier than immaterial—yet none of it irrefragable. The least we can expect of each other is repeated acknowledgment of the uncertainty, or the degrees of uncertainty, attending our claims. In this book I have attempted to meet this expectation in the following manner.

The four chapters in part 1 develop the method and approach to be used in part 2. Obviously a wide range of methods is available, and I will present an argument on behalf of my choices. In addition, I will discuss the scenario pertaining when both oral and written laws are in the picture. Basic to this scenario is the distinction between historical Israel and the biblical account.

Part 2 then develops the constructs for the three primary legal systems in ancient Israel—village culture, urban and national culture, and cultic culture. In each chapter the initial focus falls on the physical evidence for the given setting and its social makeup, and at this point we have relatively firm ground on which to stand. Archaeological excavations from the past century and a half have produced an enormous amount of information about villages, cities, and cultic places, although these findings depend on an interpretative move to draw them together and give them meaning. Thus, when I state that village population in ancient Israel averaged 75–150 people or that the central cities were primarily inhabited by the elites and typically contained less than 2,000 residents, it is a definite claim not fabricated out of whole cloth but based on strong, although not necessarily irrefutable, archaeological data.

The second part of each of these three chapters, on the other hand, represents a constructive act of a different order. It is not possible to dig customary laws out of the ground, and the extant texts or literatures, including the Hebrew Bible, do not necessarily have a direct correspondence to the actual laws functioning in that society. In proposing certain types of legal conflicts and resolutions, one should ideally include in most if not all sentences words like "probably," "perhaps," "plausibly," and the like, or use subjunctive forms like "could," "would," "might," and more. Historians face such uncertainties in most of their work, but their usual practice is to write and speak in a more straightforward manner, eschewing the tentative expressions that bog down a narrative if used in excess, however fitting they may be. I will follow a similar practice, often describing the Israelite laws and legal conflicts with a certain definiteness. Here at the start, however, I acknowledge in principle and in general the hypothetical character of these constructions, while at the same time I maintain that they are entirely plausible inferences from the social, political, and economic information available about ancient Israel.

The reader's reflex may be to dispute the details in light of past schools of interpretation. While I often depart in fundamental ways from standard lines of analysis, my basic purpose is to supplement previous understandings with new proposals. Most important to me in this book is to shift to new questions about the data. Toward this end I will progress primarily on the basis of the sociology and anthropology of law, guided by the method of ideological criticism and informed by legal realism and Critical Legal Studies.

To focus on the new questions that this combination of approaches can yield, I have deliberately decided not to engage the many proposals and issues already on the table as a result of other starting points and methods. Mine is not an undertaking in the history of legal research. Much of my previous work involves surveying and assessing past scholarship in other fields, and I relish the process of engaging with others in discussion about old and new ideas and methods. However, this present project involves striking out in a new and different direction from that usually pursued in the history of scholarship on Israelite and biblical law. I do not expect to find definitive or conclusive answers to the questions developed in this study; such answers are elusive and are not likely to come easily or quickly, if at all. To the extent that convincing answers are even possible, they will result with the assistance of other historians and interpreters. My goal for the present is to introduce novel inquiries and perspectives to the already-long list of methods and problems, not to debate other approaches or opinions.

The study of Israelite law, like the study of biblical law, is a rich, promising, and alluring field of study. I hope the reader will be as captivated by it as I have been.

PART 1

THE DIMENSIONS OF LAW

CHAPTER 1

Israelite Law and Biblical Law

The best interpreter of the law is custom.
— *Cicero*[1]

The Hebrew Bible locates the origin of Israel's law at Sinai and attributes to Moses the role of lawgiver, or rather, of mediator, since the law is held to stem ultimately from Israel's God. The law thereby acquires impressive authority and legitimacy, and violation of its precepts is intended to elicit direct and dire consequences, if not at human then at divine hands. In terms of Israel's literary heritage, the legal materials (including the religious laws and cultic ordinances) constitute nearly one-third of the entire Pentateuch—by any reckoning a significant portion for one genre. Early Jewish tradition called the entire Pentateuch "Torah," counted 613 distinct commandments and prohibitions in the "Written Torah" of the Pentateuch, and supplemented the legal legacy with the "Oral Torah," a body of legal interpretations and applications that arose in a centuries-long line stretching putatively back to Moses himself and finally becoming recorded in the Mishnah by around 200 CE. Substantial legal collections were also produced by many of Israel's predecessors, contemporaries, and successors in ancient Southwest Asia.[2]

Yet merely highlighting the enormity of the legal tradition of ancient Israel,[3]

---

1. Marcus Tullius Cicero (106–43 BCE), Paulus in Justinian's *Digest* 1.3.37.
2. The geographical term preferred in this book will be "ancient Southwest Asia" rather than "ancient Near East" inasmuch as the latter, although conventional in scholarly discussions, is rooted in the colonial period of European hegemony over the region.
3. The term "ancient Israel" is also imprecise and problematic. See esp. the discussion by Philip R. Davies, *In Search of "Ancient Israel,"* JSOTSup 148 (Sheffield: Sheffield Academic Press, 1992), distinguishing among biblical Israel, historical Israel, and the Israel as reconstructed by scholars. Part of the terminological problem is the varied use of the name with respect to different periods of history: the Israel of the Egyptian Merneptah Stela (ca. 1208 BCE), the Israel of the early monarchy, Israel as the Northern Kingdom, Israel as the equivalent of Judah to designate the Southern Kingdom, and Israel as an ideal or community concept in the Babylonian and Persian periods and later. In this book I will distinguish among these various alternatives by using appropriate modifiers or phrases, as needed, to clarify which "Israel" is intended in each discussion. Without a specific modifier, the terms "Israel" or "ancient Israel"

early Judaism,[4] and the neighboring cultures is only a first step in acquiring an appreciation for its importance. Actually, there is a prior question to face. Do the texts that have come down to us present us with actual laws that functioned and held authority among the inhabitants of ancient Israel? Or do these "legal" texts represent something other than or in addition to practiced laws? Just because a text appears to be or presents itself as a law does not oblige us to accept it as such; it may just as well be another genre or entity or combination of elements. Our own understandings of the nature and origin of law may lead to a quite different interpretation of the material than the text presents, especially since the text is not entirely forthcoming about its own intentions and character. At the outset, therefore, it may be helpful to distinguish between two phenomena that are in fact quite different from each other, even though they are often treated as being identical: Israelite law and biblical law.

ISRAELITE LAWS AND BIBLICAL LAWS

By *Israelite law* we mean the legal systems that functioned during the course of ancient Israel's history—the customary laws that emerged among the people or the regulations issued by leaders who possessed some form of legislative or judicial power; these laws thus served, or were intended to serve, as actual legal controls and judicial correctives for human behavior. *Biblical law*, on the other hand, designates the law-like materials recorded in the Hebrew Bible and is not—for several reasons—to be considered simply identical to Israelite law.[5] As they now stand, the laws in the Hebrew Bible are part of a structured literary corpus with various purposes other

---

or "Israelite" will designate loosely the span of cultures and people in the Southern Levant, including their counterparts in the Diaspora, during the period from the beginning of the Iron Age (ca. 1200 BCE) until the end of the Hasmonean kingdom and the Hellenistic period (ca. 63 BCE), by which point the bulk of the Hebrew Bible was composed, although not necessarily assembled or canonized. In Davies's terms, the "historical Israel" is ideally intended in this book, but realistically one can scarcely move beyond the "reconstructed Israel" of scholars—even with respect to the material culture, which is largely meaningless without the dates, classifications, and interpretations provided by archaeologists and other specialists. Distinguishing between "biblical laws" and "Israelite laws," which we will presently discuss, provides a further means of underscoring the difference between Israel's social history and the Hebrew Bible itself.

4. Again, the term "Judaism" implies more than can be claimed prima facie since the Second Temple period saw a variety of "Judaisms"—sects, parties, movements, and groups—some vying for religious supremacy, others more quiescent but nonetheless present, yet others opting to withdraw from the social and political fray. To some extent, we will need to attend to this diversity, whether understood as primarily religious, ethnic, or political, and in those instances descriptors will be added to clarify whichever group is intended.

5. See chap. 2 for the distinction between "law" and "laws."

than legal control, such as recounting the national history, attesting to divine revelation, regulating power relations, or legitimizing certain cultic activity. Israelite laws, in contrast, were generally not in written form but circulated quite naturally as social norms or directives during their respective periods of validity. Israelite laws are to be understood in terms of the social relations existing during their particular period of currency in Israel's history; biblical law is not intended to be restricted to single social periods but is presented as though it were applicable for all times and all people during Israelite and Jewish history. For Israelite law there is usually no identifiable legislator, while biblical law is typically promulgated by divine or legendary figures—such as by YHWH through Moses at Mount Sinai or Mount Horeb for the laws contained in the long section from Exod 20:1 through Num 10:10, or by Moses on the Moabite plains east of the Jordan River for the laws recorded in the book of Deuteronomy—thus in events that are historically unrecoverable.

Biblical law is, in a word, literature—a composition seemingly comprising Israelite laws, presented in the text as divine ordinances, woven together into a literary whole (actually, into several literary sections), and embedded in a larger narrative context, the story of the people's journey from Egypt to Canaan. As with most literature, we can make an effort to associate the corpus of biblical laws with authors, editors, readers, transmitters, preservers, interpreters, or others who may have taken an interest in it. Biblical law existed and exists as a written text. The individual laws assume any of several specific forms and various artistic features (see chap. 4 below) designed to influence or produce an effect on the reader or listener. Regarding their content, they touch on a wide variety of social and religious subjects, and even a casual reading of them will reveal substantial differences with respect to the treatment of many individual issues. As a result, it is difficult to imagine that this literature comprising the biblical laws was composed by a single person throughout, or that it was edited later by only a single individual or group aiming to eliminate any and all variations. To be sure, a common cord holds this legal literature together: the notion of theocratic rule over the unified people. Yet as a text, it exists in its own literary world, consisting of characters (e.g., YHWH, Moses, the people), setting (the mythic wilderness at one level, but all the contexts of life within settled Israel at another), plot (again, at the macrolevel the giving of the law in the wilderness, but at the microlevel all the imaginable conflicts that need adjudication), and stylistic features (the various ways through which behavior is mandated, motivated, and interpreted).

By recognizing biblical law as literature, we should at the same time be cautious not to claim too much about its relation to the functioning of law in Israelite society. This point needs to be stressed at the outset since most students of the Hebrew Bible have, quite naturally, been inclined to operate with certain assumptions and concepts stemming from modern views of law. In fact, several specific terms commonly employed today prove to be inadequate for capturing the nature of biblical law, and they should consequently be avoided:

1. A legal *code* (Latin: *codex*), in today's terminology, designates a body of laws and regulations, enacted by a monarch, an authorized legislature, commission, or other official and arranged systematically according to subject matter to ease consultation and application. Biblical scholars have conventionally used the word "code" to label the subsections of biblical law that seem to form distinct units: the Covenant Code, the Deuteronomic Code, the Holiness Code, and the Priestly Code. Even if we remind ourselves that we do not thereby mean to suggest that any of these codes was ever formally enacted by a legislative body, the impression nonetheless conveyed is that each contains laws possessing some form of official standing and that each unit may have served as an actual reference source for judicial courts of the period.

2. A better alternative, though still with its shortcomings, is to refer to the subsections of biblical law as *collections* of laws. This term has the decided advantage of avoiding the perception created by the notion of an official, systematic "code" since a "collection" does not need to be comprehensive, orderly, or official; it also acknowledges that Israelite laws were originally dispersed throughout the country and could be assembled into one place, rather than that they came into existence through legislative fiat. However, a "collection" suggests that these individual laws are here recorded in verbatim form, as if someone had traveled to the various settlements and assembled the laws found there.[6] Even if something of this sort might have been done, we have no direct evidence of it. Moreover, we cannot be sure that in each specific case the written form in the biblical text conforms precisely to the laws functioning among the people: some may have been misunderstood by the "collector," others may be a conflation of variant legal practices, and still others may be intentionally or unwittingly represented in a light different from that of the original Israelite laws on which they seem to be based. Though we will occasionally refer to these texts as collections of laws to the extent that they are presented as a series of laws and may even be incorporating some actual Israelite laws, we must not lose sight of

---

6. See the discussion in chap. 4 regarding the unlikelihood of such collecting activities.

the text's primary state as literature, a written composition including much that is not legal in character.

3. It is even less fitting to regard biblical law as a *constitution*. Note the characteristic elements of a constitution, according to *Black's Law Dictionary*:

> The organic and fundamental law of a nation or state, which may be written or unwritten, establishing the character and conception of its government, laying the basic principles to which its internal life is to be conformed, organizing the government, and regulating, distributing, and limiting the functions of its different departments, and prescribing the extent and manner of the exercise of sovereign powers. A charter of government deriving its whole authority from the governed. . . . In a more general sense, any fundamental or important law or edict.[7]

The latter meaning, labeled the "more general sense," is too vague to be useful for understanding the character of biblical law. The prior question for us is tied to the date and intention of the text. The Pentateuch presents the long section of laws as divinely ordained rules that, in *Black's* words, lay out the basic principles of the people's internal life and even describe some of their leadership institutions (such as the elders, the priests, the prophets, the king), including certain of their powers and prerogatives. According to the text's story, these laws are conveyed to the people long before they are actually needed, that is, before the people have settled the land, encountered the local populations, and established the monarchy. But if biblical law, by which we mean the literary form of these texts, stems in fact from a much later period, probably even after the demise of the monarchy, then it could at most be regarded as a constitution for the people sometime during the Second Temple period, perhaps in the Persian period but not prior to that point and quite possibly later. The text retrojects this law into the distant past, and its authors presumably hope to gain legitimacy thereby for its authority in the eyes of the Second Temple community. *Black's* also notes that a constitution derives "its whole authority from the governed." This modern democratic ideal can hardly be expected in the political system of a premodern agrarian state, which did not try to achieve popular self-governance and did not even have in its frame of reference the modern image of a constitution. Actually, the term "constitution" has rarely been associated explicitly with all of biblical law. In another sense the Ten Commandments have sometimes been regarded as a type of Bill

7. Henry Campbell Black, *Black's Law Dictionary*, 5th ed. (St. Paul: West Publishing, 1979), 282.

of Rights, a concise statement of fundamental principles underlying many of the other laws in the Hebrew Bible.[8] We will need to examine the character and function of the Decalogue at a later point, but it is enough here to indicate that it would have served poorly as a nation's "constitution" if left with no further elaboration.

4. One final distinction deserves to be made: biblical law should not be associated in any direct sense with a *transcript* of court proceedings, such as would be produced today by a court reporter. If the individual laws presented in the Pentateuch did not issue ultimately from an empowered legislature or monarch, neither did they stem directly from a judge or jury. Even the well-known judicial cases presented in the Hebrew Bible have little or no relation to a stenographic account of the interchanges among plaintiff, defendant, and judicial arbiters. In each instance another primary concern is driving the text, such as the imperative to follow the terms of the holy war and to obey Israel's faithful leaders (as in the story of Achan in Josh 7), or the glorification of Solomon and his wisdom (1 Kgs 3:16–28), or the compassion due a kin and a devoted foreigner like Ruth (Ruth 4:1–12), or the prophets' urgency to persuade Israel of its wrongdoings (in the literary form known as the prophetic lawsuit, or *rîb*). As will be further discussed below in chapter 4, these and other texts are heavily stylized literary and rhetorical renderings, bearing at most only the slightest resemblance to the proceedings of actual legal cases. We possess no reliable court records from ancient Israel, at least nothing comparable to the full, meticulous reports of today. Furthermore, they would not have been needed in ancient Israel—at most only some notation of the finding, verdict, or settlement, especially in state or commercial cases or certain other types of instances such as divorce.[9] Biblical law lies at a considerable distance from court verbatims.

We have gone to some length thus far to make the rather obvious but all too often overlooked point that "biblical law"—the texts in the Hebrew Bible that purport to present us with the rules and regulations governing Israel—does not *necessarily* reproduce the laws that actually functioned as the binding rules of action affecting the people's conduct in any of their multiple social and political life contexts. Interpreters have

---

8. Walter Harrelson (*The Ten Commandments and Human Rights*, rev. ed. [Macon, GA: Mercer University Press, 1997], 10) states it cautiously, aware of its limitation: "Put in constitutional terms, the Ten Commandments are much more like the Bill of Rights and its amendments than the United States Code."

9. Thus Deut 24:1 stipulates that a written divorce decree be handed to the divorced wife. Examples are attested in ancient Southwest Asian cultures as well.

frequently approached the biblical text as if it offered us an open window on legal affairs during Israelite history, and such an assumption can easily obscure both the special intentions of the text itself (more on this later, esp. in chap. 3) as well as the diverse legal norms and principles actually holding sway among the various groupings of people during their long history. Yet at the same time this distinction between Israelite law and biblical law does not imply that absolutely no ground is shared between the two. Biblical law had, at least in part, its source in Israelite laws, which contributed to the religious, legal, and cultural traditions that eventually became enshrined in the Hebrew Bible. Furthermore, biblical law was itself "Israelite" in the sense that it was produced by certain individuals or groups within Israel during the Second Temple period, if not before. Our primary access to Israelite law must occur to a great extent through a critical reading of biblical law, a methodological problem to which we will return in chapter 3.

Contrasting biblical law and Israelite law as we have done serves a heuristic purpose: to underscore the fact that the legal system now found in the canonized written text should not be facilely equated with the legal systems prevailing throughout Israel's long life, and conversely, that all of the laws of Israel during its history did not find their way into the biblical canon. An intriguing metaphor is offered by the great sociologist of law Eugen Ehrlich, writing in 1913, at a time when legal theorists tended to equate the whole of law with the "legal propositions" preserved in codes:

> To attempt to imprison the law of a time or of a people within the sections of a code is as about as reasonable as to attempt to confine a stream within a pond. The water that is put in the pond is no longer a living stream but a stagnant pool, and but little water can be put in the pond. Moreover, if one considers that the living law had already overtaken and grown away from each one of these codes at the very moment the latter were enacted, and is growing away from them more and more every day, one cannot but realize the enormous extent of this as yet unplowed and unfurrowed field of activity which is being pointed out to the modern legal investigator. It could not be otherwise. The legal propositions are not intended to present a complete picture of the state of the law.[10]

Our study of law will deliberately focus on the functioning of law—Ehrlich's "living law"—in Israelite society, but we will also take into account the efforts of two distinct groups that played a major role in producing

---

10. Eugen Ehrlich, *Fundamental Principles of the Sociology of Law* (Cambridge, MA: Harvard University Press, 1936; German original, 1913), 488.

the legal texts that eventually became canonized: on the one hand, the priests and scribes who composed and systematized the biblical laws into literature and incorporated this literature into the evolving biblical tradition; and on the other, the various power blocs and special-interest groups that apparently directed or influenced this recording and editing process for their own gain. The present biblical text can be used only in the most cautious and critical manner as a source for our efforts to understand the laws that existed and the legal cases that were adjudicated in ancient Israel. To reach the various elements of the complex picture we are calling "Israelite law" will require a process of reconstruction based largely on indications of the social, political, economic, and religious life of the people during their history. What is thus required is a method of triangulation, drawing on three approaches always in light of each other: a critical reading of ancient texts; an assessment of comparative evidence from neighboring cultures as well as socially and environmentally similar settings from other times and locations; and a reconstruction of Israel's social, political, economic, and religious history, elucidated wherever possible by material evidence discovered through archaeology.

LEGAL TEXTS IN THE HEBREW BIBLE

Here at the outset, it may be useful to sketch the basic tack we will take regarding the corpus of "laws" preserved in the Hebrew Bible. Nearly all of our discussion will follow the form of a sociohistorical study of the "Israelite laws" and the judicial systems in ancient Israel, but the prominent role played by the legal literature in the Bible requires some comment since I will be arguing a position very different from the usual.

For well over a century now, the study of biblical law has been dominated by an orientation that looks to historical context in order to explain content and form.[11] Scholars have sought to assign the "codes"— the Covenant Code (also known as the Book of the Covenant), the Deuteronomic Code, the Holiness Code, and the Priestly Code—as well as their individual laws to discrete historical periods, explaining the meaning of each element in terms of the political, social, and religious situation

---

11. See the summaries in, e.g., Otto Eissfeldt, *The Old Testament, an Introduction: The History of the Formation of the Old Testament*, trans. Peter R. Ackroyd (New York and Evanston, IL: Harper & Row, 1965; German original, 3rd ed., 1964), 26–29, 143–45, 212–39; Tikva Frymer-Kenski, "Israel," in *A History of Ancient Near Eastern Law*, ed. Raymond Westbrook, 2 vols. (Leiden and Boston: E. J. Brill, 2003), 2:975–81; and Frank Crüsemann, *The Torah: Theology and Social History of Old Testament Law*, trans. Allan W. Mahnke (Minneapolis: Fortress Press, 1996; German original, 1992).

of the time (or as the case may be, its later editorial reworking). Such an approach has been enormously helpful in unmasking the fiction of the text—that the laws were given by YHWH and Moses en route from Egypt to Canaan—and has instead connected the laws to later periods and diverse groups among the people. In summary form, several elements have typically characterized past and current proposals that follow this historical approach to biblical law, despite many specific differences among the various reconstructions:[12]

- According to most scholarly views, each "code" was written at a discrete time or, if at more than one time, then at a discrete time for each of its sections. Any other work on it was largely of a redactional nature, with additions and interpretations being incorporated at various later stages.
- Scholars usually associate each compilation with the end of one or the other social or political period. Consistent with our above description of the problems associated with using the terms "code" and "constitution," most of the proposals do not advocate that the various collections were enacted at the start of a new social or political period in order to provide the legal framework for the Israelites living at that time. Rather, some momentous social or political change—the founding of the monarchy, the end of Assyrian domination and the resurgence of nationalism, the exile and destruction of the temple, the restoration of the people on the land—elicited a desire to record the laws that had *previously* served as legal requirements for the preceding generations. Hence, such a move amounted to an effort to conserve the past laws, perhaps for nostalgic or preservationist or even reactionary purposes. They could serve as guides or motivation for the current and following generations, but they look back as much as or more than they look forward.
- In each case the collections are thus generally thought to be based on older legal traditions, not on newly developed laws. Most of the laws in these traditions probably circulated in oral form, and they tended to be short and independent of each other, at least at their origin. Scholars have differed widely, however, in their estimation of how successfully we

12. In most instances this overview will not refer to specific proponents of the various notions and understandings since it is not my intention here to debate them in detail.

can reconstruct any of these actual "Israelite laws" before they became recorded.

- Each of the collections is typically associated with one or the other of the major pentateuchal sources named in the documentary hypothesis,[13] even though the collections' compilation often occurred separately from the composition of the documentary sources. The Covenant Code is generally connected to the redacted JE source, the Deuteronomic Code to the D source, and the Holiness and Priestly Codes to the P source.

- The relation of biblical law to the prophets has been of critical importance in the assessment of its character and history. An idea advanced in the early nineteenth century led to a relative chronological ordering that has been followed by many if not most subsequent researchers. Drawing on a suggestion from Eduard Reuss dating back to the 1830s, Karl Heinrich Graf and then, most famously, Julius Wellhausen developed the argument that the prophets preceded the law, not that the law came before the prophets, as the biblical text states and as scholars had traditionally accepted.[14] What was meant by "the law," according to the Graf–Wellhausen hypothesis, was the priestly system dominating the Pentateuch. All agreed that laws were present in society earlier in time, but not that they were systematized and laid out to serve as the basis for the cultic community, which was thought to have been accomplished only beginning with the postexilic period.

- Most scholars have assumed that, with this succession of codes, the compilers or authors of the later collections knew the earlier ones. Those later in line did not, apparently, seek

---

13. The "documentary hypothesis," which reached its classic formulation in the late 19th c., aims to account for the formation of the Pentateuch by discerning four primary source documents that arose in different periods and became edited together into the final form of the Pentateuch: J (the Yahwistic source) in the 10th c. BCE; E (the Elohistic source) in the 9th c.; D (the Deuteronomic source) in the 7th c.; and P (the Priestly source) in the 6th–5th c. The many variations of and alternatives to the documentary hypothesis are reviewed in a wide range of publications on pentateuchal research.

14. Karl Heinrich Graf, *Die geschichtlichen Bücher des Alten Testaments: Zwei historisch-kritische Untersuchungen* (Leipzig: T. O. Weigel, 1866); idem, "Die sogenannte Grundschrift des Pentateuchs," *Archiv für wissenschaftliche Erforschung des Alten Testaments* 1 (1869): 466–77; and Julius Wellhausen, *Prolegomena to the History of Israel* (reprint, Atlanta: Scholars Press, 1994; German original, 1878).

to suppress the former codes but let them stand in their received form and then composed their own new collection as a summary of the most recent regulations. In fact, a later code could be drafted in a manner that reflects the form or content of preceding collections; the Deuteronomic Code is often cited as a prime example, in this case reworking the Covenant Code to fit the times toward the end of the monarchy.[15] Similarly, individual legal statements and principles could also be reinterpreted in later biblical texts, forming a type of inner-biblical appropriation or exegesis.[16]

• At the same time, though, in past studies we rarely observe any explicit, intensive recognition that the codes recorded only a portion, indeed perhaps only a minute portion, of all the laws that circulated in ancient Israel throughout its history. There appears almost to be a tacit assumption that the compilation of laws now present in the Pentateuch predominated in the society and that any variant legal traditions were basically deviant in comparison with these Yahwistic norms. Scholars have, in a word, tended to accept biblical law as representative of the orthodox line, if not even of the majority of the population, in each respective period. In another form of this stance, "canonical critics" have devalued the noncanonical laws as well as the prehistory of canonical laws on the grounds that the majority of believing communities basing themselves on biblical tradition during the past two millennia have esteemed only the materials retained in the canon.[17]

• It would be fair to say that the majority of biblical interpreters have attended more to theological aspects in their work on biblical law than to political and economic dimensions. On this practice we need to make two observations. First, scholars have long pursued the social contexts for many if

15. See, e.g., Bernard M. Levinson, *Deuteronomy and the Hermeneutics of Legal Innovation* (New York and Oxford: Oxford University Press, 1997).

16. Michael A. Fishbane, *Biblical Interpretation in Ancient Israel* (Oxford: Clarendon; New York: Oxford University Press, 1985); and Bernard M. Levinson, *Legal Revision and Religious Renewal in Ancient Israel* (Cambridge: Cambridge University Press, 2008).

17. The clearest articulation of this line is given by Brevard Childs, *Introduction to the Old Testament as Scripture* (Philadelphia: Fortress Press, 1979). With a different effect but also emphasizing the canon, James A. Sanders (*Torah and Canon* [Philadelphia: Fortress Press, 1972]) argues that the very recording of the Deuteronomic Code in the 7th c. BCE initiated the canonizing process that eventuated in the Hebrew Bible.

not most laws, often with valuable results, but this pursuit is not the same as pressing to determine the fundamental political and economic systems in Israel that yielded the ways in which law is now presented in the Hebrew Bible. Second, there is nothing in principle wrong with attending to the religious and theological dimensions of biblical law, nor for that matter with doing the same for any other part of the Hebrew Bible. The problem comes, however, if religion and theology are given pride of place—if interpreters, certainly not all but definitely many if not most, incline to consider first and foremost the theological or religious dimensions of biblical law. Much else is at work in ancient Israel than religion, and the reductionism involved in assuming that religiosity pervades all of life in their society results in undervaluing the influence of other factors. For many, this perspective may reflect their own personal points of view. And on that front, recent interpreters who operate within a postmodern framework have emphasized that one's own social, economic, racial, gender, and cultural rootage plays a decisive and even determinative role in one's interpretative readings: in other words, the interpreter is as complex an entity as is the text being interpreted.[18]

- Finally, ever since the discovery of Hammurabi's Code and the various other legal texts from cultures in ancient Southwest Asia, most interpreters of biblical law have drawn attention to the similarities and differences among these legal traditions. Typically, despite an effort to cite parallels to whatever biblical law or legal practice is under discussion, the differences tend to be underscored the most in order to highlight the distinctive character of Israel. It is difficult to find a corresponding appreciation, at least among biblical scholars, for the distinctiveness of those other neighboring societies. Furthermore, there has been little success, in fact little effort, in developing a plausible hypothesis for how the laws from one culture could have influenced another,

18. See, e.g., George Aichele et al. (The Bible and Culture Collective), *The Postmodern Bible* (New Haven, CT: Yale University Press, 1995); and Fernando F. Segovia and Mary Ann Tolbert, eds., *Reading from This Place*, vol. 1, *Social Location and Biblical Interpretation in the United States*; vol. 2, *Social Location and Biblical Interpretation in Global Perspective* (Minneapolis: Fortress Press, 1995).

especially when there are centuries separating the two. This problem is most notable for the Covenant Code: If it is dated in Israel's early monarchy (e.g., 10th–9th centuries BCE, as many have thought), how did Hammurabi's eighteenth-century-BCE Code reach the Israelites, especially during the premonarchic period when the individual laws in the Covenant Code supposedly arose? Moreover, how could the highland villagers, probably all of whom were illiterate, even manage to read it and formulate their own laws in light of it, even if a copy of Hammurabi's Code had made its way into their hands? Virtually all students of biblical law acknowledge the rich legal heritage of Southwestern Asia, but often it would appear as if the influence from one to the other had been breathed in with the air.

These general conceptions of and approaches to the biblical collections exhibit the historical framework that has dominated the field. Scholars have sought primarily to determine or hypothesize when each biblical law and each collection might have appeared, and a remarkable consensus, especially regarding the larger collections, has emerged—even if considerable debates continue at specific points. This near agreement regarding the delineation and the relative dating of the main legal "codices" in the Pentateuch takes the following form. As will later be clear, I am not advocating these positions but only summarizing them here as baselines for subsequent discussions.

Covenant Code

Found in Exod 21:1 (or 20:22)–23:19, the Covenant Code, also called the Book of the Covenant (see Exod 24:7 for this phrase), is generally regarded as the oldest collection of laws in the Hebrew Bible. Of all biblical law, it exhibits the strongest resemblance in both content and form to other ancient Southwest-Asian law collections. Moreover, its laws reflect more of the agricultural lifestyle than do any of the other biblical "codes," and one finds here relatively little of the concern for cultic matters that occurs elsewhere. The laws themselves regulate issues pertaining to slavery, violence, liability and restitution, social justice, marriage, the Sabbath and the Sabbatical Year, the three annual festivals, and other subjects. Most interpreters assign this legal collection to the monarchy, perhaps quite early but at least prior to the Deuteronomic Code. The laws themselves, however, are often thought to have arisen in the premonarchic contexts of local villages, clans, and tribes. According to this view, the scribes living after the emergence of the state perhaps wrote this collection of early laws in order to preserve them from being lost, and at the same time they may have sought to draw attention to the greatness of the new kingdom by celebrating its lawful and orderly heritage.

Deuteronomic Code

The Deuteronomic Code treats a wide range of subjects: religious matters regarding the central location of the cult, apostasy, impurity, tithing, the Sabbatical Year, religious festivals; leadership roles of judges, officials, kings, Levitical priests, prophets; and diverse issues concerning cities of refuge, witnesses, warfare, murder, inheritance, property, sexual matters, marriage, slavery, various "humanitarian" considerations, and more. Regarded as identical or closely related to Deut 12–26, the collection has been generally associated with historical developments of the seventh century BCE. There are numerous proposals and variations regarding its appearance. Since centralization, especially of the cult but also of political power, is a theme of many of its laws, the period of the monarchy seems to suggest itself. Moreover, the laws are connected much less to life in the agricultural villages and more to urban conditions during this period. Many interpreters have felt that these legal traditions may have stemmed from the northern kingdom of Israel and were brought south to Jerusalem by northerners who fled the Assyrian defeat of Samaria in 722 BCE; the descendants of these northerners then compiled the laws both to preserve them and also to advance them as reforming principles during the political resurgence under Josiah in the 620s. Other scholars think that the authors of the Deuteronomic Code drew on various literary sources, revising them to suit their purposes. According to some, the homiletic or paraenetic tone of the collection seems also to point toward a group, such as the prophets or perhaps the Levites, who exhorted the people in public acts of speaking; others see here the influence of scribes or sages engaged in instruction. The Deuteronomistic stream continued into the exilic period and was largely responsible for editing the Tetrateuch and Jeremiah and for drafting the great history of Israel stretching from Moses to the fall of Jerusalem in 586, now found in the books of Joshua, Judges, 1–2 Samuel, 1–2 Kings, for which the book of Deuteronomy served as the introduction and statement of principles.[19]

19. For further details, see my "Deuteronomy and the Deuteronomists," in *Old Testament Interpretation: Past, Present, and Future: Essays in Honor of Gene M. Tucker*, ed. James Luther Mays, David L. Petersen, and Kent Harold Richards (Nashville: Abingdon Press, 1995), 61–79.

Holiness Code

The collection known as the Holiness Code, located in Lev 17–26 (although some exclude Lev 17, 26, or other parts), derives its name from the repeated reference to holiness, an urgent call for moral and ritualistic sanctity. It seems to be more fragmentary and disjointed than the previous two "codes," which to most interpreters suggests that it is based on smaller collections or pieces that were linked together over time. Many of its laws may well stem from the monarchic period, but its compilation—or at least the later redactional work on it—occurred in the postexilic period. Priests in Jerusalem were likely the ones to have produced it, probably before the writing of the Priestly Code, though some would place it afterward. It seems to stem from a time when the priests believed that the people as a whole needed to be implored to do right in order for them to survive as a people living in the land. With its focus on the cult, the range of subjects treated by these laws is narrower than that of the other collections: sacrificial rules, illicit sexual practices, morality toward others, penalties for violations, qualifications for priesthood, religious festivals, blasphemy, and the Sabbatical and Jubilee Years.

Priestly Code

The remainder of the laws of Exodus, Leviticus, and Numbers, commonly called the Priestly Code, constitutes an even looser assemblage of regulations—looser in terms of its literary cohesion, but not in terms of its focus. For nearly the whole of the "code" pertains directly to the cult—and pointedly more for the ear of the priests than for the larger population. Even if some of the ordinances may date to the period before the destruction of the temple in 586 BCE, this collection of laws is widely held to be postexilic, later than the Holiness Code, in the view of most scholars. We find in it long sections outlining instructions regarding the tabernacle, the ark, and all the other accoutrements of the cult (Exod 25–31, 35–40), sacrifices (Lev 1–7), consecration of the priests (Lev 8–10, in narrative form), impurities (Lev 11–15), the Day of Atonement ritual (Lev 16), votive gifts (Lev 27), and various other laws mostly involving the cult (Num 5–6; 15; 18–19; 28–30). Some of these sections are often thought to be later additions to the Priestly Code. The disconnected nature of all these parts accounts, perhaps, for the lesser attention accorded by scholars to the Priestly Code as a whole in comparison with the other "codes." In fact, with the exception of the laws on impurities and a few specific matters about social behavior, the regulations pertaining to the setting up of the cult are typically omitted from general discussions of biblical law, almost as if they do not quite count as "laws" in the same sense as do the other directives of the legal corpora. On the other hand, the relation of the Priestly Code to the larger Priestly source has attracted attention, although not as much as the connection of the Deuteronomic Code to the Deuteronomistic History.

Decalogue

The Decalogue (found, with some variations, in Exod 20:2–17 and Deut 5:6–21) is the wild card in this historical progression of legal codes. Many interpreters tend to follow the biblical tradition and assign it to the head of the process, viewing it as the fountain of the legal principles that then became elaborated and qualified in the subsequent collections. Some set it later, but almost always earlier than the Deuteronomic, Holiness, and Priestly Codes since it is typically associated with the JE source. Its similarity to other concise lists, such as the so-called Ritual Decalogue (or perhaps twelve commandments, thus a dodecalogue) of Exod 34:13 (or 14)–26 and the list of twelve curses in Deut 27:15–26, has understandably raised questions about the function of such cataloging. Similarly, the possible relation to lists of basic standards in prophetic (Jer 7:6–9; Ezek 18:5–9), psalmic (Pss 15; 24), and wisdom (Job 31; and more) texts has invited attention. Its character as a concise inventory of fundamental principles has intrigued students of the Bible as much as anything else about it. In its present form the Decalogue is not evenly structured: four very short laws and the others of varying lengths; a mixture of prohibitions and positive commands; the first four religious and the final six social in content. Several attempts have been made to propose a uniform list that might have existed at the very outset—for example, rendering all the laws in short, prohibitive form and all with direct objects. Other scholars have sought to account for the addition or deletion of any elements that depart from such a strict format. Most have taken note of the pithy and apodictic formulation of the laws, and the difficulty of enforcing them in light of their vagueness and generality has not been lost on many. But it is the remarkable impact of the Ten Commandments as a whole on two millennia of religious and, to be sure, cultural history that has so impressed readers and has drawn their attention more to these sixteen verses than to any other single block of biblical laws—perhaps more than to any other part of the Hebrew Bible.

CRITIQUE AND PROPOSAL

This basic historical outline has served the biblical discipline as the dominant structure for interpreting not only these collections and their individual laws but also other texts that might relate to them—in the Prophets, Wisdom literature, and narratives. Personally, I have been reluctant to abandon the general schema, probably for reasons of convenience as much as conviction. Unfortunately, though, the more I think about this historical scheme, the less convinced I am that it is defensible. It may be convenient, but it is scarcely plausible. Consider several pragmatic but obvious problems.

First, who, in each of the postulated historical periods, would have written and read these collections, especially the Covenant Code and the Deuteronomic Code? Literacy at an advanced level in an agrarian society such as Israel would probably have been possessed by not much more than 1 percent of the total population, perhaps even less. Generally only professionals—scribes, archivists, certain priests, perhaps some few others—were fully literate, and only then because their work or livelihood required it.[20] Can we safely assume that at all of the historical junctures just mentioned, especially the earlier ones, there existed groups with sufficient writing proficiency to record these legal collections and with the necessary means to preserve them? And who would have read or enforced the written laws, which in their oral form carried authority by virtue of their traditional circulation among the general, nonliterate populations? Which group would have had the inclination, the financial resources, the storage space, and the continuity over time to have preserved such written documents?

Second, why should these laws have been composed in writing in the first place? Whose interests were served by having them recorded? If, as mentioned above, we were to imagine that they were composed at the end of a sociopolitical period—after the premonarchic period, or after the Assyrian invasion, or at the end of the Assyrian period, or after the fall of Jerusalem in 586 BCE—then it would appear that recording these laws served primarily the purpose of conserving them so they would not become lost or so they could provide guidance for the new sociopolitical stage. But why would a new monarchy want to retain the laws from an earlier period in which the population was not subordinated to the central power? Or why would the southerners want the northerners' laws? Or to what extent would the general populace have been interested in the details of the priests' cultic regulations and the priests' vision of an extravagant temple in the capital city, remote from the majority of the land's population?

20. See below, chap. 4, Literacy, for further discussion of this literacy rate and the main types of persons who learned to read and write.

Finally, how did these laws, especially those of the Covenant Code and the Deuteronomic Code, even become collected? Did someone, parallel to a modern ethnographer or cultural historian, circulate through the outlying villages and towns, asking people to recite their laws and judicial procedures, and then return to Jerusalem to collate them into lists? Would not such a compilation have seemed foreign to those outlying villages and towns? In light of this postulated process of literary production, *whose* laws do we really think they were? Did they fundamentally belong to the "Israelites" and reflect the values of the vast majority of the population—or do they express the viewpoints and interests of the compilers and authors?

Such questions are not easy to answer, but they have the net result of undermining our certainty about the standard historical hypotheses. On the other hand, however, generations of scholars have meticulously researched and compared the various parts of biblical law, sharpening the lines of the historical picture until it appears that we may have a near consensus about the basic lineaments of the development of the textual collections and their relation to social and religious periods in ancient Israel. Such a consensus is not easily dislodged, nor should one deal with it lightly. Yet the issues raised by the methods of social history and ideological criticism also have compelling force. I therefore propose the following alternative approach, the details of which will be developed in later chapters.

As argued above, the collections of "biblical laws" constitute literature. We have no way of testing whether or not these "laws" correspond to the laws that actually functioned among all the people throughout the country. Even with their diversity and inconsistencies, biblical laws present more of a united front than is likely to have existed throughout Israel's long and varied history and within the multiple groups and communities found throughout the country. We have to ask, therefore, about the identity of the writers of the biblical law, their reasons for producing this literature, and the social, economic, political, gender-based, institutional interests that are thereby ultimately served. The major differences among the discrete collections also need explanation, as well as the reason for their coexistence in the present Pentateuch.

What factors influenced the inclusion of certain laws and the exclusion of others? The answers should not come as a complete surprise to us if we are at all realistic both about typical legislative activity in modern societies and about the political and economic aspects of literary production: *the Hebrew Bible includes precisely those laws and traditions that in some way corresponded to the strategies and self-interests of those who drafted and compiled them.* Underlying the modern field of legal theory known as Critical Legal Studies is a simple, broad principle: all law is politics.[21] Although many of the biblical laws articulate exemplary moral principles, indeed some of the most humane social norms known to us, we should nonetheless be prepared to suspect the motives behind their compilation and to apply to the biblical text the same kind of hermeneutics of suspicion that we have learned to apply to our modern political and economic structures. For the groups in ancient Israel who would have had the training, the opportunity, the funding, and the means for preserving such legal literature must certainly have belonged to the scribal class or the priests. In both cases, according to the model of the agrarian state (see chap. 3), these groups owed their status and privileges to the central state and the governing elite, even if they could to some extent identify with the vulnerability of the masses. The composition of laws into literature would thus have served the ends of those who possessed or sought power.[22]

There was little reason for the Israelite and Judean laws to be recorded while they were "living," for the people or groups among whom they functioned were familiar with them in oral form, which counted as fully valid without formal literary codification. However, there came a time of major and thorough social change affecting all levels of society, including the elites who had previously been able to maintain a steady hold on their status and power. With the rise of the Persian Empire in the latter half of the sixth century BCE, following the devastations and social disruptions under the Neo-Babylonians, the full restructuring of life in the province of Yehud (Judah) affected all socioeconomic groups in a manner previously not experienced. Now the Persian emperor found it expedient to adopt a strategy of granting considerable latitude to remote provinces—so long as they continued to send tribute to the capital of the empire and did not rebel against the imperial authority. As will be described in detail in chapter 4, there is textual evidence that Darius I in 519 BCE instructed the leaders of Egypt to record their laws in three areas: "the law of the pharaoh, the law of the temples, and the law of the people." These he could then join with his general law for the whole empire, yielding a combination of imperial and local rules, to which the Egyptians were held. A similar tactic may well have been followed for other provinces, including Judah; we know of no reason for Darius to have treated Egypt sui generis in his empire. In this general practice early in the Persian period, we thus have a clue to what precipitated the

21. See chap. 3 for more discussion and bibliography regarding Critical Legal Studies.
22. Power relations in ancient Israel are discussed in my "Political Rights and Powers in Monarchic Israel," *Semeia* 66 (1994): 93–117.

formation of legal texts. As he did for Egypt, Darius must have turned to the Judean leaders to compile and deliver a set of laws to him. It was, one must admit, a shrewd move, which benefited imperial control of the province; at the same time it provided the new Judean elites, shortly after their return from exile, the opportunity to define the legal norms for the country and thereby secure their own interests in this period of social, political, and economic change.

The four long legal collections of the Hebrew Bible, which scholars have generally tied to widely separated periods throughout Israel's history, should thus be seen in a different light: as written products of the Persian period, probably well after Darius's initial stimulus to write laws. The biblical texts parallel tantalizingly well the three categories stipulated by Darius for the Egyptian codes: state law, religious ordinances, and customary laws. The Deuteronomic Code has the centralization of power, both political and religious, as a major theme, and it reflects more of an urban society. The Holiness Code and the Priestly Code enshrine the cultic regulations. The Covenant Code looks like customary laws, the kinds of procedures and principles one might expect throughout the numerous villages scattered over the landscape. All of these compilations contain a variety of topics, although the substantive laws *within* each literary block do not show much in the way of direct internal conflict or inconsistency. For example, the Covenant Code does not refer to different practices on any one topic, as must surely have existed from village to village, such as the amount of restitution assessed for a specific type of damage; instead, the collection implies uniformity across the country. Differences are more notable when one compares the various collections with each other in light of their social settings.

There are no conclusive grounds for assigning each collection to such distinct historical periods, as is conventionally done. Some old Israelite laws may be retained in these late compilations, especially in light of the continuity that can occur in any of these social settings, but such laws need to be identified and explained on an ad hoc basis. Attributing the initial composition of the Hebrew Bible's legal literature to the postexilic period also helps to account for the convergence between the biblical laws and the ancient legal traditions of Babylonia and Assyria, for the people of Israel and Judah became directly exposed to those laws during their long periods of vassalage. The usual hypotheses dating especially the Covenant Code and the Deuteronomic Code to the preexilic period are much less satisfactory in accounting for cultural contact with other Southwest Asian legal texts.

The basic approach taken in this study can be stated succinctly. For the "biblical laws" I will attend mainly to the special interests at work during the production of their texts. For "Israelite laws" I will primarily focus on their respective jurisdictions and social settings, in particular the rural, the urban, and the cultic contexts. And throughout, the issue of power will remain at the forefront: *Whose* law is it in each case? Who benefits and who suffers, especially along social, political, and economic lines? All of these angles of vision will converge to offer a picture of the social history of justice and injustice in ancient Israel.

CHAPTER 2

The Power of Law

The end of law is not to abolish or restrain, but to preserve and enlarge freedom: for in all the states of created beings capable of laws, where there is no law, there is no freedom.

—John Locke[1]

In legal theory it is commonplace to distinguish between positive law and natural law. *Positive laws* are explicitly enacted by a legislature or some other official or institution or, in the case of folk societies lacking a central law-making body, are developed through some accepted process among those responsible for maintaining societal order or resolving disputes between parties. These laws are generally understood to be socially constructed, even if the people governed by them hold them to be intrinsic and essential to the world as they know it, perhaps even an expression of natural law. *Natural laws*, on the other hand, include prescriptions and protections attributed through philosophical, moral, or religious conviction to the very nature of things. Usually such natural laws take the form of rather general statements of rights or duties, principles that positive laws may translate into enforceable obligations. Since by definition the natural laws are not thought to derive from a given society's legislative activity even if they are affirmed by its law, they are typically ascribed to the divine realm, or to natural realities, or to the human condition.

Societies themselves generally do not sense or articulate the difference between positive and natural laws. The relationship between the two emerges typically as a matter of debate among legal theorists, philosophers, and ethicists, often in connection with the question of human nature and human rights. As far as we know, ancient Israel did not draw a distinction between positive and natural laws. Biblical law is presented as divine law and is thus cast as being of an order different from human law, although

---

1. John Locke, *The Second Treatise of Government* (1689), 6.57.

with that self-identification its ideological leanings are not yet examined. The prophets seem to root justice in divinity—almost a type of protonatural law. Nonetheless, we can fairly note that the Israelites did not explicitly base their legal system on a doctrine of inalienable human rights.[2] Each of their many individual positive laws came into existence through one human means or the other, under one set of influences or the other, and in one sociohistorical period or the other. The same can be said of the literary rendering of laws now retained in the Hebrew Bible. Our task, then, is to understand their legal traditions—the positive laws and the ideologies associated with them—in light of the multiple factors at play. Questions of the general nature of law and its relation to, particularly, societal and political structures and values will serve as our point of departure. While focusing on positive laws, however, we also need to attend to the ways in which the ancient Israelites regarded their (positive) laws as divinely ordained and incumbent on their life in this world.

SOCIAL ORDER AND CONTROL

Every social group needs to establish and maintain some type of orderly existence for itself. To a great extent, a society—both its parts and its whole—achieves this order through informal, noninstitutional, consensual means. Parents raise their children to conform to certain modes of behavior and to avoid other types of action. The younger generation becomes gradually inculcated in the vast range of norms developed by that society for smooth and appropriate living within the group: matters of etiquette and decorum, taste and fashion, conduct befitting rank and status, physical behavior, actions condoned or forbidden in gender relationships, attitudes about institutions, religious beliefs and rituals, moral values, taboos, ideals and visions for the group and the individual, and much more that make up the culture and ethos of that society. A system of rewards and punishments—whether physical, economic, or intangible (such as honor and shame)—serves to reinforce these standards. Learned behavior of this sort is commonly called social norms or mores or, more popularly, customs. All societies operate with norms and sanctions, and each culture comprises its own unique blend of standards and expectations.

The question of norm creation belongs, properly speaking, to the fields of sociology and social psychology. We can see social norms in operation, but tracing them back to their origins is notoriously problematic. As a

2. See my discussion in "Political Rights and Powers."

general rule, a combination of factors should be expected: accommodation to the environmental demands of the people's locale, notions about the nature of the world and the people's place in it, the exigencies of finding food and shelter, negotiation of identity and community, establishment of the terms for reproduction and child rearing, and—not least—the influence of prior and alternative values and social structures. Norms do not spring de novo in a world devoid of context but respond to givens and needs, in turn facilitating social interaction. And they are constantly under construction and under scrutiny. Indeed, resistance to or violation of existing norms can lead to reform measures that relax, strengthen, or restructure those standards of behavior.

Laws should be understood within this context of the regulation of behavior, although they also differ from other types of social norms. Though the line dividing custom from law is at times subtle, we can detect the difference between the two most readily by observing the type of action triggered by a violation: an informal response for deviating from a custom and a formal action for breaking a law. In other words, infraction of a custom is not, as a rule, legally actionable: it does not lead to formal judicial proceedings initiated by the state or by the injured party against the violator. Breaking a law, on the other hand, will normally bring in its wake a judicatory process before judge or jury in order to determine guilt and punishment, or liability and remedy. This distinction is more apparent in modern cultures than in many traditional, premodern societies, as signaled by the term "customary law." Customs can assume the force of law by effectively directing, restraining, and disciplining conduct, especially in small communities or groups where behavior is closely watched. Law functions differently in that it exercises control in a formally legitimated and authoritative manner, with specific prescribed means available for dealing with violations.

At the same time, this line between the two phenomena can also shift: a custom can with time become a law, and vice versa. Especially in smaller traditional societies, laws typically originate as social norms and eventually acquire such importance that they become translated into law in order to ensure compliance with them. If literacy is extremely limited or even nonexistent, the customary laws will be preserved in largely unwritten form. Yet written or not, such laws carry equal power and authority for controlling behavior; the laws in unwritten form often prove to be even more tenacious and binding because they are owned and applied directly by the community, rather than being filed away in a legal library and often little known or understood by the people affected. It not infrequently happens that members of a social group will confuse law and custom, unaware that a given custom has no legal force or that a specific legal norm is "on the books." At any rate, the stage when customary laws prevail can be of central importance in the development of a society's legal tradition, as we will see to be the case for ancient Israel.

One specific example at this point may prove useful. The literary form used in the Ten Commandments has long been accorded special significance, primarily because of the theological and ethical meanings attached to the Ten Commandments themselves. Termed "apodictic laws,"[3] they lay out general principles, largely without punishments being specified. Albrecht Alt, in his groundbreaking study of 1934, considered this form of principle law or categorical law to be unique to Israel, and he posited that it originated in cultic worship at an early point in the people's history.[4] Decades later, Erhard Gerstenberger finally made the rather obvious observation that the apodictic statement, pronouncing a global prohibition or rule, is extremely common to the everyday life of families and clans and should therefore not be attributed to the religious realm.[5] There is no way to confirm this dictum, but plausibly all parents everywhere give their children general directives, such as "Obey your parents, Do not steal, Do not lie, Do not overstep specific sexual boundaries." In the case of many of the Ten Commandments, then, what began as domestic and social norms have merely been moved into the religious world, expanded with additional prohibitions, and placed in the mouth of the Israelite God.

Most modern large-scale societies (totalitarian states can be an exception) have legislative bodies, and laws are written in line with the legislators' findings and values, the pressures exerted by special-interest groups, or the mandates of "the people," a term often used rhetorically by politicians. This sheer complexity of interests and rights has resulted in the rise of legal professionals—not only lawmakers but also attorneys, judges, teachers, researchers, librarians, law-enforcement personnel, criminologists, and various other specialists. We all are well familiar with this situation. It is mentioned here only to highlight the fact that law and the legal professions as we know them should not govern our appraisal of law in other, "less-advanced" societies. Laws can and do exist in societies lacking

---

3. See the discussion below in chap. 4, Legal Forms.

4. Albrecht Alt, "Die Ursprünge des israelitischen Rechts," in *Kleine Schriften zur Geschichte des Volkes Israel* (Munich: Verlag C. H. Beck, 1953; original essay in 1934), 1:278–332, esp. 302–32 = "The Origins of Israelite Law," in *Essays on Old Testament History and Religion*, trans. R. A. Wilson (Garden City, NY: Doubleday, 1967), 101–71, esp. 133–71.

5. Erhard Gerstenberger, *Wesen und Herkunft des "apodiktischen Rechts,"* WMANT 20 (Neukirchen: Neukirchener Verlag, 1965), esp. 110–17.

the intricate legal apparatus with which we live, but it requires a special effort on our part if we hope to understand the workings of law in cultures drastically different from our own, societies where laws are often not codified in writing, where the legislating power is largely invisible, where legal reforms are made incrementally, and where judicial bodies are convened almost as is a militia—only as the need arises and often with nonprofessionals responsible.

RESOLVING CONFLICT

Implicit to the nature of law is *conflict between parties*, or at least the potential for a dispute. Laws serve the purpose of preventing and resolving disputes over injuries, losses, rights, obligations, relationships, and general social order. In most cases, controversies form the immediate source of laws: if there had been no conflict or potential for conflict, then most likely no need for a law would have been recognized. This circumstance seems obvious enough at one level. However, as we will see when we consider issues of power, laws can also be written or manipulated to protect those with special interests or to avert competing claims from even being presented.

Aside from claims dealing with procedural matters in the judicial process, the two basic kinds of disputes leading to court proceedings are crimes and torts. On the one hand, a *crime* is generally understood to be an offense against the state or, in a stateless society, against the community or the communal good. An explicit prohibition or requirement—a positive law—that has been enacted by the legitimate authorities is violated, and as a result the state or community can bring a legal action against the violator. If found guilty, the criminal must suffer the consequences mandated by the state or community: penalties ranging from capital punishment or imprisonment to a fine (rendered to the state, not to a private individual) or removal from office or other loss of privilege. There can be a substantial range or grade of crimes, each with its own punishment depending largely on the severity of the threat or offense to the society. A *tort*, on the other hand, is a wrong or injury that is civil or private in nature. Typically the parties involve person against person, rather than the state or community against a person. In most cases, there is some duty that the defendant has to the plaintiff, and its violation or omission is to be adjudicated not privately but through a legal process: in a trial. The remedy will take the form of damages to be paid to the plaintiff. Torts are more common than crimes in most premodern or stateless societies, which gives a special cast to those legal systems: restitution to the injured party is needed, normally not fines paid to the state.

When a controversy between two parties occurs, the judgment resolving it can be translated into more general legal form to serve as a controlling factor—as a precedent or a principle—for similar conflicts in the future. Often the creation of precedents does not occur intentionally. When two parties are at odds in a tort case, the adjudicating body will need to determine whether one party has suffered damages due to the fault of the other party and how the damages are to be remedied or compensated. A famous set of disputes found in various forms in the legal texts of three ancient Southwest Asian cultures—Sumer, Babylonia, and Israel[6]—illustrates this process well: If one person's ox has caused damage or death to another's person or property, the fault needs to be determined, any background to the fault clarified (e.g., whether the ox has a record of similar attacks in the past), liability determined, and restitution or penalty for the damages assessed. Once such a case has been adjudicated, it can serve as a basis or precedent for identical cases in the future within that community. And if future cases vary in some manner from the former incidents, those considerations will be incorporated in any new decisions. In such a manner, a precedent begins to function as an expectation of how identical or similar cases are to be handled, and the net effect is a law: a statement of what has previously been found to be a violation and how it is to be treated judicially. Ideally the law will then serve as a deterrent against similar types of damaging actions in the future.[7]

Laws, at least in traditional societies lacking formal legislatures, thus emerge typically from the ongoing day-to-day need to settle and forestall controversies. One can reasonably argue that, if a law exists, the problem it is seeking to resolve must have existed as well. Thus, if there are laws addressing the destructive actions of oxen, then it is likely that oxen in that society did damage persons and property—or such a law would not have arisen in the first place. Or to take another example, if there is a regulation prohibiting the moving of boundary markers between two properties (Deut 19:14), then probably boundary markers were actually being

6. The Laws of Eshnunna, §§53–55; the Code of Hammurabi, §§250–252; Exod 21:28–32, 35–36. See the further discussion below, chap. 5, Liability.

7. Laws have other purposes than deterrence. As we will see in chaps. 5–7, laws also seek to maintain or restore order and to punish the guilty. Rehabilitation of those convicted of crimes figures as an important feature of many modern justice systems, but it seems to have been of much less significance in ancient Israel or anywhere else in Southwest Asia.

moved or could be moved in ancient Israel.[8] As we saw in the previous chapter, biblical laws and Israelite laws are not to be equated; yet there is likely to be some referent in historical reality to what is described in the text—if not to the reality depicted (in these cases, the marauding ox or the illicit moving of boundary stones), then perhaps to an agenda lying behind the laws (e.g., a drive by those with property and livestock to preserve their holdings).

With this final observation regarding the intimate relationship between law and conflict, we touch on the issue to be addressed in greater detail in the next chapter: whatever conflict the law might purport to resolve, another quite different aim may in fact be lurking behind it. Legal rights and processes can easily be subverted by those with the power to skew justice in their favor. At one level, such manipulation can occur within a given community as those with higher status, such as males or free persons or landowners, prejudice the laws in their favor so that certain types of disputes will not even arise and others will be resolved to their benefit. At another level, an even higher authority, such as the king or others associated with centralized power, can by dint of sheer force have their own way in conflict situations by preempting the decisions that a local judicatory might reach. Both of these possibilities are cited in biblical texts, most notably by the prophets (see, e.g., Amos 5:10–12 for the former and 2 Sam 12:1–15 for the latter), as a significant cause for the unfair administration of justice among the people. By observing that conflict between parties serves as a major source for emerging laws, we are not at the same time affirming that the resulting laws or precedents necessarily enjoyed widespread support among the populace. If legal decisions are imposed by the powerful, they may indeed issue in enforceable laws, but not necessarily ones affirmed by the larger society or held by them to be consistent with natural law or with other key aspects of the legal tradition.

THE NATURE AND SOURCES OF LAW

Viewed in light of its relation to both customs and conflicts, what then is a "law"? As commonplace and self-evident as the concept may seem, legal theorists and anthropologists have been deeply divided over what precisely is meant by the term.[9] At the root of the problem is the very multiplex

8. See also below, chap. 5, Real Property, and chap. 6, Real Property, regarding differences between rural and urban landowners on this matter of boundary markers.

9. Leopold Pospíšil describes, for example, six major ways in which law has been conceived: as a cultural achievement possible only in complex or stratified societies; as a

nature of a phenomenon that in some form or another seems, as already mentioned, to be present in societies of all times and places and of varying degrees of social complexity. Indeed, "law" is so broad a category that it defies simple characterization. Subdisciplines such as the anthropology of law[10] and the sociology of law[11] have emerged to study law in terms of comparative evidence and to assess the place and role of law within a given social system. The results of such studies bear directly on the relationship between law and power in ancient Israel, the paramount focus of the present work.[12]

---

phenomenon found only in societies with a strict political structure; as a cultural characteristic understandable not through analytical or cross-cultural theories but only intrinsically, through the thought patterns and language of that particular culture; as a single aspect which, though cross-culturally identified, is too limited, vague, or widespread to be helpful, such as sanction or obligation; and as a combination of multiple attributes. Leopold Pospíšil, *The Ethnology of Law*, Addison-Wesley Module in Anthropology 12 (Reading, MA: Addison-Wesley, 1972), 5–7.

10. Seminal anthropological studies of law include Bronislaw Malinowski, *Crime and Custom in Savage Society* (New York: Humanities Press; London: Routledge & Kegan Paul, 1926); E. Adamson Hoebel, *The Law of Primitive Man: A Study in Comparative Legal Dynamics* (Cambridge, MA: Harvard University Press, 1954); Max Gluckman, *Politics, Law and Ritual in Tribal Society* (Oxford: Basil Blackwell Publishing, 1965); Leopold Pospíšil, *Anthropology of Law: A Comparative Theory* (New York: Harper & Row, 1971); and James M. Donovan and H. Edwin Anderson III, *Anthropology and Law* (New York and Oxford: Berghahn Books, 2003). Numerous other anthropological studies focus on law and judicial systems in specific cultures around the world, such as K. N. Llewellyn and E. Adamson Hoebel, *The Cheyenne Way: Conflict and Case Law in Primitive Jurisprudence* (Norman: University of Oklahoma Press, 1941); Max Gluckman, *The Judicial Process among the Barotse of Northern Rhodesia* (Glencoe, IL: Free Press, 1955); idem, *The Ideas in Barotse Jurisprudence* (New Haven, CT: Yale University Press, 1965); Paul Bohannan, *Justice and Judgment among the Tiv* (London: Oxford University Press, 1957); P. H. Gulliver, *Social Control in an African Society: A Study of the Arusha* (Boston: Boston University Press, 1963); and Laura Nader and Harry F. Todd Jr., eds., *The Disputing Process: Law in Ten Societies* (New York: Columbia University Press, 1978).

11. See, e.g., Ehrlich, *Fundamental Principles of the Sociology of Law*; N. S. Timasheff, *An Introduction to the Sociology of Law*, Harvard Sociological Studies 3 (Cambridge, MA: Harvard University Committee on Research in the Social Sciences, 1939); Charles E. Reasons and Robert M. Rich, *The Sociology of Law: A Conflict Perspective* (Toronto: Butterworths, 1978); Roger Cotterrell, *The Sociology of Law: An Introduction* (London: Butterworths, 1984).

12. Anthropological and sociological studies of law rarely take note of the legal situation in ancient Israel or ancient Southwest Asia. Such is the case in, for example, Katherine S. Newman's otherwise very enlightening study of preindustrial societies, *Law and Economic Organization: A Comparative Study of Preindustrial Societies* (Cambridge and New York: Cambridge University Press, 1983). While Roman law figures prominently in discussions of legal evolution, legal systems, and the history of civil law, scant attention is given to Israelite law, despite the substantial corpus of laws represented in the Hebrew Bible. When noted, it most commonly appears with respect to two subjects: either the practice of restitution and retaliation ("an eye for an eye . . ."), or the relationship between law and religion (particularly with respect to either the Ten Commandments or the prophetic criticism of society's disobedience of the laws). Despite the innumerable studies by biblical scholars on various aspects of Israelite law, the paucity of specialized studies placing these laws in their sociojuridical contexts perhaps accounts for the difficulties that ethnographers have in knowing how to do much more than allude in general terms to selected features of biblical laws. To be sure,

From the perspective of social anthropology, a law has four primary attributes:[13]

1. It is vested with *authority, force, and legitimacy* in the sense that the disputing parties can be expected or coerced to comply with a decision based on it. Similarly, the individual or group that renders the decision possesses the authority to do so, whether it is granted them through the people's consensus or seized through their own power to enforce the judgment. Such authority can range from a complex, formalized, bureaucratic structure to a more traditional system keyed to the status of the leaders.

2. A law incorporates *a precedent-setting or -appropriating intention.* It is normally expressed in a general or even universal manner, although its actual jurisdiction is limited to the given social group that authors or legitimates it. A decision reached by the legitimate judge(s) is not meant to resolve only that one dispute but to have relevance for other similar conflicts, whether through appropriating an earlier precedent or setting a new precedent for subsequent judicatories to appropriate. Intention may differ from actuality, and normally the legal principle will be changed if it fails for long to regulate behavior or if it lacks influence as a precedent.

3. A law defines, at least implicitly if not explicitly, *a reciprocal relationship between parties in terms of protections and duties.* It identifies what one person or group deserves (e.g., not to be robbed, not to be murdered, not to suffer loss because of another's action or neglect) and what is concomitantly required of the others (i.e., not to rob, not to murder, not to cause another's loss through action or neglect). A law thus articulates a social, legal relationship of mutuality. In the event of a violation, the plaintiff deserves to have the loss restored or to see the act punished, and the defendant is justly expected to redress the wrong or to suffer appropriate consequences.

4. Finally, a law carries with it *sanctions* that provide the legitimate consequence for any violation or omission. Usually these punishments are physical (e.g., execution, beating, imprisonment) or economic (e.g.,

anthropologists confront special problems when faced with a society that is no longer alive and subject to direct observation. However, the task is not impossible, as Gillian Feeley-Harnik ("Is Historical Anthropology Possible? The Case of the Runaway Slave," in *Humanizing America's Iconic Book: Society of Biblical Literature Centennial Addresses 1980*, ed. Gene M. Tucker and Douglas A. Knight, SBLBSNA 6 [Chico, CA: Scholars Press, 1982], 95–126) has demonstrated in her study of slavery. David Daube, approaching Israelite laws as a legal historian and a specialist in Roman law, has contributed much to the elucidation of Israel's laws, which should also prove valuable to other legal historians and anthropologists; see, e.g., *Studies in Biblical Law* (Cambridge: Cambridge University Press, 1947). By elaborating the connection of Israelite and other Southwest Asian laws to their respective social and political contexts, social historians specializing in that region and time may enhance the possibility for comparativists to consider these legal traditions more adequately in their broader studies of legal phenomena.

13. See Pospíšil, *Anthropology of Law*, 39–96.

restitution, fines), but in many societies emotional means such as public reprimand or other forms of shaming can be equally or even more effective as a form of restraint. Although normally taking the form of penalties, sanctions can also be positive in nature, offering honor, status, or other rewards for those who conform to legal requirements.

All of these attributes are evident in ancient Israel's systems of law, although frequently the elements must be surmised due to our lack of information. The laws emerged and were enforced in social contexts where authority resided in specific groups, such as the elders or household heads in a village, or in individuals or offices, such as judges functioning under royal mandate. The legal prescriptions were crafted in a generalized fashion so as to be applicable to all instances of a given offense, even though the jurisdiction in a given case might in actuality have been limited to a narrow social period or group. Though we know of no listing of legal rights guaranteed to Israelite citizens or residents—nor should we expect to find such since the jurisprudential interest in human rights is largely a modern phenomenon—the reciprocal duties and obligations bearing on Israelites are at least implicit and often explicit throughout the legal corpora. Finally, many of the biblical laws, and in all likelihood most of the Israelite laws also, specify the consequences that should follow upon violations.

LEGAL SYSTEMS

To understand laws requires more than regarding them in isolation from each other or reducing them to some abstract form. Taken together, a group of laws constitutes a legal system dependent on a given social network. The idea of a "legal system" thus connects legal studies with a concept basic to various other areas of study. Known as systems analysis, this method and perspective underlie work in a variety of social-scientific fields, including anthropology, sociology, economics, political science, and psychology; parallels are also prevalent in mathematics, physics, biology, geography, systems engineering, and information sciences. While the systems model is capable of many variations in these fields and while certain forms of it may at times be justly criticized as being overly mechanistic or even as controlling the data,[14] the basic idea is sound: the given system

14. Niels Peter Lemche ("On the Use of 'System Theory,' 'Macro Theories,' and 'Evolutionistic Thinking' in Modern OT Research and Biblical Archaeology," *SJOT* 2 [1990]: 73–88) expresses a legitimate concern about the ways in which biblical scholars, as well as specialists in other areas of the humanities, have used a systems approach as a positivistic method to bring the historical "facts" together into a hypothesis. Such an approach has often yielded a

(e.g., legal, political, religious, biological, ecological) is not a static but a dynamic entity, constantly in process, and it comprises multiple elements interacting with each other and with their larger environment. Furthermore, the system is open and adaptive in the sense that it responds to and adjusts itself in light of actions and influences, whether these come from within the system or from outside of it. When the system involves individual humans or whole societies, it represents an incredible complexity of factors, some repetitive and regular but many unpredictable and variable. Finally, a system is composite in the sense that it is made up of multiple complex subsystems, each functioning on its own as well as in the context of other subsystems and the overall system itself. Interaction among systems, such as on the international scene between two countries or social systems, can also produce significant consequences.

Israelite law constituted a subsystem of the overall social system of the country. Three cautionary observations, however, are warranted. First, the legal subsystem coexisted and interacted with other subsystems but was not identical with any one of them. The monarchic government in ancient Israel ran under its own steam, driven by various levels of officials and bureaucrats, who followed rules and protocols of more importance within their own subsystem than without; they could use the laws of the land, could often enough dictate them, but were also limited by them to the extent that they needed to accommodate the interests and customs of the people. Similarly, the religious institutions—the priesthood, the tradition of prophets, other quasi-religious entities such as the sages—each developed its own identity, norms, and culture of performance, all of which affected the distinctive way in which each related to the legal network. The world of commerce, even without an intricate market economy, involved persons who were professionally engaged, specializing in international or domestic trade, production and distribution of distinctive goods (e.g., luxury items),

───────────────

"macrotheory" or "heuristic model" that seems to take on a life of its own; the best example may be Martin Noth's amphictyonic hypothesis regarding the organization of early Israelite society (*Das System der zwölf Stämme Israels*, BWANT 4/1 [Stuttgart: W. Kohlhammer, 1930; 2nd ed., Darmstadt: Wissenschaftliche Buchgesellschaft, 1966]). Lemche rightly notes that such efforts to apply "scientific epistemology" to humanistic studies have met with increasing skepticism, in part as a result of renewed analysis of the data and in part in line with postmodernist criticisms. I am not proposing a "systems model" here in the sense described by Lemche; in fact, the old model of interpreting biblical law historically—treating the legal texts as historical sources and arranging the "codes" according to sequentially separate time periods—is in my view fundamentally problematic and insufficient. Rather, I mention systems only in the sense of structural functionalism: Laws in ancient Israel are not isolated phenomena, and they should not be abstracted from their contexts and associated primarily with only one sector, such as the religious sphere. Laws fit within social, political, and economic systems, which they intend to promote and secure—often in ways they do not explicitly acknowledge.

and even bartering at the local level; in all instances legal constraints could affect their practices, although these persons could also effect change in the laws in order to facilitate their business. The subsystem of kinship ties was especially influential in the folk culture lying at the base of community life; its rules and customs fed the store of laws as much as did any other part of the larger society, yet in turn it was stabilized and restricted by these laws as well. Any number of other subsystems with a more or less clearly distinct profile could be similarly described: the military, socioeconomic classes, groupings according to habitation (a region, a village, a city, a neighborhood), divisions defined by gender or generation, and more. If we possessed enough data, it would be possible to trace the legal subsystem longitudinally; such an effort actually lies at the base of the conventional picture of the history of the biblical law "codes." In the absence of reliable information for all historical periods, however, a cross-sectional social analysis limited to a more restricted period of time, such as the Iron Age II period of the monarchy, lies more within our grasp. Here the interactions among the legal subsystems and the other parts of the society will be especially evident, as we will see in later chapters.

Second, Israelite law is by no means homogeneous: it should not be regarded as *a* subsystem but as subsystem*s* within the larger society. Reducing law to a single entity—as if there were only one law of the land at any given time—has led interpreters to project onto it an unrealistic degree of uniformity. In all likelihood, legal practices and principles diverged widely between city and countryside, if for no other reason than because of the different means of subsistence prevalent in each context. Furthermore, laws could vary substantially even from village to village, especially with the absence of any controlling interregional body to oversee and standardize local practices.[15] Under the monarchy the state had minimal involvement in the folk laws, other than to control actions that touched directly on governmental interests: the command economy, taxation, the corvée, military conscription, rebellion or resistance, and the like.[16] The increasingly powerful priesthood centered in the Jerusalem cult sought, so it seems in several biblical texts, to stamp out local cults and to control the access of Levites and others to priestly prerogatives—all of which implies that a multiplicity of cultic norms and practices existed across the country and that the central priesthood tried to regulate it.[17] The interaction among the various legal subsystems should not, in other words, be idealized as

15. See chap. 5.
16. See chap. 6.
17. See chap. 7.

congenial in all cases, for antagonism and competition for control can be observed or suspected in various contexts.

Finally, to speak of *the* social system of the country in which the subsystems of law figure is only a form of shorthand. Entirely too much variation in societal structures existed over time and space to warrant any suggestion of uniformity. Ancient Israel did not take shape as a monolithic social structure, neither at any one time nor in any one sphere throughout the generations.[18] We can rightly class it as a traditional, preindustrial, small-scale agrarian folk society,[19] but in so doing we should not think of it as simple, lacking in complexity. The very absence of effective communication or control across the territories meant that each region and each hamlet had the chance to develop its own "social facts," to use Durkheim's term.[20] The terrain and ecological conditions varied substantially from region to region, which by itself had a significant impact on the options for living and associating within each community. The individual social systems had an internal integrity: each "worked" as a social entity and changed or adapted as new circumstances required. But despite all the similarities that certainly existed in the various social systems throughout the country, they were not all identical. To regard the entirety of Israel as a closed society is a convenience for us that is neither historically accurate nor analytically productive.

We are thus faced with a dizzying set of variable systems, permitting a seemingly infinite number of permutations in their interrelationships: multiple subsystems of law functioning in multiform social contexts. One may be tempted simply and doggedly to impose a picture of social uniformity across the country, but such an approach would misrepresent the complexities and differences that must certainly have prevailed. We cannot know all we might wish about the various subsystems of laws and judicial practices, but we can be certain that they constantly needed to interact with a wide variety of social, political, and economic realities. Law is by no means a constant or ready phenomenon and—to appropriate Mary Douglas's comment about primitive cosmologies—"cannot rightly be pinned out for display like exotic lepidoptera, without distortion to the nature of a primitive culture."[21] It can be studied, but viewing it, as one

18. For details, see Paula M. McNutt, *Reconstructing the Society of Ancient Israel*, LAI (Louisville, KY: Westminster John Knox Press; London: SPCK, 1999).

19. The characterization of Israel as an agrarian society will be elaborated in chap. 3.

20. Émile Durkheim, *The Rules of the Sociological Method*, ed. and introduced by Steven Lukes, trans. W. D. Halls (New York: Free Press, 1982; original ed., *Les règles de la méthode sociologique* [Paris: F. Alcan, 1895]), 50–59.

21. Mary Douglas, *Purity and Danger: An Analysis of Concepts of Pollution and Taboo* (London: Routledge & Kegan Paul, 1966), 91.

might any zoological specimen, outside its intricate natural environment will inevitably present limits to our chances for understanding the nuances of all its interrelationships.

There is one further important point deriving from this systems approach to law, which bears as much on our own contemporary appropriation of legal traditions from ancient Israel as' on the interpretation of laws in the ancient world. Taking a single law out of its social-legal complex and comparing it with a law or laws from another society's legal systems is at its base a problematic enterprise since its elements can easily, even unwittingly, be manipulated and distorted when they are removed from their natural contexts. For this reason the temptation, not often enough resisted, to compare laws from various societies—as on property rights or sexual offenses or capital punishment—can yield intriguing but largely inconclusive results if the various laws stem from legal and social systems that are basically dissimilar. The character of the social system is therefore as important as the individual law itself in making such comparisons. It makes a difference whether the social system is preindustrial or industrial, pastoral or sedentary, rural or urban, traditional or progressive, simple or complex. In terms of their political base, laws issued by the ruler can scarcely be equated with the customary laws stemming from the ruled, or those from imperial powers with those from the colonial provinces, or those from a militaristic state (e.g., the Middle Assyrian laws) with those from a more peaceful, nonexpansionist state. To be sure, in all of these instances some power structure functions within the second half of the equation just as it does in the first half—among the "ruled," in a colony, or in a nonbelligerent state—but this recognition only heightens our point that the social and political dimensions of any given law must necessarily be considered. Merely laying out on the table all the laws of Southwest Asia, or for that matter the laws from the Hebrew Bible or those from any other culture, and comparing them flatly with each other will not promote an adequate appreciation of their meaning and place in legal or social history.

The implication of this point touches us directly if we should wish to draw on biblical or Israelite laws as guides for our own legal values today. For example, one might take the position that capital punishment is acceptable today because the Bible orders and sanctions this response to certain types of criminal behavior. However, such direct importing of a legal custom rarely considers the social, political, economic, and even psychosocial differences between that ancient society and modern countries, especially in the West. In ancient Israel, prisons were not an option on the local level, and there is even little evidence for them in the state system. Today we have the economic and social means to support a penal system in which persons convicted of crimes can be detained for any period of time. We have also developed strategies to foster the rehabilitation of convicted criminals, and many of us today find it unconscionable not to make this effort even if societies in the biblical period did not. Furthermore, many of the biblical commands to execute wrongdoers must have been driven by the special interests of certain groups, who through rhetoric and threat, if not actual action, hoped to control types of religious behavior (e.g., idolatry, sorcery, work on the Sabbath), sexual conduct, disrespect toward parents, and more. Many other examples could be cited as cases in which the social dimensions of Israelite and biblical laws vary sharply from the situations facing us in the modern world: ecological matters, sexual issues, gender roles, slavery, production, commerce, and the like. At all of these points, appropriating a law without regard to the differences between the ancient and the modern social systems will appear as little more than an arbitrary act, faithful neither to the biblical world nor to our own. No one, to my knowledge, advocates importing Israel's whole social structure or entire legal system into today's world. Selecting one or the other law to appropriate from the biblical period, or to exclude, thus represents an arbitrary choice and is likely driven by a desire to legitimate one's own prior values.

LAWS AND LEGAL SYSTEMS OF ANTIQUITY

Do most traditional, premodern societies, including ancient Israel, tend to hold in common certain general characteristics of law? On the face of it, premodern societies seem to contrast much less with each other than they do with the socially complex, technologically advanced, and globally interconnected nation-states of today. It would be strange indeed to suppose that any one of those societies, in this case ancient Israel, is so radically distinctive from the others that it must be treated in a class of its own in a way that other societies do not also deserve. To declare a society unique is a tautology, and to pronounce it special and unrivaled is to privilege it unduly, a chauvinism that effectively insulates it from comparative studies. Yet ancient Israel and the Bible have all too frequently been treated in this manner, largely because of the veneration accorded them by religious communities over two millennia. They are often held to be so unusual and so influential as to be sui generis. According to such notions, the legal traditions from that culture would then, by implication if not assertion, also rise above those of all other lands or deserve to be treated in some special manner.

Actually, every society possesses distinctive traits and thus is unique. By dint of the sheer unpredictability and complexity of the human beings who form it, social systems are capable of infinite variations, and no two systems are fully parallel, much less identical to each other. Comparative studies seek both to expose the elements resembling each other as well as to ferret out the distinctive points. The specific task facing us, therefore, involves learning the legal traits typical in comparable societies without assuming that all of these elements were necessarily present in ancient Israel—or, for that matter, in any other single society either. Or to put the issue differently, Israel's legal systems were unmatched in the same sense that every culture's legal systems comprise unique combinations of ingredients and ideologies. Yet common ground can also be found with other ancient or premodern societies' legal traditions. We can go even further: In all likelihood, there is no single legal ingredient or ideological element in ancient Israel that cannot be found in some other setting, not necessarily in another part of ancient Southwest Asia but in some other culture in world history. How the various elements came together in Israel defines its distinctiveness, as is the case for all societies.

The traditional term for referring to the legal systems of premodern societies is "ancient law" or "primitive law." Since the nineteenth century and largely because of the groundbreaking work in 1861 of British jurist Sir Henry Sumner Maine,[22] interest in the field has increased considerably, especially in anthropology and certain branches of legal scholarship. Drawing on his familiarity with ancient Roman law, the laws of India, other Western and Eastern legal traditions, and some "primitive"[23] legal systems,

22. Henry Sumner Maine, *Ancient Law: Its Connection with the Early History of Society and Its Relation to Modern Ideas* (1861; reprint, with foreword by Lawrence Rosen, Tucson: University of Arizona Press, 1986).

23. In anthropology, the notion of "primitivism" is largely associated with 19th- and early 20th-c. theories about an early stage in the evolutionary development of culture (as outlined by, e.g., E. B. Tylor and Lewis Henry Morgan) or an early way of thinking (see, e.g., Lucien Lévy-Bruhl and G. van der Leeuw; and for critique, E. E. Evans-Pritchard). A primitive society was not necessarily inferior to modern cultures (although some evolutionists did seem to think so), but simply earlier on an evolutionary line. Such cultures are generally small, stateless, not complex in institutional structure, somewhat simple in material culture, and either preliterate or mainly illiterate. Since they represent a societal stage rather than a time period, they are not restricted to antiquity but can designate societies in modern times as well. "Primitive law," as used by Maine (*Ancient Law*) and others, refers to the legal systems of societies with such characteristics. In many respects, the prestate peoples living in the Canaanite highlands fit this anthropological model of a primitive society, but the situation shifts somewhat with the advent of the Israelite monarchy—although not thoroughly since villagers, who constituted perhaps 80–95% of the country's population, could maintain much of their traditional legal system even after and despite the centralization of the state. Basic to primitivist theories is the notion that primitive societies can be detected in fossilized forms within later societies. With regard to our specific topic, "primitive law" can thus appear in vestigial form in modern law,

Maine argued that law had developed along evolutionary lines together with the growth of society. Since later law was thus an outgrowth of early law, the study of legal history was in his view directly pertinent for the understanding of law in modern times, a point that ran counter to the opinions of most law scholars of his era. He conceived of law, however, in a rather strict form, disallowing its existence until society had become relatively complex.

In Maine's view, social evolution proceeds through several stages, each occurring at different points in world history depending on the society in question: first the family, in particular the extended family ruled by its patriarch; next what he called the "Gens or House," a type of clan comprising an aggregation of families; then the tribe, a collection of clans; and finally the state, which various tribes living in a territory combine to form. Kinship in blood, whether actual or fictive, is usually asserted in primitive societies as the basis for cohesion from the first to the last stage. However, the state finally succeeds in shifting the sense of community from the principle of consanguinity to the principle of "local contiguity," whereby polity and law become oriented to the fact that the people are sharing common space and thus need to have a more effective foundation for coexistence than the kinship structure alone promotes. For Maine, law does not exist until society in a given locale reaches the concluding phases of the tribal stage and, then fully, the state stage. During the earlier stages, social control is based on the dominant structure of the family: the patriarchal head exercises the authority to keep behavior within the limits he sets, which limits normally conform to the customs and traditions of the group. But when the society reaches a certain geographical range and social complexity because of the combination of not only families and clans but also multiple tribes, law needs to come into existence to effect order among groups not easily managed by a patriarchal figure.[24]

Maine succeeded in bringing "primitive law" to the attention and appreciation of legal scholars, although his notions of social evolution are no longer viable in light of subsequent anthropological work. Furthermore, he applied an understanding of law that was overly restrictive, failing to recognize the intimate connection between it and general social control. One might be willing to agree with him that rules and punishments within

---

which is precisely what Maine maintained. In the absence of a perfect alternative for the term "primitive" and in light of its often pejorative connotations, I will generally use words such as "ancient," "premodern," "preindustrial," or "traditional," recognizing that these latter terms are also not without their own problems.

24. Maine, *Ancient Law*, 93–141.

a family are private in nature—so long as they do not violate certain community values or standards (as in avoiding incest or providing for the children's welfare, for example); the very presence of such community standards and values regarding family life suggests social norms or incipient laws. Nonetheless, to achieve social control in circles wider than the family requires a measure of consensus, negotiation, or power among parties, each of whom possesses some autonomy and authority at the basic level of the family. Even if the society is ruled by a chief who serves as both legislator and judge, the community overtly or tacitly acknowledges this person's jurisdiction and the validity of the rules. Virtually any group the size of a village or larger will be guided not only by customs but also by laws according to which behavior is regulated and disputes are settled; the fact that these laws may not be written does not detract from their authority or function in that setting. A territorial state's laws will be developed and enforced in a more complex manner than may be needed in the smaller group, but that does not mean that the seemingly insignificant, semiautonomous hamlet cannot also have a fully operating, cohesive, and effective legal system in its own rights. Despite the conceit apparent in Maine's higher regard for written over unwritten law, his attention to the ancient roots of modern laws governing contracts, property, crimes, inheritance, and more set the stage for further anthropological and sociological studies of law.

There are other typical characteristics of premodern, preindustrial legal systems (i.e., ancient or "primitive" law) to note, many of which appear in the legal traditions of ancient Israel. Anthropological studies of legal structures have often indicated that some of the greatest differences between premodern societies and modern, complex civilizations are the procedures of administrating justice, not just the substantive laws themselves. In societies lacking centralized political authority, each kinship group adjudicates its own conflicts, based on a type of private law accepted by the society at large. Conflicts within a lineage are resolved by the head of the household, the patriarch of the kinship group. Disputes between parties not belonging to the same lineage, however, are typically handled either by a chief or by some kind of judicial council made up of all the heads of the families, convened on an ad hoc basis to deal with problems encroaching on the community's welfare. Here we can observe a type of public law, designed to prevent, among other things, the destructive and interminable feuds that have occasionally cropped up between lineage groups. There is little evidence, as has been supposed by some, that without such a legal system a community would devolve into continuous and excessively violent feuding.

Even with the autonomous nature of lineage groups, it is in the larger community's interest to maintain a mutually beneficial and harmonious, or at least stable, system. Nonetheless, vengeance and feuds certainly can constitute real threats in social settings, and some acceptable means need to emerge to keep all parties from simply annihilating each other. To this end, the principle of "an eye for an eye and a tooth for a tooth" represents a decisive effort to set limits on vengeance: only *one* eye for an eye, only *one* tooth for a tooth. Yet such public law is at the same time moderated by private law: many of the controls and conflicts regarding interests or injuries will be handled within the lineage group.

Premodern legal systems are often willing to assess guilt collectively in those cases where modern legal systems would punish only a single violator. Tending to treat legal violations more as torts than crimes,[25] premodern systems are not so much bent on punishing lawbreakers as they are oriented toward restitution of losses and restoration of social relations. Imprisonment is rarely practiced since it does not immediately serve such ends. It is more important that remedies be designed to repay injured parties for their loss, which will help them to regain their prior status and material welfare in the community. If the violator is shamed as a result, that sanction can function as part of the rectification process. The death penalty is reserved for socially dangerous acts, not only for homicide but often for incest, adultery, "sorcery" (an unclear phenomenon in the Hebrew Bible), and more. In some instances banning or shunning can take the place of capital punishment. Though the violator's state of mind or intent is sometimes considered to be a mitigating factor, the very fact that a social norm has been broken requires an appropriate judicial or ritual response, or the entire legal system and thus the health of the community may be jeopardized. When a judicial decision is reached or carried out, the parties or the community may engage in a type of public ritual to underscore the fulfillment of justice and the restoration of community relations.

The politics of law does not seem to be much recognized within premodern legal systems. There can be criticism from the outside, as in the case of the Israelite prophets who charge the people or their leaders with disobedience to the laws, but one rarely finds expressions of cynicism regarding the ways in which the powerful manage to effect and secure their will through substantive and procedural laws. Rather—and in fact precisely to this point—the authority of both the laws and the judges is generally grounded in religious terms, with the legal codes "pretending

25. Ibid., 307–8.

to supernatural origin," as observed by Maine.[26] In many such systems a god or goddess of justice inspires the laws and exacts punishment in the event of violations. Where the positive laws are not regarded as divinely ordained, the given society at least holds them to be natural and normal, consistent with the very order of life. In such settings, the rules of evidence in a trial can allow for oaths, ordeals, sacred lots, and other such devices that invoke the supernatural or the natural world.

Yet even in avowing the divine origin of law, premodern societies are able to accommodate change in their laws, whether it comes as a result of technological innovations, exposure to other cultures, or internal political shifts. The law, as powerful and permanent as it may appear as a means to regulate behavior, is thus not static. In cases such as conquest by a foreign power, the adaptations may be compelled from without. But fundamentally there is an "open texture"[27] to laws in these legal systems, with considerable discretion granted to judges to interpret the laws and adjust them for new situations. Thus a general law prohibiting theft may be inflected according to circumstance (e.g., does the thief break and enter a house during the daytime or during the night?), or intent (e.g., was the killing of a person intentional or accidental?), or status (e.g., was the killer, or the one killed, a slave or a free person?). However, legal reform, both for a whole legal system or for individual laws, will normally not be acknowledged as such since continuity and longevity in the legal tradition, with its roots reaching back to the "supernatural origin," belong to its legitimization; Maine refers to this factor as "legal fiction," the society's notion, because of a "superstitious disrelish for change,"[28] that its laws do not shift with new social or political conditions.

These various features of premodern legal systems, or what is frequently called ancient or "primitive" law, will not, as indicated above, be present in every small-scale, nonurban, decentralized, largely illiterate, preindustrial culture. A given society may possess certain elements but not others, and each culture must be examined on a case-by-case basis to determine the details of its legislative and judicial traditions. Nonetheless, as already noted, premodern legal systems will generally share more in common with each other than they will with the legal systems prevalent in modern industrial states. For this reason alone if for no other, perspectives resulting from the comparative study of law in other premodern, preindustrial societies provide a valuable context for analyzing the situations pertaining in ancient Israel.

26. Ibid., 22.
27. H. L. A. Hart, *The Concept of Law*, 2nd ed. (Oxford: Clarendon Press, 1994), 124–36.
28. Maine, *Ancient Law*, 22.

THE LAW AND THE LAWS

For both premodern and modern societies, much of the power of law resides in its symbolic meaning. When compared to anarchy and arbitrariness, a legal order represents a far preferable system for most social groups. A more transparent though invidious dimension of law is evident in our own day in the way in which the phrase "law and order" is used as a type of political rallying cry, often capitalizing on and even heightening fear about minorities, whose behavior is cast as threatening. There is no inherent problem with either "law" or "order" as such, but both can be manipulated to further the agenda of those in power or to assist others in gaining control. The critical issue, then, lies in the specific meaning or import attributed to law, and in particular its relation to other symbolic expressions current within the given social group.

To this point, we have been referring without clear distinctions to two different entities, "the law" and "the laws" (or "a law"), and we need now to articulate the difference between them. "The law," often rendered as a capitalized word in the phrase "the Law," carries an abstract sense, denoting a system of legal order. As the sum total of all legitimate components of legal control within the society in question, it embraces and yet also transcends the mass of individual positive laws. Termed *jus* in ancient Roman law, "the law" possesses symbolic power insofar as it expresses the ideological objectives of social harmony, or minimally the sense that one should not interfere with or injure other members of the community. To "break the law" amounts to more than merely violating a single rule; societal order is thereby transgressed, and some form of punishment or restitution must follow in order to restore the harmonious state of life in that social group. *Jus* thus possesses an ideological valence in addition to its juridical sense since it symbolizes the social order and relationships that ought to exist. To the extent that religion, ethos, and ideology are symbolic forms or expressions of a cultural system, "the law" represents their enforcement.

While "the law" in this sense is abstract, "laws" occur normally in concrete form, proscribing specific conduct or imposing certain duties and stipulating the consequences of violation. A law—*lex* (plural, *leges*) in Roman law—has an explicitly juridical function. Its moral character is ancillary, though morality may underlie it as a reflection of the values and strategies of that social group for establishing rights and responsibilities. Such laws can be aggregated into collections, although the extent to which they are systematized or codified in an orderly manner will depend on the given society. As "positive laws," the *leges* are generally contrasted with "natural laws," which are thought not to have been enacted or produced by the social group but to be inherent to the nature of humans or the world.[29]

Biblical Hebrew does not have a strict correspondence to such terms as *jus* and *lex*, yet there is a near equivalence to *jus* in the word תורה, *tôrâ*, which is itself set off from such other legal terms as "precept" (פקוד, *piqqûd*), "statute" (חק, *ḥōq*), "commandment" (מצוה, *miṣwâ*), and "judgment" (משפט, *mišpāṭ*). Occurring by far most frequently in biblical texts in the singular form (208 out of 220 times), *tôrâ* seldom appears within any of the biblical laws themselves: it occurs twenty-one times formulaically ("this is the law . . ." or "these are the laws . . .") in Leviticus and Numbers to introduce or conclude ritual or cultic ordinances on various subjects, and then notably three times in Deut 17 to refer to the law of the priests and the law of the king. Primarily it functions as a theocratic symbol—to affirm that the legal order is ordained by God and, at least by implication, that the leaders of the country or the priests are its caretakers. The few cases of nontheocratic usage of *tôrâ*, primarily in the Wisdom literature, where it is generally understood to designate sagacious teachings (e.g., Prov 3:1; 13:14; Job 27:11), may point to its nonreligious origins in the contexts of family and clan socialization.

However, the word possesses another aspect that is especially revealing. Virtually every study of biblical law, it seems, rushes to emphasize that *tôrâ* in the Hebrew Bible does not mean "law" in its usual sense (presumably the contrast is with *lex* and maybe even with *jus* as well) but rather has the basic meaning of "instruction." According to this conventional explanation, the legalistic dimensions are much lessened in favor of a benign, necessary teaching function. Biblical law, it follows, should not be depicted as an onerous structure imposed on the people, but rather as a gift for the benefit of the people from their caring God. It should be heeded in its entirety and without question.

It is true that forms of its verbal root ירה (*yārâ* III; e.g., מורה, *môreh*, "teacher") refer explicitly to the teaching activity carried out by parents, sages, priests, friends, and the Israelite God, and the same valence attaches to *tôrâ*. The presumed didactic function, however, is not usually of the type witnessed in a school setting but takes the form of inculcating the fundamental terms governing life in the Israelite community. Such teaching also occurred in Israel within the trades, in the family, and in other contexts, where the content embraced the more pragmatic matters of daily life. When the priest, the prophet, or Israel's God conveys these instructions, a

29. See above, chap. 2.

religious tenor prevails. However, it was probably not until the exilic and postexilic times, when the religious establishment appropriated the concept and limited it primarily to doctrines about cultic practices and God's will, that *tôrâ* acquired a distinctly theological meaning. But such was not its original import. From the earliest point in Israel's history and on to its conclusion, teaching in the ways of living—both in the sense of social norms and in the pragmatics of life—persisted as an inevitable component of Israelite existence, just as would be expected in most societies. The processes of socialization and training underlie the notion of law as "instruction," and the everyday context of living in ancient Israel constituted the normal sphere in which it occurred.

We thus need to be mindful of two primary contexts in which *tôrâ* could appear. On the one hand, we can see it functioning in the Hebrew Bible as a potent, compelling symbol: the law originates with Israel's God, denoting the set of expectations that have religious weight attached to them, and the people are "instructed" to comply with them or face dire consequences. This very compulsion and the threat of punishment, whether for cultic or for more secular offenses, provide the ideological critic the means for inquiring into the social, political, economic, and religious stakes that certain groups may have attached to compliance by the populace, as we will discuss in more detail in the following chapter.[30]

On the other hand, we also need to consider Israelite laws, not just biblical laws. In the real world of person-to-person interactions, dispersed settlements, urban enclaves, and central powers, it is difficult to imagine a term like *tôrâ* functioning in quite the same way as it can in a text. Laws existed in the Israelite society to settle actual conflicts or to deter conflicts from occurring. Although we are not likely to recover the practice of instruction in detail, inculcation occurred in family and community settings at the local level, just as central powers pressed their will on the populations scattered throughout the country. But neither of these forms has the look of the "instruction" ascribed to the biblical tradition. The people's customs constituted a body of practices and values into which the younger generation was trained or socialized. But laws go beyond customs in terms of their judicial enforceability, and they are immediately relevant to those who can be held legally liable: the adults. A parent can instruct a child with the warning that one must not steal, but the court is convened not in the first instance to instruct but to punish or to seek remedies from those who steal. It was not until late in Israelite history, during the Persian or even as

30. See below, chap. 3, Torah as "Instruction."

late as the Hellenistic era, that there was a single corpus of "literary laws," and then it was more the product and possession of the priests and leaders than it was a shared heritage of the people at large. *Tôrâ* is religious literature, to be read by the literate or recited authoritatively to the nonliterate.

LAW, MORALITY, AND RELIGION

The question of the relation between law on the one hand and morality or religion on the other has been much debated, and legal specialists, ethicists, philosophers, theologians, anthropologists, and cultural critics—to name just a few of the obviously interested parties—vary widely in their estimation of the relationship. Even compiling a mere list of issues in the debates can prove frustrating since the issues often prove to be discipline specific or at least are weighted heavily in terms of the larger concerns of a given field. The more useful course for us in this context will be to remain with the methods and perspectives followed in this study—social history and ideological criticism—in assessing the situation that pertained in the world of ancient Israel.[31]

One may be inclined simply to equate the legal system with the moral and religious systems. "Equate" is not the correct word to use, though, since each system has its particular character, role, and components. Perhaps "overlay" or, colloquially, "map onto" or just "overlap" would be preferable to express their substantial convergence. Alternatively, one could speak of the moral or religious dimension of law, or of the legal aspects of morality and religion. The interrelationship of primary components in a society or culture belongs to a fundamental insight of theoretical sociology and social anthropology, as developed since the early part of the twentieth century. Biblical laws must certainly have coincided with moral practices or ideals in ancient Israel—or at least in large part, one would think. Moreover, the laws are so closely connected with religious matters—whether in ordaining proper cultic and pious behavior or in finding in religion the rationale for moral ideals or the justification for types of punishment—that one is scarcely conceivable without the other.

A larger conceptual framework in ancient Southwest Asia and ancient Egypt may account for the interlocking relationship among these domains of law, morality, and religion: the notion of order, which underlies or

31. See also my article "The Social Basis of Morality and Religion in Ancient Israel," in *Language, Theology, and the Bible: Essays in Honour of James Barr*, ed. Samuel E. Balentine and John Barton (Oxford: Clarendon Press, 1994), 151–69; also K. van der Toorn, *Sin and Sanction in Israel and Mesopotamia: A Comparative Study* (Assen: Van Gorcum, 1985).

should underlie all that exists and which is created and maintained by the gods. Egypt's goddess Maʿat, the daughter of Re and the guarantor of justice, represents the order of the Egyptian kingdom, of morality, and of the world. At a person's death the heart is weighed in a balance against a feather, the symbol of Maʿat, and woe to the person whose heart, burdened with selfish and evil deeds, tips the scale against the feather. This order extends to the cosmic sphere, the natural world, the political institutions, and the religious contexts. Just as the king is the enforcer of the principle of order in the political domain, so also the priests ensure that rituals and observances are properly conducted in the cult. Any act that disrupts the order must be appropriately countered, whether by punishment or by ritual. Laws fit into this whole as the means by which obligations are fulfilled and conflict within the orderly running of the social and religious domains is minimized or managed.[32]

There are, however, two basic problems with a facile, close linkage among law, morality, and religion in ancient Israel. The first has already been addressed and need not be treated in further detail: the difference between Israelite law and biblical law. Several recent studies have made the point effectively that popular religion differs significantly from the state cult.[33] Archaeologists' findings confirm that a popular, domestic, village-oriented cult flourished throughout the country of ancient Israel, even after a temple and central sacrificial cult became established.[34] Some of the religious notions prevalent among the general populace may also have been at odds with the religious beliefs and practices advocated in Jerusalem or other cultic centers.[35] Could there have been a comparable division between the popular morality at home among the people throughout the land and the moral stances advocated from the leaders at the center? If so, there was probably diversity in this popular morality even among the nonurban settlements across the land as well.

Consequently, if we want to argue for a strong convergence between

32. For more discussion of the concept of order and its significance in Israel and elsewhere in ancient Southwest Asia and Egypt, see Hans Heinrich Schmid, *Gerechtigkeit als Weltordnung: Hintergrund und Geschichte des alttestamentlichen Gerechtigkeitsbegriffes*, BHT 40 (Tübingen: Mohr [Siebeck], 1968); and my "Cosmogony and Order in the Hebrew Tradition," in *Cosmogony and Ethical Order: New Studies in Comparative Ethics*, ed. Robin W. Lovin and Frank E. Reynolds (Chicago and London: University of Chicago Press, 1985), 133–57.
33. For further discussion and bibliography, see Patrick D. Miller, *The Religion of Ancient Israel*, LAI (Louisville, KY: Westminster John Knox; London: SPCK, 2000). See also chap. 7 below.
34. Some of the material evidence is cited in Philip J. King and Lawrence E. Stager, *Life in Biblical Israel*, LAI (Louisville, KY, and London, UK: Westminster John Knox Press, 2001).
35. See below, chap. 3, The Cult, as well as chap. 7; also James L. Crenshaw, *Prophetic Conflict: Its Effect upon Israelite Religion*, BZAW 124 (Berlin: de Gruyter, 1971), esp. 23–38.

laws on the one hand and religion and morality on the other, we need to specify which laws and which religion and morality: for the former, the Israelite laws or the biblical laws; and for the latter, the popular or the state-sanctioned? Although it seems simplistic, it is most likely that the customary laws of the villages converge mainly with popular religion(s) and popular morality(ies), while the biblical laws reflect mainly the forms of religion and morality at home among the elites, the national leadership, and the central priesthood. Thus the question of the relationship among these three domains—law, religion, and morality—requires a differentiated answer depending on the social and political context of each.

The second problem is more subtle, not least because it involves deconstructing the biblical text. According to the Hebrew Bible, the laws stem from Israel's God and thus presumably embody or promote divine values. Though the Pentateuch overwhelmingly supports this notion, at the same time it acknowledges the presence of humans in the process of receiving and recording the laws. The laws are not conveyed to the Israelites in the form of a heavenly book untouched by human hands.[36] The stone tablets containing the "ten words" (presumably referring to the Ten Commandments) are written not in heaven but on earth, either by God (Exod 24:12; 31:18; Deut 4:13; 5:22; 9:10; 10:2, 4) or by Moses (Exod 34:28). In other texts Moses is the one who writes (Deut 31:24) or recites (Exod 24:7; Deut 5:1; 12:1) the laws, and Joshua later copies them (Josh 8:32). Moses teaches the people "statutes and ordinances" (חקים ומשפטים, ḥuqqîm ûmišpāṭîm, Deut 4:5), a task that is later continued by the priests (Jer 18:18). Humans, in a word, play a distinctive role at the origin of the laws and in their transmission and interpretation, according to the biblical tradition itself.

Even more pointedly, these leaders are presented as imperfect humans. At the sight of Israelites worshiping the golden calves, Moses flies into a rage and destroys the two tablets containing the Decalogue (Exod 32:19; Deut 9:17). His flaws become enough for God to prohibit him from entering the land of Canaan: he lacks trust in YHWH (Num 20:10–12); he rebels (Num 20:24; 27:14); he fails to maintain God's holiness among the people (Deut 32:51); he triggers God's anger against him (Deut 1:37; 3:26; 4:21); he becomes bitter and rash (Ps 106:32–33). Joshua, for his part, is the leader under whom the people suffer a disastrous loss against Ai because of Achan's perfidy (Josh 7), and he lets himself be duped by the Gibeonites (Josh 9). These acts stem from fully understandable circumstances with

36. Geo Widengren, *Religionsphänomenologie* (Berlin: de Gruyter, 1969), 569.

which we can identify; yet in showing the human side of these mediators of the law, the text at the same time undermines the notion of an inviolate law. Jeremiah's charge against the priests, "those who handle the law" (2:8), reflects the ongoing problems associated with those to whom the law is entrusted.

Extending this observation almost to the breaking point, an isolated prophetic text seems to undermine—at least from our perspective—the notion of the complete morality (in a normative sense) or sanctity of biblical law. Ezekiel 20:25–26 contains the following statement:

> I also gave them laws [חֻקִּים, *ḥuqqîm*] that were not good, and statutes [מִשְׁפָּטִים, *mišpāṭîm*] by which they could not live. I defiled them by means of their own gifts when they sacrificed their firstborn, so that I might horrify them, in order that they would know that I am YHWH.

This extraordinary assertion stands out as an unexpected confession, by Israel's God through the prophet Ezekiel, that immoral or harmful—literally, "not-good"—laws were intentionally included in the legal corpus for the purpose of drawing, or driving, the people to God. The referent for this admission is notoriously difficult to identify; it could be that it alludes to the law in Exod 22:29b (22:28b MT): "You shall give to me the firstborn of your sons," which the Israelites could construe as a command to sacrifice rather than to dedicate the firstborn son to God. More likely this statement stems from the prophets' frequent practice of selecting themes or motifs from earlier tradition and developing or, as here, reversing them for rhetorical effect.[37] Yet even if this explanation accounts for this text, it constitutes a remarkable acknowledgment that the law could contain devious elements.

Perhaps even more striking is another prophetic utterance, the well-known promise of writing the law on the people's hearts (Jer 31:33; cf. also Ezek 11:19–20; 36:26–27). This statement is normally interpreted as a hopeful assurance—not least in the New Testament (Heb 8:6–13)—that the law can one day be declared obsolete and will be superseded by a new set of circumstances. In the context of the book of Jeremiah, however, the prophet is not announcing the eventual obsolescence of the law but is criticizing the people of his time: they are so intractable in their sinful, rebellious ways that there is no chance they can reform on their own, and

---

37. Walther Zimmerli, "Prophetic Proclamation and Reinterpretation," in *Tradition and Theology in the Old Testament*, ed. Douglas A. Knight (Philadelphia: Fortress Press; London: SPCK, 1977; reprint, Atlanta: Society of Biblical Literature, 2007), 69–100; and Rudolf Smend, "Das Nein des Amos," *EvT* 23 (1963): 404–23.

it would take divine surgical intervention to refashion their hearts (i.e., their will and their intentions) if they are to do good.[38] The law, in other words, is not the problem; rather, it is the people themselves. Even so, the law is thereby also changed inasmuch as it becomes a different kind of phenomenon—an internal will of the people.

The Hebrew Bible quite uniformly ties the law to high morality and proper religious practice; Ezek 20:25–26 is the only suggestion that there is deceit in the law. Moreover, compliance with the terms of the law is commanded, not made optional. In his study of the use of the word for love, אָהֵב, 'āhēb, especially as it is used in the book of Deuteronomy, William Moran argues that it is to be understood not as an emotional sentiment but as a political and legal act of compliance with the requirements of an overlord, a sense well understood in ancient Southwest Asia.[39] When love is commanded, it is obedience that is expected, specifically obedience to the laws. Note, for example, Deut 13:3b–4 (13:4b–5 MT):

> YHWH your God is testing you to determine whether you love YHWH your God with your whole heart and your whole life. You shall follow YHWH your God and fear him, keeping his commandments, obeying his voice, serving him, and remaining loyal to him.

At the same time, obedience to the law is also portrayed as being for the good of the Israelite people themselves.

These affirmations notwithstanding, it remains to inquire into the types of social and political contexts in Israel lying behind such injunctions to comply with the law and honor authority. We turn to this question in the next chapter.

---

38. See my discussion in "Jeremiah and the Dimensions of the Moral Life," in *The Divine Helmsman: Studies on God's Control of Human Events; Presented to Lou H. Silberman*, ed. James L. Crenshaw and Samuel Sandmel (New York: Ktav, 1980), 104–5.

39. William L. Moran, "The Ancient Near Eastern Background of the Love of God in Deuteronomy," *CBQ* 25 (1963): 77–87.

CHAPTER 3

The Law of Power

Laws grind the poor, and rich men rule the law.
—Oliver Goldsmith[1]

Inasmuch as laws do not emerge in a vacuum, disconnected from cultural and social contexts, they originate and endure with the interests of certain persons or groups at stake. At the broadest level, a nation's legal system aims to stabilize its society in general, ensuring an orderly structure so that its members will be able to live in community according to predictable standards, protections, and duties. The absence of such overall order usually conjures up images of anarchy and chaos, the rule of might over right or of heterodoxy over orthodoxy—a circumstance perhaps contemplated by a later generation of ancient Israelites in their reference to Israel's premonarchic period: "In those days there was no monarch in Israel; everyone acted according to one's own judgment" (Judg 17:6; cf. 18:1; 19:1; 21:25). The mark of civilization, it is often claimed, lies in the very existence of laws, the establishment of legitimate means for making and enforcing the regulations necessary to curb any attempt to disrupt social organization. Laws, according to this notion, protect the populace from obstructions and violations stemming from its own membership or from others living or operating within its territory. The judicial establishment thus functions as the domestic counterpart to the military and diplomatic corps, which on the international plane aim to protect the nation from external threats and to represent the nation's interests beyond its borders.

Yet such a view of law is idealistic at best, and naive if not insidious at worst. While societies do need a means for regulating internal order, the sheer variety of the types of order represented in various nations or groups should convince us that a given legal system is far from neutral in terms of who is benefited and who is disadvantaged as a result of its establishment.

---

1. Oliver Goldsmith, *The Traveller, or, A Prospect of Society: A Poem Inscribed to the Rev. Mr. Henry Goldsmith* (London: J. Newberry, 1765), 19.

Do the laws represent the will of the whole people? *Or* the preferences of only or mainly a small and privileged group? Rarely, if ever, is it possible for the interests of absolutely all the people to be reflected fully and equally in laws and policies, despite the commonly heard political rhetoric that cites "the will of the people." One should with good reason approach such rhetoric with suspicion, whether it be within texts like the Bible[2] or in our own contemporary world. Some political, economic, or ideological gain for certain special-interest groups is likely to be at stake, and soliciting the support or compliance of the larger populace will legally serve the ends of those in power.

THE POLITICS OF LEGISLATION: WHOSE LAWS? WHOSE BENEFITS?

An understanding of the character and structure of Israel's social systems provides us with the means for connecting lawmaking and preservation to certain specific groups that had the opportunity and the motivation to draft legal traditions into literature. It makes a difference for our interpretations whether a given law stems from the lower class or the upper class, from the powerless or the powerful, especially if the law appears on its face to be advancing the cause of, for example, the poor and defenseless, but at another level may deliberately not be accomplishing this goal at all.

Such possibilities raise profound questions about the social role and function of law, issues that have been treated by the school of thought in legal theory known as Critical Legal Studies, or CLS.[3] A progressive, and for some even a radical, movement in legal theory, CLS is a direct outgrowth of Critical Theory on the one hand, and the various political

2. One example is the notion of "all Israel," in contrast with the Israelite tribes seen separately. Martin Noth (*A History of Pentateuchal Traditions*, trans. Bernhard W. Anderson [Englewood Cliffs, NJ: Prentice-Hall, 1972; German original, 1948], 42–45) has drawn attention to this notion as a stage in the development of the Pentateuch when smaller, independent traditions circulating among various tribes were later brought together and reconceived as the literary heritage of all of Israel. Noth does not, however, pursue in depth the ideologically motivated groups of society that may have had a special interest in this synthesis of disparate traditions.

3. Among the studies devoted to CLS, see Roberto Mangabeira Unger, *Knowledge and Politics* (New York: Free Press, 1975); idem, *The Critical Legal Studies Movement* (Cambridge, MA, and London, UK: Harvard University Press, 1986); various essays in David Kairys, ed., *The Politics of Law: A Progressive Critique*, rev. ed. (New York: Pantheon Books, 1990); the articles reprinted in James Boyle, ed., *Critical Legal Studies* (Aldershot: Ashgate/Dartmouth, 1992); Costas Douzinas and Adam Gearey, *Critical Jurisprudence: The Political Philosophy of Justice* (Oxford, UK, and Portland, OR: Hart Publishing, 2005); and the extensive bibliography in Richard W. Bauman, *Critical Legal Studies: A Guide to the Literature* (Boulder, CO: Westview Press, 1996).

upheavals of the 1960s and 1970s on the other. It first appeared in the mid-1970s in the United States and soon thereafter in Britain, Germany, France, and elsewhere. Its roots can be traced to the legal realism of the 1920s–30s, which had observed that law has political and other dimensions and needs therefore to be studied by the social-scientific methods then on the rise. As much as influence, however, the theoretical critique of gender, race, and class during the second half of the twentieth century stimulated CLS thinking, as the study of social systems shifted from surface-level problems to systemic defects and injustices. In addition, CLS shares common ground with impulses in deconstruction and postmodernism.[4] In a word, it submits the very character of law as well as the conventional reasoning of its professionals—legal theorists, lawyers, and jurists—to radical scrutiny. The statement of principle at the Critical Legal Conference in Britain in 1984 sums up its point of departure and its goal:

> The central focus of the critical legal approach is to explore the manner in which legal doctrine and legal education and the practices of legal institutions work to buttress and support a pervasive system of oppressive, inegalitarian relations. Critical theory works to develop radical alternatives, and to explore and debate the role of law in the creation of social, economic and political relations that will advance human emancipation.[5]

As may be deduced from such a statement, CLS advocates have often been discontent with theoretical scholarship and have turned to activism in the cause of establishing an egalitarian society and reforming legal education. Recent years have seen a decline in CLS publications and a discrediting of what some regard as its more radical principles, resulting then in a more moderate position.[6] Nonetheless, certain of its emphases—especially the attention to gender, race, and class—have continued with a life of their own. At the same time, its insights about the fundamental nature of law are likely to outlive the movement itself. While CLS theoreticians concern themselves primarily with contemporary legal systems, elements of the approach

4. See, e.g., Costas Douzinas, Ronnie Warrington, and Shaun McVeigh, *Postmodern Jurisprudence: The Law of Text in the Texts of Law* (London and New York: Routledge, 1993), and note particularly chap. 11, "The Books of Judges: The Shibboleths of Justice"; Jerry Leonard, ed., *Legal Studies as Cultural Studies: A Reader in (Post)modern Critical Theory* (Albany: State University of New York Press, 1995); and Helen M. Stacy, *Postmodernism and the Law: Jurisprudence in a Fragmenting World* (Aldershot: Ashgate/Dartmouth, 2001).

5. Quoted in *Critical Legal Studies*, ed. Peter Fitzpatrick and Alan Hunt (Oxford: Basil Blackwell Publishing, 1987), 1–2.

6. See, e.g., the response to "the CLS attack on the liberal embrace of the rule of law" by Andrew Altman, *Critical Legal Studies: A Liberal Critique* (Princeton, NJ: Princeton University Press, 1990), 13.

can also be applied to the study of law in premodern cultures, including ancient Israel. Perhaps it may hold the key for a fresh assessment of the literary expression of Israelite legal traditions in the Hebrew Bible, which has typically been driven by mainly theological concerns.

At one level, to be sure, CLS may not appear to offer much that is novel. Historians and social scientists have long understood that a country's laws are formed in light of that culture's character and needs, that social as well as ideological—including religious—factors leave their imprint on procedural and substantive aspects of the law. By the same token, lawyers (or their premodern counterparts, if they existed in a given culture) as well as their clients are equally aware of the prejudices that can infect the system in multiple ways. But the sociolegal approach represented by CLS in its more radical form penetrates to a deeper level, reaching the very core and character of a given legal system. Three of its basic principles have the potential of recasting our understanding of Israelite law:

1. *All law is politics.* On their face, laws seem merely to be what the legislators enact or the judges decide. However, behind every legal prescription, interpretation, and adjudication lies someone's or some group's self-interest. As befits political manipulations, the pressures exerted on the legislative and judicial processes generally go unnoticed until, eventually, a benefit clearly accrues to certain persons or a disadvantage to others. No law is free of bias, and we only demonstrate, or participate in, its partisan effectiveness by disavowing its political motives. The laws of ancient Israel are no exception. They are not ethereal products, the mere rendering of deep ethical insights in legal form, although they often do espouse humanitarian causes of equality, fairness, and community responsibility. For all of the appeal that certain biblical laws may have for many people today, it would be disingenuous of us to suppose that those laws do not reflect the calculations of certain groups or individuals in antiquity, even if those people are no longer identifiable. Consider, for example, the scant biblical material on homosexuality—obviously not a major issue for groups in ancient Israel but milked and manipulated to oppressive ends today. The laws were and still are political, benefiting certain groups over others even as they appear to be the innocent or simple means to establish social order. There may well be additional factors to consider, as the critics of the CLS movement have emphasized, but the political character and purposes of law must not be overlooked or underestimated. Stated differently, laws are social constructs and need to be understood as such.

2. Not only are laws produced through the leverage or mandate of certain groups, but they also reflect the *systemic dominance of classes or*

other status entities. Laws, in other words, secure the power relations fundamental to the society in question. For example, as has been argued by feminist legal theorists,[7] a patriarchal society is likely to produce laws in which males are advantaged over females, often in ways that are not at all transparent but that have the net effect of depriving women of some of the rights, privileges, options, or protections afforded the males. Or again, the laws of a monarchic state, whether constitutional or despotic, will safeguard the royal house, legitimate certain powers and privileges of the monarch, sanction the hierarchical political structure, and usually ensure that there is a clear division between monarch and subject or citizen. Another example is the institution of slavery in the United States, which depended on its social context and the laws in place to ensure the status quo of inequality and oppression,[8] in sad irony legitimated often through appeal to biblical tolerance of slavery. The "rule of law," much touted in the tradition following the Magna Carta of 1215, does represent a compelling alternative to anarchy and arbitrariness, but at the same time it reflects the values of the group that enacts and enforces it. All of these examples display the approaches of CLS and its predecessor, legal realism.

3. A primary issue in CLS legal theory is *the law's indeterminacy:* the law does not comprise a body of authoritative principles that can in themselves define or determine the results in a legal conflict. This principle disputes the common notion that legal professionals—lawyers, elders, judges, legal philosophers, and others operating within the spheres of lawmaking and law application—can function in a relatively apolitical and objective manner, in control of pressures on them and unmoved by ideological disputes. According to this disputed notion, it should be possible for professionals to perform within an authoritative legal tradition, interpreting, supplementing, or applying it fairly to the conditions of the day. The touchstones of the legal tradition, then, would acquire an almost unassailable status at the core, and new laws and judgments become presented as ongoing reforms and improvements. CLS, however, fundamentally challenges this objectivist notion that laws reflect and regulate a moral social order and that those applying or enforcing the legal system are simply acting in a manner consistent with this putative moral order, with "the rule of law." Too much is left to interpretation, by both the lawyers and the judges, to suggest that

7. See, e.g., various articles in Katharine T. Bartlett and Rosanne Kennedy, eds., *Feminist Legal Theory: Readings in Law and Gender* (Boulder, CO: Westview Press, 1991).
8. For a description of slavery and antislavery from the perspective of legal realism and CLS, see Robert M. Cover, *Justice Accused: Antislavery and the Judicial Process* (New Haven and London: Yale University Press, 1975).

adjudication follows a straightforward process of applying the law to a given case. The question thus shifts to the specific influences affecting this interpretative act.

Laws, just like gender and racial conceptions, are social constructions and are accordingly subject to the usual realities and pressures—political, social, economic, religious, psychological, and more. While CLS in its more radical form tends to focus primarily on the political and economic influences, its moderate position attends to the other factors as well, which is the tack we will take in the present study. Nonetheless, issues of power and control—interests and benefits—lie at the heart of these approaches, and we will turn our attention to them directly. But first a sketch of the political and economic structures in ancient Israel will provide a backdrop for the discussion of how power, political and otherwise, affected the emergence and application of laws.

THE SOCIAL STRUCTURE OF POWER IN ANCIENT ISRAEL

The sovereign states of Israel and Judah largely fit the macrosociological pattern termed the agrarian state or society. The agrarian state[9] is known to us from many areas and periods throughout the world, from large empires such as the Roman, Byzantine, Ottoman, and Chinese Empires to more limited nation-states such as ancient Israel and Judah. Substantial variation exists among the political structures identified with this model, but they share several characteristics in common, elements evident in Israel from the onset of the monarchy and forward.

Fundamental to the agrarian pattern is a pronounced social inequality in power, privileges, and honor, and the centralized state itself functions as the immediate source of this disparity. Monarchs view the state as their own property to use as they will, and any archives they leave behind tell mainly about themselves, their wars, their building projects, and other matters of state—and almost nothing about the lives of the common people except insofar as they intersect with the interests of the monarchic government. However, in addition to the royal house there is also an elite or governing

9. A detailed description of agrarian societies is provided by macrosociologist Gerhard Lenski, *Power and Privilege: A Theory of Social Stratification* (Chapel Hill: University of North Carolina Press, 1966, 1984). The following discussion builds on portions of my article "Whose Agony? Whose Ecstasy? The Politics of Deuteronomic Law," in *"Shall Not the Judge of All the Earth Do What Is Right?" Studies on the Nature of God in Tribute to James L. Crenshaw,* ed. David Penchansky and Paul L. Redditt (Winona Lake, IN: Eisenbrauns, 2000), 97–112; revision and translation of "Herrens bud—elitens interesser? Lov, makt, og rettferdighet i Det gamle testamente," *NTT* 97 (1996): 235–45.

class, a small minority normally less (often much less) than 2 percent of the whole population, which exercises political and economic power at the national level: high state officials, chief military officers, large landowners, wealthy merchants, priestly leaders, and others to whom the monarch grants land, offices, or special rights. The balance of power between these two groups—the monarch and the royal government on the one hand, and the ruling class or elites on the other—can fluctuate: each will often try to dominate the other and thereby gain the upper hand in controlling the country and its economy. But more important, they generally collaborate to hold the populace in check, both the peasants in the countryside and the artisans and laborers in the cities, in order to extract from them as much of their economic surplus as possible. The result is that typically less than 2 percent of the total population will receive in excess of 50 percent of the national income.[10]

There is essentially no socioeconomic class in agrarian states comparable to the independent middle class in modern industrial states. Instead, a small group of specialists enjoys some status and privilege in comparison to the exploited masses: bureaucrats, functionaries, retainers, merchants, and priests. This dispersed group, usually only 5–10 percent of the total population, is dependent on the elite or the government for their position and income, and they are employed to manage the affairs of government, collect taxes and rents, and generally make life comfortable for the royal house and the governing class. Ultimate power resides securely in that top 1–2 percent, and all others are largely at their mercy—especially the peasants and craftspeople, who make up the bottom 90 percent and can barely survive in the subsistence economy. Additional characteristics of the agrarian society include technological advances, quite frequent wars and internal conflicts, urban domination of the countryside, diversity of specialized professions, trade and commerce conducted by a merchant class, and a religious institution intermeshed with the centralized state and often afflicted with internal strife.

On the whole and on the basis of our current knowledge, monarchic

10. Lenski, *Power and Privilege*, 212–19; see also Janet Richards and Mary Van Buren, eds., *Order, Legitimacy, and Wealth in Ancient States* (Cambridge: Cambridge University Press, 2000). By way of comparison, the estimates of wealth distribution in the United States show that in 2009 the top 1% of the population held approximately 37.1% of total private wealth while the top 5% controlled 65% of private wealth; see Edward N. Wolff, *Recent Trends in Household Wealth in the United States: Rising Debt and the Middle-Class Squeeze—An Update to 2007*, Working Paper No. 589 (Annandale-on-Hudson, NY: Levy Economics Institute, Bard College, March 2010), http://www.levyinstitute.org/pubs/wp_589.pdf.

Israel and Judah fit this heuristic model of the agrarian society quite well, so long as one makes some necessary adjustments to the pattern in light of specific situations and regions in the various periods. While the monarch was on the throne, resources and power were held mainly by the relative few who belonged to the royal house or the elite sector, resulting in a glaring disparity in wealth and options between them and the vast majority of the people.[11] Recently scholars have debated whether or not there was an actual class system in ancient Israel. The question depends in part on one's understanding of "class," in part on one's use of sociological methods, and in part on one's interpretation of the textual and material record of ancient Israel.[12] Whatever the outcome of the discussion, no one contests that there was an uneven distribution of wealth and power during ancient Israel's monarchic period and that these uneven circumstances resulted from or were reinforced by the economic and political structures of the society.

THE PLAYERS AND THEIR POWERS IN ANCIENT ISRAEL

To understand the character of the legal systems in ancient Israel, we need to consider the types of social groups and political and institutional structures in which laws arose and functioned. The most typical way of approaching biblical laws has been to imagine a chronological progression from the earliest to the latest, in terms of both the larger blocks of laws and, ideally, also as many of the individual laws as possible.[13] While such a historical orientation has attended to the laws' social and religious settings, it has been less attuned to the political dynamics that spawned laws and legal collections, precisely the kind of issues that CLS has underscored. Throughout Israel's history, the various legal conflicts that arose were resolved through leadership or control by certain groups or individuals, not by the populace as a whole, which had no practical means to express their collective opinions. Furthermore, even in the absence of a legal conflict, these power centers or factions were able to influence the customary

11. David W. Jamieson-Drake, *Scribes and Schools in Monarchic Judah: A Socio-Archeological Approach*, JSOTSup 109 (Sheffield: Almond Press, 1991), 107–35; Timothy Mark Green, "Class Differentiation and Power(lessness) in Eighth-Century-BCE Israel and Judah" (Ph.D. diss., Vanderbilt University, 1997).

12. Norman K. Gottwald, "Social Class as an Analytic and Hermeneutical Category in Biblical Studies," *JBL* 112 (1993): 3–22; and the essays in Mark R. Sneed, ed., *Concepts of Class in Ancient Israel*, South Florida Studies in the History of Judaism 201 (Atlanta: Scholars Press, 1999).

13. See above, chap. 1, Legal Texts in the Hebrew Bible, for a description of the conventional schematization of historical settings and law collections.

laws and manipulate legal procedures to their benefit, whether for material or economic gain or for enhanced prestige and standing.[14] While the CLS statement "All law is politics" may be overstated—legal traditions and other factors also play a role—there is no question that political and economic aspects are present, even dominant at times, and should be identified in a study of Israelite laws.

To function as an effective legal control, a law must carry authority and social legitimacy.[15] Such authority generally derives from specific persons by virtue of their social standing or office or acquired power, yet it can also be conferred by a group, however constituted. In each case the jurisdiction of the individual or group is delineated according to social, political, institutional, or geographical domains. To identify the holders of power and authority in ancient Israel, I propose to follow a division that highlights three primary contexts as the crucibles for the Israelite laws and, to an extent yet to be determined, for the biblical laws as well: the village, the city and state, and the cult or worship setting. For all the differences that existed in ancient Israel over time regarding each of these categories, each domain shared more similarities internally—among the actual examples within the type—than it did with either of the other two categories. Each domain, however, was not fully distinct from the others; in addition to some nesting or overlapping, they continually exerted a reciprocal influence on each other. Each also had multiple subcomponents. In a moment we will identify those categories of persons or groups where the power to make and enforce laws was concentrated. Later, in chapters 5–7, we will again look at each in much more detail in an effort to determine the content and application of laws in the respective settings. At this juncture we focus on the "legislators," as anachronistic as that term may seem for ancient Israel, and on the administrators of justice. As we will see, in no cases are we able to pinpoint an individual Israelite lawmaker by name; rather, our only recourse is to identify roles played by unknown individuals or groups.

The Hebrew Bible makes no effort to describe the legislative process other than to project it onto YHWH, with Moses as the intermediary. In so doing, it seeks to persuade readers and hearers alike that the laws in Exodus, Leviticus, Numbers, and Deuteronomy bear the highest possible authorization and are to be followed in all their detail. Similar legitimization,

---

14. John H. Kautsky, *The Politics of Aristocratic Empires* (Chapel Hill: University of North Carolina Press, 1982), 211–29, discusses what he calls the "stakes of aristocratic politics" as being position and rank, symbols, and wealth.
15. See above, chap. 2, The Nature and Sources of Law.

in the name of other gods and leaders, prevailed among neighboring cultures. The lack of specificity beyond such mythic or supreme sanctioning
constitutes one of the most glaring examples of "measurable absences" in
the Hebrew Bible, a circumstance similar to that for other legal collections
in ancient Southwest Asia as well. The notion of "measurable absences"
belongs to the ideological criticism advanced by Terry Eagleton.[16] In his
view, texts reflect and are produced by real people in real time, and con-
cealing information about specific individuals or groups is likely to be a
result of a deliberate effort by them or by others who do not want their
identity and agenda known. In the case of the Hebrew Bible, why are we
not provided with a description of the process by which the biblical laws
developed and were recorded? And why are the persons or groups responsible for their emergence not identified? The very absence of such obvious
information invites suspicion that the responsible parties, not wanting their
identities disclosed, attributed the laws' origins to the Israelite God and the
legendary Moses. The next chapter will pursue this question in more detail
and offer a proposal about the reason for this glaring absence in the written canonical texts.

At this point we limit ourselves to identifying the likely producers of
Israelite laws—not those who wrote the collections of biblical laws, but
those responsible for the "living" laws regulating social, political, economic,
and religious affairs during ancient Israel's history. The following construction of the personnel and their powers is hypothetical, yet plausible in my
view. Scholars have attained a basic sense of the nature of society, religion, and politics in ancient Israel, pieced together from textual comments,
archaeological finds, and comparative ethnographic information. Inevitably
it is often necessary to speculate to fill the gaps since our historical knowledge of ancient Israel is surprisingly limited despite the extensiveness of
the Hebrew Bible. As already mentioned, the writers of the Hebrew Bible
chose not to tell us all we may want to know about its history and its
historical contexts. For the task at hand, we will try to imagine the kinds
of players who had a role in the production of Israelite laws. Those identified as primary authorities in each setting are the ones who likely had
the most immediate responsibility for articulating or determining the laws.
Those with secondary influence may in some cases have been positioned
as superior powers (such as the monarch), while others (such as wives or

16. Terry Eagleton, *Criticism and Ideology: A Study in Marxist Literary Theory* (London:
Verso Press, 1976). For an application of this method to the Hebrew Bible, see Norman K.
Gottwald, "Social Class and Ideology in Isaiah 40–55: An Eagletonian Reading," *Semeia* 59
(1992): 43–57.

other household heads) may have had powers to sway but not to determine the legal norms. Many more details about the following three settings will be provided in later chapters, and here I will mention only enough about each to provide a basis for hypothesizing the identity of the leaders and influential parties.

First is an overview of the factors and figures involved, followed by a clarification.

Table 3.1   Schematic of Legislative and Judicial Authority and Power

Jurisdictional Setting	Types of Legal Conflicts Controlled by Laws	Primary Legislative and Judicial Authority	Persons or Groups Exerting Secondary Legal Influence
Family (found throughout the country)	Actions internal to family	Household head	Other adults in family; neighboring families
Clan (found in villages and less so in urban residential areas)	Social and economic affairs within clan	Clan elders, or ad hoc gathering of household heads	Other adults in clan; neighboring clans
Tribe (generally located in a distinct territory)	Social and economic affairs within tribe not satisfactorily resolved by clans; intertribal affairs	Ad hoc gathering of representatives of clan elders	Other adults in tribes; neighboring tribes
Urban residential neighborhood	Social and economic affairs among neighbors (sometimes clan based)	Ad hoc gathering of household heads	Other adults in neighborhood; other neighborhoods; monarch; elites
Administrative and royal cities	State and commercial affairs	Monarch; elites	Bureaucrats; other functionaries

Jurisdictional Setting	Types of Legal Conflicts Controlled by Laws	Primary Legislative and Judicial Authority	Persons or Groups Exerting Secondary Legal Influence
Royal house	Palace affairs	Monarch	Other adults close to monarch, especially queen, queen mother, counselors, heir apparent
Nation-state	Matters of state (governmental, economic, social)	Monarch and royal judges	Counselors; elites; central priests
Empire	Imperial affairs (governmental, economic, cultic)	Emperor	Counselors; high officers; provincial governors; elites
Commerce and property ownership	Commercial and property affairs	Elites	Monarch; temple priests
Domestic cult	Cultic matters in the family	Nonspecialist leader	Other members of family
Local cult	Local cultic matters	Nonspecialist leader (probably household head)	Other community members, especially household heads
Regional cult	Tribal or regional cultic matters	Nonspecialist leader (probably household head)	Other household heads
State cult	Religious issues of the state	High priest	Monarch; elites; other priests
Imperial cult	Religious issues of the empire	High priest	Emperor; other priests

The Villages

Before any monarch sat on a throne in Israel and then later throughout the entire monarchic and colonial periods, the vast majority of the people were dispersed over the landscape in villages and small towns. This non-urban population ranged between 80 and 95 percent of all the inhabitants of the land, depending on the period and the region. Modern scholarship has tended to downplay their importance, not as much through intention as through default. The culture, architecture, literature, and political events associated with the cities have seemed much more compelling to historians, probably for reasons residing as much in the modern researchers themselves as in the ancient phenomena.[17] Whatever the reason, the life, institutions, customs, and perspectives of villagers have remained largely invisible, at least until more recent times, when new attention has been drawn to them. Since the 1960s archaeologists have deliberately sought to uncover material evidence of the nonelite population,[18] and new interest in popular culture and popular religion has resulted. Many scholars now inquire into the hidden or suppressed histories of peasants, women, the impoverished, the oppressed, the powerless. All of these groups are mostly to be found in the villages.

The first two or three centuries of the Iron Age, beginning ca. 1200 BCE and leading to the founding of the monarchy, preceded the agrarian-state period as described above. The absence of a centralized governing body and an elite sector with widespread impact on the nation's economy constituted the primary difference between the premonarchic and monarchic political systems as experienced by villagers. Throughout Israel's history, village inhabitants struggled to survive in a subsistence economy, which normally based itself on a combination of agricultural and pastoral means of production. The centralization of political and economic control during the monarchy made a command economy possible, with the resources, surpluses, and labor of the villages redirected at the behest of those holding overarching powers. Yet whatever circumstances prevailed at the national level, villages still remained throughout all of Israel's history as the most populous residential option.

The villagers developed schemes of social organization to match their family and kinship ties and to accommodate their subsistence options and

---

17. See esp. Gottwald, "Social Class as an Analytic and Hermeneutical Category," 3.
18. William G. Dever, "Syro-Palestinian and Biblical Archaeology," in *The Hebrew Bible and Its Modern Interpreters*, ed. Douglas A. Knight and Gene M. Tucker, BMI (Philadelphia: Fortress Press; Chico, CA: Scholars Press, 1985), 31–74, esp. 36–53.

environmental conditions.[19] The family (בֵּית אָב, *bêt ʾāb*, "house of the father") constituted the most basic social unit in ancient Israel, with the father as the household head. More of an extended or compound family than a nuclear family, the *bêt ʾāb* could embrace children, wedded sons with their families, unwedded or widowed elders, together with the central couple, and the head of the household was the oldest male—the father or, presumably if still competent, the grandfather. The clan (מִשְׁפָּחָה, *mišpāḥâ*), the next largest social unit, consisted of several such families in a lineage system living in a single village or in several nearby villages, and authority rested with the elders, the gathering of the household heads. Larger yet was the tribe (שֵׁבֶט, *šēbĕṭ*; מַטֶּה, *maṭṭeh*), composed of a number of clans that actually or supposedly shared lineage connections, and its most obvious characteristic lay in its location in a distinct territory generally identifiable by topographical contours or delineations. Again the heads of households of various, though probably not all, clans would convene to decide on issues of common interest, including legal disputes that could not be settled at the clan level.

This type of social structure in ancient Israel is known as a segmentary society: a system comprising kinship units, each with some self-sufficiency but also closely aligned with other similar units.[20] The segments coexisted and cooperated because, if for no other reason, it was to their mutual benefit to do so. The village society was acephalous, with no powerful head in the form of a chief or a monarch. In all likelihood, toward the end of the premonarchic period more of a ranked social system began to evolve, in large part because of the emergence of a class of persons with more property holdings than others. Such a shift may also have fostered a chiefdom, which eventually gave way to the monarchy and the agrarian state.[21]

While power was more evenly dispersed within the village society than it was in the country as a whole after the monarchy took hold, villages

19. Numerous studies, many of them based directly on modern ethnographic research, are devoted to kinship—its structures, features, and meanings. For a general discussion and bibliography, see Robert Parkin, *Kinship: An Introduction to Basic Concepts* (Oxford: Basil Blackwell Publishing, 1997). The situations in ancient Israel and the larger region are discussed in King and Stager, *Life in Biblical Israel*, 36–61; Lawrence E. Stager, "The Archaeology of the Family in Ancient Israel," *BASOR* 260 (1985): 1–35; J. David Schloen, *The House of the Father as Fact and Symbol: Patrimonialism in Ugarit and the Ancient Near East*, Studies in the Archaeology and the History of the Levant 2 (Winona Lake, IN: Eisenbrauns, 2001); and Niels Peter Lemche, *Ancient Israel: A New History of Israelite Society*, trans. Fred Cryer, Biblical Seminar 5 (Sheffield: Sheffield Academic Press, 1988; Danish original, 1984), 75–117.

20. See the overview in McNutt, *Reconstructing the Society of Ancient Israel*, 78–85.

21. James W. Flanagan, "Chiefs in Israel," *JSOT* 20 (1981): 47–73; and idem, *David's Social Drama: A Hologram of Israel's Early Iron Age*, SWBA 7 (Sheffield: Almond Press, 1988).

were no bastions of egalitarianism.[22] As a general principle, we can probably assume a certain communitarian orientation since it was only through strategies of shared labors that those in such precarious ecological and political circumstances would be able to subsist.[23] As has been argued by several,[24] the standing of women within local village contexts was probably higher than it was at the national level because the local community's well-being undeniably depended on women's economic and social contributions. Nonetheless, patriarchalism and hierarchy were not inventions of the state;[25] adult males in the villages had more public roles than did women, for example, through serving as elders of the village to adjudicate conflicts or to make decisions affecting the village as a whole. Within a given family or household, the father served as the head,[26] although in practice power was likely shared between the parents. As a rule, consensus and negotiation among village members, rather than heavy-handed authority, presumably served as a precondition for smooth relations among members of these hamlets.

In such a situation, then, who would have served as the "legislators" and administrators of justice, possessing the authority and power to determine the legal traditions for the community? Insofar as laws by their very nature must exist and function publicly, those playing public roles were clearly involved. By tradition such public figures were probably the adult males, the household heads. They may have been enslaved by the monarch or trapped in indentured service to a large landholder, but if all others in the village had a comparable status, these adult males would as a general principle have had more public status than women and minors. This surmise is based on the functioning of other known patriarchal societies and on the

22. Norman K. Gottwald argues for a primarily egalitarian ethos and social organization during the Iron I period; *The Tribes of Yahweh: A Sociology of the Religion of Liberated Israel, 1250–1050 B.C.E.* (Maryknoll, NY: Orbis Books, 1979).

23. For more details on agricultural challenges and solutions in this region, see David C. Hopkins, *The Highlands of Canaan: Agricultural Life in the Early Iron Age*, SWBA 3 (Sheffield: Almond Press, 1985).

24. Carol Meyers observes also a chronological and political development: women were largely on a parity basis with men during the prestate society, but the monarchy fostered a distinct hierarchical and patriarchal structure at the national level, which was then followed by misogyny in the postbiblical period. See her *Discovering Eve: Ancient Israelite Women in Context* (New York and Oxford: Oxford University Press, 1988).

25. In her historical survey of ancient Southwest Asia, Gerda Lerner traces the rise and establishment of patriarchy as a dominant social force. See her *The Creation of Patriarchy* (New York and Oxford: Oxford University Press, 1986).

26. Use of the term "paterfamilias" is problematic here since, unlike the situation in Rome and Roman law, the household heads in ancient Israel did not necessarily have a recognized standing as landed citizens. Their sphere of influence was local, not national.

biblical description of adult males as the only ones involved in the promulgation and enforcement of laws.[27]

The adult males in a village, however, were not remote from their neighbors, as might be the case with lawmakers at the national level. Because of contiguous living and shared economic interests, the other villagers had an indirect or even a direct impact on the village's laws. Some allowance for this effect can be recognized within social relations, as Max Weber indicated in his much-discussed distinction between "authority" (*Herrschaft*) and "power" (*Macht*).[28] Women, for example, may not have had the public roles that men traditionally enjoyed (Weber's "authority"), but they could nonetheless have affected societal affairs, customs, and laws through more private influence (Weber's "power") vis-à-vis the men. Similarly, even with the authority vested in a household head, he is likely to be sympathetic to his kinfolk, which can then translate into legal positions with an in-group bias. Similarly, the endogamous customs within a tribal group will affect the laws dealing with forbidden sexual relations (incest, for example), inheritance, property, and more. Thus, even if the adult males are the public players in the making and enforcing of village laws, the needs and values of the wider society of clan and tribe are implicitly reflected in the decisions.

One further issue needs attention: the jurisdiction of the lawmakers and enforcers in these local contexts in ancient Israel. In all likelihood, their range of authority was coterminous with their village or with several villages connected largely by kinship ties. A single body of "legislators" to set the laws for all village life throughout the whole land did not exist. It is inconceivable that all or even most of Israel's heads of households ever collected in one place as if in a national assembly, and even just a representative group of them at the tribal level would have been rare, occurring only on an ad hoc basis when needed to settle some dispute or reach a consensus about a dire situation faced by a group of villages. No political system existed to organize and legitimate such a gathering. Some scholars, most notably Martin Noth,[29] have argued for the presence of an amphictyonic league during the prestate period, a rather loose confederacy

27. A figure such as Deborah (Judg 4–5) fits more the role of a charismatic military leader than that of a lawmaker, despite the label of "judge."

28. Max Weber, *The Theory of Social and Economic Organization*, trans. A. M. Henderson and Talcott Parsons, ed. Talcott Parsons (New York: Oxford University Press, 1947; German original, 1920), 152–53 and passim. Meyers (*Discovering Eve*, 40–45) applies this distinction to Israel's patriarchal society.

29. Noth, *System*.

of tribes: its functions were claimed to include maintenance of a cultic center, cooperation in holy war against foes, leadership centered in a rotating office of "judge," and—of special importance for our study—the promulgation of divine law. As intriguing as such an institution may appear, Noth's thesis is overly speculative and impractical. In my view, its primary weakness resides in the notion that an overarching political structure could have established itself by the end of Iron I without the heavy hand of a monarch, supported by a burgeoning military and administration, to control its formation. With respect to the laws, it is much more plausible that bodies of customary laws arose in all the various villages throughout the land, produced, remembered, and applied primarily by the household heads, not by some central authority.

Legal conflicts were resolved as locally as possible, without recourse to more-remote judicatories. If, for example, damage to property or livestock occurred within a village, the elders or household heads of that village gathered to hear both sides of the conflict and to adjudicate it according to their legal precedents. If the two parties in the conflict were from neighboring villages (both of which may be in kinship relations), the elders from both villages would presumably meet to find the remedy and, if warranted, the punishment: a classic case involving an unsolved murder discovered in the open country is described in Deut 21:1–9. A similar solution would have been negotiated on an ad hoc basis for cases involving even more greatly removed parties. Despite Noth's amphictyonic construct, there is no evidence for a standing, nonlocal institution until the rise of the state. Even during the monarchic period, legal disputes involving local matters were typically handled by the villagers themselves. The state and the central cult intervened only if their own interests were at stake. For life in the villages and towns, the local residents, through their adult male heads of households, retained immediate judicial authority.

The Cities, States, and Empires

In contrast to villages, with their few inhabitants and their vulnerable exposure, cities denote power, no less in ancient Israel than in other cultures. After the period of Iron Age I, during which the increase in population focused almost exclusively on the rise of villages and towns, starting in Iron Age II urban centers prevailed in more senses than just one—still not as the home of the majority of the country's population, which remained scattered throughout the multitudinous villages during all of Israel's history, but as the epicenters of wide-reaching power. Their existence continued hand in hand with the rise and fortunes of both nation-states and empires, and together they offered the opportunity for the promulgation of laws on a wide scale. This linkage between urbanism and statism is not surprising. A nation-state depends on the consolidation and organization of its powers, and cities offer precisely this opportunity. Even though ancient Israelite cities were very small by today's standards, in comparison to the villages around them they loomed as centers of power and resources, visibly evident in their fortifications, gates, palaces, temples, public spaces, and wealthier dwellings.

In our later discussion of substantive laws in the cities and states,[30] we will differentiate among various types of cities found in ancient Israel. For now, however, we focus on the kinds of powerful urban groups and individuals who served as the sources of the laws emanating from these centers. As might be expected, a substantial variety existed from one city to another, and even within a given city. There is not much firm evidence of lower-class residential districts in Israelite cities until the seventh century BCE, following the fall of the north, and even then the poorer populations probably lived outside the walls, where archaeologists have found traces of built-up areas. Some limited neighborhoods of bureaucrats, laborers, artisans, and other defined trades may have existed inside the walls. If so, they could have been knit by kinship relations if there was sufficient dwelling space for the relatives of a worker. The elders or household heads in such a subcommunity had the power to establish the legal norms for their group and to adjudicate conflicts within the neighborhood.[31] It constituted a form of autonomous local management, which however should not be confused with sovereignty or independence. In monarchic and imperial times, all cities, towns, and villages were subservient to the central powers, to which allegiance, obedience, taxes or tributes, and military and labor service were due. But aside from such matters touching on state interests, the inhabitants of urban neighborhoods in ancient Israel managed their own affairs. So long as they did not run afoul of the royal house and its representatives or of those who held economic power over them, the people could develop

30. See chap. 6.
31. Many parallels from other cultures, ancient and contemporary, can be cited. For example, as I discovered while teaching in Kyoto, the *chōnai-kai* existing in Japanese cities are efficient, semi-autonomous organizations of all households in a neighborhood. Each forms a tightly knit community, bonded together to ensure safety, maintain neighborhood sanitation, offer mutual aid, prepare for emergencies, promote cultural activities, and set expectations about behavior. Large residential districts can in this way become honeycombed with many of these *chōnai-kai*, resulting in an orderly environment throughout the entire area. Rooted in a tradition reaching back to feudal times, these neighborhood groups have evolved in response to social and political changes, and they still persist and function in cities today. Ancient Israel's urban neighborhoods were likely not so formally structured, but they found their own means to maintain order and manage affairs of local concern.

their own legal standards and judicial procedures. We should thus expect that the laws of any lower classes living in or near cities shared more in common with the laws of the villagers than they did with those of the upper classes in the cities. For the lower class, the heads of households together held primary public authority, and we have no evidence of a role played by the tribe within urban neighborhoods.

The other legal and judicial constellation in cities comprised the upper class: the royal house and the governing class or elites, as mentioned above in the description of the agrarian state. Here also the hierarchical principle prevailed. The monarch[32] had ultimate authority over the royal house and the courtiers, though certainly with the aid of counselors, administrators, and officers. Rules controlled the terms of succession and inheritance, the women and children of the palace,[33] the privileges and limitations of the court attendants, and many other aspects of royal functioning. Are such rules to be considered laws? Although they appear to be merely internal regulations, the monarch's status as the supreme authority in the land, indeed with despotic powers when desired, gave special weight to palace norms, and they were presumably enforced rigorously, with punishment meted out as deemed fitting. Although the royal house represented a limited world, with relatively few actors, its relation to—and general exclusion of—all nonroyals meant that its practices had at the minimum an implicit bearing on the affairs of the rest of the population. Certainly the story of the intervention of Bathsheba, the queen mother, in securing Solomon's succession to David's throne (1 Kgs 1:11–31), and then Solomon's brutal slaying of any possible threats to that throne (1 Kgs 2:13–46)—these stand out as dramatic object lessons about the ways in which palace affairs could exist as a closed jurisdiction, with no need to answer to another legal body.

Outside the royal palace and beyond the personnel attached to it, the monarch had final authority over the legal system of the state. With familial and other local conflicts handled by traditional authorities within the clans, villages, and urban neighborhoods, the monarch's legal power focused on state interests. The monarch certainly had the power to intervene in local matters and perhaps did so in certain instances, but on the whole there was little royal interest in local conflicts so long as they were settled at that level

32. Of the 42 monarchs of Israel or Judah described in the Hebrew Bible, only one was female—Athaliah, queen of Judah ca. 842–837 BCE. According to the descriptions in 2 Kgs 11:1–20 and 2 Chr 22:10–23:21, Athaliah exercised every bit as much power as did any of the kings—and ruthlessly so.

33. For more discussion of the status and roles of women in the royal house, see Elna K. Solvang, *A Woman's Place Is in the House: Royal Women of Judah and Their Involvement in the House of David*, JSOTSup 349 (London and New York: Sheffield Academic Press, 2003).

and did not impinge upon national affairs. The monarch could appropriate land for the crown, even if it was necessary to go through the motions of a sham trial; the story of Ahab and Jezebel's seizure of Naboth's vineyard (1 Kgs 21:1–16) could have been played out by any number of monarchs. The extent of their power is evident, for example, in the list of the high officials on whom David (2 Sam 8:15–18; 20:23–26) and later Solomon (1 Kgs 4:1–19) reportedly relied in governance. Royal judges could also act on behalf of the monarch in administering justice, but again they limited their cases to matters of state interest—and certainly personal interest as well, given the number of biblical allusions to the bribery of judges.

Furthermore, according to the tradition of royal ideology in the region, the monarch was envisioned as the judicial head and preserver of justice throughout the land; texts from Mesopotamia to Egypt, and Israel in between, often refer to the symbolic and actual roles of monarchs in law-making and law enforcing.[34] The Hebrew Bible does not attribute any of the biblical laws to the kings: they are proclaimed by Moses, the people's chief leader at that time. But while called a prophet, Moses' leadership style matched that of a monarch: the military commander, the jealous guardian of centralized power (note, e.g., the uprising subdued in Num 16), the chief administrator of justice, the leader of the cult. To the extent that traditions about a legendary lawgiver such as Moses circulated during the monarchy, inhabitants of the royal throne could point to this figure as the warrant for their political and judicial powers. According to biblical reports, prophets such as Nathan, Elijah, Micaiah ben Imlah, Elisha, Isaiah of Jerusalem, Jeremiah, and others voiced resounding critiques of royalty on theological and ethical grounds, but the actual extent to which kings and queens were influenced by these religious leaders was, while no longer measurable, probably not significant. Monarchs had supreme power in their lands.

Among the governing class or elites, the group of powerful and privileged persons alongside but separate from the monarch,[35] there may have been less need for rules or laws than was the case for the monarch. They were subject to the precepts of the monarch, from whom they derived benefits as a result of the patron-client relationship.[36] Presumably their personal and familial situation was defined along patriarchal lines, with a male head of household in the dominant role, similar to the rest of the Israelite society.

---

34. See Keith W. Whitelam, *The Just King: Monarchical Judicial Authority in Ancient Israel*, JSOTSup 12 (Sheffield: JSOT Press, 1979); and Westbrook, ed., *History*, passim.

35. See discussion above, chap. 3, The Social Structure of Power in Ancient Israel.

36. Niels Peter Lemche, "Kings and Clients: On Loyalty between the Ruler and the Ruled in Ancient 'Israel,'" *Semeia* 66 (1994): 119–32.

Amos (4:1) suggests, however, that wives in these wealthier contexts could also exercise substantial power within the family, although no mention is made of the legal sphere in this context. Aside from the familial structures, the primary concerns of the governing class were likely focused on property ownership and commercial transactions, for which they determined acceptable practices and saw to the punishment of violations. Members of this governing class enjoyed considerable latitude of action, limited only by the monarch and each other. With their prestige and standing in the circles of power, they probably carved out for themselves a relatively insulated sphere of legal protection: holding themselves above the peasants, they did not consider themselves subject to the same laws and the same courts that governed the lives of the lower class. Within their own guarded world this elite class lived according to their own laws, privileges, and protections.[37] Such a situation is consistent with the prophets' excoriation of the wealthy and the powerful, who showed little concern for the poor and manipulated justice to their own ends. It is also reflected in the many laws elsewhere in ancient Southwest Asia that punished ordinary citizens and slaves more harshly than free property holders, especially if the latter were the victims of the crime.

Finally, when the Israelites were subjected to imperial powers—in succession, the Neo-Assyrians, the Neo-Babylonians, the Persians, and the Hellenists—they effectively lost all sovereign power and control over their political world, at least in terms of the final political authority. From the perspective of the various emperors, once the wars of conquest had been completed and the subjugated countries were incorporated into the empire, the primary concern lay in maintaining the empire's position of dominance over the provinces and keeping a steady stream of tribute and other resources coming into the imperial treasuries. In some cases they allowed a degree of latitude to the provinces, so long as they remained compliant. This situation especially marked the early part of the Persian Empire under Darius I, which is the time most likely for the initial production of a written legal text in Palestine, as we will elaborate in the next chapter. Then, and generally under other empires as well, the imperial law was geared toward ensuring the supreme authority and power of the emperor. Legal issues faced within local communities were left to the communities themselves— to families, clans, tribes, villages, and cities—to resolve, so long as they did not impinge on the well-being of the empire. The emperors thought globally; their subjects acted locally.

---

37. Kautsky (*Politics*, 197–205) discusses such circumstances at the imperial level, but they existed within monarchies such as Israel's as well, albeit on a smaller scale.

One feature often overlooked in this structure is the role of the elites in the provinces. With their own monarch out of the way or at least in a position of diminished power, the elites had the opportunity to increase their fortunes and privileges by collaborating with the imperial representatives in the management of the province. As we have seen for the agrarian state, the competition for advantage between the monarch and the elites or governing class meant that each sought to maneuver for better position than the other whenever possible, so the demise or restriction of monarchical power by an emperor provided an advantageous opening of this sort for the elites. The period following the Babylonian exile presented them with a quintessential opportunity.

Against this background, it is clear that the emperor held highest authority in the determination of laws and the administration of justice in the realm, though in all likelihood the day-to-day affairs of the larger population in the provinces occupied little imperial attention. Those matters, especially in the villages and in kinship groupings, continued to be handled according to traditional procedures in place for centuries. Administrators in a given province—governors or satraps, officers, tax or tribute collectors—shared some powers with the elites, but again affairs in the villages were likely of little consequence to them. From the perspective of the villagers, they still faced a hierarchy above them, all the more formidable because it functioned at two levels: the internal provincial powers, and the more distant but also more daunting imperial center.

The Cult

The world of religious practice represents a sphere that in some senses is distinct from, yet in other senses is inherently related to, the social, political, and economic domains of everyday life. Religion can position itself in opposition to any of the other areas, but then the same can be said of the other domains as well. Similarly, a structure of reciprocal support can and usually does exist among these focal aspects of life. Within the religious world, consequently, it should be no surprise to find a pattern of authority and obedience, or dominance and subservience, that coincides with patterns seen elsewhere in the society.

The cult[38] was observable at a variety of places throughout the land,

38. "Cult" will be used here to refer to a particular group's enactment or celebration of their religious practices and beliefs, especially with the help of designated officiants and symbolic paraphernalia. It also denotes the physical place or setting where such enactment routinely occurs. For more on the definition and significance of "cult" in the history of religions, see

adapting as necessary to the specific circumstances of the given context.[39] Its most basic and most ubiquitous form was the *domestic cult*. Many if not most houses probably had a niche reserved for a household god or gods and other venerable objects, which the family members tended with care and regularity in order to ensure the family's well-being. Family and clan tombs also served as places for ritual and reverence. A *local cult* was maintained by a village or several villages in tandem, or by neighborhoods in towns and cities.[40] Termed in Hebrew בָּמָה, *bāmâ*, "high place" (plural בָּמוֹת, *bāmôt*), these local cults may traditionally have been situated on a hill in the vicinity, probably with nothing more than an open-air altar, where villagers gathered for religious festivals and other rituals. Later these terms designated almost any worship site, sometimes one that had been built on an artificial mound. A *regional cult* served an area larger than just a few villages, perhaps a tribal territory. Less is known about this form just as less is known materially about tribes than about villages in ancient Israel, despite the considerable interest in tribes in the Hebrew Bible. The *central cult*, especially the *state cult*, constitutes the final and most influential context of formal religious activity. Many scholars have postulated the existence of central cults during the premonarchic period—for example, at Shechem, Bethel, Mizpah, Gilgal, Shiloh, Beersheba, Dan—and have associated them especially with the development of the local and national traditions.[41] Some of these sanctuaries may have actually served as regional cult sites. The primary examples of the central cult were associated with the monarchies, and the temples in the capital cities of Samaria and Jerusalem, although not yet discovered, would have served as the central locus of the state cult, providing a close interweaving of religion and politics. When the country was colonized by the Assyrians—the north repopulated and the south transformed to a vassal state—the national cult accommodated the new masters during especially the seventh century BCE, whereas the

---

s.v. "Kult/Kultus," *RGG*, 4th ed. (Tübingen: J. C. B. Mohr [Paul Siebeck], 2001), 4:1799–1809. Chap. 7 below provides more details about the cultic types described here.

39. Descriptions of various types of cult forms, some using different categories than those presented here, can be found in a number of publications. See, e.g., Miller, *Religion*, 62–105; and Rainer Albertz, *A History of Israelite Religion in the Old Testament Period*, 2 vols., OTL (Louisville, KY: Westminster John Knox Press, 1994).

40. A version of this phenomenon still continues in most if not all cultures of the world, in some places more obviously and actively than in others. From a tiny neighborhood shrine to a tall-steeple church to a national temple, they represent the respective community's impulse to worship and to keep the deity or deities in their midst.

41. See discussions in my *Rediscovering the Traditions of Israel*, 3rd ed., SBLSBL 16 (Atlanta: Society of Biblical Literature; Leiden: E. J. Brill, 2006), passim. This tendency to connect the history of traditions so intimately with cultic sites, especially during the premonarchic period, has waned in recent decades.

Babylonians' destruction of the temple in 586 BCE led to a reorientation of Yahwistic worship, as well as a rebuilding of the Jerusalem temple in Persian times.

To appreciate this disbursement of cultic activities requires us to distinguish between a popular and an official cult. This distinction is commonly made, despite several basic problems that it presents: an element that is condemned at one time or place can be accepted in another setting, or vice versa; and religion in Israel, as in most environments, is fundamentally syncretistic.[42] One problem generally not recognized about this distinction is the issue of perspective: official or orthodox is normally associated with the state or centralized cult, while the popular or heterodox is then relegated to the lower classes, the powerless, and the rural. However, poor villagers, believing in transcendent powers that bring help or cause detriment, may well not have known, and much less honored, the pronouncements of a central priesthood: what those villagers regarded as acceptable and efficacious was in effect orthodox for them, even if the central priesthood denounced it as heterodox. To be more specific, many of the religious practices condemned in the Hebrew Bible—worshiping gods other than YHWH, venerating idols and figurines, enacting rituals in sites other than in the temple of Jerusalem (the Deuteronomists' preference), not keeping certain "purity" laws, consulting a medium—may have been perfectly acceptable to Israelites outside Jerusalem, perhaps even to the majority of the population. So what we regard as central or orthodox probably represented a minority perspective that sought in vain to steer the beliefs and practices of the majority. This problem, as we will see in chapter 7, will have a direct bearing on the question of religious laws.

In light of these considerations, the authorities behind Israel's religious laws were cultic leaders of either the professional or nonprofessional (also termed specialist or nonspecialist) order. The term "nonprofessional" designates a cultic officiant who has another primary role in the economy and life of the community, alongside serving the cult. Such a person, for example, worked mainly as a farmer, artisan, merchant, or the like yet would then be acknowledged as the normal officiant whenever the cultic ritual begins. In contrast, the professional has no other business or profession than to serve in the cult. The nonprofessional leaders were to be found in the domestic and local cults and probably in the regional cults as well, although some

---

42. For the larger discussion of official vis-à-vis popular religion as it applies to ancient Israel, see Miller, *Religion*, 47–62. For an early and basic discussion of syncretism, see Gösta W. Ahlström, *Aspects of Syncretism in Israelite Religion*, trans. Eric J. Sharpe, Horae Soederblomianae 5 (Lund: C. W. K. Gleerup, 1963).

traditional group such as the Levites may have played a role at this regional level, and then eventually in the state cult as well. The professionals occupied the central roles of priests and other cultic functionaries in the official state cult.[43] The central priesthood developed its own hierarchy, headed by the high priest. Males presumably had the positions of highest authority and were the primary public officiants, especially in the regional and state cults. Women, however, had roles in all of the cultic levels and were possibly most active and most responsible in the domestic cult.[44] While much has been made of certain dynastic lines in the Jerusalem priesthood, especially the "Zadokites," the evidence for such a dynasty is scantier than is generally acknowledged.[45] Nonetheless, a father typically trained his son, and a mother her daughter, in their respective occupations in ancient Israel, and many children of cultic officiants probably followed their parents into these roles. There were always other influences on the cultic leaders, most notably the worshipers themselves as well as other cultic functionaries. The monarch could exercise control over the state cult; the governing class had additional influence by virtue of its wealth and prestige. The emperor was the key external figure for the imperial cult.

TORAH AS "INSTRUCTION": WHO INSTRUCTS WHOM—AND TO WHAT END?

As indicated in the previous chapter, one of the most common elements in the standard interpretation of biblical law centers on the word תורה, *tôrâ*, a term frequently interpreted to mean "instruction." In light of the discussions in this chapter, the underlying structure of this word deserves a second look. The word *tôrâ* does mean "instruction," but what kind of instruction? and for what purpose? The hermeneutics of suspicion, when applied to this phenomenon, raises profound questions.

In 1968, at the height of the social unrest and reforms sweeping North and South America and Europe, the Brazilian Paulo Freire published a book in Portuguese that was to become an influential, much-studied text among

---

43. See esp. the discussions in Joseph Blenkinsopp, *Sage, Priest, Prophet: Religious and Intellectual Leadership in Ancient Israel*, LAI (Louisville, KY: Westminster John Knox Press, 1995), 72–98.

44. Phyllis A. Bird, *Missing Persons and Mistaken Identities: Women and Gender in Ancient Israel* (Minneapolis: Fortress Press, 1997); also Miller, *Religion*, 201–6; and most recently, Saul M. Olyan, "What Do We Really Know about Women's Rites in the Israelite Family Context?" *Journal of Ancient Near Eastern Religions* 10 (2010): 55–67.

45. Alice Hunt, *Missing Priests: The Zadokites in Tradition and History*, LHBOTS 452 (New York and London: T&T Clark, 2006).

movements for liberation and human rights. *Pedagogy of the Oppressed*[46] stemmed from a world of oppression and illiteracy, which Freire and others sought to counter. In his book Freire argued that education is anything but a neutral enterprise, that it inevitably occurs with political and economic goals in mind even if these remain hidden from public sight, and that in an oppressive context it becomes an effective tool in maintaining the status quo. Preceded in his ideas of a critical pedagogy by the Italian political theorist Antonio Gramsci, Freire maintained that, when education is conducted as if all knowledge resides in the teacher and the students are empty vessels to be filled, then such instruction "attempts to control thinking and action, leads men [*sic*] to adjust to the world, and inhibits their creative power."[47] The better and far preferable approach, he advocated, envisions education as a process of posing problems to the students as a means of instilling in them a sense of competence, a critical capacity, and a posture of responsibility. Freire thus promotes "education as the practice of freedom—as opposed to education as the practice of domination."[48]

Such an understanding of education will probably strike many readers as modern, idealistic, and thus irrelevant to the ancient world. However, we must remember that Freire's own world was one of poverty, exploitation, widespread illiteracy, and oppression of the masses by the few—probably not all that dissimilar from the situation facing the majority of ancient Israelites during the monarchic and imperial periods. While our own contemporary approach may regard instruction as a necessary and appropriate process of socialization, of acquiring scientific and humanistic knowledge, and of developing a creative and critical posture, a subtle, more sinister form of education can easily instill in the students a restrictive attitude of compliance, conformity, submission, and resignation. Not only students in a formal classroom but also an entire population or an economic class can be formed in this way—as much in antiquity as in the modern world. Those who occupy positions of power can inculcate ideology, values, acceptable behavior, ritual practices, an attitude of compliance or criticism—all for the benefit of the larger whole *or* to the gain of the few. Lenski observed it in his study of how power and prestige are secured and sustained in social groups; his examples are taken primarily from modern industrial societies with a formal educational system.[49] Even in a culture that lacks widespread

---

46. The English translation appeared as Paulo Freire, *Pedagogy of the Oppressed*, trans. Myra Bergman Ramos (New York: Seabury Press, 1970).
47. Ibid., 64.
48. Ibid., 69.
49. Lenski, *Power and Privilege*, e.g., 53, 261–62, 329–30, 389–95.

formal education, as was the case in ancient Israel, norms—and thus also laws, as well as a sense of "rights" and protections—are conveyed by means of informal instruction, in one way within a communitarian context and in another way within a monarchy. The empires that controlled Israel also had it within their power to exploit instruction to indoctrinate the colonies, as postcolonial criticism has argued.[50]

But was law really used to such ends in Israel, and is *tôrâ* to be understood as an authoritative pedagogy? The above discussion of the players on the legal scene, if it is correct, points primarily to power holders within their respective social, political, economic, and religious contexts as the ones who directly determined the legal traditions in those contexts, with some secondary influence by others. It stands to reason, then, that the interests of the power holders will be served by their laws—except to the extent that these individuals or groups can transcend their self-interests and act for the good of others. Although even altruism can incorporate an element of self-interest, there is little to be gained in pressing that point now. The much more significant conclusion for the understanding of law is that, inasmuch as power underlies instruction, so also does it infuse the notion of *tôrâ*. If biblical laws are conceived of as "instruction" (= *tôrâ*), those laws are the product of power. They stemmed from those who sought to control their worlds.

Yet not all hierarchy is oppressive. Instruction in a communitarian context—in a village of ancient Israel, for example—may be overseen by the male household heads, but mothers and others in the community participate fully in the upbringing of the children, not only in training them to be productive contributors to the group but also in grooming them in the ethos and traditions of the community. When, however, one group of adults sought to control or manipulate another group of adults, as happened under the monarchy and within the sphere of commerce and economics, the process and result can be all the more objectionable because of the inequalities inherent to the system. Even in the cultic sphere, the actions of priests to define correct ritual, to set the terms for access to communal worship, to require offerings from which the priests will materially benefit, and to punish those who depart from certain norms—all such cultic laws reflect a hierarchy built on power and control. The worshipers may accept all these regulations just as the subjects of a king may obey all royal orders, but such compliance does not lessen the fact that those in power

50. Jon L. Berquist, "Postcolonialism and Imperial Motives for Canonization," *Semeia* 75 (1996): 24–26.

have determined what is acceptable and have "instructed" their audiences accordingly.

There is another context for law and instruction, however, a more formal setting though still one with an ideological, controlling bent. Some scholars have maintained that the coherence, subtleties, and interactions within the legal texts of the Hebrew Bible should be attributed to the presence of a scribal tradition, a setting in which Israelite scribes, trained in both copying and interpreting, used legal texts as a means of learning to reproduce and engage the traditions. Their education occurred through the process of preserving and engaging the legal tradition. In some cases they might have been compelled to reproduce this tradition faithfully; in other settings they sought to use it as a means of reconceiving and reapplying the inherited legal principles—by means of a "hermeneutics of innovation," as has been attributed to the writers behind the book of Deuteronomy.[51] Evidence of this scribal activity, it is thought, appears in the various editorial devices used in reformulating earlier legal texts. Such a process of scribal education is entirely plausible: scribes had to learn their trade in some manner. The deeper question, though, is the character of the ideological, political, economic, and religious interests driving that education. The training of specialists thus parallels the larger critical issue regarding the ways in which "law" is to be understood as "instruction."

CONCLUSION

One final word about the law of power is appropriate. The biblical tradition of social and political morality and accountability has figured prominently in political theology and ethics for many years. British socialism of the late nineteenth century drew on it, as did the social-gospel movement in the United States early in the twentieth century. It served as a guiding point in the World Wars, in the opposition to National Socialism, and in the rebuilding efforts after the World Wars. Direct appeal to biblical moral principles is especially apparent in liberation thought of many forms—in the fight against poverty in Latin and Central America and elsewhere, in the efforts for freedom and self-determinacy in Asia and Africa, in the civil rights movement in the United States, in reform of the justice system, in feminist movements, and in gay rights efforts in the West and elsewhere in the world. The Hebrew Bible articulates a high ethic, one that may be impossible to institute fully but that can serve well as a goal and ideal in the building of a just society.

51. Levinson, *Deuteronomy*, 17.

The argument presented in this chapter is not meant in the slightest to undermine these efforts but rather to bring them to a new level of awareness and to show how power functions. In modern times these movements have struggled with multiple forms of power, and the social and political ethics of the Hebrew Bible has been mined to good effect. Those who advocate change by drawing on liberation thought have employed a "hermeneutics of suspicion," a questioning of the agendas and ulterior motives of those with power and means, thus critiquing the societal institutions they use to their benefit. I am suggesting here that the same hermeneutics of suspicion be applied to the biblical tradition itself. The Hebrew Bible is not in some fashion remote from the realities of politics, economics, and social processes—but is the very product of these structures. Rather than simply appropriating the biblical ideals uncritically, we should at the same time be aware of the special interests that produced biblical pronouncements in the first place. If today we can be suspicious of the motives of our own politicians and power centers, it is appropriate for us to be equally suspicious of comparable behind-the-scenes interests and practices during ancient Israel's history as well. If we gain some understanding of ways in which laws served to bind—especially when on the face of it they appear to be releasing—the powerless in that ancient context, we may sharpen our ability to understand parallel circumstances in our own settings. The biblical traditions can thus continue as a source of guidance and inspiration, but with the chastened realization that they were subject to forces comparable to those that prevail today. The roots of our own heritage—and probably the heritage of all peoples as well—should not be shielded from suspicion and scrutiny.

CHAPTER 4

Speaking and Writing Law

Rechtswerdung ist ja grundsätzlich ein Vorgang nicht des litera-rischen Schaffens, sondern des gelebten Lebens.
—*Albrecht Alt*[1]

To function as intended, laws must be articulated clearly, enforced effectively, and preserved indefinitely. Whether they stem from the general populace or from the elite centers of power, they must follow conventions acceptable in the given society, or their legal force may not be recognized. Oral settings—where laws are retained in memory and recited in public, usually without the aid of written documents—will conform to their conventions as much as do literate settings, which depend on the written word. The mere difference between oral and literate environments does not alter the need to communicate in a traditional and unambiguous manner; actually, the oral world may in some cases be more stringent than the written world in expecting conformity.

The spoken law does not naturally evolve into the written law. Many, perhaps even most, societies in human history have existed without a high level of literacy, depending instead on the oral word for all of their interactions and traditions. Even in societies where literacy predominates, an oral world continues alongside the written and can vary quite significantly from the literary records. This circumstance exists today, just as it did in antiquity. The customary laws in oral form are the only legal terms for a social group that does not use written means for its laws, whereas laws that are issued and stored in written form in another social or political context will not necessarily eliminate all customary laws in pockets of the populations within their territory. A central government may claim sole jurisdiction over all inhabitants in the country, but it is rarely successful in stamping out all

---

1. "The making of law is basically not a literary process at all, but part of the life of a community." Alt, "Ursprünge," 1:284; translation in "Origins," 110.

other practices regulating and punishing behavior at the local levels. Thus we should not expect to find a linear, inevitable progression from oral to written laws but more of a dynamic, variable interaction or even coexistence among these forms of expression.

LEGAL DISCOURSE

Two elements common to legal articulations are vocabulary and form, and both have been the focus of considerable attention in the study of ancient law.

Legal Vocabulary

How are we to recognize legal discourse in an ancient society? One possibility is that it will be identified as such for us. Yet even if a text classifies itself as a law or a legal decision, it does not mean that it necessarily satisfies our four defining conditions for laws: authority, force, and legitimacy; precedent-setting or -appropriating intention; reciprocal relationship between parties in terms of protections and duties; and sanctions.[2] Despite its claims, the text may reflect more of an idealistic or fictional agenda and not record actual laws, as indicated in chapter 1, above. Nonetheless, in the inevitable absence of transcripts of actual oral discourse from ancient Israel, the Hebrew Bible may at least suggest some of the terms or concepts associated with law. Especially noteworthy is the semantic field of "law" in the biblical texts, including several polysemous words stemming originally from nonlegal contexts.

Consider, for example, a text of a clearly nonlegal genre, Ps 119, a paean to the divine law, which throughout its 176 verses repeatedly refers to the law, using at least nine different terms to express it. Most are readily identifiable as expressions denoting legally binding directives: "law" (תורה, tôrâ), "precept" (פקוד, piqqûd), "statute" (חק, ḥōq), "commandment" (מצוה, miṣwâ), and "judgment" (משפט, mišpāṭ).[3] In addition, this psalm contains nearly as many terms used as synonyms for law that are not at all limited to the legal context but stem from or are fully at home in nonlegal speech. Frankly, if the reader of Ps 119 did not approach the text with the prior, conventional notion that each of its 176 verses contains a reference

---

2. See above, chap. 2, The Nature and Sources of Law.
3. I will not comment in detail on the meanings and usages of these various terms since my focus falls more on the social and political than the philological dimensions. For discussions of the words and further bibliography on each, see articles in *THAT* (English: *TLOT*) and *ThWAT* (English: *TDOT*).

to law, in all likelihood many of the uses of the following surrogates would be interpreted as referring to something else than law:

Thus the noun דבר (*dābār*) occurs twenty-four times in the Ps 119 with apparently this meaning of "law" (e.g., in vv. 9, 130, 160), although several times it seems to connote "promise" or "trust" or "hope" (e.g., in 25, 28, 114). The common term for "word" or "thing," *dābār* would not necessarily connote laws except for its occurrence in a setting where laws are otherwise indicated, as in the phrase "these words," often used to refer to a collection of laws (e.g., in Exod 20:1; 34:27; Deut 5:22; 6:6; 12:28). Much more frequently, however, it serves in narratives to indicate a set of events, matters, or statements (e.g., Gen 22:1; Num 14:39; Josh 24:29; 2 Sam 13:21).

Somewhat similarly, אמרה (*'imrâ*, 19 times in Ps 119) designates something said and is usually translated simply as "word" or "promise." It differs from the preceding term in that *'imrâ* indicates more the content of speech, while *dābār* tends to emphasize the act of speaking, including the proclaiming of specific types of content.[4] But again, it is not a technical legal term, nor is it used exclusively or even predominately in legal contexts.

Another substitute for "law" in Ps 119 is דרך (*derek*, "way," 13 times as a noun in Ps 119). Frequently it is used alone in Ps 119 to refer to "my ways" (vv. 5, 26, 59, 168) or the "ways" of YHWH (vv. 3, 37). Almost as often, it is combined with a legal term: "the way of your decrees" (v. 14), "the way of your precepts" (v. 27), "the way of your commandments" (v. 32), and "the way of your statutes" (v. 33). The word implies a course of action, almost a moral pattern of behavior consonant with the law. This meaning is a semantic shift from its designation as a literal road or journey.

The final and most allusive of the surrogates reveals the religious symbolism attaching to law in certain Israelite circles. Both forms from the same root, עדת (*'ēdōt*, always in the plural form, 14 times in Ps 119) and עדות (*'ēdût*, 9 occurrences in Ps 119, all of them plural except for the singular form in v. 88), normally carry the meaning "testimony" or "testimonies," but they are commonly so identified with the law that they are translated "decree" or "decrees" (so NRSV and NJPS for all 23 occurrences of these words in Ps 119, for example). Both forms are related to עד (*'ēd*), the common word for "witness," especially a judicial witness. The step from "testimonies" to "laws," however, is not a natural or obvious move. The Akkadian *adû*, to which the Hebrew *'ēd* is etymologically related, designates a written agreement established with binding force and generally secured by religious or magical means, but it nowhere

---

4. *THAT* and *TLOT*, s.v. דבר *dābār*.

carries the meaning of "decrees."[5] In what sense are the laws of the Hebrew Bible a witness of or to the divine? Laws in ancient Southwest Asian texts are conventionally associated with deities, which obviously lends the laws extraordinary weight and legitimacy. The religious symbolism at work involves, then, viewing the laws as testimonies of divine will and intervention in mandating specific behavior. As such, they are not to be trifled with, nor are those who administer or interpret the laws to be challenged.

Just on the basis of this one nonlegal biblical text, a praise of the biblical laws and the divine lawgiver, we can thus see an expressive vocabulary including both technical and metaphorical terms. Remarkably, however, a key word is virtually missing: only in Ps 119:154 do we find רִיב, *rîb*, which occurs 136 times in the Hebrew Bible to designate the legal process of bringing a suit against an individual or a group or of arguing the case in court. And even here in v. 154 it appears that the person pleading for protection is not necessarily poor and vulnerable but pious. This slight allusion to settling a legal conflict is in no way proportionate to the people's experience of law in real life, in which they were familiar with the need to resolve legal claims or conflicts between two or more parties. They may even have sensed the manipulation that could occur when those with power used the *tôrâ* to "instruct" the people.[6] In Ps 119's extended praise of law, we see instead a theologized version of the legal corpus: the literary corpus and not the undefined, uncollected assemblage of customary laws circulating among the majority of the people. To be sure, the general populace may also have regarded their own laws and customs as heaven sent, but they would have primarily expressed them in terms usable for settling actual cases and not in vague, abstract notions.

Legal Forms

The starting point for form criticism of laws has been the written text—both biblical and cognate texts from ancient Southwest Asia. Since they were not deduced primarily from knowledge of the oral world, the literary genres should not be presumed to match the oral genres, the forms taken by customary laws. If the question of genre had started with the context of living-but-unwritten law, the results may well have been different from what was proposed for the literary forms. Or stated differently, can we know or postulate the conventional forms of village laws, where writing

5. *CAD*, s.v. *adû*.
6. See the discussion above, chap. 3, Torah as "Instruction."

did not prevail, as the standard form of communication and preservation? We begin with an overview of the literary forms—not the contents but the structures of the written laws.

Most frequent are the *casuistic laws*, sometimes referred to as case laws or conditional laws. The form comprises two parts—the protasis ("If . . ." or "When . . ."), which specifies the offense; and the apodosis ("then . . ."), which prescribes the consequence, usually a punishment. For example, "if someone steals an ox or a sheep and slaughters or sells it, then the thief shall pay five oxen for the ox or four sheep for the sheep" (Exod 22:1 [21:37 MT]). Sometimes it can be more complex, with additional stipulations or consequences (e.g., 21:22), or it can be nested with others to describe a string of conditions and the consequence for each (e.g., 21:28–32, the well-known case of the goring ox). It is also the most common form in other Southwest Asian law collections. Casuistic laws serve well in resolving legal conflicts since they can record precedents, complete with punishments. They are not necessarily based on a set of legal principles or rights, such as a constitution or a declaration of rights; the Ten Commandments is too limited in coverage to serve such a role. Case laws lend themselves to becoming remembered and collected.

The second form is the *apodictic laws*, sometimes known as principle laws or categorical laws. Unlike the casuistic laws, they take the form of direct personal address: "You shall not . . ." Circumstances, degrees of guilt, or personal motives are not taken into consideration, nor is punishment specified for the guilty one. They tend to be so general in nature that they require interpretation in order to function in adjudication. Thus, for example, the apodictic law "You shall not kill" (Exod 20:13) does not allow for nuances such as accidental killing, capital punishment, or killing in war, and a given court would need to interpret the general principle in order to determine how it applies to these and other circumstances. In its simple form, it gives an authoritarian, absolutist air, more so than do casuistic laws, which suggest a deliberative process of adjudication and selection of remedy. While apodictic laws fit well in a religious context, the form itself probably stems from a family or clan setting, where parents direct their children not to lie, or steal, or behave in any other manner frowned upon by the community.[7]

The third form is known as *participial law*, so-called because in Hebrew it begins with a participle, often translated into English as "the one who

7. See above, chap. 2, Social Order and Control, regarding Alt's and Gerstenberger's positions on this issue.

does . . ." or "whoever does . . ." Because of the general character of its beginning, it has sometimes been connected with the apodictic law. However, it specifies the consequence or penalty of a violation and thereby is similar to the casuistic form. With elements suggestive of both other types, it deserves to be classed as distinct from the others. Like the casuistic, it lends itself to refraction in light of ancillary conditions. A good example is Exod 21:12–14, which starts with a participial law followed immediately by two casuistic laws: "Whoever strikes a person fatally shall be put to death." Then the first casuistic law adds a provision regarding unintentional manslaughter, followed in turn by another casuistic law specifying further details about intentional murder.

Additional types of laws or legal formulations exist in the biblical texts: motive clauses, additions to laws that seek to motivate compliance; cultic laws, directives regarding matters pertaining to religious behavior; procedural laws; laws embedded in narratives; and commercial laws and contracts.[8]

What can we speculate about the *Sitze im Leben* of the primary conventional legal forms, the life settings in which they thrived and survived? With an absolutist style that brooks no exceptions, the apodictic form conveys a stronger tone of authority than do the casuistic and participial forms. A parent, a monarch, a high priest, a powerful member of the elite, or a god can proclaim sweeping, unequivocal demands in this manner, leaving the details to be worked out by others. The casuistic and participial forms also speak authoritatively, but they imply not a unilateral order by fiat but a judicial process: they do not simply forbid some generalized action but show that there must be a finding of guilt for each case and then an application of a punishment or remedy. "If someone steals an ox . . ." implies that the theft is not taken for granted simply because it has been charged or suspected. The proper judicial body or judge must establish the guilt before the punishment is carried out. Even when an apodictic pronouncement is made in a village or domestic context and conveys the authoritative status of the parent or village leader who is speaking, it lacks the specificity necessary for adequate application. Thus the practical intention of the apodictic form is to affect general behavior, while its political or ideological intention is to ensure recognition of authority. In comparison, the casuistic and participial forms are intended to guarantee at least some minimal form of judicial process leading from a charge or complaint to a resolution and remedy.

8. On the latter, which are especially plentiful in other Southwest Asian cultures, see the discussions below, chap. 6, Marriage, and Contracts.

In written dress, these forms seldom occur in isolation but mainly in lists, often quite lengthy, in both biblical and extrabiblical literature. Such compilations stem immediately from the literate world of scribes, priests, and government officials—not directly from the highest authorities themselves but, at most, recorded and disseminated at their direction or, alternatively, from individuals or groups aspiring to prestige and power. Some lists, probably rather limited and in each case focused on a specific type of crime or tort, are also thinkable in the oral settings of the villages. The household heads or the elders, the ones most publicly involved in adjudicating legal conflicts, developed the judicial precedents and could have remembered them in small groups of laws, such as interrelated precedents dealing with personal injury (as in the combination of participial and casuistic forms in Exod 21:12–27), or those about a goring ox (e.g., 21:28–32, 35–36), or those about property loss and restitution (e.g., Exod 21:1–15 [21:37–22:14 MT]). I am not suggesting that these texts preserve the actual laws in the villages or elsewhere, only that they show how laws about a related subject and expressed with the conventional forms could have crystallized into short lists at the oral level and been remembered in that manner long before they were ever written. Apodictic laws may have been somewhat different in this respect: each one may have originated in isolation from other such laws (e.g., a monarch issues an edict, or a parent tells the children not to lie, or male priests declare what renders women unclean culticly), yet they can be brought together in a list to emphasize basic principles and to highlight the authority of the lawgiver (e.g., the Ten Commandments in Exod 20:1–17, set in its final written form within the context of a theophany).

WRITING LAWS

Literacy

Writing has a long and complicated history in ancient Southwest Asia, dating at least from the third millennium BCE in the southern Mesopotamian region of Sumer. Close to that same period, a system of recording appeared in Egypt as well, in all likelihood independent of influence from Sumer. From the following two millennia, archaeologists have uncovered hundreds of thousands of stone surfaces, clay tablets, potsherds, bones, metals, papyrus, leather, and other objects used to retain markings and scripts conveying some meaning or message in a variety of languages. Though the majority of these texts are economic or administrative in nature, writing developed relatively quickly to the degree that it could also record the intricate nuances of literary texts: narratives, poetry, and laws as well.

Late on the scene, the Hebrew script evolved out of protoforms that emerged in the course of the second millennium BCE and are retained in several inscriptions found from the period. The notable feature was the move toward an alphabetic script, in which each sign represents not a syllable (as in the cuneiform from Babylonia and Assyria) but a phoneme, a single articulated sound. The cuneiform alphabet from mid-second-millennium-BCE Ugarit in the northern Levant was succeeded first by the noncuneiform, linear script of Phoenicia sometime during the eleventh and tenth centuries BCE and then finally by Aramaic and Hebrew in the tenth and ninth centuries BCE. The sheer complexity of scripts decreased from several hundreds of syllabic cuneiform characters required to be literate in Akkadian, to thirty alphabetic cuneiform characters in Ugaritic, to twenty-two alphabetic noncuneiform characters in Phoenician, Hebrew, and Aramaic.

Inscriptional evidence in the southern Levant rose significantly with the eighth century BCE as Aramaic and Hebrew become more distinguished from Phoenician, and the number of inscriptions increased even further in the following two centuries. Still, most of the extant writings are relatively short, and it is not until the Persian period that we begin to find longer texts. Aramaic had often been used in the Assyrian Empire for international communication, both written and spoken, and the Persian Empire adopted it as one of its official languages and scripts, especially in their western provinces, including Yehud (the Persian province of Judea). The Aramaic script also supplanted the old Hebrew script in most cases, and by the Hellenistic period virtually all Hebrew texts, including the writings at Qumran, were rendered in the square Aramaic letters.[9]

However, beyond the techniques and materials of writing, literacy raises social, economic, and political questions as well. Who learned to write and read, and for what purposes? Who did not learn, and why not? Literacy, to be sure, should not be regarded as an either/or but as a continuum stretching between mainly oral at one end and highly literate at the other.[10] Some individuals, for example, were only able to make simple markings to signify numbers or objects or persons, and others knew enough signs to write a

9. The literature on the history of writing in ancient Western Asia is vast. For a summary description and bibliography, see William D. Whitt, "The Story of the Semitic Alphabet," *CANE* 4:2379–97. For a recent collection of Hebrew inscriptions, see F. W. Dobbs-Allsopp, J. J. M. Roberts, C. L. Seow, and R. E. Whitaker, *Hebrew Inscriptions: Texts from the Biblical Period of the Monarchy with Concordance* (New Haven, CT, and London, UK: Yale University Press, 2005).

10. Susan Niditch, *Oral World and Written Word: Ancient Israelite Literature,* LAI (Louisville, KY: Westminster John Knox Press, 1996; London: SPCK, 1997), 44–59.

simple message. Or again, some were trained to conduct administrative work in written form, while others could write fine literary pieces. The point is that literacy is not a single, absolute attribute but one with variations and degrees. Just as important, the oral world and the written word coexisted in ancient Southwest Asia, as in many other traditional societies. A narrative, poem, proverb, or law, for instance, may be created in oral form and be transmitted for decades if not centuries in that state. Recording it in writing does not necessarily freeze it, for it can continue to live orally alongside the written, with both forms undergoing gradual change and perhaps moving away from each other. Although the written word may for some carry a near magical or religious or monumental significance, the spoken word will for others be virtually the only dynamic currency they know and value.[11]

It is easy, as many have done, to confuse the mere presence of script with widespread literacy. After the so-called Gezer Calendar, dating from the late-tenth century BCE and written in what seems to be an early form of Hebrew, was discovered in 1908, a number of scholars concluded from it that literacy was well established in ancient Israel at an early point. It is much more likely, however, that—using the notion of a continuum—very few, well under 5 percent and probably even less than 1 percent of the population, possessed high-level competence in writing and reading, as was also the case in both Mesopotamia and Egypt.[12] Even if the rate was as high as 5 percent, it can be safely assumed that the majority of those who received an education to become literate were destined to be professional

11. Knight, *Rediscovering the Traditions of Israel*, 236; and various other studies of orality, including Niditch, *Oral World and Written Word*, 54–59; Burke O. Long, "Recent Field Studies in Oral Literature and Their Bearing on OT Criticism," *VT* 26 (1976): 187–98; idem, "Recent Field Studies in Oral Literature and the Question of *Sitz im Leben*," *Semeia* 5 (1976): 35–49; Robert C. Culley, *Oral Formulaic Language in the Biblical Psalms*, Near and Middle East Series 4 (Toronto: University of Toronto Press, 1967); and David M. Carr, *Writing on the Tablet of the Heart: Origins of Scripture and Literature* (Oxford and New York: Oxford University Press, 2005).

12. See Niditch (*Oral World and Written Word*, 39–45) for references, although she does not venture to estimate the percentage. Regarding the rate of 1% or less for ancient Egypt during all of its periods except the Greco-Roman period, see John Baines, "Literacy and Ancient Egyptian Society" (33–62), and John Baines and Christopher Eyre, "Four Notes on Literacy" (63–94), both articles published in John Baines, *Visual and Written Culture in Ancient Egypt* (Oxford: Oxford University Press, 2007). Karel van der Toorn sets the figure for Egypt at about 5%; see his *Scribal Culture and the Making of the Hebrew Bible* (Cambridge, MA, and London, UK: Harvard University Press, 2007), 67. The situation in Mesopotamia is treated in a number of recent studies, which generally recognize the literacy continuum as well as the limitation of advanced literacy to professional and elite circles; see the summary by Jack M. Sasson, "Comparative Observations on the Near Eastern Epic Traditions," in *A Companion to Ancient Epic*, ed. John Miles Foley (Oxford: Basil Blackwell Publishing, 2005), 218–19, especially his observation that all such percentages are speculative at best.

scribes. In a word, there was no reading public in the cultures of ancient Southwest Asia. As evidenced in many tablets discovered in the larger region, scribes in training often copied and recopied existing contracts, small series of laws, and sets of legal phrases and terms—probably so they would later be able to write contracts themselves. While some texts from the region contain boasts by kings who claimed they were proficient in reading, there is little evidence that kings and other wealthy elites were routinely trained to read and write at this advanced level, and they had little need for it if they had slaves or administrators who read to them. Advanced literacy was primarily a requirement for professionals or a privilege for the elite, and it was largely to be found only in the urban contexts of palace, temple, and administration.[13] Little more than rudimentary writing and reading can be expected among the rural populations.

The significance of these considerations for the study of ancient Israel's laws is substantial. As will be discussed in the following chapters, the majority of the population living in the rural villages had a flourishing tradition of customary laws, but they possessed neither the competence nor the need to commit to writing their store of rules and legal decisions. These laws lived on in oral form and counted as fully valid in that condition because the oral world was the familiar, accepted context for the villagers. Differences among villages in terms of their legal practices caused little concern unless conflicts arose between them that needed to be adjudicated. Customary laws among certain population groups in the cities also survived long in oral tradition, and most were probably never recorded; if any did become written, only the urban elite and their functionaries controlled the means to do so. The cultic laws were developed, transmitted, and finally written by the priests or their designates.

Both conservative and adaptive tendencies affect oral traditions in general, and customary laws experience the same forces on them: they tend to remain constant over time, but new social or political circumstances will trigger revision and reform when needed. Conversely, written laws might seem to be permanently fixed, but they also can be revised to suit new

---

13. For details about Egypt and Southwest Asia, see van der Toorn, *Scribal Culture*, 51–73; and about ancient Israel and the biblical evidence, ibid., 75–108 and passim. Carr (*Writing on the Tablet of the Heart*, 119, with his emphasis) draws the regional evidence to bear on the situation regarding education, literacy, and class in ancient Israel: "The issue in Israel is not mastery of an esoteric sign system to achieve literacy but use of literacy to *help* enculturate, shape the behavior, and otherwise mentally separate an educated upper class from their non-educated peers." Christopher A. Rollston argues that the consistency found in early Hebrew writing points to formal education for the scribal elites: "Scribal Education in Ancient Israel: The Old Hebrew Epigraphic Evidence," *BASOR* 344 (2006): 47–74.

times. In both settings, however, the general principle applies: laws first tended to arise and survive in unwritten form until some stimulus, such as a demand by an emperor, led to the drafting of texts.[14] Even collecting them into lists, whether at the oral or the written stage, is a later development, and laws functioned as well or better when not collated than when some individual or group assembled them and produced texts of them.

Alternative Scenarios

Two alternative scenarios are worth considering before proposing what to my mind is most likely the first step in the writing of laws in ancient Israel. We begin with the question of how the laws of the villages might have become recorded. An intriguing analogy comes from nineteenth-century Germany: Jacob and Wilhelm Grimm's *Kinder- und Hausmärchen*,[15] the collection of German fairy tales that belongs among the best-known and most-influential publications of folklore in the world. There is a wide-spread notion concerning its origin, and I confess to sharing this view until only recently upon reading several current studies. According to the legendary account, the Brothers Grimm collected their fairy tales by painstakingly crisscrossing Germany, visiting out-of-the-way settlements and succeeding in getting the local peasants to recount their stories. In smoky cabins and in small outside gatherings of children and adults, they heard storytellers, especially housewives, spin the tales that had existed only in oral form for generations and centuries, and the two brothers assiduously committed them to writing. Back in their homes, they collated the various renditions of each tale, producing eventually their classic of world literature in 1812–15.

Such a romantic legend is, however, "patently false."[16] Far from ranging through the countryside to find stories among the common folk, the two brothers largely heard the tales in their own urban settings. Rather than collecting them from unknown informants, they learned about many of them from groups of friends and other acquaintances. Their informants were not

---

14. For some parallels with the situation in ancient Greece, see Michael Gagarin, *Writing Greek Law* (Cambridge: Cambridge University Press, 2008).

15. A recent English edition is Jacob and Wilhelm Grimm, *The Complete Fairy Tales*, with an introduction by Padraic Colum and a folkloristic commentary by Joseph Campbell (London and New York: Routledge, 2002; German original in 1812–1815).

16. Walter Scherf, "Jacob and Wilhelm Grimm: A Few Small Corrections to a Commonly Held Image," in *The Brothers Grimm and Folktale*, ed. James M. McGlathery (Urbana and Chicago: University of Illinois Press, 1988), 187. For further discussion of the details of the Grimms' sources and methods, see other articles in this same volume, particularly Heinz Rölleke, "New Results of Research on *Grimms' Fairy Tales*," 101–11; and Linda Dégh, "What Did the Grimm Brothers Give to and Take from the Folk?" 66–90.

quaint, wizened specimens from another age, but generally younger persons in their teens, 20s, and 30s who were recalling stories they heard as children. Instead of the image of illiterate, uncultured peasants, a scene with mainly middle- and upper-class, educated urbanites appears more appropriate. Furthermore, Jacob and Wilhelm Grimm searched through older written sources for tales that could be adjusted to conform to their notion of charming little narratives. Even the idea that the stories represent old Germanic traditions is incorrect since a good number of them have a French or Italian origin. The Grimm brothers did not intentionally deceive their readers concerning their sources, although they left the impression that their folktales were to be found natively in rural, tradition-oriented settings. Scholars have only rather recently managed to cast doubt on their legendary activities through a careful analysis of both external records and indications as well as internal comments made by the Grimms themselves in their writings.[17]

Who in ancient Israel would have been motivated to assemble the customary laws of the villages—whether in the legendary or in the more probable manner of the Grimms—and then to write them down and preserve them? The villagers themselves, who hardly possessed literacy equal to this task, had little reason to engage in such a painstaking process for their own benefit. Each community had its own legal customs, which were sufficient to get them through crises until some new conflict arose that required fresh adjudication by the villagers themselves. They had no need of, nor could have read, a written code of their laws, much less a compendium of laws from other villages around the country.

Just as numerous variations for most of the stories were identified by the Grimms, so also there could hardly have been full uniformity in the legal traditions of the multitudinous small Israelite settlements, which had virtually no direct contact with each other except for those closest at hand. From discussions of the laws in the Covenant Code (Exod 21–23), we often receive the impression that they constitute a collection of rural legal practices. It strains credulity, however, to propose that they reproduce or encapsulate rules that enjoyed widespread legal acceptance across the land. How could they have acquired such broad currency? With no central authority during the prestate period, no legislative arm, no agreed-upon place to which the disparate villages might have sent representatives to form a grassroots national assembly—these scattered communities had no

---

17. Others have collected oral traditions from the speakers who were accustomed to reciting them to audiences. See, e.g., Albert B. Lord, *The Singer of Tales*, Harvard Studies in Comparative Literature 24 (Cambridge, MA: Harvard University Press, 1960; 2nd ed. with CD, ed. Stephen Mitchell and Gregory Nagy, 2000).

means to settle upon a set of laws authoritative for all of them. It is difficult to conceive of the hamlets in even just one region collaborating, whether out of necessity or desire, to compile such a legal code for themselves. Even during the later state period, the villages were largely independent and relatively isolated from settlements at a greater remove, and each sought to maintain its tightly knit, kinship-centered, tradition-oriented, subsistence-level existence. The state officials and the economic elite, centered largely in the cities, needed to employ strict measures if they hoped to extract anything from the villagers—taxes or tributes, military conscripts, labor gangs, resources and produce for an urban or national market. The people in the hamlets faced enough difficulties in surviving from one year to the next, and they had little use for those on the outside who sought to drain them of their meager holdings.[18] Similarly, there was no good reason for them to share their legal traditions with others, and they must certainly have been amused, if not suspicious, if a governmental authority or religious representative sought to record their laws. Any of the biblical laws that happen to match real-life rural laws are, if not coincidental, then occasional but not extensive materials in the Pentateuch. We have no extant compendium of village laws, and it is hard to imagine that it ever existed. Most if not virtually all of the villagers' laws were lost to history.

The second scenario involves laws arising in urban and national settings during the Iron II period, the years of the monarchies in northern and southern Israel. Here, not in the agricultural villages, is where we might expect to find the advanced levels of literacy necessary to record laws with nuances of judicial import. But were laws issued initially in writing? Certainly edicts and directives from the kings and emperors needed to be promulgated, which was probably accomplished in written form and distributed to officers and governmental heads, but they then needed oral means to reach the nonreading public, the people who did not have sufficient literacy to read them. But such royal decrees—and we can only speculate since we have no such inscriptions from Israel's monarchic period—must have appeared only occasionally, when significant matters of state were at stake.

Did the kings or, for that matter, some group of elites produce a corpus of laws regulating crimes, torts, contracts, procedures, penalties, and the like—for example, the types of laws now retained in Deut 12–26? We can grant that they had at their disposal the literacy, the writing materials, the

---

18. For a description of attitudes in modern villages in the region toward outside political and economic interference, see C. A. O. van Nieuwenhuijze, "The Near Eastern Village: A Profile," *The Middle East Journal* 16 (1961): 295–308.

archives, and the scribes to accomplish it. However, there is no indication and little likelihood that kings drafted the laws or dictated them to scribes.[19] Furthermore, it is equally improbable that a monarch would voluntarily have commissioned scribes, judges, or priests to produce a new set of laws for the kingdom. What might have motivated a king or queen to do so? Those who were in positions of power in the cities and nation-states had little interest in overseeing daily affairs among the larger populace—so long as their taxes (in-kind food supplies, for the most part) and conscripted labor were forthcoming. Faced with a challenge to or a conflict involving national or urban interests, the king or the judges whom he may have appointed were available to dispatch the threats to the system.

The Hebrew Bible itself does not attribute legislative powers to the kings, although prophetic and other texts are quick to criticize them for judicial corruption and other manipulations, especially when the vulnerable suffer from it.[20] In all likelihood the Assyrians, who had their own legal traditions, would not have tolerated any effort in Judah to draft laws for their own small kingdom. The story of finding "the book of the law" (ספר התורה, sēper hattôrâ, 2 Kgs 22:8–13) during the refurbishing of the temple is a linchpin in the Deuteronomistic History inasmuch as it not only lionizes Josiah as a model king but also especially highlights the principles of cultic centralization and fidelity to YHWH as spelled out in Deuteronomy. However, there is no extrabiblical evidence corroborating this story, and it is much more likely that it stems from a much later time frame, during the Persian period at the earliest, when the historical narrative running from Joshua and Judges to 1–2 Samuel and 1–2 Kings was composed, and with it the prose and laws of Deuteronomy. The figure of Josiah and "the book of the law" function then as legitimizing devices for the Deuteronomic laws and the Deuteronomistic theology, not as evidence of written compilations of law during the monarchic period of ancient Israel.

Consider a second variant of this scenario: rather than being drafted

19. As Whitelam (*The Just King*, 209–18) indicates, our assumptions about the Israelite kings are very much influenced by the theology of the Hebrew Bible, according to which the laws have a divine origin, not a royal origin. Nonetheless, the biblical texts also often refer to the kings' involvement in adjudicating specific cases, issuing decrees, and—ideally—maintaining justice in the land. Thus, Whitelam hypothesizes, "the king was probably the greatest contributor to the developing system of law necessary in such a dynamic society as that of monarchical Israel" (217).

20. For allusions to judicial corruption, see, e.g., 1 Kgs 21:8–13; Qoh (Eccl) 5:8 (5:7 MT); Isa 29:20–21; Jer 22:15–17; Mic 3:1–3, 9–11; 7:3. Other types of manipulation and exploitation by the royal house are referenced in, e.g., Deut 17:16–17; 1 Sam 8:10–18; 2 Sam 12:1–15. Other texts speak of rendering justice fairly, especially by kings or royal judges, such as Deut 16:18–20; 17:18–20; 2 Sam 15:2–4; 1 Kgs 3:16–28; 2 Chr 19:5–7; Prov 29:4; Jer 21:11–12; and Zech 8:16.

anew, could the laws of the cities and states have been simply collected and recorded from the customary laws operative within the cities? As I will argue in chapter 6, below, we must not think that the urban and national domains were devoid of customary laws, any more than was the case within the villages. Legal disputes over property, contracts, injuries, marriage and divorce, slavery, and much more certainly arose and needed to be adjudicated. Some of these cases could be settled among the parties and their peers, while others were appealed to the priests or the monarch. A system of precedents and principles resulted, parallel to the evolving legal systems in villages during this period. Even with writing available, such legal processes remained mostly at the oral level. It is difficult to imagine why kings would routinely intervene by ordering that these customary laws be recorded in writing. Contracts (involving, e.g., sales, property, inheritance, loans, marriage, adoptions) may have been written, but not their underlying contract law. As long as the formal and informal judicial systems worked adequately to resolve disputes, no written code was needed.

Thus in neither village nor city should we expect laws functioning during Iron II Israel to have been compiled in writing during that same period. Similarly, many or even most of the legal codes produced in other ancient Southwest Asian cultures have more of a monumental purpose than the practical goal of regulating behavior. Those codes, such as the one preserved on Hammurabi's famous stela, are not even directly referenced in court documents or contracts of their period.[21] If some Israelite king ever erected such a monument containing laws, it has not survived, and we have no reason to think we will ever discover it.[22] We need to look elsewhere to hypothesize a starting point for writing laws in the southern Levant.

The Emergence of Written Laws

The question is thus not simply when the biblical laws were written but whether laws were in writing at all during most of Israel's history. During

21. As indicated by Niels Peter Lemche ("Justice in Western Asia in Antiquity, or: Why No Laws Were Needed!" *Chicago-Kent Law Review* 70 [1995]: 1695–1716, esp. 1698), this absence of references to the codes has long been recognized, especially with respect to Hammurabi's Code.

22. Gary A. Rendsburg's suggestion that royal inscriptions are lacking in Israel because of the humility of the kings, in accord with the teachings of the Hebrew Bible, is ideologically speculative and highly unlikely. Would not the praise poured on David, Solomon, Hezekiah, and Josiah in 1–2 Samuel, 1–2 Kings, and 1–2 Chronicles have accordingly been discouraged or eliminated if the kings were so humble? Cf. Rendsburg, "No Stelae, No Queens: Two Issues concerning the Kings of Israel and Judah," in *The Archaeology of Difference: Gender, Ethnicity, Class, and the "Other" in Antiquity: Studies in Honor of Eric M. Meyers*, ed. Douglas R. Edwards and C. Thomas McCollough, AASOR 60–61 (Boston: American Schools of Oriental Research, 2007), 95–107.

all of its existence from the Iron I through the Iron II periods, from 1200 to 586 BCE, the entire population in the country was able to manage well with their bodies of customary laws. It is likely that various legal systems flourished across the land, but no written codes were needed as long as legal conflicts could be settled according to traditional, local means. The legal systems in the cities and at the state level probably varied from those in the villages, but they sufficed in both contexts. Even if some group in the cities ever thought to write down their own laws—which was unnecessary for legal processes since the traditional system functioned adequately on its own—there is no reason to assume that it ever occurred to them to impress this code of legal texts on the whole country.

Colonial circumstances, however, introduced a change in the internal operations of the country, especially after the fall of Jerusalem. Following the demise of the northern kingdom in 722 BCE, the Assyrians had held strict control over Judah just as they did over the other vassal states in their empire, and the Judeans had little chance to introduce changes in the legal structure of their country. Then the situation began to shift after the fall of the southern monarchy in 586 BCE. Now the elites and the royal house were exiled en masse to Babylonia, where they were settled in various areas to work as farmers, artisans, merchants, cultic officials, and the like, according to biblical and a few Babylonian sources.[23] They were not dispersed throughout the empire and their identity intentionally dissolved as had happened under the Assyrians a century and a half earlier. Rather, while languishing in Babylonian exile, they understandably could have reminisced about the power, property, and prestige they had enjoyed during their earlier lives in Judah, and they passed on to their children the history of dominance and entitlement they had enjoyed shortly before their fall into subservience to the Babylonian emperor. Their descriptions of their former properties, their luxury items, their slaves, their standing, their leisure, their access to realms of power—probably all such stories not only fed their nostalgic visions of utopia but also engendered desires among the new generation to reclaim, if they had the chance, what they felt to be rightly theirs.

When the Persians supplanted the Neo-Babylonians as the imperial power, circumstances took a new turn with Cyrus's edict in 539 BCE,

---

23. A recent history of the Neo-Babylonian exilic period, including a comparison with the Neo-Assyrian exile, is offered by Rainer Albertz, *Israel in Exile: The History and Literature of the Sixth Century B.C.E.*, trans. David Green, SBLSBL 3 (Atlanta: Society of Biblical Literature, 2003; German original, 2001), 70–138. Albertz (89–90) calculates a higher number of exiles, ca. 20,000, than many other historians have suggested.

recorded on the famous Cyrus Cylinder,[24] allowing those in Babylonian exile, from a variety of lands, to return to their respective home countries. While a sizeable community of former Judeans apparently opted to remain longer in Mesopotamia, many others made the long journey back to the southern Levant, to the Persian province now known as Yehud. There they discovered not the idyllic land their parents had described, but a harsh, deurbanized, largely rural environment inhabited by descendants of those who had been the compatriots of their parents, albeit largely of a much lower class. Tensions and outright hostilities between those who had remained in the land and those who had returned from exile arose and persisted well into the fifth century BCE, as described in Ezra and Nehemiah regarding the rebuilding of the Jerusalem temple and fortification wall. Even if the details of the controversy are stylized in these texts, including a dramatic description of builders working with one hand and holding a weapon with the other (Neh 4), the basic conflict or resistance is under-standable as a fear among the rural population that the cities, the traditional "power containers,"[25] would again become established and would seek to extract from the villagers their labor and their meager produce. A sign of this tension may be reflected in a specific development dating to the early years in the reign of Darius I (ruled 522–486 BCE), an occurrence that may double as the earliest writing of laws in the Israelite tradition.

The social and political dynamic is the realignment of power relations and the rise of a new elite among the people of Yehud: diverse religious and political factions competed for the upper hand following the return of the exiles.[26] The old elite from Israel's monarchic period had employed blatant power to effect their will, but now that power had been shifted to the imperial center, leaving an uncertain situation among the indigenous residents and the returnees in Yehud. To claim the position of prestige held

24. *ANET* 315–17; *COS* 2:314–16.
25. See below, chap. 6.
26. A discussion of early postexilic factions is present in Morton Smith, *Palestinian Parties and Politics That Shaped the Old Testament* (New York: Columbia University Press, 1971), 62–112. Several more-recent studies of the ideology of texts from this period have also taken up the question of power maneuvers by the elite in connection with the people's return to the land. See, e.g., Gottwald, "Social Class and Ideology in Isaiah 40–55"; Robert P. Carroll, "The Myth of the Empty Land," *Semeia* 59 (1992): 79–93; and Frank Crüsemann, "Israel in der Perserzeit: Eine Skizze in Auseinandersetzung mit Max Weber," in *Max Webers Sicht des antiken Christentums: Interpretation und Kritik,* ed. Wolfgang Schluchter (Frankfurt am Main: Suhrkamp, 1985), 205–32. For further discussion of local elites within the Persian Empire, see Pierre Briant, *From Cyrus to Alexander: A History of the Persian Empire,* trans. Peter T. Daniels (Winona Lake, IN: Eisenbrauns, 2002; French original, 1996), 43–61 and passim; Jon L. Berquist, *Judaism in Persia's Shadow: A Social and Historical Approach* (Minneapolis: Fortress Press, 1995), 131–46; and Lester L. Grabbe, *Judaism from Cyrus to Hadrian,* vol. 1, *The Persian and Greek Periods* (Minneapolis: Fortress Press, 1992), 103–19 and passim.

by their ancestors and to cloak it with legitimacy, the new elite needed to transform the old force into a new authority and the old might into a new right. Or to use the metaphor of the great Italian sociologist Vilfredo Pareto, "the lions" of the old order became "the foxes" of the new.[27] This new kind of elite in the postexilic period was driven as much by self-interest and partisanship as had been the governing class during the monarchic period, but the new elite, like the fox, had to operate with more cunning than had previously been necessary when power and force were centralized in the monarchy. Such maneuvering was all the more crucial for them now since acceptable relations could be negotiated with the imperial government, giving these aspirants a certain standing as leaders of the Yehud province, at least in the eyes of Darius. How to position themselves vis-à-vis the larger populace of Yehud, the vast majority of which was agrarian, certainly represented a more difficult task, yet one they did not need to resolve immediately in order to gain recognition from the Persian powers. These new elites could draw on their knowledge, gained during their Babylonian exile, of the Mesopotamian tradition of justice sanctioned by the king, such as was present in Hammurabi's Code. Thus it is likely that they included some laws mentioning the justice due to the powerless, for which parallels already existed in the numerous villages of the country, as we will see in the next chapter. The social values of the many thus became manipulated to the benefit of the few.

The Persian Empire, in a word, handed these would-be elites the perfect tool for securing the power and status they sought. As the Persian court planned to ensure stability in the realm by fostering stability within each province, including Yehud, they adopted a policy of tolerance toward ethnic religions but insisted that these cults in the various provinces be "well organized under responsible leadership."[28] One means to show this tolerance and to shore up the native leadership was to support the rebuilding of cities and the construction of temples. While the Persian emperor thereby sought to co-opt the Yehudite leadership, these new elites took advantage of imperial policy in order to regain their birthright of power and prestige in the land.

For our purposes, the Persian imperial policies have direct implications

27. Vilfredo Pareto, *The Mind and Society*, vol. 4, *The General Form of Society*, trans. Andrew Bongiorno and Arthur Livingston, with the advice of James Harvey Rogers (New York: Harcourt, Brace & Co., 1935; original, *Trattato di sociologia generale*, 1916), §2178. Cited and discussed in Lenski, *Power and Privilege*, 50–58.

28. A. T. Olmstead, *History of the Persian Empire* (Chicago: University of Chicago Press, 1948), 304.

for the writing of laws, for it is in this period—and more particularly during Darius's reign—that we can best locate the origin of a written trajectory that eventually and after many changes found its way into the Hebrew Bible canon. Persian sources relate that Darius caused laws to be drafted for his entire realm. Some thirty meters (100 feet) above the base of the mountain of Behistun (or Besitun) in modern-day Iran is an imposing relief with a trilingual inscription from Darius, written in the Old Persian, Akkadian, and Elamite languages. The lengthy description of Darius's royal line and incidents early in his rule contains this statement: "By the favour of Auramazda, these peoples [the 23 provinces listed in the inscription] respected my law; in accordance with what was said to them by me, they acted."[29] Whether "my law" refers to an actual written code issued by Darius or rather to the general authority of his imperial kingdom[30] is debatable. No extant copy of this law remains today, but in ancient times Darius's role as legislator gained such a reputation that it was still cited centuries later. Plato praised him for "enacting laws into which he introduced some measure of political equality," which contributed to the success of his rule.[31] Diodorus of Sicily (1st c. BCE) even counted Darius among the six greatest lawgivers of Egypt because he, the only non-Egyptian on the list, is credited with having studied and supported the traditions of the land.[32]

A third-century-BCE papyrus document, reportedly obtained in 1801 during Napoleon's Egyptian campaign and now preserved in the Bibliothèque nationale in Paris (BN 215), retains a key piece of information pertinent to the question of recording laws in writing. On one side of the papyrus is the Demotic Chronicle, apparently an oracle foretelling the disaster awaiting the bad kings of late Egypt. On its reverse side, along with a few other

29. Translation from the Old Persian text by Amélie Kuhrt, *The Persian Empire*, 2 vols. (London and New York: Routledge, 2007), 1:143, §8. The Babylonian text reads slightly differently: "Under the protection of Ahura Mazda I made my laws effective within these lands. That which is ordered from my own presence that they perform whether by night or by day"; Elizabeth N. von Voigtlander, trans., *The Bisitun Inscription of Darius the Great: Babylonian Version*, Corpus inscriptionum iranicarum, Part I, Inscriptions of Ancient Iran; vol. 2, The Babylonian Versions of the Achaemenian Inscriptions, Texts 1 (London: Lund Humphries, 1978), 54. For further discussion of the inscription with respect to issues of writing and power, see Donald C. Polaski, "What Mean These Stones? Inscriptions, Textuality, and Power in Persia and Yehud," in *Approaching Yehud: New Approaches to the Study of the Persian Period*, ed. Jon L. Berquist, SemeiaSt 50 (Atlanta: Society of Biblical Literature, 2007), 37–48.

30. Briant (*From Cyrus to Alexander*, 511) and Kuhrt (*The Persian Empire*, 1:152 n. 10) argue the latter.

31. Plato, *Laws* 3.695c; trans. R. G. Bury, *Plato: Laws, Books 1–6*, LCL 187 (Cambridge, MA, and London, UK: Harvard University Press, 1926 and 2001), 228–31. For another favorable reference to Darius, see Plato, *Phaedrus* 258c.

32. C. H. Oldfather, trans., *Diodorus Siculus*, vol. 1, *Books 1–2.34*, LCL 279 (London: William Heinemann; New York: G. P. Putnam's Sons, 1933), §95 (pp. 324–25).

short pieces, is a copy of an order by Darius, recording that in 519 BCE he sent the following decree to his Egyptian satrap:

> Have them bring to me the scholars [. . .] among the soldiers, priests and scribes of Egypt [. . .]. They are to write the law of Egypt from olden days until Year 44 of Pharaoh—life, prosperity, health—Amasis—life, prosperity, health!
>
> The law . . . [. . .] of the temples and the people, have them brought here . . . [?] a papyrus until Year 19 [. . .] Egypt. They were . . . [. . .] (in) Year 27. He wrote matters [. . .] in the manner [?] of the law of Egypt. They wrote a copy on papyrus in Assyrian writing and in documentary writing. It was completed before him. They wrote in his presence; nothing was left out.[33]

Though the text is fragmentary and its meaning at times elusive, Darius's decree in the third sentence above, following the reference to the pharaoh in the previous sentence, presumably read something like this: "The law of the pharaoh, the law of the temples, and the law of the people—have them brought here to me [Darius]."[34] The reference to Amasis (more commonly known as Ahmose II), the pharaoh who ruled 570–526 BCE and is named by Diodorus as another of the six great lawgivers of Egypt, represents Darius's shrewd acknowledgment of Egypt's legal and royal heritage. Deceptively simple in its instructions, Darius's order explicitly concerns only the province of Egypt. According to the papyrus, the laws were recorded over a sixteen-year period, from 519 to 503 BCE, and were written on papyrus in both the Aramaic (= "Assyrian") and the Demotic (= "documentary") languages.

This directive to Egypt raises the obvious question of whether Darius required the same of all or many other provinces as well. Although little evidence has appeared elsewhere than in Egypt, this new drafting of local laws is consistent with Darius's general strategy of allowing each province considerable latitude in restoring its religious and social traditions, even to the point of giving support to rebuild its temple and capital city. Such a policy is one of several possible strategies available to a new empire that needs to make the transition from a conquest mode to an administrative mode in order to secure the ongoing stability and funding of the realm. By

33. Translation by Kuhrt, *The Persian Empire*, 1:125. See also the critical edition by Wilhelm Spiegelberg, *Die sogenannte demotische Chronik des Pap. 215 der Bibliothèque nationale zu Paris, nebst den auf der Rückseite des Papyrus stehenden Texten* (Leipzig: J. C. Hinrichs, 1914), 31.

34. Spiegelberg (*Chronik*, 31) translates: "Das . . . Gesetz des Pharao, der Tempel (und) des Volkes <möge> man es hierher bringen" = "<Let> them bring to me the law of the pharaoh, of the temples, <and> of the people."

requiring from each province a written copy of its legal traditions, Darius put himself in a position to combine these local laws with his empire-wide decrees and establish or authorize them as enforceable norms for the respective province.[35]

The categories named in the papyrus cover the various types of provincial laws: state laws (= "pharaoh"), religious ordinances (= "temples"), and popular customary laws (= "people").[36] Specifically including the people's laws is significant since it seems to acknowledge the existence of legal norms and procedures outside the state's purview, or at least the development among the people of judicial traditions that had not been crafted by the central government but that persisted alongside the laws of the state. Furthermore, Darius perceives that, even with the Egyptians' beliefs in the intimate connection between the pharaoh and the divine world, the political establishment and the religious establishment were discrete enough to have developed their respective sets of laws and customs.

It is tempting to see in these distinctions among state, temple, and people a parallel set of legal systems preserved in biblical law: does the Deuteronomic Code record the laws of the state and the urban centers, the Priestly Code retain religious norms and practices, and the Covenant Code represent the laws at home among the general populace? In my view, however, the period of Darius I is entirely too early to associate with the written production of the legal texts in the Hebrew Bible. It is all the more unlikely that, as has been advocated by some, the whole Pentateuch was drafted in response to Darius's order, who then authorized it.[37] While it is reason-

---

35. The notion of "authorization" of local laws by the Persian imperial center stems from Peter Frei, who discusses not only the BN 215 papyrus but also several other instances in which Persian authorities specifically legitimate the legal rulings or other actions occurring in the provinces. See Frei, "Zentralgewalt und Lokalautonomie im Achämenidenreich," in Peter Frei and Klaus Koch, *Reichsidee und Reichsorganisation im Perserreich*, 2nd ed., OBO 55 (Freiburg, Switzerland: Universitätsverlag Freiburg; Göttingen: Vandenhoeck & Ruprecht, 1996); the 1st edition of 1984 is supplemented in the 2nd edition with a long discussion by Frei (36–131) of responses to his initial edition. See also Peter Frei, "Persian Imperial Authorization: A Summary," in *Persia and Torah: The Theory of Imperial Authorization of the Pentateuch*, ed. James W. Watts, SBLSymS 17 (Atlanta: Society of Biblical Literature, 2001), 5–40.

36. Briant (*From Cyrus to Alexander*, 474) identifies the three categories as "public (or constitutional) law," "temple law," and "private law." Donald B. Redford ("The So-Called 'Codification' of Egyptian Law under Darius I," in *Persia and Torah*, ed. Watts, 135–59) argues that Darius did not "authorize" or "codify" the Egyptian laws but merely caused their regulations pertinent to wealth production to be translated into Aramaic, the new imperial language: "It served as a means of instructing the new authority in its attempt to control that wealth through tapping into the laws and statutes of the administration of the pharaohs, the lay-community, and *especially* the temples" (ibid., 158, with his emphasis).

37. See, e.g., Erhard Blum, *Studien zur Komposition des Pentateuch*, BZAW 189 (Berlin: de Gruyter, 1990), 333–60; also the discussions in various articles in Watts, ed., *Persia and Torah*.

able that he had some interest in the local laws, the full narrative expanse of the Pentateuch held much less importance for him, and "authorizing" it would have produced no gain for him or for the provincial government in Yehud. Both the legal and the nonlegal texts in the Pentateuch required a long period of literary development to reach their present form. What we can perceive as an unintended effect of Darius's policy, however, is the first step taken in Israel to record oral laws in writing. The intent of this early action also differs from that of a collection of laws written later for internal purposes within the Jewish community: if some group produced an assemblage of laws in the late sixth century BCE, it was to satisfy Darius's imperial requirement, not to preserve Israelite traditions as such. And significantly, it also served the special interests of the new elites in early Persian Yehud, who were all too ready to respond to Darius's command, thereby gaining his recognition as leaders in this province and, with it, the grants of land and privileges typically bestowed by an emperor on his clients and collaborators.

Furthermore, the precedents for written laws in Yehud were not some putative collections from the Israelite monarchy (e.g., the Covenant Code and the Deuteronomic Code) but the texts, some of them observable as monumental inscriptions, that these new elites could have seen or heard about during their years in Babylonian exile. That direct contact, presumably preceded by earlier generations' acquaintance with Assyrian laws, also accounts for the adoption of the casuistic form so well known from those earlier legal collections in ancient Southwest Asia. New texts written in response to Darius's command would correspond in this and other respects to the legal discourse already familiar in the realm. Regarding the content, the new elites would have had little trouble collecting or creating laws and attributing them to the state, the temple, and the people. They did not need to be comprehensive or to record actual legal practices: what they sent to Darius needed only to *appear* to represent the laws of the land. But with this beginning, with laws now rendered in written form, the stage was set for later groups, leaders, priests, scribes, or others in the postexilic community to craft their own legal texts, which in turn eventually evolved into the legal literature now retained in the Hebrew Bible.

This proposal for the initial appearance of written laws in ancient Israel is surely hypothetical. But so are the long-standing notions that attribute the Covenant Code to the early monarchy, or the Deuteronomic Code to the seventh century BCE, or the Priestly Code to the exilic or postexilic period, or any other such attribution of biblical laws to specific points in the long history of ancient Israel, from the putative time of Moses in the Late Bronze

Age to the Hellenistic period. In favor of the proposal described here is the discovery of this text, BN 215, describing a policy issued by early Persian authorities that required the Egyptian province to deliver a written copy of their laws. Even though no explicit parallel exists for Yehud or other provinces, it is reasonable to assume that a similar policy extended to them as well, resulting in the turn toward writing laws in ancient Israel. Previous proposals have been postulated without the benefit of extrabiblical evidence, but here we find a stimulus that, so far as we know, did not exist before the time of Darius. As we will see in the next three chapters, laws flourished during the preceding centuries in the villages, the cities, the states, and the cults of ancient Israel, functioning with authority in oral form. Now in the Persian period, some group was expected to produce a written set of laws. Then during the following centuries, perhaps in conjunction with the work of Ezra and Nehemiah, a written tradition evolved, eventually resulting in a canonized text of biblical laws.

CULTURAL MEMORY

As a subject of considerable interest in recent years, cultural memory refers to the convergence, generally over centuries or even millennia, of the notions, perspectives, experiences, histories, verbal articulations, and commemorative symbols that combine to form a people's identity and distinctiveness.[38] It extends beyond the synchronic limits of social memory and is much more than an individual's memory, yet cultural memory cannot exist without the memory of many individuals and the functioning of a society. For most scholars studying this phenomenon, the turn toward writing is a decisive step in the development of cultural memory inasmuch as it thereby becomes fixed, concretized, and stored (e.g., in libraries), whereas the memory of an "oral society," even with its conservative character, can change when necessary, shifting with alterations in the political and social environment.

38. Key studies on cultural memory include Maurice Halbwachs, *The Collective Memory*, trans. Francis J. Ditter Jr. and Vida Yazdi Ditter (New York: Harper & Row, 1980; French original, 1950); Jan Assmann, *Das kulturelle Gedächtnis: Schrift, Erinnerung und politische Identität in frühen Hochkulturen*, 2nd ed. (Munich: Verlag C. H. Beck, 1999); idem, *Religion and Cultural Memory: Ten Studies*, trans. Rodney Livingstone (Stanford, CA: Stanford University Press, 2006; German original, 2000); Jan Assmann and Tonio Hölscher, eds., *Kultur und Gedächtnis* (Frankfurt am Main: Suhrkamp, 1988); Aleida Assmann and Dietrich Harth, eds., *Kultur als Lebenswelt und Monument* (Frankfurt am Main: Fischer Taschenbuch, 1991); Astrid Erll, Ansgar Nünning, and Sara B. Young, eds., *Cultural Memory Studies: An International and Interdisciplinary Handbook*, Media and Cultural Memory 8 (Berlin and New York: Walter de Gruyter, 2008); and Philip R. Davies, *Memories of Ancient Israel: An Introduction to Biblical History—Ancient and Modern* (Louisville, KY, and London, UK: Westminster John Knox Press, 2008).

To consider the place of laws in cultural memory warrants a return to the fundamental principles of ideological criticism, legal realism, and CLS: *Whose* laws are being presented as part of the cultural memory? *Whose* memory is thereby represented? And what political, economic, and social interests are reaping benefits as a result? More specifically, do only written laws count? Or stated more generally, is there an even distribution of Israelite experiences and legal traditions in this cultural memory, or does it represent mainly the viewpoints of the writers and their patrons?

The main point I have proposed and will be illustrating in further detail in the next three chapters is that a significant variety in laws and legal adjudications must have existed across ancient Israel—not just in the prestate period, when there was no centralized power in the land, but also throughout the entirety of that culture's history, from prestate, to monarchy, to colonial vassalage, to exile and the Diaspora. The differences were social and demographic on one level, and ideological on another. To write laws under those circumstances involved selecting or inventing some laws and excluding others, and it could hardly have been otherwise so long as the writers had in mind to produce a manageable collection rather than a limitless assemblage of all laws with any judicial force in any corner of the country during any time in Israel's history. Even if some group had taken it upon themselves to produce such a massive compilation, would it represent cultural memory? For many who study cultural memory, the answer would need to be no. For them, only a portion of the mass of cultural experiences and representations can become the focus of the cultural memory: the rest languishes in storage or is forgotten in the everyday oral world. The process has been referred to as "excarnation":[39] when the lived experience (including the living oral tradition) is rendered in written form ("excarnated"), it becomes a visible artifact, separate from the prior experience and from those who lived it. The written word may have carried near-magical significance at the dawn of writing, but it lost this weight as it became more commonplace. At the same time, though, a text could acquire authority and new normative status of its own as it became the object of study and interpretation—as happened with the canonical form of the biblical laws. The other laws, those not retained in the written cultural

39. Aleida Assmann, "Exkarnation: Gedanken zur Grenze zwischen Körper und Schrift," in *Raum und Verfahren*, ed. Alois Martin Müller and Jörg Huber, Interventionen 2 (Basel: Stroemfeld/Roter Stern, 1993), 133–55; and with special reference to biblical laws, Eckart Otto, "Exkarnation ins Recht und Kanonsbildung in der Hebräischen Bibel," *ZABR* 5 (1999): 99–110.

memory of ancient Israel, became lost because their oral form did not make the transition to written record.

However, the oral legal traditions, even if not written, quite certainly continued to evolve and to function among the general populace, which did not necessarily regard the urban written tradition as normative for their lives. We recognize this phenomenon even in our contemporary world; surveys have often shown that many laypeople, unaware of fundamental laws underlying our legal system (e.g., regarding rights), think they are being faithful to their legal tradition even though they advocate principles directly opposed to constitutional law. Thus the place of laws in cultural memory is not uniform, but it is significant. In the oral world of ancient Israel, legal provisions and principles belonged to the stock of traditions that governed everyday life, and they were as varied as were the social groups: the farmers and the city dwellers, the destitute and the wealthy, the military and the bureaucracy, the priests and the merchants, the royal house and the slaves. Each such grouping developed its own identity and ethos, its own internal norms and procedures for dealing with violations. A state-level or empire-level of mandates had the capacity to overrule them but normally did not bother to do so if affairs moved smoothly at the lower levels. So the cultural memory during this oral period was not shared across the whole country: it was plural and multiform, reflecting the respective social subgroups. Did those who had no use for written texts have a cultural memory? To be sure, yes, but it did not survive intact because it was not recorded and preserved by those who favored another memory.

When the biblical laws were first written, which in my view was highly unlikely before the middle of the Persian period, these statutes represented primarily the parochial interests of the priests and the elites. They became part of a wider cultural memory, not immediately but only gradually, as an increasing number of the Judean descendants in the southern Levant and in the Diaspora identified themselves with it. Various Jewish sects appearing during the Persian, Hellenistic, and Roman periods deviated from each other in one respect or the other, but the cultural memory survived, especially in its written form. The laws of the Pentateuch became defining components for later generations. However, we have no grounds for supposing that these pentateuchal laws are identical with the written laws produced for Darius I in the late sixth century BCE nor, for that matter, with pre-Persian legal collections. Whatever it was that Darius received from the new elites of Yehud was drafted primarily for his goals of imperial governance, not for preservation of the Jewish heritage. Darius's order resulted in a novel move in terms of recording laws at all in Israel, but several more centuries during the remainder of the Persian and into the Hellenistic periods were needed for priests, scribes, and other traditionists to develop the pentateuchal legal texts, as well as the rest of the Hebrew Bible, and to lend them the authority necessary for their eventual canonization.

PART 2

LAWS IN THEIR CONTEXTS

CHAPTER 5

Law in the Villages

*India lives in her 700,000 villages—obscure, tiny, out-of-the-way
villages, where the population in some cases hardly exceeds a few
hundred, very often not even a few score. I would like to go and
settle down in some such village. That is real India, my India.*
—*Mahatma Gandhi*[1]

The settings in which by far the greatest population of ancient Israel was
located are also the contexts about which we are least informed.[2] That gap
in our knowledge is being closed somewhat as archaeologists and historians
attend increasingly to life in the countless small villages of the land,[3] but
too little remains from most of those settlements to cast significant light on
their inhabitants' lives, circumstances, ideologies, conflicts, and laws. Their

1. Mahatma Gandhi, *Harijan*, 7 April 1946.
2. The discussion in this chapter builds on portions of my article "Village Law and the Book
of the Covenant," in *"A Wise and Discerning Mind": Essays in Honor of Burke O. Long*, ed.
Saul M. Olyan and Robert C. Culley, BJS 325 (Providence, RI: Brown Judaic Studies, 2000),
163–79. While that article focuses on the Covenant Code, here I will discuss village law more
generally.
3. Among recent studies describing details of daily living drawn from the archaeological
record and other sources, see King and Stager, *Life in Biblical Israel*; McNutt, *Reconstructing
the Society of Ancient Israel*; S. Bendor, *The Social Structure of Ancient Israel: The Institution
of the Family (beit 'ab) from the Settlement to the End of the Monarchy*, Jerusalem Biblical
Studies, 7 (Jerusalem: Simor, 1996); Victor H. Matthews and Don C. Benjamin, *Social World
of Ancient Israel, 1250–587 BCE* (Peabody, MA: Hendrickson Publishers, 1993); and Thomas
E. Levy, ed., *The Archaeology of Society in the Holy Land* (New York: Facts on File, 1995). For
comparable recent portrayals of social life in Mesopotamia, see Karen Rhea Nemet-Nejat,
Daily Life in Ancient Mesopotamia (Westport, CT, and London, UK: Greenwood Press, 1998);
Daniel C. Snell, *Life in the Ancient Near East, 3100–332 B.C.E.* (New Haven and London: Yale
University Press, 1997); Daniel T. Potts, *Mesopotamian Civilization: The Material Foundations*
(London: Athlone Press, 1997); and Marc Van De Mieroop, *The Ancient Mesopotamian City*
(Oxford: Clarendon Press; New York: Oxford University Press, 1997). For a comparative
and methodological discussion of issues involved in the archaeological study of villages
and cities, see *Archaeological Views from the Countryside: Village Communities in Early
Complex Societies*, ed. Glenn M. Schwartz and Steven E. Falconer (Washington and London:
Smithsonian Institution Press, 1994); and especially on villages: Uta Zwingenberger, *Dorfkultur
der frühen Eisenzeit in Mittelpalästina*, OBO 180 (Freiburg, Switzerland: Universitätsverlag;
and Göttingen: Vandenhoeck & Ruprecht, 2001).

relative poverty meant that they could not afford to construct and maintain buildings similar to the monumental urban edifices or the houses of the elite. As additional evidence of village layout, housing, everyday pottery pieces, tools, storage areas, and more comes to light, our picture fills out with details that provide us with an ever-better sense of their terms of living than we have previously possessed. Nonetheless, there will always be distinct limits to the extent and depth of how much we can know about these villagers. Much of their everyday lives left little or no trace in the material or textual record.

The effort to reconstruct the legal systems in Israelite villages needs to start with a brief description of village life in ancient Israel, in particular the physical features of villages, their typical number of inhabitants, and the social structures underlying community existence. The premonarchic settlements alone are not the focus: villages from all periods, the entire Iron Age as well as the Persian and Hellenistic periods, present situations where behavior needed to be regulated. Chapter 3 above identifies the holders of power and authority within the villages. On this basis I now propose to reconstruct the kinds of legal issues and conflicts that probably occupied the villagers' attention. Finally, in light of the distinction made above (chap. 1) between Israelite laws and biblical laws, I will also turn to biblical and other ancient texts that purport to contain laws or to describe legal conflicts. After listing criteria to use in identifying any village laws preserved in these texts, I will try to give as much content to the legal systems as is reasonably possible. The next two chapters will follow a similar structure, first for the city and state and then for the cult. However speculative and hypothetical these efforts must remain, shifting the focus thus to the "Israelite laws" themselves is a legitimate undertaking in historical reconstruction. As indicated above (chap. 3), we are hereby engaging in a hermeneutic of recovery, trying to retrieve what has been lost to history in large part due to the efforts of those with power, whose own interests prevailed. Nowhere in the study of ancient law is this loss more evident than in the legal systems that evolved among the villagers and guided their everyday lives.

VILLAGE LIFE

Historians of ancient Southwest Asia have accorded the village far less significance than they have the city on the one hand and the nomadic/semi-nomadic life on the other. Such, at least, is in large part the net result of a focus, for the city, on matters of national consequence or, for the nomadic life, on exotica from the Western point of view. Cities, virtually by definition, constituted the locus of public, wide-ranging, and powerful interests, the driving factors behind national politics and economics. In contrast, village life thrived on its relative isolation from the wider universe of the nation-state, and indeed from urban life in general. These circumstances present us with a clear caveat: the study of ancient Israel should not simply privilege the urban, public, and national activities, for the terms according to which villagers sought to order their lives belong equally to the landscape of that ancient people, even if the rural ethos did not attain the normative status granted to the urban tradition in the writings of the Hebrew Bible. Because relatively little modern attention has been paid to villages, at the outset we need to take time to understand the character and viability of village life in ancient Israel. We will then be in a better position to consider the kinds of legal problems and strategies taken in these innumerable hamlets, and their relation to the literature of law in the Pentateuch.

The following discussion can provide only the barest sketch of the character of these settlements during Israel's history, with little attention to the many differences among various areas of the land. The differences constitute part of the argument: entirely too wide a range of small, disparate, and often isolated settlements persisted throughout ancient Israel's history for us to suppose that their legal customs could have been captured in pentateuchal law, much less in a single corpus such as the Covenant Code. Much the same can be said of the relation of villages to legal texts found elsewhere in ancient Southwest Asian cultures. At the same time, we should not suppose that we can easily characterize village society, which itself was likely as varied as were the settlements. Nonetheless, a certain typification of these settings provides a basis for assessing their legal systems—the legal conflicts, principles, and precedents involved in social order and redress in the villages.

In terms of sheer numbers the villages occupied a remarkable position in Israel's social history. Although the evidence is and will remain incomplete, it appears that the vast majority of the region's population—probably 80–95 percent, depending on the period and the region—resided in these villages, scattered by the hundreds over the countryside. The occasional cities and towns were not so populous in size as to amount to a total census of inhabitants close to that of the rural population. However, the power wielded by these urban centers was disproportionate to their numbers, a situation quite common in cultures both ancient and modern, deriving in the main from the city's ability to act in concert in pressing its demands and interests onto those sectors of the population too diffuse to resist effectively or to exert a comparable set of influences. Even nomadic groups, less susceptible to urban controls, could bring villagers to their knees if that was their intent. Note the text in Ezek 38:11, speaking of Gog and his army: "You will say, 'I will go up against a land of unwalled villages [פרזות, pĕrāzôt]; I will go against the undisturbed people dwelling in safety, all of them living where there are no walls or bars or gates.'"

An old adage has it that the city taxes the village and the nomads raid it. While too generalized and simplified to serve as a historical summary, this observation amply describes the vulnerability of villages—as well as their frequent antagonism toward outsiders and suspicion of them, which was often enough justified, as things happened. Defenseless and exposed, villagers could scarcely resist anything larger than a small raiding party.

The Location of Villages

Archaeologists, particularly during recent decades, have conducted extensive surveys of the countryside on both sides of the Jordan River in an effort to find evidence of ancient settlements.[4] The resulting picture indicates that villages were distributed in considerable number throughout many regions of the land, beginning early in the Iron I period and stretching down to the Greco-Roman period and later. To be sure, the settlement situation during the twelfth and eleventh centuries BCE has attracted the greatest attention due to modern interest in uncovering details about Israel's beginnings.[5] Village life on the whole, however, thrived unabated throughout the millennium beginning in 1200 BCE even though individual villages disappeared and emerged with some frequency. To a great extent, these hamlets are the unseen and unsung actors in Israel's history.

The Iron Age I saw a dramatic increase in the number of villages in the highland region, from about 30 villages in 1200 BCE to more than 250 by the year 1000 BCE. Significant numbers have also been identified in other regions of the country.[6] On average, there was an increase of approximately eight

    4. See, e.g., the volumes in the series Archaeological Survey of Israel, edited by Zvi Gal and published by the Israel Antiquities Authority. Other surveys and analyses have continued the studies in detail; examples include Israel Finkelstein, Zvi Lederman, and Shlomo Bunimovitz, *Highlands of Many Cultures: The Southern Samaria Survey: The Sites,* 2 vols. (Tel Aviv: Tel Aviv University, 1997); Adam Zertal, *The Manasseh Hill Country Survey,* 2 vols., CHANE 21 (Leiden and Boston: E. J. Brill, 2004 and 2008); and Israel Finkelstein, Baruch Halpern, Gunnar Lehmann, and Herman Michael Niemann, "The Megiddo Hinterland Project," in *Megiddo IV: The 1998–2002 Seasons,* ed. Israel Finkelstein, David Ussishkin, and Baruch Halpern (Tel Aviv: Emery and Claire Yass Publications in Archaeology, 2006), 2:705–76.
    5. See the recent discussion in Avraham Faust, *Israel's Ethnogenesis: Settlement, Interaction, Expansion, and Resistance* (London, UK, and Oakville, CT: Equinox Publishing, 2006).
    6. According to recent counts, which in most cases have not yet been completed for all territories and will eventually produce even higher numbers, 240 Iron I sites have been identified in the central highlands: 122 in the territory known by the tribal name of Ephraim, 96 in Manasseh,

times more than the number of villages known from the end of the Late Bronze Age (LB). Moreover, roughly half of these villages were founded on sites where there had been no previous settlement. This relatively short period of only two centuries was thus witness to a major demographic shift that became decisive for the remainder of Israel's social history. The origin of this increased population, however, is anything but clear—whether escapees from Egypt (as the biblical story presents it, although it cannot be verified independently from external sources or the archaeological record), or an immigration of diverse peoples from the surrounding region (which is plausible since the Canaanite highlands at the time were relatively open for new settlers), or an increase in the indigenous population (perhaps plausible in part but not realistic alone in these numbers).

Although cities were later built in these same highland areas during Iron II, the proliferation of villages continued, although not at the same rate as had occurred in Iron I. In the traditional tribal territory of Ephraim alone, the number of villages nearly doubled in the course of Iron II, and at the same time their average size increased as well. Statistics for the distribution of village sites during Iron II and later periods are not yet as readily available as they are for Iron I, perhaps because archaeologists and historians have typically been much more intrigued by the processes of urbanization and statehood during the Iron II period.

The demographic character of Judah takes a decided shift as one moves from the start of the Neo-Babylonian period into the time of the Persian Empire. From the end of the seventh century to the middle of the fifth century BCE, the overall size of the settled area declined by 72 percent, a drastic decline by any standards. Only a small area southwest of Jerusalem escaped this near depopulation, and the area of Benjamin, north of Jerusalem, suffered only a 56 percent reduction. In general, the number and size of the

---

and 22 in Benjamin and Judah. This total number in the central hill country during Iron I rose to 254 in a report by the end of 1992; see Israel Finkelstein, "The Emergence of Israel: A Phase in the Cyclic History of Canaan in the Third and Second Millennia BCE," in *From Nomadism to Monarchy: Archaeological and Historical Aspects of Early Israel*, ed. Israel Finkelstein and Nadav Na'aman (Jerusalem: Israel Exploration Society; Washington: Biblical Archaeology Society, 1994), 153–71. In addition, evidence of at least another 68 villages from this period has emerged in Galilee, upward of 60 in the Jordan Valley, and some 73 in Transjordan (I. Finkelstein, "Emergence," 162, sets the number in Transjordan during Iron I at 218, as of 1992). These data are based on surveys published in the Archaeological Survey of Israel series and elsewhere, e.g., Israel Finkelstein, *Archaeology of the Israelite Settlement* (Jerusalem: Israel Exploration Society, 1988); Stager, "Archaeology of the Family"; and James A. Sauer, "Transjordan in the Bronze and Iron Ages: A Critique of Glueck's Synthesis," *BASOR* 263 (1986): 1–26. For historical, political, and social assessments in light of these findings, see Gösta Ahlström, *The History of Ancient Palestine* (Minneapolis: Fortress; Sheffield: Sheffield Academic Press, 1993); and Levy, *Archaeology of Society*.

larger settlements—the cities and towns—decreased dramatically while villages proliferated.[7] For our purposes, village life thus became not less but more important in the Persian period.

In general, we can conclude that living in villages was the survival strategy most practiced by Israelites throughout the people's entire history. War wreaked the greatest havoc on larger cities, while villages—though vastly less defensible—were as a group more likely to survive the invasion of foreign troops, such as occurred during the eighth and sixth centuries BCE. Passing armies could easily commandeer agricultural resources and compel villagers to join them as slaves or soldiers, and since a village can scarcely offer resistance, there was little reason to attack and destroy it rather than to exploit it. In this respect the formidably walled cities proved more prone to destruction than did the villages.

Settlements were normally not scattered indiscriminately over the landscape. Rather, several key factors affected the location of villages: permanent and reliable water supply, preferably within a distance of one kilometer but often farther away;[8] habitable terrain; proximity to the means for subsistence, mainly pasturage or arable land; availability of materials suitable for building houses, making pottery, and meeting other common needs for implements and the like; and relative safety, probably less from military forces than from marauding raiders. One or more of these factors might be sacrificed if others proved more inviting. Quite clearly, the means for subsistence ranked as being of chief importance, and it should come as no surprise that villages situated themselves most frequently next to arable land. Yet one finds settlements in all types of terrain, from the desert fringes to very rocky regions. In periods when a centralized state and economy could dictate it, a village might be compelled to specialize in the production of one or the other commodity, depending especially on what was conducive to its environmental context. Villages were much less likely than were cities to be situated near the well-traveled roads; one can speculate

7. Oded Lipschits, "Demographic Changes in Judah between the Seventh and the Fifth Centuries B.C.E.," in *Judah and the Judeans in the Neo-Babylonian Period*, ed. Oded Lipschits and Joseph Blenkinsopp (Winona Lake, IN: Eisenbrauns, 2003), 323–76, esp. 355–66. See other articles in the same volume for further discussion and other perspectives; and more recently, see Lipschits, *The Fall and Rise of Jerusalem: Judah under Babylonian Rule* (Winona Lake, IN: Eisenbrauns, 2005), passim, esp. 258–71; and Lipschits and Manfred Oeming, eds., *Judah and the Judeans in the Persian Period* (Winona Lake, IN: Eisenbrauns, 2006), esp. 19–52. Cf. also Kenneth Hoglund, "The Achaemenid Context," in *Second Temple Studies*, vol. 1, *The Persian Period*, ed. Philip R. Davies, JSOTSup 117 (Sheffield: Sheffield Academic Press, 1991), 54–72.

8. I. Finkelstein, *Archaeology*, 194–98. A number of village sites in the Ephraim area, for example, were 2 km (1.25 mi.) or more removed from water sources, especially in the highland areas with substantial rock formations. Cisterns as well as storage jars provided the inhabitants with the necessary means for procuring and maintaining a water supply.

that the reason lies in the need either for safety or for food production. Villagers sought a place where they could subsist and survive, as a rule by their own hand. Notable exceptions were the villages deliberately situated near larger cities in order to supply these urban centers with needed agricultural and pastoral produce. Known as the בנות (bānôt, "daughters")[9] of the cities, these outlying satellites represent either an accommodation of the typical village to the market potential provided by population centers, or a coercive move by the urban powerful to satisfy the needs of those in the city.[10]

Especially because of kinship ties among their residents, villages presumably associated most compatibly with nearby villages like themselves. Density figures alone are rather revealing.[11] By the latter part of Iron I, the average for all types of topography throughout the entire central highlands of Israel was at least 1 village per 18 square kilometers (7 sq. mi.); as more villages are discovered, this number will fall even further. During Iron II the density almost doubled, but then receded somewhat throughout later periods before rising to its greatest level in the Roman and Byzantine periods.[12] Considering only the Iron I ratio of 1 village in 18 square kilometers, the distance between villages would average a mere 4 kilometers (2.5 mi). Villages tended to cluster in hospitable terrain, and roughly 2 kilometers (1.25 mi.) or less between them was not uncommon. In other words, quite typically two or more villages would be within eyesight of each other or only a short walking range apart. Such physical proximity suggests the need for some shared strategies and structures in the social, political, and economic—and thus also legal—arenas if the villages in a given area were to coexist and thrive.

Yet villages were by no means exclusively located in isolation from larger settlements. As indicated, cities usually had villages around them to help supply their needs for food and other products. Even in the absence of a city, a given region often had at least one town that was more populous than the other settlements and to which the smaller hamlets were subordinated, even if in only informal ways. Such a situation suggests a hierarchy

9. Consider the metaphorical use of English "outskirts" to refer to a city's edges.

10. Frank S. Frick (The City in Ancient Israel, SBLDS 36 [Missoula, MT: Scholars Press, 1977]) emphasizes that an antagonism did not necessarily exist between city and countryside since the inhabitants of each needed the other for survival. There was, nonetheless, a difference between them in interests and powers; see my essay "Political Rights and Powers."

11. According to I. Finkelstein's study of the territory of Ephraim (Archaeology, 190), Iron I villages in the central range occurred as frequently as one per 10 sq. km (3.9 sq. mi.), while in the western slopes the density thinned to one village for every 34 sq. km (13.25 sq. mi.).

12. Stager, "Archaeology of the Family," 4–5. On the process of ruralization during the Persian period, see Hoglund, "The Achaemenid Context."

of interests and power, which could variously constitute or enhance the cooperative strategies within a village or among contiguous villages of similar size. If life for the vast majority of Israelites transpired in the context of small villages, these villagers were normally impacted by the presence of larger settlements—if not in their immediate vicinity, then at a further distance away but nonetheless powerful and demanding.

Size and Population

The Israelite villages were generally small in size, on average only 0.3–0.6 hectares (= 0.75–1.5 acres) and very often not more than a cluster of just a few homes. A convenient system of classifying settlements, to be extended below for cities, distinguishes between two sizes for villages:[13]

- Very small sites of 0.1–0.3 hectares (0.25–0.75 acres), the mean size being 0.2 hectares (0.5 acres).
- Small sites at 0.4–1.0 hectares (1.0–2.5 acres), the mean size being 0.7 hectares (1.75 acres).

In comparison, settlements of 2–5 hectares (5–12 acres) qualify as regional towns, and larger than that would be a city (Megiddo: 10 hectares [25 acres]; Jerusalem at the time of Josiah: 60–65 hectares [150–160 acres]). On average, only about half of a village's total space was occupied by residences. Thus a settlement encompassing one acre, for example, contained roughly 20–30 houses, although individual villages could be more or less densely inhabited.

Calculating the population of settlements is fraught with difficulties, and several different methods have been proposed, each with inherent problems.[14] Best estimates indicate that a village typically comprised 75–150

13. Magen Broshi and Israel Finkelstein, "The Population of Palestine in Iron Age II," *BASOR* 287 (1992): 48. For the Iron I period in the territory of Ephraim, I. Finkelstein (*Archaeology*, 192) distinguishes among three sizes of villages: a large central village, covering at least 0.5–0.6 hectares (1.25–1.5 acres); a small village of some 0.3–0.4 hectares (0.75–1.0 acres); and a grouping of only a few houses (or tents?). For the area between Shechem and Ramallah, he indicates (in "Emergence," 162–63) that 23% of the sites during Iron I were over 0.5 hectares (1.25 acres) compared to 66% in Iron II, and 50% of the sites during Iron I were only 0.1–0.2 hectares (0.25–0.5 acres) compared to 34% in Iron II. Cf. Stager, "Archaeology," 3.

14. For a survey and critique of various methods of estimating the population of ancient Israel, see esp. Yigal Shiloh, "The Population of Iron Age Palestine in the Light of a Sample Analysis of Urban Plans, Areas, and Population Density," *BASOR* 239 (1980): 25–35. The main methods are these: reasoning from water resources or agricultural potential of the area; applying a formula based on roofed living space (usually one inhabitant per 10 sq. m [108 sq. ft.] of an enclosed dwelling) or a family coefficient (usually four persons per home); or calculating on the basis of a density coefficient per square meter of the whole settlement in question, a figure reached in light of multiple factors including the number and size of houses, the amount of public space, and the nature of the settlement. Israel Finkelstein (*Archaeology*, 331–32) considers a

people, but frequently even less than 75. Sites with only a few houses clustered together were not uncommon; during times such as the Iron I period
in the territory of Ephraim,[15] virtually half of all the known sites were very
small, embracing fewer than 50 inhabitants each. All villages taken together
yield the following totals: around 21,000 sedentary Israelites living west of
the Jordan about 1150 BCE, and around 51,000 about 1000 BCE.[16] During
Iron II the total village population increased appreciably, as did the number and size of cities. One recent estimate[17] of the total population when
the Assyrians arrived in the eighth century is around 460,000, of which
350,000 were in the North and 110,000 in the South. Of importance for our
purposes, approximately 68 percent of the population east of the Jordan in
Iron II and 71 percent in Judah lived outside the larger settlements. With
the population decline during the sixth century BCE, the total number living
in the Persian province in the fifth century was only approximately 30,000,
mostly in small settlements.[18] All of these figures underscore the prevalence
of village life throughout the country, but ironically not its dominance over
the culture. A hidden world, all too frequently undervalued if not underestimated by students of antiquity, confronts us here.

Social Realities

Summarizing the social makeup, institutions, and traditions of so many
tiny settlements disbursed over the landscape is a daunting and precarious enterprise. This very fact should caution us against assuming that the
laws in texts such as the Pentateuch faithfully reflect the legal practices of
Israelite village life. There were far too many villages, too little direct contact among them, too wide a territory, and too long a time period for us
to assume that we can with much certainty know them and their customs.
Any suggestions we make about village society must consequently be very
general in scope and tentative in nature. In chapter 3, in the context of
determining where legislative and judicial power resided within villages,
we provided an overview of key social structures within Israelite villages.
Now we need to consider their basic social realities, which serve as a

---

reasonable, conservative density coefficient to be 25 inhabitants per 1,000 m² (= 100 people
per acre). Shiloh ("Population") works with too high a number, 40–50 persons per 1,000 m² (=
160–200 people per acre). For his calculations about the Neo-Babylonian and Persian periods,
Lipschits ("Demographic Changes," 326) accepts the figure of 25 persons per dunam (= 1,000
m² = 0.25 acre).

15. Israel Finkelstein, *Archaeology*, 192–93.
16. Ibid., 330–35.
17. Broshi and I. Finkelstein, "Population," 54.
18. Lipschits, "Demographic Changes," 363.

backdrop for understanding the laws that kept order and adjudicated conflicts in the villages of the land.

Of crucial importance was the small-scale nature of village society in ancient Israel—around 75–150 inhabitants in each hamlet, often even fewer. This size, however, does not mean that the society was therefore simple, only that it was less complex than that of the urban centers, where multiple circles or layers of interactions and interests prevailed. Yet within villages there could be nuances in the relationships among people that heightened the potential for severe conflicts. In other words, we should be cautious not to romanticize the life of the ancient Israelite villagers. For them, as for most others in ancient times and still all too many in modern times, their very existence matched the well-known phrase of Thomas Hobbes: life is "poor, nasty, brutish, and short."[19]

Four social realities dominated the scene: family and kinship matters; the imperatives of subsistence and production; the threat, and usually the actual presence, of outside powers or pressures; and an ideology that fostered and legitimated their life on the land. Regarding the first, most or all of the inhabitants of a village were likely to be bound to each other as kinfolk, ties that often extended to neighboring villages as well. Dwelling as extended or compound families was commonplace, and with it the possibility for tensions and the need for strategies to minimize or handle them. Endogamous marriage with others in the clan or tribe secured property within the group and stabilized relations as well. Villages at a far remove, however, did not have the same connections with each other, even if their social structures were basically similar. An individual's identity was derived primarily from one's family, village, or region—and much less so from a national consciousness. The construct of tribe, whether based on real or putative blood ties, fits well the affinity of villages located within a territorial region. Local conflicts were handled locally—within the families, villages, clans, or if necessary, tribes. Virtually all aspects of life for villagers were probably conducted within a short distance of where they were born and normally lived all of their lives.

Second, villagers had to direct the majority of their time and energy toward production. Their subsistence economy meant just that: their life centered on a struggle to subsist and survive from one harvest to the next. Families and clans constituted the fundamental economic machines in the countryside. Each had to be largely self-sufficient in food production, maintenance of shelter, and manufacture of everyday tools and utensils. At

---

19. Hobbes, *Leviathan* (1651), chap. 13. Hobbes was referring mainly to the effect that a state of war could have on people, but the phrase can aptly describe also the general conditions of peasants in a subsistence economy.

certain times in history some specialization in production did occur, such as in iron making or in raising crops more conducive to the climate in one area rather than in another. The monarchy was able to establish such a command economy to maximize production across the country—for example, organizing grain cultivation in the Shephelah, viticulture and olive planting in terraced highlands, herding sheep and goats in the less arable areas, mining where the ore was found (e.g., copper in the Beersheba Valley and at Timna ͨ, in the Arabah, ca. 30 km [20 mi.] north of Eilat]). Villages could adapt to such demands, but in doing so they also became dependent on the circulation of goods they could not themselves produce. Without a centralized power to command specialization, each hamlet held more naturally to its own locale, producing all that it consumed and needed. In doing so, each community diversified in order to reduce risk, for example, by combining agriculture with herding, and transhumance was practiced by others.[20] Production was labor intensive, requiring as much involvement as possible from both genders and all ages in a family. Children could be more useful in herding than in heavy fieldwork. The elderly might take care of the young while all others were working outside the village during the daytime. As a rule, the villagers enjoyed no surplus. Each village and clan generally shared the same fate together: in good seasons they ate equally well, and they suffered together when the crops failed or other circumstances weighed heavily on them, such as war or taxation. This experience of shared fortune accounts as well for the concern for the poor and the vulnerable as found in various laws and traditions of biblical and other literature. Villages were not communal in structure, but they tended to be communitarian in ethos.

Third, pressures external to the villages, mainly from urban, national, and imperial power centers, affected the people in substantial and often unpreventable ways. Taxation and wars, as mentioned above, are only two obvious forms the pressures could take. The command economy set in motion by the royal house was another. The exploitative practice of corvée drained the villages of labor at times in the year when the adults were most needed at home to tend their crops. Large landowners could also take advantage of villagers' hard times, trapping them in a spiral of debt and eventually foreclosing on their inherited property, which in turn compelled the people to work as tenants on what had previously been their own lands—or even set them adrift as the poor of the land. All such incursions on the life and livelihood of the villagers drained them of their

20. See the larger discussion about agriculture in D. Hopkins, *Highlands of Canaan*, passim.

scant resources, and it should not surprise us that they preferred to be left alone in their hamlets.[21] We should thus not expect to find laws in these contexts that served the interests of the power centers, except insofar as such legal norms were imposed from the outside.

Finally, the religious ideologies of villagers issued primarily from their own local culture. The national ideology, focusing on the religious practices and traditions of the central cult, could at most only be grafted onto the village culture, and at that not permanently. Being dependent on the fecundity of the ground and the livestock meant that the villagers saw their fate in the hands of deities that could bring bounty or withhold it, and these gods were at home among them, not resident only in some distant cultic site. Furthermore, the cosmic and natural order established and maintained by the gods required a counterpart within the human sphere: if humans act counter to the principle of order, they should expect things not to go well for them, while actions in harmony with the divine and natural order would bring them blessings.[22] These actions involved right cultic performances, but in large measure they also included social and legal behavior. Thus the system of laws and mores was thought to be connected intimately with the gods, who legitimated it and ensured its continuation. The same structure of divine justification of laws and the administration of justice prevailed also in the cities, the nation, and the central cult; the differences resided primarily in the interests of those whose laws were being justified. As indicated previously, we should also be cautious not to regard all villages scattered throughout the land as being ideologically homogeneous. Despite the assertions by many scholars, the people were not politically or ideologically united—especially not during the prestate period. Villagers developed their ideologies and their laws locally, at times under the influence of others but generally in an autonomous manner.

THE LAWS

In its own way, the Hebrew Bible is extremely problematic as a reliable resource for understanding customs in these small, innumerable settlements dispersed over the countryside. As indicated above in chapters 3 and 4, the biblical text stems immediately from groups and individuals that possessed or controlled a high level of literacy as well as the means, both

---

21. For a description of contemporary village attitudes, see van Nieuwenhuijze, "The Near Eastern Village," regarding the tendency of villagers, when visited by a representative of the government, to become deferential and accommodating in an effort to be quit of the functionary as soon as possible so they can return to their own way of life.
22. See above, chap. 2, Law, Morality, and Religion.

financial and institutional, necessary for carrying out the tasks of writing and preserving such extensive literature. Neither this literacy nor means was normally to be found in the villages but only in cities with their own political and economic interests or in communities, such as Qumran, dedicated to sectarian interests. In all likelihood, the Hebrew Bible therefore emerged out of primarily urban or sectarian settings. Before the final compositional stage, traditions—stories, proverbs, songs, laws, and the like—circulated in a variety of settings, including the rural districts, above all in the oral mode. To the extent that any such materials reached written form, in the process they most certainly underwent significant modification, if not even full transformation. Thus the Hebrew Bible does not contain the direct expressions of village life, but at most only the city dwellers' own viewpoints as well as their perceptions of village life.

This situation pertains especially for the laws. The Covenant Code (CC, or Book of the Covenant) serves as a good example. The laws recorded in Exod 21–23 are commonly held to represent the legal traditions of Israel before the monarchy. Since Israelite urbanization began in full force only during Iron Age II, in the time of the centralized state, a premonarchic origin would place these laws squarely in the social period when villages served as virtually the only context of human settlement in the land, apart from the Canaanite and Philistine city-states in the coastal region and certain inland areas. Many of these laws in the CC are preoccupied with agricultural matters and give sparse evidence of centralized powers; hence, many scholars see all this as reinforcing the notion of its rural provenance or roots. Even if one supposes that the CC was recorded after the advent of statehood and by persons living in the city of Jerusalem, it is assumed—sometimes tacitly but often explicitly—that the laws it contains derive from communities located outside the cities.

Frankly, in my view the Deuteronomic laws are much more plausibly connected to cities than the CC laws are to villages and towns—certainly in their present form as a law collection, but probably also as individual laws. How might the CC laws have been collected? The countryside contained many hundreds of tiny settlements. If we are to think of the CC laws as the laws of rural society, then we ought to present a plausible means whereby they became assembled. Yet it is hard to imagine that someone roamed over the land, asking villagers to recount their laws and recording them for the benefit of either the villagers themselves or others.[23]

---

23. See the above discussion on this point (chap. 4, Alternative Scenarios) in light of the work of the Gebrüder Grimm.

One detail is certain: the CC *in its present form* does not coincide with village law. As argued in chapter 1 above, one confronts the text now as literature, the product of urbanites. Even if it reflects laws that are thought to be the result of legal traditions brought by rural persons who relocated into cities, there are still questions of how, by whom, and for what purposes the legal norms of various villages became recorded in their new social contexts. To press further on the question of the relation between village law and biblical law, we thus approach a double-blind situation: on the one hand, the paucity of information about village life in Israel; and on the other, the activity of city-dwelling elites and literate specialists in producing the text that worked its way down to present times.

Identifying Ancient Village Laws

To determine the legal traditions operative within the villages of ancient Israel requires attention to the specific characteristics of their society—to the extent that we can recover or reconstruct them. Three types of sources are available, each presenting its own special difficulties: (1) the texts of the Hebrew Bible, which must be critically interpreted because they stem immediately not from the villages themselves but from people in the cities who purport to be writing in part about nonurban life; (2) the material culture, the mute and circumstantial evidence uncovered by archaeologists and studied by historians interested in the lifestyles and events of antiquity; and (3) comparative information from other ancient as well as more-recent cultures, stemming from anthropologists or historians but not necessarily representative of circumstances prevalent in ancient Israel.

Twelve criteria strike me as fitting in the effort to reconstruct village laws. These criteria should be at work both in the interpretation of textual records, including the biblical laws, and also in the constructive effort of understanding the legal issues and social structures of the village communities:[24]

1. Village laws reflect and promote the social customs and traditions of the community. Representing what is often called customary laws, they are developed and transmitted in oral form.
2. Village laws recognize the social and political hierarchy basic to village life and kinship groups, especially the patriarchal structure and local leadership.

24. See the appendix for a comparison with the criteria used in identifying urban/national laws and cultic laws.

3. Village laws seek to ensure cooperation and eliminate discord among members of the community. They attempt, as needed, to resolve conflicts, to remedy losses and injuries, and to clarify liability.
4. Village laws are especially concerned with matters affecting the family, kinship groups, marriage, and sexuality.
5. Village laws do not contemplate the more-complex, layered society found in cities or at the national level.
6. Village laws tend to be oriented toward life on the land, toward agricultural or pastoral existence.
7. Village laws are more likely than urban or national laws to be responsive to conditions of vulnerability among the lower classes, as in the case of persons who suffer from hardships, death of a provider, or natural catastrophe.
8. Village laws foster the interests of the given village and, usually, those of nearby or similar villages as well, especially those with which there may be kinship ties.
9. Village laws rarely involve any formal institutions larger than kinship ties, at most only an ad hoc deliberative gathering of village or regional elders.
10. Village laws do not support the diversion of the community's produce or resources to cities or other parts of the country, except insofar as a direct benefit (e.g., trade or security) can come to the villagers as a result.
11. Village laws are sensitive to the priorities and perils inherent to a subsistence economy.
12. Village laws tend to exclude or give limited protection to outsiders.

Not all of these criteria will be evident in each law. However, it is difficult to imagine any given law originating in a village that runs directly counter to these criteria. Again, for all the diversity presumably prevailing among the villages spread across the land of ancient Israel, the kinds of circumstances or orientations reflected in these criteria seem to be fundamental, especially since they allow each separate community substantial latitude to develop its own customs. Villages with laws deviating significantly from these norms were most likely located close to cities and were thus under their influence, or were in existence during those monarchic or imperial times when overlords, large landowners, tax collectors, military and labor conscriptors, and others representing outside interests interfered in village affairs to a greater

extent than the villagers probably desired. We cannot expect absolute economic and political equality within a given village, but we can expect much
less of a disparity than prevailed between large and small settlements.

Admittedly, a considerable amount of speculation has contributed to
this list of criteria, and others might construct a list quite different from
this—or refrain altogether from even trying. In my view, however, the
enterprise is warranted for four fundamental reasons: (1) Many hundreds
of villages existed throughout the country and throughout Israel's history
and contained the vast majority of the population, which should be reason
enough for the historian to pay them attention. (2) Even despite the variety
among them, they must have shared much in terms of their social structure and social values because of similarities in their cultural backgrounds,
their means of livelihood, their coping with outside pressures, and their
response to the natural environment. (3) Enough information has now
become available, especially from archaeology and anthropology, to give
us a reasonable sense of issues and priorities in small-scale communities
of this type. And (4) customary laws develop quite naturally in such social
groups in order to maintain order, resolve conflicts, and maximize the
chances for survival of the group and its individual members. It is therefore
legitimate to inquire into the nature of village laws, despite the absence of
documents recording them explicitly.

We thus embark on a process of recovery and reconstruction, drawing
on the sources as described but venturing further as needed. Even the identification of legal issues and potential conflicts, without full knowledge of
the substantive laws that regulated them, can represent an advance in our
understanding of Israelite legal systems. The above criteria do not immediately spell out the content of the laws, but rather indicate their tendencies
and their aversions. They point not so much to moral values as to actionable offenses. Our goal is not to formulate the wording of laws, which
is impracticable at our distance and with insufficient data, but to identify
some of the legal conflicts plausible in Israel's village societies and to imagine the kinds of resolutions needed for the societies to endure.

Substantive Law in Israelite Villages

What laws regulated behavior and settled disputes in the villages of ancient
Israel? At this point we will focus on the substantive laws, with some reference to procedural laws as well. The difference between substantive and
procedural laws is basic to legal thought, even though the two categories
overlap and intersect in essential respects. Substantive laws designate rights,
duties, obligations, and criminal offenses, often with penalties or remedies

specified for their violation. Procedural laws, on the other hand, detail the means according to which the substantive laws are to be enforced, a breach of them is to be prosecuted, or redress is to be obtained. In the following sections we organize the substantive laws according to general legal issues and areas of conflict, schematized under the basic spheres first of social life and second of economic life. Religious laws will be treated separately in chapter 7, where the circumstances of villages, cities, state, and empire can be compared.

Social Life

Kinship. Family and kinship constituted the fundamental structures of social relationships in Israel's villages, and maintaining their stability and order rivaled the importance of securing the community's economic means of subsistence. No written legal text from Israel or other ancient Southwest Asian cultures provides a full picture of kinship organization, which was surely complex in light of the many possible permutations as kinfolk interacted. Nonetheless, numerous specific aspects do emerge.

Marriage. Issues of marriage and sexuality functioned as defining social indicators in villages, and controls arose to keep the lines clearly drawn. Marriage was typically *endogamous*, within a given clan or tribal entity: among village communities located in a distinct territory and self-identified as descended from a common ancestor. Marrying outside one's own clan or tribe meant that ownership of inherited property could be at risk of devolving to an outside group. The story of Abraham's search for a wife for his son among "my own kindred" (מולדתי, *môladtî*, Gen 24:4), rather than among the people indigenous to the land of Canaan, indicates the custom at a broader ethnic/national level, even if it was by no means always practiced according to biblical traditions (e.g., Judah and the Canaanite woman, Gen 38:2; Moses and Zipporah, a Midianite, Exod 2:21; Solomon and his foreign wives, 1 Kgs 11:1–10; and the intermarriage problematized in Ezra 9–10). The need to keep marriages—and thus inherited land—within a specific tribe is articulated in the accounts involving the daughters of Zelophehad (Num 36:1–12; also 26:33; 27:1–11). Considering endogamy as little more than a "custom" diminishes its legal force within village cultures, where marriage and property ownership were of such vital significance for the continuance of society as to warrant the strictest of safeguards.

The same can be said of *levirate marriage*, the practice of marrying a widow to her late husband's brother in order to produce an offspring in the name of the deceased and to keep the property within the family or clan; the story of Judah and Tamar (Gen 38) serves as a classic account of the practice and its violation. The text in Deut 25:5–10 detailing it in legal fashion has the flavor of urban and national society, to the point even of warning that all of Israel will be aware of the stigma attached to anyone who refuses this levirate responsibility. *Polygyny* was legally permitted, though in all likelihood rarely practiced among the peasants; the multitude of wives attributed to the kings critiques the monarchy and its oppressive demands on the people (Deut 17:17). Similarly *concubinage* existed as an acceptable option, yet it is doubtful that it would have been much found among villagers if for no other than economic reasons. Virtually all of the cases cited in the Hebrew Bible involve men of some standing or wealth: Abraham, his brother Nahor, Jacob, Caleb, Gideon, Saul, David, Solomon, and Rehoboam, among others.

On the whole, it is safe to assume that a *patriarchal* system prevailed in village society as it did in urban contexts, but probably without the same stringency since all parties in a subsistence economy needed to contribute as much as possible to their mutual continuation. Marriages in Israelite villages were as a rule *patrilocal*, even though the significance of this arrangement was somewhat lessened in such contexts where the wife's parental home was typically in close proximity—in a neighboring village if not even in the same village. Several biblical texts allude to the practice, or to variances as in cases where a wife could return to her home of origin because of her husband's death (Ruth, who famously opts not to do so) or for some other reason (e.g., Moses' wife Zipporah, Exod 18:2–6; Samson's wife, Judg 14:19–15:2).

The custom of a *bride-price* was probably widespread, though we know little about it other than a few references (the gifts on behalf of Rebekah, Gen 24:53; Jacob's work for Laban, a prepayment so he can marry Leah and Rachel, Gen 29; the text in Exod 22:16–17 [22:15–16 MT]; see also LH 159–161 and MAL A 30 for examples from elsewhere in Southwest Asia). For peasants in a subsistence economy, this bride-price can only have been quite meager, especially in comparison with what was possible among the upper class. *Divorce* must have occurred quite seldom in the villages. Families and clans living in such close contact with each other had the chance to support married couples and intercede when problems arose. Positively, the centrality of families for the maintenance of society in village contexts made it necessary and possible for marital relationships to be affirmed and reinforced.

The Covenant Code—conventionally associated with life in the countryside, especially during the premonarchic period,[25]—contains only the

---

25. See above, chap. 1, Covenant Code.

slightest references to marriage. One case focuses on marriage involving slaves (Exod 21:2–11), a social phenomenon reflecting a wealthier economy than villages typically managed. A slight hint of the vulnerability in such a marriage is expressed by this law, suggesting perhaps the viewpoint of the underclass: the slave owner benefits whether or not the male slave chooses to remain with his enslaved family. The only other marriage law in the CC (Exod 22:16–17 [22:15–16 MT]) deals with the seduction of an unengaged virgin daughter.[26] For all the importance that marriage and family must have had in village society, the paucity of CC laws controlling their diverse aspects is a curiosity. Did the drafters of the CC not understand the nuances of kinship laws within the villages? Or was there too much variety from place to place to allow for a reasonable representation in this literature?

Reproduction. Fertility of the family, just as fertility of the land, constituted an imperative for survival.[27] The fertility cult, castigated and fought by a mono-latrous Yahwistic priesthood, represented precisely the kind of religion that appealed to those immediately dependent on the productiveness of the land. We will discuss the importance of the domestic and local cults[28] below, in chapter 7, and it may suffice now simply to allude to the considerable archae-ological evidence of fertility figurines from Iron Age Israel. Narrative and prophetic texts of the Hebrew Bible confirm the prevalence of worshiping other gods; not only Asherah (e.g., Judg 6:25–28 MT) and Astarte/Ashtoreth/Ashtaroth (e.g., Judg 2:13) but also the Queen of Heaven (Jer 7:18; 44:15–19, 25) are all related to fertility cults. The Israelites, especially those living in vil-lages across the landscape, counted on these deities to ensure fecundity. The text of Gen 1:28 directing the people to "be fruitful and multiply" amounted to an ideal that they could not fulfill simply by giving it their best effort, for too many other factors militated against successful reproduction.

There are no specific biblical laws regulating or proscribing either birth control or termination of a pregnancy, although both became widely dis-cussed in later Jewish and Christian traditions. Efforts at *contraception*, the intentional intervention in normal reproductive processes in order to prevent conception, are known from ancient Egypt, Greece, and Rome,

---

26. See the following section.
27. For a recent wide-ranging treatment of topics and problems related to fertility and birth in ancient Southwest Asia, see Marten Stol, *Birth in Babylonia and the Bible: Its Mediterranean Setting*, Cuneiform Monographs 14 (Groningen: Styx, 2000).
28. Also the purity laws will be treated in chap. 7, where they can be situated within the larger context of cultic practices and demands.

as Plato, Aristotle, and other texts from those periods indicate.[29] Several medical texts contain recipes to provide women with the means of birth control, even though some of the potions may have had little chance of succeeding—or at least their efficacy has not yet been established. As is the case with a variety of herbal and other alternative medical treatments,[30] certain chemical properties may be active in them that have not yet been scientifically tested. There is good reason to suppose that various contraceptive methods belonged to the traditional lore circulating among Israelite women of all classes. Preparations made from plants such as pomegranates, saffron, the seeds of Queen Anne's lace, juniper, rue, ferula, some types of myrrh, and other natural substances have been widely used in other cultures as antifertility means; knowledge about them was shared within the company of women and not necessarily recorded in writing. Various types of suppositories (wool, honey, gum, crocodile dung) were also thought to be effective contraceptive means.[31]

In Israel and elsewhere in antiquity, though, the preeminent concern probably focused on increasing rather than decreasing the birth rates. Villagers in ancient Israel faced a similar situation: they would have had little inclination to limit their chances for conception if they had not been able to give birth as they wanted, and legal strictures to block contraception are unlikely. They faced a natural inhibitor inasmuch as a woman who exclusively breast-feeds an infant has a significantly reduced chance (up to 98%) of conceiving during the first six months after birth. Illness and other life-threatening circumstances, for either the man or the woman, struck frequently enough to reduce the chances of conception further without deliberate intervention. The coitus interruptus described in Gen 38:9 is condemned and punished not because it represented a form of birth control but because Onan violated the levirate obligation to impregnate Tamar, his brother's widow, and thereby give his deceased brother a child that would be considered that brother's offspring.

Abortion also occurred seldom if at all in the villages. As with contraceptives, abortifacients such as pennyroyal and saffron were also known

29. Robert Jütte, *Lust ohne Last: Geschichte der Empfängnisverhütung von der Antike bis zur Gegenwart* (Munich: Verlag C. H. Beck, 2003), 27–35.

30. Erica Reiner describes the range of the herbalist's craft in ancient Mesopotamia in *Astral Magic in Babylonia*, Transactions of the American Philosophical Society 85/4 (Philadelphia: American Philosophical Society, 1995), 25–42.

31. See the discussion and bibliography in John M. Riddle, *Contraception and Abortion from the Ancient World to the Renaissance* (Cambridge, MA, and London, UK: Harvard University Press, 1992), 16, 19–20, 57–62; and Stol, *Birth*, 37–39. Unfortunately, we often do not know the specific species to which the words for plants refer in the ancient sources.

in antiquity, and thus perhaps in Israel as well.[32] The biblical law in Exod 21:22–25, which has parallels in several other ancient Southwest Asian legal collections,[33] speaks not of abortion but of a miscarriage caused by injury to a pregnant woman during a fight involving others, and the punishment against the one who struck her is monetary unless there is further harm to her. Notably, it is not considered a capital crime in any of these laws (except MAL A50) if only the fetus dies, but it usually is if the pregnant woman dies. For our purposes at the moment, at any rate, we can conclude that abortion scarcely existed as an issue with which village law needed to deal.

Sexual Relations, Offenses, and Illicit Sexual Behavior. The regulation of sexuality represented a primary component of the ordering of village life in ancient Israel. Its enormous importance in the Hebrew Bible shows in the ways in which sexuality and reproduction are associated with YHWH, who created the primordial couple (Gen 1–3) and ordained laws identifying illicit actions for the Israelites. In the villages legal protections developed to ensure the preferred nature of marriage, and any breach of these obligations met with censure in the form of restitution or punishment. The basic principle governing human sexuality was that licit sexual relations occur between a husband and a wife. Any variation from this structure can raise legal as well as social problems, even though it is often difficult to know whether males had more of an acceptable latitude in this regard than did females.

Adultery (נאף, *nāʾap*) is generally thought to refer to sexual relations only between a married woman and a man who is not her spouse, or between an engaged woman and someone other than her fiancé.[34] In other words, in light of the linguistic usage of this term in biblical texts, adultery does not occur if the woman is not married or engaged, nor is the term used to describe sexual relations between two unmarried or unengaged persons, nor for sexual relations with a prostitute. It is difficult to know the extent to which such texts describe rural or urban life, but in all likelihood the expectations were very similar in both contexts, differing primarily in terms of the class distinctions presented by urban and national economic

32. See, e.g., Riddle, *Contraception and Abortion*, passim; and Stol, *Birth*, 39–48.
33. LL d–f; SLEx 1′–2′; LH 209–214; MAL 21, 50–52. Note the difference in punishment depending on whether the pregnant woman is of the upper class, a commoner, or a slave. See also Stol, *Birth*, 39–47; and Raymond Westbrook, "Lex talionis and Exodus 21,22–25," *RB* 93 (1986): 52–69.
34. For an early articulation of this principle with reference primarily to Mesopotamian laws, see Jacob J. Finkelstein, "Sex Offenses in Sumerian Laws," *JAOS* 86 (1966): 355–72.

and political systems.[35] Considering the close proximity of families and clans living in the villages, any known violation of the monogamous standard had extraordinarily disruptive consequences.[36] The provision of the death penalty for cases of adultery signals the severity of this offense, even if we find no instance in the Hebrew Bible where such an execution was carried out.[37]

Sexual relations, whether consensual or not, between two unmarried or unengaged persons of different genders would have been of concern as well, even though no biblical laws speak explicitly to it.[38] Again, the tightly knit social structure in the villages, with considerable oversight and control regarding the younger generation, made such liaisons unlikely. In the event that it occurred and was discovered, however, it most likely would have resulted in the two getting married, with a bride-price paid to the woman's parents. Execution in such a case was unlikely in light of the importance of continuing the family line and the need for workers.

It is entirely possible that there was an economic basis for laws involving marriage and adultery: that a wife and an unmarried daughter were considered to be the property of, respectively, her husband or her father, and that he experienced loss—economic loss in the sense of the productive value of either as a key member of the family, or loss of his own honor and standing in the community—if the wife were to step outside the marriage bond or if the unmarried daughter compromised her virginity. Nothing explicit in the texts supports this economic interpretation. We do find that a monetary exchange is required if a man has sexual relations with a young woman who is neither engaged nor married (Exod 22:16–17 [22:15–16 MT]; Deut 22:28–29; cf. also MAL A 56); in these cases the man's penalty takes the form of payment of essentially the bride-price to the father and marriage to the woman (though the latter is not stipulated in the Middle Assyrian law).

Among the most notable of boundary lines between licit and illicit sex

35. Other Southwest Asian cultures provide more-explicit information than do biblical texts about class distinctions, but parallel structures are likely in Israel as well. See the next chapter for details.
36. The text of Lev 20:10 includes a verbatim repetition of several words, generally deleted by textual critics on the grounds of dittography even though there are scant textual witnesses to support the deletion. However, considering the severity of adultery in that social world, it is quite possibly an intentional, rhetorical repetition to highlight the offense: "If a man commits adultery with the wife of, *if a man commits adultery with the wife of* his neighbor, the adulterer and the adulteress shall be executed."
37. Even the incident of the woman charged with adultery in John 8:3–11 did not result in her death.
38. The man in Exod 22:16–17 (22:15–16 MT) and Deut 22:28–29 may have been married, not unmarried or unengaged.

are *incest* laws, which, though not identical in terms of the forbidden relations, are found widely among societies in human history. The Hebrew Bible has its own list, but curiously it is not to be found among the laws generally associated with village and urban affairs, but rather among the religious laws of the so-called Holiness Code. Thereby, however, they are given special legitimacy: that the people are to avoid incest if they wish to be holy and remain in the land (e.g., Lev 18:28–30). The typical euphemism for incest is to "uncover the nakedness of" someone (as in PN עֶרְוַת לֹא תְגַלֵּה, *'erwat PN lō' tĕgallēh*, "Do not uncover the nakedness of PN"). In certain cases the prohibition names that person's spouse first: thus Lev 18:7 states, "You shall not uncover your father's nakedness, that is, your mother's nakedness; she is your mother—you shall not uncover her nakedness." In some cases (e.g., Lev 18:17–18, using the word תִּקַּח, *tiqqaḥ*, "you take") the incestuous relationship involves marriage, not merely a onetime or occasional sexual act. The two passages devoted to incest prohibitions (Lev 18:6–18, 20 and Lev 20:11–12, 14, 17, 19–21) describe a range of forbidden relationships, reorganized in the below table by category. Instances of duplication result from two separate texts that treat the violation differently. In each case the law is directed to the party first mentioned (i.e., the person preceding the ampersand below). We present these details here not because they all necessarily functioned as the legal norms of the villages; rather, with this overview we will be in a better position to distinguish the rural from the urban laws in ancient Israel:

Prohibition	Penalty
WITH OLDER GENERATION	
Son & mother[39]	Banishment[40]
Son & father's other wife[41]	Banishment
Son & aunt[42]	Banishment or childlessness
A man & his father's wife[43]	Execution of both
WITH SAME GENERATION	
A man & wife of his kinsman[44]	Banishment
Brother & sister[45]	Banishment

39. Lev 18:7.
40. Banishment ("vomit out," "cut off") is named in Lev 18:28-29 as punishment for all these offenses.
41. Lev 18:8.
42. This liaison is mentioned in both Lev 18:12–14 and 20:19–20, in the latter case with unspecified punishment in v. 19 and with childlessness as punishment in v. 20.
43. Lev 20:11 refers to either the son's mother or his stepmother.
44. Lev 18:20. The word עֲמִית, *'āmît*, can mean fellow citizen, not necessarily kinsman.
45. Lev 18:9; 20:17.

Brother & stepsister[46]	Banishment
Brother & half sister[47]	Banishment
Brother & brother's wife[48]	Banishment or childlessness
WITH YOUNGER GENERATION	
Grandfather & granddaughter[49]	Banishment
Father & daughter-in-law[50]	Banishment or execution of both[51]
WITH MULTIPLE RELATED PARTIES	
A man & a woman plus her daughter[52]	Banishment
A man & a woman plus her granddaughter[53]	Banishment
A man & two sisters[54]	Banishment
A man & a woman plus her mother[55]	Execution of all by burning

Several observations are noteworthy. Although these laws in Leviticus bear signs of editorial organization and are given a decidedly religious cast, on the whole they represent the kinds of customary laws plausible in the villages as well as in the cities of ancient Israel. As indicated earlier in this chapter, relatives typically lived in close proximity to each other, often as an extended family in the same house or as two or more related families in a compound. They thus had frequent and easy access to each other. Furthermore, the age difference between generations could be only a few years. For example, if a woman married around age 13 or 14 and had a child by 15, that child reached puberty not long after its parents' younger siblings; hence the easy possibility of a sexual encounter between a nephew and aunt, or a niece and uncle.

Finally, the biblical incest laws are by far the most detailed of all the laws so far discovered in ancient Southwest Asia. The only other list is from the eighteenth-century Code of Hammurabi, which specifies five forbidden liaisons (§§154–158):

46. Lev 18:9; 20:17.
47. Lev 18:9 seems to refer first to a sister and then to a stepsister or half sister, and 18:11 to a half sister—a sexual liaison with both being proscribed. There is another reference to the stepsister or half sister in 20:17.
48. Both Lev 18:16 and 20:21 refer to this relationship, in the latter case with the statement that they shall both remain childless.
49. Lev 18:10.
50. Lev 18:15.
51. Lev 20:12.
52. Lev 18:17.
53. Ibid.
54. Lev 18:18.
55. Lev 20:14.

Prohibition	Penalty
WITH YOUNGER GENERATION	
Father & daughter	Banishment
Father & daughter-in-law after son has had sex with her	Execution of father by drowning
Father & daughter-in-law before son has had sex with her	Monetary restitution to her
WITH OLDER GENERATION	
Son & his mother after the father's death	Execution of both by burning
Son & his father's principal wife after the father's death	Disinheritance of son

Perhaps the most distinctive difference is that a sexual relationship between father and daughter is strictly prohibited in Hammurabi—and is actually listed first among the five laws—while it is not even mentioned in the biblical texts. Was it in any way condoned in ancient Israel, or could it rather have been so obviously odious as not even to merit mention? The latter seems more likely for the Israelites, certainly for those in a tightly knit village context, but its absence in the texts is indeed perplexing. Another noticeable omission in the biblical laws is any prohibition against first cousins marrying. Since it is described without comment in the case of Isaac and Rebecca and then again for Jacob's marriage with Leah and Rachel, we might conclude that it was commonplace or at least not unusual in ancient Israel, particularly since it ensured that inherited property would remain within the clan. Since first-cousin marriage did not qualify as incest, the other customary laws regarding engagement and marriage applied to cousins as to others.

Homosexual acts are considered illicit according to Lev 18:22 and 20:13. No mention is made of lesbian relations, only of same-gender intercourse involving males. Whether legal proscriptions against homosexuality existed in village contexts is impossible to know. Opportunities for such relationships must have been plentiful, and one can imagine that the strictures involving heterosexual relations made alternative options likely. The ancient texts give us no indication of the modern concept of "sexual orientation." It seems probable, at any rate, that the two laws in Leviticus express later religious perspectives and motivations that were not shared broadly among villagers, for whom homosexuality may have been tolerated as long as it did not interfere with family relationships.

A similar point can be made about *bestiality*, which is unequivocally prohibited in Exod 22:19 [22:18 MT] and Lev 18:23; 20:15–16. The Leviticus laws explicitly address both men and women, while the Exodus regulation uses only the masculine pronoun. Following our principle that the existence of a legal prohibition means that what was prohibited was in fact being practiced or it would not have needed to be proscribed, then bestiality laws suggest that engaging in sexual acts with animals must have occurred, especially in rural contexts. Availability was no problem since many families herded sheep or goats. Villages may not have bothered to proscribe bestiality if it was not uncommon behavior since penalizing numerous offenders would have affected the livelihood of the whole village.

Despite the modern caricature of *prostitution* as "the world's oldest profession," it is hardly conceivable that it could have been economically viable within a village with such limited population and traditional family structures. Virtually all of the references to prostitution in the texts of the Hebrew Bible and other Southwest Asian cultures presume an urban culture and will be treated in the next chapter. Nonetheless, to the extent that they had the financial means for it, villagers could have visited prostitutes wherever they were, as did others in the general populace. While certain religionists in Israel may have argued against prostitution, we possess no evidence that it was illegal in either villages or cities. The same applies to cultic prostitution, which aimed to ensure fertility of land and family, although it was probably practiced only at central shrines where the priestly staff and the temple income were sufficient to accommodate it.

Children and the Elderly. Although numerous social customs must have affected both minor children and the elderly, few of them would have risen to the level of actionable offenses. Both demographic groups held extremely high value in the village community. *Children* represented the future of the group and the prolongation of the family line. The ancestral legends of Genesis depict graphically how urgent it was for the wives to give birth: the "barrenness"[56] of Sarah, Rachel, and Leah drives large parts of the narratives, as do the life threats to the sons Isaac, Jacob, and Joseph. With infant and child mortality rates at 50–60 percent,[57] every

56. The biblical texts associate infertility only with women; no notion that the problem may have stemmed from their husbands can be observed.

57. Several studies of premodern, preindustrial societies have posited mortality rates in this general range. For discussion and further bibliography, see, e.g., Arnold A. Lelis, William A. Percy, and Beert C. Verstraete, *The Age of Marriage in Ancient Rome*, Studies in Classics 26 (Lewiston, NY; Queenston, ON; and Lampeter, UK: Edwin Mellen Press, 2003), 2–3; and William Petersen, "A Demographer's View of Prehistoric Demography," *Current Anthropology* 16, no. 2 (1975): 227–45. Note, for example, the following summary of the findings in a burial cave at Meiron: "Skeletal remains of all age groups and both sexes were found, both in the *Kokhim* and central chamber. . . . In all, the remains of 197 individuals were identified, of

surviving child must have been highly prized. In addition, they served essential roles in the family's economy, laboring as early as possible as herders, fieldworkers, and performers of sundry chores and later providing for the well-being of their elderly parents. For these reasons infanticide is unlikely, and we have no biblical texts mentioning it in terms of exposure of newborn babies. Several texts forbid it as a form of sacrifice (e.g., Deut 18:10; 12:31), although it is difficult to know if such allusions were more a part of religious rhetoric or if they referred to actual practices among the Israelites. Disciplining the children could be expected and was presumably condoned.[58] We have no evidence of physical abuse by villagers of their children; if it ever occurred, intervention by the community may have ensued, either informally or formally by the parents or a group of household heads.

The *elderly* were due respect for their cumulative contributions to the community, for their knowledge in the areas of production and domestic life, and for their ongoing status as heads of the household.[59] We know of no cases of abandonment of one's parents, and a village would probably have taken action against anyone who did so. The Decalogue's injunction "Honor your father and your mother" (Exod 20:12) probably focuses primarily on the adult children's respect and care for their elderly parents, the only means of support on which the older generation could count. Such expectations derive as much as anything from their role of most elderly in their extended families, which continued until the authority needed to be handed to a son due to the advanced age and probably infirmity of the father. "Advanced" age, we must remember, was far short of what we expect today. Given the problems of malnutrition, food shortage, disease, hard labor, war, death in childbirth, and more, life expectancy scarcely reached 40 years and was often closer to 30.[60] The elderly probably needed

whom 95, nearly 50%, had died before reaching the age of 18. Within this age range, the highest mortality occurred within the first five years of life (70% of all childhood and adolescent deaths). The figures are high, but probably represent normal morbidity statistics in this period" (i.e., from the 1st c. BCE to the 4th c. CE); Eric M. Meyers, James F. Strange, and Carol L. Meyers, *Excavations at Ancient Meiron, Upper Galilee, Israel, 1971–72, 1974–75, 1977* (Cambridge, MA: American Schools of Oriental Research, 1981), 110.

58. Note the wisdom saying in Prov 13:24: "Those who withhold the rod are being hateful to their children, but those who love them are sure to discipline them." Other texts in Proverbs reinforce a strict form of upbringing, though primarily, it would seem, in order to produce a type of obedience consistent with the religious allegiance advocated for the children being taught by the sages.

59. Lev 19:32a: "You shall rise before the aged, and show honor to the old."

60. Lelis, Percy, and Verstraete (*Age of Marriage*, 3) in fact set life expectancy between 20 and 30 for ancient Rome. For methods used in determining age at death for people in the premodern period, see Santiago Genovés, "Estimation of Age and Mortality," in *Science in Archaeology: A Survey of Progress and Research*, ed. Don Brothwell and Eric Higgs, rev. ed.

the support of their families because of poor health, not so much because of their age.

Personal Injury and Death. Inevitably personal injuries, whether accidental or intentional, will occur in societies, and the villagers of ancient Israel needed to develop means for dealing with the problem, as do other groups. Biblical laws cite only a few instances, most of them plausible in a rural context. Fighting between two individuals could well result in either or both parties being injured. If the injured person died, the relatives presumably had grounds for seeking revenge in the form of killing the one who caused the death. Whether there were any circumstances that could have mitigated the family's reaction to the death—for example, who initiated the fight, what reasons occasioned it, or how the brawl proceeded—is unknown, but some form of response was certainly expected of the relatives, though not by the state. A fight that ended with injury but not death would be judged according to the severity of the damage. Exodus 21:18–19 indicates that the penalty for striking another person severely enough to send the injured to bed will be lessened if the wounded person recovers enough to move around with the aid of a staff; restitution for lost time and recovery costs are, though, still due to the injured. From this text one receives the impression that an injury to either party was handled in this manner, regardless of any other considerations. Other causes of injuries certainly existed in the life of villagers, such as negligence or accident, but fighting between two men receives explicit attention in biblical laws.

Cases of *homicide* show sensitivity to degrees of culpability. Normally the killing of another was a capital offense, to be followed legitimately by an act of blood vengeance executed by a close relative of the victim.[61] The lengthy discussion in Num 35:16–34 stems from an urban or cultic context, yet it probably reflects widely shared notions that anyone wielding an iron piece or stone or lethal weapon against another should be held accountable for the resulting death, unless the community decides that the stone incident happened by accident. Thus only if the killing occurred by misadventure (*per infortunium*) was some latitude warranted. Exodus 21:13 attributes such an accident to God, according to the notion that the divine world must have caused the death if no human was responsible. Another

---

(New York and Washington, DC: Praeger, 1969), 440–52; and Petersen, "A Demographer's View of Prehistoric Demography."

   61. While some scholars describe blood vengeance as a form of "private" justice, it is actually not private insofar as the community has legitimated it as an appropriate remedy for the crime of homicide.

hypothetical situation is described in Deut 19:4–6, an incident in which two men are chopping wood in the forest and the axhead of one slips off the handle and strikes the other man, killing him. Such cases show the need for cities of refuge (Num 35:9–15; Deut 19:1–13; Josh 20) to be established as safe havens for these killers, who could otherwise be the victims of blood vengeance even though their act was accidental and not premeditated. Another innocent form of homicide is self-defense, an example of which is one's house being broken into at night; yet if the thief is killed while (*flagrante delicto*) burglarizing during the daytime, it is a capital offense (Exod 22:2–3 [22:1–2 MT]).

All such examples reveal the importance of culpability in Israelite law, yet also the effort to make allowance for homicide that is not willfully and intentionally committed. The legendary story of the murder of Abel by his brother Cain (Gen 4) demonstrates the complexity of personal injury and homicide cases in local rural communities. While a family is expected to carry out blood vengeance against the murderer of one of their own, a family on the other hand is also required to defend their own members against external forces. It is not possible, however, for the parents both to protect their son Cain and to kill the murderer Cain, so Cain is instead sent away, banned from continuing to live among his clan.[62] Throughout these instances runs the consistent notion that homicide is treated as a tort, not a crime. Restitution or vengeance are the normal remedies, not state-initiated trial and incarceration or execution.

At a minimum, the community as a whole has a certain accountability for justice in the case of a capital offense, which could scarcely be more effectively presented than it is in the extended text of Deut 21:1–9. Here we read of a hypothetical case in which the corpse of a person who met with a violent death is discovered in the open country and the assailant is not known. In such an instance, the elders are to pace off the distance from the corpse to the nearest towns to determine which is closest, and that town must then perform a sacrifice of forgiveness "in order to eradicate the guilt of innocent blood from your midst" (Deut 21:9). The text in its present form reflects more of an urban than a village social structure, but it is probably based on a practice known to villagers and tribal elders. If a murderer cannot be found and punished, the people on the whole will suffer from a festering evil unless it is ritually purged.

62. Isaac Schapera, "The Sin of Cain," *Journal of the Royal Anthropological Institute* 85 (1955): 33–43; reprinted in *Anthropological Approaches to the Old Testament*, ed. Bernhard Lang, IRT 8 (Philadelphia: Fortress Press; London: SPCK, 1985), 26–42.

Economic Life

The domain of economics contains substantial issues that warrant legal controls and adjudication. While economic relations at the national and international levels may seem to be of greatest importance and to possess the most intense complexity, we must not underestimate the intricacy of circumstances at the local level as well. Villagers in a context such as ancient Israel would generally have known all other members of their own village, which (as we have seen) typically had only 75–150 inhabitants. Similarly, they would have been familiar with many living in nearby villages, often only 2–4 kilometers (1.25–2.5 mi.) away. Not only did parties know each other; they also counted many of them among their kinfolk. In such a situation disputes over property and commercial transactions were urgent and sensitive, needing rapid resolution in order to minimize acrimony and contention and to keep affairs running smoothly within the community.

Real Property. The system of land tenure common among ancient Israelite villages blended individual and kinship ownership rights.[63] The close connection among families, as we have described, does not mean that all the land around the village was communally owned by the families clustered there. Various efforts and proposals have tried to clarify ancient social and economic systems. In theorizing about the evolution of such systems, Karl Marx proposed the notion of an "Asiatic mode of production," which he regarded as a special form distinctive to certain Asian empires and thus different from his usual developmental scheme. This notion has been much discussed and revised in subsequent research, especially as a result of ethnographic work. According to Norman Gottwald,[64] the premonarchic period saw a form of, if not an egalitarian system, then at least a communitarian society with an agrarian base; with the onset of the monarchy, a tributary structure emerged

---

63. The problem of land ownership in ancient Israel has attracted considerable interest. From among the many available publications, see esp. Raymond Westbrook, *Property and the Family in Biblical Law*, JSOTSup 113 (Sheffield: Sheffield Academic Press, 1991); and Jeffrey A. Fager, *Land Tenure and the Biblical Jubilee: Uncovering Hebrew Ethics through the Sociology of Knowledge*, JSOTSup 155 (Sheffield: Sheffield Academic Press, 1993).

64. Gottwald was among the first to consider this model for ancient Israel. See his "Early Israel and 'the Asiatic Mode of Production' in Canaan," *SBLSP* 10 (1976): 145–54; idem, *Tribes of Yahweh*, passim; and David Jobling, "Feminism and 'Mode of Production' in Ancient Israel: Search for a Method," in *The Bible and the Politics of Exegesis: Essays in Honor of Norman K. Gottwald on His Sixty-fifth Birthday*, ed. David Jobling, Peggy L. Day, and Gerald T. Sheppard (Cleveland: Pilgrim Press, 1991), 239–51.

as those living in the countryside were obliged to send taxes (in-kind goods), rents, and labor to the state and the elite class, and eventually to far-removed imperial centers.

Whatever may be made of these and other theoretical models, it is clear that legal title to arable land could rest with private persons. Obviously, without a modern title office to preserve detailed survey records of property, issues of boundaries as well as ownership could arise. Villagers encountered several different categories of real property:

1. Locally owned plots of arable land. Such parcels were handed down as inheritance for perhaps many generations, and the effective owners were thus families rather than isolated individuals. Houses and residential spaces in villages were also part of the property conveyed from parents to children.

2. Community property, available for common use. Included here were local threshing floors, storage areas and cisterns constructed by the community, water sources, open areas where small children were tended, paths, dumps, and the like. Probably some of the open grazing areas for sheep and goats were also understood to be available for common use.

3. Land accumulated by large landowners, mainly as a result of foreclosures on the debts of the private individuals described in category 1 (above). While not much of this migration of land resources into the hands of a few occurred during the early settlement period of Iron I (1200–1000 or –900 BCE), it increased shortly before the advent of the monarchy and then continued throughout the monarchic and colonial periods. The loss of patrimony and the increase in latifundia (large landed estates) were thus realities for many if not most villagers in Israel's history.

4. Crown land. Hand in hand with the transfer of land to the elites, the holdings of the monarch were as extensive as the power the king exercised. While a despotic king or emperor managed to acquire land at will, even less overbearing rulers held property to supply their needs and benefit the royal coffers. The story of Ahab's expropriation of Naboth's land (1 Kgs 21:1–16) makes the point effectively that private land is not safe from state interests. In this case, though, Naboth was likely a large landowner or a person of the elite class insofar

as his land, a valuable vineyard, is reportedly adjacent to the king's summer palace. Villagers knew that they were much more vulnerable than the privileged few and could not have resisted a king who coveted their land.

5. Temple land. Judging from the situation in other ancient Southwest Asian areas, we can assume that substantial tracts of land were also owned by the temples. These holdings provided income and resources needed for the operation and maintenance of the temples as well as for the support of the priests, other cultic officiants, laborers, and slaves. The temples acquired this land either through gifts or grants from the king or through financial dealings similar to those of the large landowners. And as with the previous two categories, the temples also depended on tenant farmers, hired laborers, and slaves to work the land and manage their herds of sheep, goats, and cattle.

Legal issues and conflicts that arose regarding categories 3–5 (above) were resolved not by villagers but were handled in the jurisdiction of the elites, the royal administration, and the cultic officials.[65] Even with the presence of reformers and social critics such as the prophets depicted in the Hebrew Bible, in an agrarian state the royal house and the ruling elite held the power to ordain the legal controls and to affect the outcome of judicial proceedings touching on their own interests.[66]

Among the villagers themselves, one of the most basic issues, though perhaps rarely contested, was the delineation of the *boundaries* of each family's or person's property, especially the arable land. Thus Deut 19:14 makes a clear statement of the regulation: "You must not move your neighbor's boundary [generally understood as the 'boundary stone' or 'marker'], which former generations established on the property you inherited in the land YHWH your God gives you as your own." Such a law probably reflects more the interests of the wealthier class, if the following logic holds good: Villagers would have been very familiar with the extent of their own small plots, and any effort to encroach on the space of a neighbor must have been readily noticed not only by the owner of that property but also by others in the community, whose families had for generations remained in close proximity and probably even had helped work each other's land

65. See chaps. 6 and 7 for discussion.
66. See above, chap. 3.

at various points in the year.[67] Wealthier landowners, on the other hand, especially those living in towns or cities and thus removed from their holdings, were not nearly so familiar with their lands and thus depended on boundary markers to denote the extent of their territory. Their interest in keeping the boundary lines inviolate was no more real than that of the villagers; the difference was that villagers would have been instantly alert to changes in the size of their plots and could have counted on their neighbors to corroborate their claims. In this sense a legal proscription regarding the moving of boundary lines is conceivable among villagers, though it was probably rarely needed—which may explain why no remedy is provided for its violation, only a religious motive clause.

Residential dwellings in the villages belonged also to families and in many cases were occupied not by nuclear families but by extended or compound families.[68] In the case of an extended family, ownership was not likely to be contested since anyone living in the household besides the nuclear family was there because they lacked the resources for independent living—elderly parents, unwed siblings, the physically handicapped, and the like. A compound family situation, however, depended on the force of custom and law to maintain lines of possession and authority: with two or more houses in the compound, each occupied by a male sibling and his family, or one perhaps also by their parents, some conflict is conceivable, but the tradition of having authority lodge in the eldest male sibling, or in the elderly parents until death or incapacity, served as a deterrent to contested ownership claims. The compound of closely related families worked efficiently if the lines of authority were respected.

Potentially contentious, however, were *inheritance* practices involving real property. Biblical texts, especially in light of the description of the case reportedly brought to Moses by the daughters of Zelophehad, indicate that a son was to be the primary inheritor of his father's estate, followed in sequence by—if living—a daughter, then the father's brothers, then his

67. An analogy taken from modern-day circumstances in the Sinai peninsula may be useful. The whole of the Sinai is traditionally divided into discrete areas, each occupied by one of some twenty-five different Arab tribes. (The figure is sometimes set lower, around twelve, the difference stemming from how one defines and counts various tribal subdivisions.) While on an extended back-country camel trip in the Sinai in 1982, I learned from our Bedouin guides that tribal members, who tend to spend all of their lives there, are intimately familiar with the extent of their tribal land, and they refrain from passing into another tribe's territory without good reason or permission. If such precise social knowledge can work for a larger tribal area, it is all the more likely that the tiny arable plot cultivated by a family in ancient Israel was intimately familiar to both that family and their neighbors. Boundary markers were scarcely needed, and moving them would not have gone unnoticed.

68. Stager, "Archaeology of the Family," 17–23; King and Stager, *Life in Biblical Israel*, 28–40.

paternal uncles, and finally his nearest kinsman in the clan (Num 27:7–11). Furthermore, the principle of primogeniture was to obtain as a general rule, with the firstborn male receiving a double portion[69] of the inheritance (Deut 21:17). It is difficult to know the extent to which the villages of Israel followed such customs and laws, however. Despite the legendary fecundity of Jacob and his wives (twelve sons and an unknown number of daughters) and Job and his wife (seven sons and three daughters—two sets of such: Job 1:2 and 42:13), the high rate of infant mortality at 50–60 percent, coupled with the severe health risks to the mother during pregnancy and delivery, must have meant that the average number of offspring a couple expected to reach adulthood was closer to two, one of each gender. Since a daughter conventionally left her home of origin upon marriage and a son brought his wife into the family household, there may have been relatively few cases where the inheritance had to be divided among two or more sons. When it was necessary, a double inheritance to the eldest would have put the other sons and families at severe risk in a subsistence economy. Consequently, it is more likely that a villager with minimal landholdings and with more than one son followed the principle of partible inheritance: arable land as well as residential space was divided equally among the sons (assuming that the daughters had relocated at marriage to live with their husbands), or among the daughters if there were no living sons.[70] As will be observed in the next chapter, the wealthier Israelites, many of whom held large estates, may have been the ones who tried to keep their land, or the majority of it, in the hands of a single offspring.

Movable Property. Villagers also typically had much fewer belongings and little of great worth in comparison with the elites of the country, yet what they possessed was all the more valuable and essential to them. Legal constraints against theft of movable property—any animate or inanimate item capable of being moved from one place to another (thus, not real property)—are therefore to be expected in villages. However, laws such as those present in the Covenant Code do not quite match the rural conditions where only 75–150 people were clustered in a community, with everyone knowing well what others possess. It would be hard for one villager to

---

69. The Hebrew in Deut 21:17 reads פִּי שְׁנַיִם (*pî šĕnayim*), translated by some as "two-thirds" but more likely meaning "two portions" or "a double portion," as in the LXX (διπλᾶ, *dipla*, "double").

70. A literary topos in the Hebrew Bible, stories about younger sons superseding older brothers—such as Isaac, Jacob, Joseph, David, Solomon—also contravene the practice of primogeniture.

get away with stealing a neighbor's animals (Exod 22:1–4 [21:37–22:3]), and breaking into a home is only slightly more thinkable among neighbors (22:2–3a [22:1–2a MT]). Either these laws were designed to specify punishments that would affect primarily outsiders coming to the village, or they point to urban contexts where such theft stands a better chance of success.

Production. Villagers probably had little in the way of legal agricultural regulations. The life of the farmer was filled with traditional knowledge and lore about the cultivation of the land,[71] but it is hard to imagine that any of it would have been legally actionable if not carried out. Those who deviated from the practices inherited from previous generations ran the risk of losing the whole crop—punishment enough for the family that depended on it. Biblical laws include a number of agricultural commands, but that does not necessarily mean that they governed the villagers' behavior, unless they were perhaps prescribed by large landowners for their tenant farmers. The laws about fallowing (Exod 23:10–11; Lev 25:1–7) have more of a didactic and religious than a legal intent; if farmers knew the value of fallowing, they would have practiced it without someone from the outside mandating and enforcing it. Similarly, the laws in Lev 19:19 and Deut 22:9—stipulating that a piece of land was not to be planted with more than one crop at a time, and that the entire yield was to be forfeited if anyone did it—reflect more of a cultic concern with boundaries than a peasant's need to produce food, and community consensus at the local level could override laws from the temple or the palace that were not backed up with enforcement.

Most of the biblical laws regarding *treatment of animals* address problems involving the liability or theft of work animals and cattle, and we can expect that it was similar for the customary laws in the villages. The religious ordinances involving the Sabbath extend to the work animals (Exod 20:10); the text in Exod 23:12 casts it in terms of the consequences of the behavior mandated of the people: when their owners eschew work on the Sabbath, the animals will have the rest they also need. In all likelihood, though, the practice of giving a restorative break to the animals certainly preceded the religious strictures evident in the Exodus laws, with the theological legitimation coming later, when the idea of the "Sabbath" was extended to the work animals. Yet even if work animals could get a

71. For detailed discussions about farming and animal husbandry in ancient Israel, see D. Hopkins, *Highlands of Canaan*; King and Stager, *Life in Biblical Israel*, 85–122; and Oded Borowski, *Agriculture in Iron Age Israel* (Winona Lake, IN: Eisenbrauns, 1987).

day off in this manner, those tending them could not abandon the animals' needs for food and milking on every day of the week. In general, animals are to be treated humanely by, for example, helping a donkey or ox that has fallen under its burden (Exod 23:5; Deut 22:4), or not muzzling an ox while it threshes (Deut 25:4), or taking only a bird's eggs or young and not the mother bird as well (Deut 22:6–7). Cruelty or negligence involving one's own work animals or those of others may well have prompted a community response in the form of a judicial sanction if the incidents were egregious or habitual and harmful to group ethos. The villagers' meager means of subsistence required that their resources be preserved and maximized, and it was counterproductive for any owner of work animals or food animals to diminish the well-being of these animals.

Slavery. Laws about slavery could hardly have been commonplace in villages, where subsistence needs were met with only considerable difficulty. To be sure, slaves in the ancient economy did not always denote luxury since persons could become enslaved through a variety of means, including birth, hardship, or capture in wartime. Yet in village contexts the average family did not have the means or the opportunity to acquire slaves; the greater danger was that these villagers would fall into debt and have no other recourse than to sell themselves into slavery. The impulse toward benign treatment of slaves and toward release of slaves after six years, as advanced in several biblical laws (e.g., Exod 21:2; Lev 25:39–55; Deut 15:12–15; 23:15–16 [23:16–17 MT), conforms to the self-interests of villagers who could so easily become indentured. Stated differently, villagers would have known all too well the hardships of life on the land, including the threats of indentured servitude, and any mechanisms or provisions that could lessen their obligations to others, including debt slavery, would have been welcomed. The release laws in the Hebrew Bible, while not within the power of the villagers to enact, reflect their ideals and hopes. In the next two chapters we will return in more detail to the subject of slavery: the city, state, and cult are the most likely contexts where slavery occurred and was, if at all, regulated.

Liability. Several forms of liability in the economic sphere demanded legal attention in the village context. Liability for movable property held for another person (e.g., Exod 22:7–8, 10–15 [22:6–7, 9–14 MT]) applies in both rural and urban contexts. When livestock is the property in question, the village is the most likely setting. Borrowing an ox belonging to a neighbor, for example, may have been commonplace for farmers who did not own one and needed it for certain tasks. On the other hand, if the property actually belonged to a large landowner who lent it to a tenant farmer, then these laws betray less a village ethos than a class division. Many of the laws in the Hebrew Bible and in ancient Southwest Asian texts regarding the protection of property are most likely intended to benefit the wealthy rather than the villagers and peasants, as will be argued in the next chapter.

Construction liability, attested in other ancient Southwest Asian societies, was not likely to have been as much of a legal problem in villages as it was in cities, as we will see in more detail in the next chapter. In contexts where people were at a subsistence or near-subsistence level, the houses were self-built by those who planned to occupy them, or by their relatives. As a result, there was no nonrelated, third party to hold liable for damages consequential to inferior construction or substandard building materials. Moreover, houses, if kept in good repair, could be used for several generations, which meant that the original builder was quite likely no longer living at the time of a building collapse or construction failure. The law in Deut 22:9 requiring house owners to add a parapet on the flat roof is plausible in both villages and cities, and an owner could incur bloodguilt if someone were to fall from the roof and die.

The issue of *negligence* becomes especially evident in cases involving *animals*. One identified in various legal collections from ancient Southwest Asia[72] is the case of the goring or marauding ox, which could cause severe harm not only to persons but also to other animals and property.[73] Exodus 21:35–36 portrays such a case of an ox that kills another person's ox. In one of the variations named, it is the first time that the ox has acted in this manner, and as a result the surviving ox is to be sold and the sale price divided between the two owners of the oxen. Though it is not mentioned, that ox will presumably be known thereafter as a dangerous animal and will require due diligence for the protection of others. In the second case, the goring ox has a history of goring, yet its owner has neglected to restrain it; as a result, this owner must replace the dead ox and then is allowed to keep the carcass of the dead animal for food or other use. Exodus 21:28–32 considers both cases in the event of a person as the victim: in the first instance where the ox had not caused violence previously, the ox is to be

72. LE 53–55; LH 250–252. Liability in the case of a biting dog owned by another is treated in LE 56–57. In all of these early Babylonian laws, only monetary restitution is expected, and the owner of the ox or dog is not to be executed if the victim is a person.

73. For a comparative study of such laws within ancient Southwest Asia, see Jacob J. Finkelstein, *The Ox That Gored*, Transactions of the American Philosophical Society, new series, 71/2 (Philadelphia: American Philosophical Society, 1981).

stoned to death for killing a person, but the owner has no other liability; but if the ox had previously caused damage, then the owner of the ox that kills a person is to be executed, unless a monetary ransom is imposed (by whom is not explicitly stated) or unless the victim is a slave. Liability in cases not involving personal injury does not extend beyond restitution and has no other punitive dimension, presumably on the grounds that the villagers knew well that animals could not be expected to control themselves, though their owners should make every effort to keep them from doing damage to other animals or property.

Villagers were also liable for damage they caused to the *crops* of others. Exodus 22:5 (22:4 MT) describes a situation in which the livestock of one person is allowed to graze in another's field or vineyard; in such a case, the defendant must pay restitution in the form of the best produce from one's own land. Recompense is also due to the owner of stored grain if someone else has caused its loss by fire (Exod 22:6 [22:5 MT]). The story of Samson's setting fire to the Philistines' fields by setting loose three hundred foxes with lit torches attached to them (Judg 15:4–5) may have struck some Israelites as an appropriate attack on their enemy, but villagers who lived with the threat of total loss of the harvest must have viewed the prospect with some anxiety. Another biblical law deals with negligence that results in the death of an animal, as can happen if a pit is left open and someone's livestock falls into it and dies, which deserves restitution to the animal's owner (Exod 21:33–34).

All such instances—and many others are conceivable in the life of the villagers—reflect the basic principle that no person should need to suffer loss of produce or work animals as a result of someone's negligence. Punitive measures against the one who caused the damage were not needed. Reasonable restitution from that person was sufficient and would probably have served as an adequate deterrent against similar behavior in the future since the guilty person and family thereby suffered substantial loss of their own annual produce from the negligent act.

One other cause for loss comes to mind, though I must say that I have found no clear example of it in the extant texts of ancient Southwest Asia. *Vandalism*, malicious and wanton destruction of property, outside of the context of war, for little reason other than the delight of the destructive act itself, was not likely to have occurred in those socioeconomic settings. For villagers barely subsisting on the edge of survival, there would have been no tolerance for such behavior. For example, the construction and maintenance of terraces in the highlands required labor-intensive effort over generations, involving all able-bodied persons in the community. These terraces, formed by stacking the plentiful rocks into retaining walls to form narrow arable spaces, constituted essential resources for village economy. They may have been torn down by an invading army intent on decimating the population's means of existence, and goats and other animals could have damaged them while climbing. However, it is unthinkable that anyone in the village would have caused such destruction willfully, especially not if they had been involved in building or maintaining them. The same can be surmised for other forms of vandalism that had direct consequences for the livelihood of neighbors and kinfolk.

Responsibilities toward the Vulnerable. Whole village populations could at times become vulnerable to passing armies, to famines and droughts, to diseases, to heavy taxes and tributes, or to other onerous pressures. The threat of becoming heavily indebted and finding no recourse but to sell family members and oneself into slavery loomed more frequently during the monarchic period than we might realize. A culture of concern for the vulnerable may thus have emerged among villagers, not because of some idealism or ideology but simply due to the reality of living with relatives and neighbors whose situation could easily become more tenuous than that of others in the community. The biblical laws providing for the protection of strangers, widows, orphans, and the poor[74] mirror the vulnerability of individuals and groups alike in the villages. Biblical prophets such as Amos and Micah reinforce this picture of desperation and need on the one side, and greed and exploitation on the other. Various texts conjure up the image of a poor person as laboring for a day but not being paid at sunset,[75] a destitute widow needing to give her garment as security for a loan,[76] a borrower confronted with a lender who enters the house to seize some collateral item[77] or even retains the sole means for warmth at night,[78] a borrower facing usurious interest rates for a loan,[79] another with the prospect of endless indebtedness,[80] a slave faced with interminable servitude,[81] a landless person with no hope of recovering the ancestral property,[82] or a poor person who has no chance even for the meager leavings in the

74. Exod 22:21–24 (22:20–23 MT); 23:9; Lev 25; Deut 14:28–29; 24:19–22; 26:12–13.
75. Deut 24:14–15.
76. Deut 24:17b.
77. Deut 24:10–11.
78. Exod 22:26–27a (22:25–26a MT); Deut 24:12–13.
79. Exod 22:25 (22:24 MT); Lev 25:36–37; Deut 23:19–20.
80. Deut 15:1–11.
81. Lev 25:39–43; Deut 15:12–18.
82. Lev 25.

field during the fallow year or after the harvest.[83] The only recourse for the defenseless in such situations is apparently to appeal to YHWH;[84] in Weber's terms, "the curse of the poor" is the "weapon of democracy."[85]

While empathic concern may have been ultimately rooted in the villagers' own experiences and values, the texts themselves seem to have the ring of rhetoric and exhortation, not of functioning and enforceable laws and customs. Furthermore, moneylending, the taking of collateral, and the owning of slaves point to the presence of wealthier persons, such as were to be found in cities or large estates. In the next chapter we will return to this subject in an effort to assess the extent to which such laws that appear to help the vulnerable might actually have benefited the wealthy as much as or even more than they did the weak.

CONCLUSION

Not many of the biblical laws can be traced unequivocally to the villages of ancient Israel. As a whole, the Pentateuch is a literary artifact, and its parts do not necessarily bear close resemblance to any actual legal formulations or practices of the Iron Age. Just because certain texts take the form of directives, restraints, prohibitions, and sanctions does not mean that we have in them a record of living laws, nor even of a promulgated code. To assume, as has been the practice of many modern interpreters, that any of these statements reveal legal controls actually at work in one or the other social context of ancient Israel goes beyond the evidence we possess—and is just a modern assumption on our part.

The best we can manage in testing for correspondence between the text and social norms of the period is to apply a principle of plausibility, based on a mixture of textual, material, and comparative indications. On these terms, internal indications point toward an urban provenance for most if not all of the biblical laws, and much the same can be said of the laws extant from other ancient Southwest Asian countries. The institution of slavery, the presence of both wealth and poverty, houses large enough to be burglarized while the residents sleep, a judge who can be bribed, a leader who should no more be reviled than should the deity, a formalized cult to which sacrifices are expected to be brought—all such phenomena are scarcely imaginable in villages averaging 75–150 inhabitants, most

83. Exod 23:11; Deut 24:19–22.
84. Exod 22:23–24, 27b (22:22–23, 26b MT); Deut 24:13.
85. Max Weber, *Ancient Judaism*, trans. and ed. Hans H. Gerth and Don Martindale (New York: Free Press, 1952; German original, 1917–19), 256–57.

of them agriculturalists or pastoralists barely surviving in a subsistence economy.

On the other hand, however, some vestiges of customs and values conceivable in such villages can perhaps be detected in biblical laws: some theft controls, some marriage and sexuality customs, liability specifications, instructions on treatment of work animals, sanctions against violence, guidelines for religious veneration that use simple materials and the fruits of rural production, and concern for the vulnerable, both slaves and poor. Yet in no case are these topics treated fully enough in the biblical texts to count as adequate protections or provisions for the ordering of life in the villages. The writers of the Pentateuch have at most incorporated highly selected legal traditions that *may* have been operative in *certain* villages. Surely there were also agriculturalists living in or just outside of the cities who could have served as a source for these notions of laws of the land. The villagers did not produce this text, not even something amounting to a first draft. Too many indications of city interests and too few of the villagers' must lead us to conclude that the pentateuchal laws, from their first appearance onward as literary documents, were a product of the city.

For what reason is it even worthwhile to consider the terms of village life when Israel's most notable cultural remnants—the texts, the monumental buildings and fortifications, the impact on history—stem from cities? Two compelling grounds suggest themselves. First, a social history seeking to appreciate the terms of living faced by the majority of the population, those who do not count among the powerful and influential, rounds out our picture of that culture. Although our efforts at historical recovery are severely hampered because of the inadequacy of the sources, we should try to identify conditions and perspectives different from those dominating the relatively few cities of Israel—or at least question whether urban viewpoints coincide with the interests and customs of those living elsewhere. Second, this larger sociohistorical picture provides insight into the agenda of the writers of our texts, which were produced by, and in all likelihood mainly for, persons situated in the cities. The agricultural and pastoral economy depended on the work of all the villagers across the land, but as long as the persons at the nation's center were able to control the economic and political systems, which a monarchic structure facilitated, it was not a high priority for them to cater overmuch to the interests of these villagers.

Both of these reasons should affect the way we think about the texts and culture of ancient Israel. Specifically, we can expect the legal literature to retain not much more than only occasional traces of village practices and values, mediated always through the experiences and self-interests of urban, literate, largely upper-class or privileged groups. Nonetheless, whether or not they were appreciated by urbanites, the villagers themselves had to find order for their own social existence, which necessitated legal norms and structures for them to deal with disruptions and conflict. Contrary to conventional assumptions by modern interpreters, these villagers would have found little benefit in contributing to the production of the legal texts that evolved into parts of our present Pentateuch. Their primary interests lay not in texts but in their own traditions and in their survival in the face of often extraordinary political, economic, and environmental odds.

CHAPTER 6

Law in the Cities and the States

Cities are power containers which, in conjunction with their relations to the countryside, generate the structural nexus of the state form.

—*Anthony Giddens*[1]

Although the greatest portion of the population in ancient Israel, from the beginning of the Iron Age around 1200 BCE through the Hellenistic period (to 63 BCE) and even later, lived in the villages scattered throughout the land, the cities represented an imposing and powerful force in the country—economically, politically, ideologically, socially, and religiously. Life proceeded in a notably different manner in the urban areas than in the rural settings, despite many points of commonality. In this chapter we attempt to reconstruct the terms of city life in Israel and then assess the legal systems operative there. One of many distinctive ways in which cities differed from villages was their range of influence: while villages had little chance, and probably little inclination, to affect the lives and livelihood of others throughout the land, cities depended on villagers for their means of existence and thus sought continually to control them in order to keep a steady stream of resources, including food and labor, coming from the countryside into the cities. This control showed itself not only in terms of taxation, conscription, and the command economy but also in the effort to regulate the villages' legal systems at the points where they had a bearing on urban and national life. In short, the Israelite cities, just as other cities in the region, constituted "containers of power," to use Giddens's phrase. To appreciate their capacities to exercise this power, we need to examine not

---

1. Anthony Giddens, *The Constitution of Society: Outline of the Theory of Structuration* (Berkeley and Los Angeles: University of California Press, 1984), 195. See also Ze'ev Herzog, *Archaeology of the City: Urban Planning in Ancient Israel and Its Social Implications*, Tel Aviv University, Sonia and Marco Nadler Institute of Archaeology Monograph Series 13 (Tel Aviv: Emery and Claire Yass Archaeology Press, 1997), 6–7, 278.

only the infrastructure of the cities but especially their tendency to reach out beyond themselves and dominate the lives of others.

URBAN LIFE

Just as we needed to reconsider the implications of rural demographic distribution, with the vast majority of the country's population scattered in the countless tiny villages of ancient Israel, we must also adjust our notions of scale regarding "urban" settlements. Cities in Israel were very small in comparison with those of modern times; to us they would appear to be little more than towns, some of them even very small towns.[2] In fact, they also paled in comparison with some of the great ancient Southwest Asian cities. The seventh-century-BCE Neo-Assyrian capital city of Nineveh, the largest known city in Mesopotamian antiquity, covered an area of about 700 hectares (= 1,730 acres) inside the city wall and could have held upward of 250,000 inhabitants, although probably many fewer lived there because so much of the space was devoted to royal, administrative, and military purposes.[3] According to one estimate,[4] early Mesopotamian city-states settled almost 80 percent of their total population in cities, many of them farmers. While that distribution would constitute a dramatic difference from the situation prevailing in Iron II Israel, we should withhold conclusions until more Mesopotamian villages from antiquity have been excavated.

We will follow the convention of using the term "city" for the largest Israelite settlements for two simple reasons. First, even though their population size was small, the physical structures seemed enormous relative to the average size of the Israelite villages. The fortified walls surrounding the cities lent them an aura of superiority and impregnability, all the more imposing because the majority of them were located high on multilayered mounds or on hilltop sites. The luxury of their buildings and homes also far outstripped the modest, even meager habitations of the villagers. Second

2. In light of their size, C. H. J. de Geus opts to use the word "town" rather than "city" in his monograph *Towns in Ancient Israel and in the Southern Levant*, Palaestina antiqua 10 (Leuven: Peeters, 2003).

3. Elizabeth C. Stone, "The Development of Cities in Ancient Mesopotamia," *CANE* 1:247. Jack M. Sasson (*Jonah: A New Translation with Introduction, Commentary, and Interpretation*, AB 24B [New York: Doubleday, 1992], 311–12) reports that Simo Parpola's calculation sets the Nineveh population at more than 300,000. Parpola uses a much higher residential rate of 630 inhabitants per hectare (252 per acre), compared to the figure of 200 per hectare (80 per acre) used below for Israelite cities.

4. Bruce G. Trigger, "The Evolution of Pre-Industrial Cities: A Multilinear Perspective," in *Mélanges offerts à Jean Vercoutter*, ed. Francis Geus and Florence Thill (Paris: Éditions recherche sur les civilisations, 1985), 343–53; idem, *Understanding Early Civilizations: A Comparative Study* (Cambridge and New York: Cambridge University Press, 2003), 123–25.

and more significantly, the Israelite cities, like their modern counterparts, functioned as economic and political centers, possessing the power to affect greatly the lives of those living at a substantial distance from them, unlike the limited reach of each individual hamlet.

Yet ancient Israel's cities do not deserve greater regard merely because of their size and functions. Their aggregate population amounted to no more than some 20 percent of the whole population of the region, and considerably less in most periods. Even the culture they produced—the grand buildings, the political and religious institutions, the texts—though seemingly far more impressive than that of the multitudinous poor rural villages, should not be privileged as of a higher order, for the very means of survival developed and transmitted by those who lived off the land represented a remarkable accomplishment in its own right. While cities played an important role in the overall social history of the people, villagers must have regarded their own contexts as of ultimately more significance. Our task as social and legal historians is to grant each setting its own due and to understand their interactions.[5]

Three great periods of urbanization occurred in the eastern Mediterranean region: the Early Bronze Age (esp. after ca. 3000 BCE), the Middle Bronze Age (starting ca. 2000 BCE), and Iron Age II (900–586 BCE). In seemingly cyclical fashion, a period of mainly village settlements and pastoralism was followed by development of urban centers and cultures, which in turn eventually gave way to a decline of the cities and the ruralization of the region, followed later by a new wave of urbanization.[6] In the southern Levant, the Late Bronze Age (1550–1200 BCE) was the period of urban decline.[7] Most of the once-great Canaanite city-states were abandoned or were reduced to poor settlements, with few buildings and limited habitation. Egyptian forts appeared on some of the sites. Megiddo and Hazor

5. For a discussion of the problems inherent to a division between "center" and "periphery," see my "Political Rights and Powers," 99–100.

6. I. Finkelstein, "Emergence of Israel," 150–78; Ferdinand Braudel, "La longue durée," *Annales économies, sociétés, civilisations* 13 (1958): 725–53; idem, *Civilization and Capitalism, 15th–18th Century*, 3 vols. (London: Collins; New York: Harper & Row, 1981–84); idem, *The Mediterranean and the Mediterranean World in the Age of Philip II*, 2 vols. (New York: Harper & Row, 1972–76). For further discussion of urbanism in the region, see Van De Mieroop, *The Ancient Mesopotamian City*; and the articles in *Urbanism in Antiquity: From Mesopotamia to Crete*, ed. Walter E. Aufrecht, Neil A. Mirau, and Steven W. Gauley, JSOTSup 244 (Sheffield: Sheffield Academic Press, 1997).

7. Rivka Gonen, "Urban Canaan in the Late Bronze Period," *BASOR* 253 (1984): 61–73; Niels Peter Lemche, *Prelude to Israel's Past: Background and Beginnings of Israelite History and Identity*, trans. E. F. Maniscalco (Peabody, MA: Hendrickson Publishers, 1998; German original, 1996); Herzog, *Archaeology of the City*, 164–89; Shlomo Bunimovitz, "On the Edge of Empires—Late Bronze Age (1500–1200 BCE)," in Levy, *Archaeology of Society*, 320–31.

were the main exceptions to this pattern: both cities were occupied continuously in the fourteenth and thirteenth centuries BCE, with new buildings (palaces, temples, administrative centers) and residential areas for urban elites (esp. at Hazor) reflecting a form of city planning.[8] Many of these fortified cities of the Bronze Age, including Megiddo and Hazor during certain periods prior to Iron II, existed as city-states, autonomous political entities including their outlying feeder villages and generally operating on the basis of autocratic royal and elite powers.[9]

With the onset of the Iron I Age in 1200 BCE in the southern Levant, we meet a situation ripe for change. As noted above in chapter 5, the greatest social development during that period occurred with the proliferation of small villages over much of the landscape. Against this background and following the urban decline in the Late Bronze Age, it took time before the land of Israel was reurbanized. In addition to the Philistine cities of Ashdod, Ashkelon, Ekron, Jaffa, Timnah, and Gath in the coastal region, a few other settlements—such as Megiddo, Beth-Shean, and Gezer—survived or were rebuilt, if only in a reduced state, as Iron I continuations of the urban tradition.[10] The tremendous increase in the number and population of villages, as noted in the previous chapter, formed the most distinctive characteristic of Iron Age I. The third wave of urbanization in the region began in Iron II, contemporaneous with the rise of the monarchy.[11]

8. Israel Finkelstein and David Ussishkin, "Archaeological and Historical Conclusions," in *Megiddo III: The 1992–1996 Seasons*, ed. Israel Finkelstein, David Ussishkin, and Baruch Halpern (Tel Aviv: Institute of Archaeology, Tel Aviv University, 2000), 2:592–95.

9. Political and socioeconomic dynamics in the Mesopotamian city-states of 2700–1600 BCE are discussed in Elizabeth Stone, "City-States and Their Centers: The Mesopotamian Example," in *The Archaeology of City-States: Cross-Cultural Approaches*, ed. Deborah L. Nichols and Thomas H. Charlton, Smithsonian Series in Archaeological Inquiry (Washington and London: Smithsonian Institution Press, 1997), 15–26.

10. The history of urbanization and the description of individual sites can be found in multiple publications; see, e.g., Ze'ev Herzog, *Archaeology of the City*; idem, "Settlement and Fortification Planning in the Iron Age," in *The Architecture of Ancient Israel from the Prehistoric to the Persian Periods: In Memory of Immanuel (Munya) Dunayevsky*, ed. Aharon Kempinski and Ronny Reich (Jerusalem: Israel Exploration Society, 1992), 231–74; idem, "Cities," *ABD* (1992), 1:1031–43; de Geus, *Towns*; Volkmar Fritz, *The City in Ancient Israel* (Sheffield: Sheffield Academic Press, 1995); Frick, *The City in Ancient Israel*; McNutt, *Reconstructing the Society of Ancient Israel*, 143–81; and Giorgio Buccellati, *Cities and Nations of Ancient Syria: An Essay on Political Institutions with Special Reference to the Israelite Kingdoms*, Studi semitici 26 (Rome: Istituto di Studi del Vicino Oriente, Università di Roma, 1967). For a focus more on the representations of the city in the Hebrew Bible, see Jon L. Berquist and Claudia V. Camp, eds., *Constructions of Space II: The Biblical City and Other Imagined Spaces*, LHBOTS 490 (New York and London: T&T Clark, 2008).

11. The traditional date of the early 10th c. BCE for the inception of the Iron II period and of the monarchy has been challenged by Israel Finkelstein, who cites substantial archaeological reasons for moving the date to the early 9th c. BCE; see esp. I. Finkelstein, "The Archaeology of the United Monarchy: An Alternative View," *Levant* 28 (1996): 177–87; and idem, "Hazor and the North in the Iron Age: A Low Chronology Perspective," *BASOR* 314 (1999): 55–70.

The Iron II age possesses special significance for us in our effort to reconstruct the legal systems because the states of Israel and Judah were sovereign during this period until Assyria conquered the northern kingdom of Israel in 722 BCE and subjected Judah to a century of vassalage. This era, from the tenth or ninth century to the early sixth century BCE, presents us with the urban and national counterpart to the domain of villages with their own laws, as discussed in the preceding chapter. At the same time, this monarchic context can also be contrasted with the colonial periods—Assyrian, Babylonian, Persian, Hellenistic—when sovereignty resided ultimately with remote imperial forces, even though the Judean structures and traditions could continue to function to a greater or lesser degree, depending on the will of the empire.

Size, Types, and Location of Cities

Cities can be described in terms of both size and function. Regarding their size, the cities of ancient Israel were very small in comparison with both their modern counterparts and the imperial cities of antiquity, but they functioned politically, economically, and symbolically in similar ways. Settlements larger than villages during the Iron Age II period fall into three groups according to surface coverage:[12]

- Medium sites of 1.1–4.9 hectares (= 2.7–12.1 acres), the mean size being 3 hectares (= 7.4 acres).
- Large sites of 5.0–9.9 hectares (= 12.4–24.5 acres), the mean size being 7 hectares (= 17.3 acres).
- Very large sites of 10 hectares (= 24.7 acres) or more.

Though the physical extent or perimeter of a city can be estimated in light of the distribution of material evidence for a given stratum, excavations have rarely exposed enough of a whole stratum to determine the full makeup of the settlement. Furthermore, it is a mistake to assume that the entire area of a city was devoted to residences, any more than is the case in modern cities. Common, nonresidential spaces included streets and paths, marketplaces, plazas and other gathering spaces, monuments, and storage areas. Depending on the role of a given city in the administration of the state, there could also be palace grounds, temple grounds, administrative buildings, areas for the military, and open spaces for celebratory functions. Consequently, the mere physical expanse of a city does not alone indicate

12. Broshi and I. Finkelstein, "Population," 48. See above, chap. 5, Size and Population, regarding the two smaller sizes, which qualify as villages.

the size of the population inhabiting it. The agricultural capacity of the immediate vicinity for producing crops and raising livestock, as well as the presence of adequate water resources, can also affect population density. The first step in demographic assessment with the aid of archaeology involves inferring the function of the city at a given period, after which the ratio of residential quarters to nonresidential areas can be postulated.

In light of such considerations, a reasonable average for calculating population size is 200 inhabitants per hectare (= 80 per acre) of built (sometimes called "built-up") urban space.[13] By "built space" is meant the full size of the site, whether occupied by buildings or open areas. The proportion of the residential sectors to the overall scope of the city, as we will see shortly, varied substantially depending on the function of the given city. The largest cities in surface area do not seem to have been appreciably more populous than the towns: capital cities and "royal cities" had so much space devoted to royal, religious, administrative, and ceremonial purposes that typically less than 25 percent of the area within the city walls was used for actual dwellings during the Iron II, Assyrian, and Persian periods. An exception may have been Jerusalem during the seventh century BCE, after the influx of northerners following the Assyrian conquest of Samaria.

The following discussion of urban life will focus primarily on the Iron II period (ca. 900–586 BCE) and the political, economic, and cultic dynamics of the cities during those centuries. I am not suggesting that the biblical laws stem from the Iron II period; to the contrary, I think they were written no earlier than the Persian period. The purpose of focusing in this chapter on the monarchic period is to assess the impact of the political and economic powers on the rest of the country, especially on the legal principles and practices among the elites, on one hand, and the commoners, on the other. The cities served a key function in this exercise of power during Iron II. Four different types of cities existed in this period; variations occurred during the following Babylonian, Persian, and Hellenistic periods. The key

13. Broshi and I. Finkelstein ("Population," 48) propose 250 per hectare (= 2.5 acres), as does Lipschits (*The Fall and Rise of Jerusalem*, 259–61; his figure is 25 per dunam, or 250 per hectare). In a private communication (7 April 2008), however, I. Finkelstein, citing ethnoarchaeological and ethnohistorical data (see also I. Finkelstein, "A Few Notes on Demographic Data from Recent Generations and Ethnoarchaeology," *PEQ* 122 [1990]: 47–52), argued that 200 per hectare is more probable. In contrast, Shiloh ("Population," 29–39) operates with an average twice as high: 400–500 per residential hectare (= 160–200 per acre). (Shiloh's figure is stated in terms of a dunam, which equals 1,000 square meters, or 0.25 acre; thus he estimates 40–50 inhabitants per residential dunam.) He arrives at this number by assuming a high family coefficient of 6–10 people inhabiting each dwelling. However, an average of five or slightly less per family is more likely in light of health considerations, social circumstances, and typical house size; hence the population coefficient of 200 per hectare (or at most 250 per hectare, as proposed by Broshi and I. Finkelstein) is preferred.

criteria distinguishing them relate not so much to their physical size or the number of inhabitants, but to their function and the extent to which each type was centrally planned and controlled. Settlement hierarchies, such as are found in ancient Israel, are a sure sign of political and economic inequalities.[14]

Residential Cities or Towns

The residential city or town falls within the above category of a medium-sized site, generally with 2–5 hectares (5–12.5 acres) of inhabited space and thus a population ranging from 500 to 1,250 persons. These towns were scattered unevenly across the countryside, by far the greatest number of them in the central highlands, where they ranged in frequency from one per four villages in Samaria to one per 2.5 villages in Judea (including the Shephelah) during the middle of Iron II (8th c. BCE).[15] Proximity to the political and economic forces in the capital cities of Samaria and Jerusalem probably accounts for their frequency within these regions. The Jezreel Valley, with its relatively flat land and major east-west trade route, had a ratio of almost one such town to one small village. In most other regions, though, these towns occurred much less frequently in comparison to the numerous small villages.

Small cities or towns of this type evolved gradually to meet local and regional needs in production and trade. Agriculturalists lived here and worked the surrounding lands, just as did the villagers in their own settings, but these towns also lent themselves well to small-scale manufacture of goods such as pottery, textiles, and metal objects. Their grain storages, winepresses, and olive presses served the villages in the region, and probably the royal house as well. Little if any organized urban layout existed in these towns: houses clustered as space permitted, and streets or paths ran randomly throughout each settlement. More-spacious houses for elites, such as larger landowners, could exist alongside the modest dwellings of the general population. No public buildings were needed, and city walls occurred only occasionally. These cities were not deliberately founded by a central state authority to serve administrative functions of the government,

14. See Paul K. Wason, *The Archaeology of Rank* (Cambridge: Cambridge University Press, 1994), 127–52. The following urban categories draw on those of Herzog, "Settlement and Fortification Planning"; idem, "Cities," 1038–41; idem, *Archaeology of the City*, 276; and Fritz, *The City in Ancient Israel*, 117–18. Others have proposed comparable classifications, e.g., Shiloh ("Population," 28): royal centers (including capital and royal cities); provincial towns (comparable to the local administrative or military city); and rural settlements, estates, and central fortresses (similar, in part, to the residential cities).

15. See the overview in Broshi and I. Finkelstein, "Population," 50–52.

although each such town would be more susceptible to state attention in the form of conscription and taxation because it contained more inhabitants than did a tiny village.

Local Administrative Cities

To serve the needs of the monarchy and the elites, a number of local administrative cities were apparently founded or rebuilt throughout the country.[16] The archaeological evidence is less than certain since they cannot always be clearly distinguished from royal cities or residential cities, but some type of intermediate regional centers seems likely in order to conduct the administrative tasks of the kingdom. Some of the sites filling these functions were not much more populous than the residential towns, while others ranked as relatively large sites, upward of 8 hectares (20 acres) and with a population of 1,500 or more. Unlike the residential towns, they contained public buildings and seem to have benefited from urban planning. Approximately 25 percent of the total space was devoted to buildings and spaces for the state's administration of local affairs, especially the collection and storage of agricultural produce as taxes for the king. Grain silos of various sizes, storehouses (מסכנות, miskĕnôt, e.g., in 2 Chr 32:28), and treasuries (אוצרות, 'ôṣārôt, e.g., in 1 Chr 27:25) for supplies of foodstuffs and other goods were under the control of the state administrators living there. A military presence, at least of modest size, could also be accommodated. Fortifications—city walls, gates, towers—lent a measure of protection and an aura of power, reminding the subjects in the vicinity that they owed allegiance as well as taxes to the reigning monarch. If we understand correctly their place in the governmental hierarchy, these administrative cities ranked higher than the residential cities mentioned above, yet below the royal cities. They also occurred less frequently than the residential cities but more so than the royal cities.

Beersheba serves as an ideal example of these administrative cities. The eighth-century BCE settlement, identified archaeologically as Stratum II and founded on previous levels of habitation, functioned as a southern administrative center until its destruction by the Assyrians in the late eighth century. Occupying a small space of slightly more than one hectare (= 2.5 acres), it was efficiently planned to maximize its utility to the state of Judah as one of its southern outposts and storage centers. Built into the casemate-style fortification walls around the city was a band of houses and official

---

16. See Herzog, "Administrative Structures in the Iron Age," in Kempinski and Reich, *Architecture of Ancient Israel*, 223–30; for more details about the urban layout of this and the following two types of cities, see also idem, *Archaeology of the City*, 221–58.

buildings, bordered toward the interior by a street that circled through the full city parallel to the exterior wall. An inner street spaced inside the ring of the first street allowed another band of houses and buildings in the center of the city. A four-chambered city gate opened to a small plaza, and directly beside the city gate were three large tripartite buildings that probably stored the in-kind taxes collected from villages in the vicinity. One corner of the city was devoted to a remarkable water storage system, accessed by steps leading down to five large cisterns. The buildings functioned for administrative purposes and as residences for those in service to the state—officials, bureaucrats, tax collectors, military officers, merchants, and priests. The careful arrangement of these structures contrasted with the haphazard assemblage of houses in typical villages and residential towns. Small in size, Beersheba contained only about 75 houses and some 300–350 residents, including the family members of the royal administrators. Yet while such a population amounted only to the equivalent of three or four average-sized villages, its importance and power far outweighed its physical and human dimensions. It represented the state, had military support if needed, was enclosed by impressive walls, and was organized to control the surrounding local population and extract the taxes needed by the state. Those who lived in Beersheba were not agriculturalists but Judean officials and functionaries.[17]

Royal Cities

Second only to the capital cities, the so-called royal cities constituted the primary loci for the state's control of the various regions of the country during the eighth-century Iron II period. Only a handful of such cities have been extensively excavated: Megiddo, Hazor, Gezer, and Dan in the more populous and economically stronger kingdom of Israel in the north, and Lachish in the kingdom of Judah to the south. Other major tells (mounds) have not yet been sufficiently investigated and may turn out to be of this type also. As a rule, these royal cities had the monumental buildings and accoutrements befitting the monarchy:[18] palace, temple or other conspicuous cultic site, various administrative buildings, open ceremonial spaces, strong fortifications, the distinctive six- or four-chambered gates (the

---

17. Herzog, *Archaeology of the City*, 244–47; and idem, "Settlement and Fortification," 258–61.

18. The importance of monumental structures for signaling, both domestically and internationally, the power of the state is well known. See recently, e.g., J. Bretschneider, J. Driessen, and K. van Lerberghe, eds., *Power and Architecture: Monumental Public Architecture in the Bronze Age Near East and Aegean*, OLA 156 (Leuven: Uitgeverij Peeters, 2007).

so-called Solomonic gates, once thought by some to have been built by Solomon in the 10th c. BCE but more likely constructed one or two centuries later),[19] quarters for the military, stables, water systems, storehouses, court-yards, and the like. Some could have had special functions; for example, Megiddo may well have been a large breeding and training center for horses, some to be used by the northern monarchy and others to be traded to nearby clients, especially Assyria.[20] All of these cities were built accord-ing to comprehensive plans developed by official architects working in the service of the king. Viewed from both the outside and the inside, these cities were imposing, impressive structures.

Significantly, though, they were not meant to be occupied by many people, only by those involved in state administration, cultic officiants, the elite, and their servants. Upward of 75 percent of the land space was devoted to state matters, leaving only small sections for residential use. For example, both Megiddo (Strata V–IV) and Lachish (Strata IV–III) during this period probably housed fewer than 500 permanent inhabitants each, not counting military or merchants who stayed there temporarily.[21] By contrast, if cities of their size had been devoted to residential use, their populations would have been more in the vicinity of 2,500–4,000. A sizeable workforce was needed to construct the buildings, walls, and roads —slaves, war captives, and farmers conscripted from villages in the region as corvée labor. During the construction season the villagers lived in mud huts or other temporary dwellings outside the city walls, if they could not com-mute daily from nearby villages. The types of domestic architecture found

19. David Ussishkin, "Was the 'Solomonic' City Gate at Megiddo Built by King Solomon?" *BASOR* 239 (1980): 1–18. Deborah O. Cantrell and Israel Finkelstein ("A Kingdom for a Horse: The Megiddo Stables and Eighth Century Israel," in *Megiddo IV*, 2:654–55) demonstrate how the chambered gates could be used as hitching stalls for the horses as they were hitched and unhitched from chariots.

20. Cantrell and I. Finkelstein ("A Kingdom for a Horse," 656–60) argue that the substantial stables and supply areas of 8th-c. BCE Megiddo could have accommodated approximately 450 horses within the city. See also Deborah O. Cantrell, "Stable Issues," *Megiddo IV*, 2:630–42; idem, "The Horsemen of Israel: Horses and Chariotry in Monarchic Israel (Ninth–Eighth Centuries B.C.E.)" (Ph.D. diss., Vanderbilt University, 2008); and Lawrence A. Belkin and Eileen F. Wheeler, "Reconstruction of the Megiddo Stables," *Megiddo IV*, 2:666–87.

21. Herzog, *Archaeology of the City*, 229, 242. Megiddo of the 9th c. BCE (Stratum V) has revealed more domestic space than its 8th-c. counterpart (Stratum IV). I. Finkelstein and Ussishkin ("Archaeological and Historical Conclusions," in *Megiddo III*, 2:597) refer to Iron II Megiddo as an administrative center "with very limited habitation quarters." Shiloh ("Population," 29–31 and n. 22) states that only 50%, not 75%, of the royal cities constituted public spaces and public buildings, but he then proposes a population for Iron II Megiddo of 4,000–5,000 (for a space of 100 dunam = 10 hectares = 25 acres, using his density coef-ficient of 40–50 per dunam)—instead of a population of 2,000–2,500 if only half of the space was residential. Both of his calculations appear to be excessive now in light of more-recent determinations.

in these cities ranked mostly as upper-class dwellings, with some houses of noticeably lesser quality situated nearby for slaves, bureaucrats, and lower functionaries. With no place for the urban poor these royal cities were, in a sense, gated communities for the powerful and the wealthy.

Capital Cities

Finally, the two capital cities during Iron II—Samaria in the north and Jerusalem in the south—represented the pinnacle of governmental power and prestige, and all other cities were subordinate to them. Physically they were also the largest of the cities, fortified with gates, towers, and massive city walls. Samaria was founded as the northern capital by Omri after he ascended the throne in 876 BCE (see 1 Kgs 16:24), and it went through several later building phases until it was conquered and destroyed by the Assyrians in 722 BCE. With some remains of Middle Bronze monumental buildings lasting to Iron I, Jerusalem emerged from a small settlement[22] in the tenth–ninth centuries BCE to become capital of the sovereign southern kingdom until 722 BCE and thereafter vassal to Assyria until the 620s BCE, when it reestablished itself as independent for a short period until its destruction by the Babylonians in 586 BCE.

During the eighth century BCE, Samaria, as capital of the larger of the two kingdoms, covered substantially more area—perhaps some 40–50 hectares (= 100–125 acres), or even up to 60 hectares (= 150 acres)—than did Jerusalem, with about 30 hectares (= ca. 75 acres). Samaria also exceeded its southern counterpart in monumental, luxurious structures. Only after the fall of the north did Jerusalem expand considerably, with the rebuilding by Hezekiah and Manasseh, and reach some 60–65 hectares (= 150–162.5 acres) in size.[23] The influx of new immigrants to Jerusalem during the last quarter of the seventh century stemmed presumably from the northern kingdom of Israel after its fall and from the western parts of Judah ceded by Sennacherib to the Philistines. The new inhabitants settled largely in

22. The extraordinary archaeological effort throughout all parts of biblical Jerusalem with the exception of the Temple Mount, which for religious and legal reasons cannot be excavated, has not produced evidence of Solomon's ambitious building projects as described in the Hebrew Bible. At most only a small settlement on the hill known as the City of David, above the Gihon spring, seems to have existed in the early Iron Age until a fortified city was constructed in the 8th–7th c. BCE. David Ussishkin argues this point in his overview, "Solomon's Jerusalem: The Text and the Facts on the Ground," in *Jerusalem in Bible and Archaeology: The First Temple Period*, ed. Andrew G. Vaughn and Ann E. Killebrew, SBLSymS 18 (Atlanta: Society of Biblical Literature, 2003), 103–15.

23. Herzog, *Archaeology of the City*, 220, 229, 236–37, 249; Broshi and I. Finkelstein, "Population," 51–52. Not much of Samaria has been excavated to date, primarily only the acropolis area. Jerusalem has also not yielded significant material evidence from the 10th–8th c. BCE, although much of its basic perimeter is known.

contiguous areas outside the city of Jerusalem, swelling its overall size to 60–65 hectares.[24]

The same kinds of monumental buildings and spaces mentioned above for the royal cities filled the capital cities, although here they were even more numerous and impressive in size and appointments. Especially conspicuous in Samaria, an acropolis with an encircling wall contained the royal residence, the primary palace for the kingdom. A comparable acropolis and palace, though undiscovered, may have existed in Jerusalem during the eighth–seventh centuries BCE. Temples from the Iron II period, to be expected in the capitals while the states were sovereign, have also not yet emerged. Other governmental buildings housed the many persons involved in state affairs and administration. Jerusalem's famous water tunnel, attributed to Hezekiah (2 Kgs 20:20; 2 Chr 32:30), was also dug at this time, replacing the Middle Bronze tunnel system already there.

As with the royal cities, the population size in the capitals was limited by the royal and administrative buildings and open spaces occupying the majority of the urban space, altogether some 75 percent of the area enclosed by the city walls. Assuming a density of 200 inhabitants per hectare (= 80 per acre), we can estimate that during the eighth century until its destruction in 722 BCE, Samaria with its 60 hectares had about 12,000 permanent inhabitants while Jerusalem with 30 hectares held about 6,000. In the following century and until the fall of Jerusalem in 586 BCE, its population increased to about 13,000.[25] One estimate puts the increase of Jerusalem's population from about 6 percent to about 23 percent of the total population of Judah by the late seventh century BCE.[26]

24. M. Broshi, "The Expansion of Jerusalem in the Reigns of Hezekiah and Manasseh," *IEJ* 24 (1974): 21–26; Lipschits, *The Fall and Rise of Jerusalem*, 215–18. Nadav Na'aman attributes the increase not to refugees from the north but refugees from Judean settlements destroyed by the Assyrians; "When and How Did Jerusalem Become a Great City? The Rise of Jerusalem as Judah's Premier City in the Eighth–Seventh Centuries B.C.E.," *BASOR* 347 (2007): 21–56.

25. The size of Jerusalem's population during the monarchic period remains elusive despite scholars' efforts to resolve it. For the late 7th c., estimates range from 15,000 (Israel Finkelstein and Neil Asher Silberman, *The Bible Unearthed: Archaeology's New Vision of Ancient Israel and the Origin of Its Sacred Texts* [New York and London: Simon & Schuster, 2001], 3; King and Stager, *Life in Biblical Israel*, 219) to 24,000 (Broshi, "Expansion of Jerusalem," 23). While part of the difference stems from the density factor used in calculating the population, the other part derives from varying projections of how much of the area within the walls was in fact residential. Most important, there is a fourfold difference between applying the coefficient of 200 per hectare to the entire space of the city (e.g., 65 hectares for 7th-c. Jerusalem yields 13,000 inhabitants) or just to the postulated size of the residential quarter (25% of 65 hectares, or 16.25 hectares, at 200 per hectare, yields a total population of 3,250).

26. Israel Finkelstein, "The Archaeology of the Days of Manasseh," in *Scripture and Other Artifacts: Essays on the Bible and Archaeology in Honor of Philip J. King*, ed. Michael D. Coogan, J. Cheryl Exum, and Lawrence E. Stager (Louisville, KY: Westminster John Knox Press, 1994), 177.

The cities did not fare well with the conquest of the land by the imperial powers in the eighth and sixth centuries BCE. The Assyrians under first Shalmaneser V and then Sargon II[27] laid waste to Samaria in 722 BCE after a three-year siege. Either during this campaign or in the previous one under Tiglath-pileser III against the Syro-Ephraimite coalition in 734–732 BCE, several royal cities—Megiddo, Dan, Hazor, Gezer—also succumbed. The elites who dwelled in the urban centers, probably along with some inhabitants of villages and towns, were deported—27,290 in all, according to Sargon's Annals.[28] Some of the cities, including Samaria and Megiddo, were rebuilt by the Assyrians, who constructed more residential quarters than these cities had during the period of the northern kingdom.[29] Nearly one and a half centuries later, the invasion of Judah by the Babylonians under Nebuchadnezzar resulted in the devastation of the urban centers there as well. Jerusalem withstood an eighteen-month siege, but the Babylonian army eventually breached the walls and proceeded to destroy the city entirely—palace, temple, governmental buildings, residences, and fortifications—leaving the former capital uninhabited until the Persian period. Lachish was also reduced to ruins. Apparently only the royal family and the elites were exiled to Babylon, not many of the local population. The Babylonians developed Mizpah (Tell en-Naṣbeh), about 13 kilometers (8 mi.) northwest of Jerusalem, as their own provincial capital and administrative center for the entire period of their occupation of the land.

The overall demographic picture after the Babylonian invasion and until the beginning of the Persian period in 539 BCE shows a marked change in the settlement pattern of Judah. Altogether, the inhabited space, both cities and villages, decreased some 70 percent; in fact, in the area of Jerusalem and east toward the Dead Sea, as well as in the Shephelah, it reached a 90 percent reduction from the population size of the seventh century BCE.[30] In terms of raw numbers, it meant a decline in Judean population from about 110,000 at the end of the monarchy to 30,000–40,000 under the Babylonians. Most of the populace lived in villages, primarily in the tribal area of Benjamin and in the Judean hill country. For all practical purposes, urban culture ceased in Judah during the Babylonian period. During the following Persian period, from 539 to 331 BCE, some cities were rebuilt,

27. The relationship between these two rulers, including the question of which one was responsible for the conquest of Samaria, has long been disputed. See, e.g., the brief discussion and references in Ahlström, *History of Ancient Palestine*, 669–75.

28. *ANET* 284–85; *COS* 2.118D and 2.118E.

29. Ahlström, *History of Ancient Palestine*, 666–67.

30. Lipschits (*Fall and Rise of Jerusalem*, 206–71) presents the data region by region.

but their major increase in size occurred during the Hellenistic and Roman times, and again substantially more in the Byzantine period. Jerusalem was repopulated under the Persians, though with scarcely more than 3,000 inhabitants, and it did not become a city of much political or economic significance during that period.

One other power dynamic remains to be highlighted. Throughout the majority of ancient Israel's history, the country did not enjoy sovereignty but owed allegiance and tribute to one or the other imperial power—Neo-Assyria from 722 BCE to the late seventh century, Neo-Babylonia during 586–539 BCE, then Persia 539–331 BCE, the Hellenists 331–63 BCE, and finally the Romans. In each case the Palestinian region ranked as a provincial territory in a much larger empire, with the center of power situated in the imperial capital— Asshur or Nineveh under the Assyrians, Babylon under the Babylonians, Susa under the Persians, mainly Alexandria or Antioch under the Hellenists, and Rome under the Romans. These empires varied from each other in significant and substantial ways;[31] yet from the perspective of the residents of Palestine, the situation was one of vassalage to a distant power, subservience to the imperial representatives in their own land, loss of any autonomy they earlier had under what could itself be an oppressive homegrown monarchy, and an obligation to send tribute and other resources (including human, for the military and the labor gangs) to the emperor. The supreme authority of the emperor's law and court system was inescapable.

Residential Groups in the Cities

The above picture, based primarily on archaeological findings, offers a quite different image of urban populations than what we know from other times, including our own. The cities of ancient Israel were not teeming with masses of people—especially not the urban poor nor the middle class observable in many other urban contexts. Rather, with the two exceptions to be described shortly, cities in Israel served primarily as the place of residence and work for most of the elites and powerful figures in the country. The characterization of cities as "containers of power"[32] suits well the circumstances prevailing in ancient Israel.

The first exception, the only type of city not fitting this characterization or, rather, fitting it less so than the others, was the *residential city*, which

---

31. Recent descriptions of the history and governance of these various empires are available in Marc Van De Mieroop, *A History of the Ancient Near East, ca. 3000–323 BC*, 2nd ed. (Malden, MA, and Oxford, UK: Basil Blackwell Publishers, 2007); Briant, *From Cyrus to Alexander*; Grabbe, *Judaism from Cyrus to Hadrian*; and various essays in *CANE*.
32. Giddens, *The Constitution of Society*, 195.

served the interests of centralized power but was not inhabited mainly by the powerful and the elite. In these cities the population represented a wider range of professions and classes, including farmers, artisans, merchants, slaves, as well as retainers for those who possessed more wealth or power. In addition, perhaps, were some governmental functionaries—administrators, tax collectors, keepers of the storehouses, a posting of soldiers, and probably some priests. Here were the markets where villagers bartered or sold their produce, acquired goods and products, and found a context for social interaction beyond their own hamlets. The inhabitants of these towns also included their family members, young and old. The buildings and residences were not laid out by urban planners commissioned by the central monarchy; the haphazard assemblage of structures and open spaces points more to a gradual evolution as the towns grew to become local or regional hubs for commerce and storage. The monarchy thus found in them convenient bases for collecting taxes and managing the population of the surrounding villages.

The local administrative cities housed a concentration of governmental officials and their families, and probably few others. Here would have been offices for record keeping, particularly for taxes, crown-land holdings, construction projects, commercial dealings affecting the monarchy, and various correspondence. The governmental officials oversaw all of these functions, ensuring that the region served by the given city continued to deliver the taxes and manpower expected by the royal house. Laborers served specific needs, such as management of foods stored in the silos. They, just as others involved in construction of buildings, roads, and fortifications, most likely lived in outlying villages rather than within the city walls. Retainers, on the other hand, must have resided in the city, close to the officials and the wealthy whom they served. A noticeable military presence could also be expected in order to ensure regional compliance with state orders and also to give some immediate protection against raiders. While the officers may have lived within the city, the limited space there meant that the rank and file were bivouacked outside it.

In contrast to the makeup of the other two city types, the several royal cities and the two capital cities were inhabited by those at the head of or directly responsible for the four major types of institutions centered here: the palace, the temple, the governmental administration, and the military. We can speculate[33] that each of the four institutions had a cluster of homes

33. As noted by Israel Finkelstein in private correspondence with the author on 7 April 2008, at this time there is not enough archaeological evidence to be certain of the makeup of the residential groups in the cities. My inferences are drawn from the presence of the country's

where those occupied with them dwelled: courtiers, advisers, and clients near the palace; priests and other cultic functionaries and laborers near the temple; administrative staff near the governmental buildings; and officers near the military headquarters. The picture provided in 1 Kgs 4:1–19 of Solomon's administration, though quite certainly stylized in a later time, identifies the types of high officials that were needed in most administrations, all subsumed here under the king and each presumably over a distinct body of functionaries: high priest, chief scribes, recorder, head of the army, overseer (perhaps of the provincial governors), the "king's friend" (probably his closest counselor), superintendent of the palace, and supervisor of the forced labor. The twelve provincial governors then named presumably lived in administrative cities or royal cities in their respective districts, though they may well have had a residence in the capital as well. Another group of city dwellers included those who owned extensive property in the countryside and those who had become rich through trade and commerce. Also housed in these areas were the retainers and slaves who saw to the needs of the wealthy and powerful in each context. Family members lived in all of these households, though it is less likely than in villages that extended clan members could have been accommodated. These mighty cities, however, did not welcome those from the lower classes. In this sense, as mentioned previously, the urban contexts amounted to "gated communities" where only the select could reside, well protected and among their own.

We have already mentioned one of the two exceptions to the norm that cities were mainly occupied by the powerful and the elites: the residential cities, which were inhabited by a variety of classes and professions. The second exception was a variation of the capital-city type, caused by the historical circumstances of the Assyrian period. Jerusalem of the seventh century, which abruptly increased in size and population due to the conquest of the north and the west, had to absorb immigrants from those areas, probably the majority of them not of the upper class. Archaeological excavations have confirmed this urban expansion to the west and southwest, much of it outside the city walls. Yet even with this increase the capital, especially within its fortified area, continued to be the residence of the country's royal, commercial, and cultic elites.

This picture of the kinds and numbers of urban dwellers, derived from both inference and archaeological evidence, coincides remarkably well with the model of the agrarian society described above in chapter 3.

---

powerful institutions in the cities and the relatively circumscribed residential areas there due to the space needed for monumental structures and open areas.

According to this model, the royal house and the elites constitute together some 1–2 percent of the total population, while those who serve them and this political, economic system—the merchants, bureaucrats, functionaries, retainers, and priests—form another 5–10 percent of the population. If we estimate their combined size at 8–10 percent and if the total population of the eighth-century-BCE northern and southern kingdoms approximated 460,000,[34] then we would expect between 36,800 and 46,000 in these groups of the powerful and the privileged, most of whom resided in the cities. That range corresponds quite well with the combined population estimated for the three powerful types of urban centers—the two capital cities, the few royal cities, and the administrative cities. While they contained some governmental and commercial functionaries, the more-numerous residential cities were largely populated by agriculturalists and artisans not counted among the privileged groups. From their urban base, the upper class wielded power and influence effectively, whereas the vastly larger and poorer portions of the population were dispersed over the countryside, unable to exploit their greater numbers vis-à-vis the cities.

THE LAWS

In the previous chapter we sought to reconstruct some of the laws that plausibly functioned in the villages of ancient Israel, and there our primary obstacle was the absence of textual sources recording the laws and legal practices prevailing in hamlets around the country. When we now turn to identifying the laws of the ancient Israelite cities and states, our task is quite different though no less difficult, for the problem is not the paucity but the presence of writings purporting to represent centrally mandated laws. These legal texts in the Hebrew Bible do not present themselves explicitly as the legislation of cities and states, but rather as divinely ordained and humanly mediated proscriptions, principles, and punishments. Nonetheless, for more than a century modern scholars have, in effect, attributed them to urban or state activity, and quite rightly so. The task we now face, though, is to determine the intent and purpose of these biblical texts, as well as the plausibility of their actually having functioned as laws in living communities. At the same time, we need to consider whether other laws, not represented in the Pentateuch, should be expected in these settings.

To the extent that literacy existed in ancient Israel, it was present in urban contexts or under the control of urban powers. Not much more than

34. Broshi and I. Finkelstein, "Population," 53.

1 percent of the country's total population is likely to have been literate enough to read and write literary pieces. Those who possessed such skills were themselves not necessarily elite or royal. The wealthy and the powerful had the means to hire or enslave scribes and archivists to carry out any writing they needed. Not only the ability to write but also the means to store the texts—especially bulky clay tablets—was within the reach of the upper class, and archaeologists excavating in Southwest Asian sites have uncovered substantial libraries and archives in palaces, temples, and upper-class homes. Correspondence, contracts, and record keeping were the primary tasks required by the elites, while the king needed in addition to have royal archives, taxation records, and other administrative materials kept up to date. However, very few of these texts have survived in Israel, and we can only surmise that such materials in fact existed and simply were destroyed over time or have not yet been discovered. The Hebrew inscriptions still extant and stemming from the Iron II period and later are generally only short notations, often in fragmentary form.[35] There is nothing from the Iron II period of the northern and southern kingdoms to compare with the massive finds elsewhere in the ancient Near East—hundreds of thousands of tablets unearthed in Ebla, Sumer, Mari, Babylon, Nuzi, Nineveh, Nimrud, Sippar, Asshur, Ugarit, and elsewhere, as well as papyri and inscriptions from Egypt. The literary texts from those cultures—though not as plentiful as their economic records, administrative texts, and royal inscriptions—carry special significance since they retain classic myths, legends, wisdom materials, and songs. Whether any portions of what later became the Hebrew Bible were recorded and preserved in the Iron II kingdoms of Israel and Judah is notoriously difficult to ascertain. The biblical legal texts, as I have argued, did not originate until later, at any rate.

Identifying the Laws of the Cities and the States

The state was primarily interested in laws that secured its own powers, protection, and fiscal support. To the extent that it could prove useful in gaining the compliance of the wider populace, officials were also concerned with the ideological basis of the state's powers, not least through claiming its divine legitimacy and blessing. The legal systems in cities were consistent with the state's interests inasmuch as the urban dwellers saw their own self-interests guaranteed as long as the state remained sovereign and in control of the populace. At the same time, these powerful inhabitants of the

---

35. See most recently the collection by Dobbs-Allsopp, Roberts, Seow, and Whitaker, *Hebrew Inscriptions*.

cities could also be in conflict with each other over any number of claims, and a legal system was needed to keep the peace and resolve conflicts.

The following criteria can assist us in identifying or reconstructing laws in the urban and national contexts of ancient Israel. While there may well be some overlap or duplication with practices prevailing in various villages, especially with respect to legal conflicts at the social level, we are here particularly interested in conditions that vary noticeably from the village laws. The distinction between urban laws and state laws reflects the two legal systems originating in the cities: The *urban laws* regulate behavior and settle disputes primarily among the city residents but also for nonresidents who are temporarily in the cities. The *state laws*, normally issued by or in the interests of the king, govern behavior anywhere in the kingdom. In the following list, the first eleven have counterparts in the list of criteria for identifying village laws.[36]

1. Urban laws will rarely assume written form during the periods in which they are functioning as living law, except insofar as they are reflected in contracts and other legal documents. On the other hand, state laws, while quite minimal and general, may be written in the form of proclamations and administrative procedures.

2. The patriarchal structure prevails also within urban families, perhaps ameliorated somewhat by the increased status and wealth of the whole family, including the wife.

3. The composition of the nonroyal urban population is primarily determined not by kinship and clan ties or by long-standing family associations but rather by the power and prestige acquired and held by its inhabitants. Consequently, urban laws are less likely than village laws to seek to secure restitution and restoration for a wronged neighbor whose loss threatens their subsistence and participation in the community.

4. A variety of the conflicts seen in villages occur also in cities: issues involving marriage, family, sexuality, personal injury, and property loss or damage.

5. Urban laws reflect and reinforce the large-scale institutions based in cities, including the monarchy, the central priesthood, the governmental administration, and the military.

36. Above, chap. 5, Identifying Ancient Village Laws. Also see the appendix for a comparison with the criteria used in identifying village laws and cultic laws.

6. Though village laws are oriented toward life on the land, such as agriculture, pastoralism, and supporting functions, urban laws focus heavily on commercial and property issues. The scale of these economics is not merely local—as in the case of peasants, who at most own only their mud-brick dwelling and the small arable plot they have inherited—but extends well beyond the cities to encompass landholdings accumulated in the countryside, often from those same peasants, as well as merchant activity with others in the country or even with traders and suppliers in distant lands.

7. Urban and state laws are less responsive to the vulnerability of the lower classes than are village laws.

8. State laws, which may generally not be overly complex in an ancient agrarian kingdom, are oriented toward two ends: establishing and preserving the preeminent power of the monarch and securing the crown property and the ongoing revenue desired for the comforts of the royal house.

9. Taxation, military conscription, and labor conscription are determined by the state, effected by the bureaucracy, and enforced by the military.

10. State laws normally do not interfere with legal cases at the local levels unless there may be an impingement on state interests.

11. Much more so than is the case in villages, socioeconomic status and political position affect the legal rights and prerogatives of urban dwellers.

12. State laws will seek, where possible, to use legal as well as political means to contain the powers and influence of the nonroyal elites.

13. While absolute power lies in the hands of the monarch, it is potentially curbed by the interventions of the commercial, military, or priestly elites.

14. State laws prescribe hereditary royal succession and yet need to adjust to coups d'état when they prove successful.

15. State laws must yield to imperial laws during periods of colonization.

Similar to our analyses of village contexts, we are here engaging in historical reconstruction based on what we know and can surmise about the functioning of cities as power centers in ancient Israel. The texts of the Hebrew Bible provide us with scant evidence of the actual processes employed by the holders of power, and we lack the vast store of administrative, economic, and epistolary records that archaeologists have uncovered in other ancient Southwest Asian and Northeast African cultures. The limited, elite residential populations in the cities, their control of the much-larger rural populace from whom goods and services were extracted, their manipulation of persons granted certain privileges in exchange for assistance in this extraction (retainers, merchants, priests, military officers)—all such circumstances in a society with wide-ranging inequality meant that the laws and legal procedures issuing from these political and economic centers served not the general good but furthered the interests of those in power. The extent to which these legal traditions found their way into the biblical "laws" deserves close scrutiny.

Substantive Law in the Cities and the States

Employing these criteria and drawing on the distinction between substantive and procedural law used above for the village laws, we can propose the following legal principles at the urban and national levels, organized according to the general rubrics of social and economic affairs.

Social Life

Class. The principle of kinship as an organizing and defining social reality in village societies had as its counterpart in urban contexts in ancient Israel the structures of socioeconomic and political class. Kinship remained a relevant factor in cities inasmuch as family units could include relatives beyond the nuclear family. Related families, especially those whose wealth and status derived from their inheritance, may well have resided close to each other. Yet while such blood ties can account for certain social and legal behaviors, class seems to be more fundamental as a determinant of who inhabits the cities and who does not. As recognized above, the monarch and the elites, along with their families, comprised the core of the urban population. They were supplemented by retainers, bureaucrats, merchants, officers, priests, and slaves—all of whom found their right to urban residence arising from their roles of serving the wealthy and the powerful.

While class divisions, with the exception of the royal house, are less transparent in the Hebrew Bible, we see clearer evidence of them in other ancient Southwest Asian and Egyptian documents. The eighteenth-century-BCE Code of Hammurabi uses the term *awīlu* to refer to a free person of high standing, a "gentleman," while *muškēnu* designates a free person of subordinate standing, a "commoner" who has certain rights and privileges but not as significant as those of the *awīlu*. Yet lower was the slave (the male *wardu* and the female *amtu*). Quite probably the various artisans, laborers, and other professionals belonged to the *muškēnu* class, while those with specialized skills may have been directly in the employ of the palace or the temple and derived some standing from that association. The Middle Assyrian laws from the fourteenth to the eleventh centuries BCE focus on two classes, the free person (the male *a'īlu* and the female *sinniltu*) and the slave (male *urdu* and female *amtu*).[37] The Hittite laws, which date variously to the period from the seventeenth to the twelfth centuries BCE, reveal elements of social stratification in some of the fines assessed for violations: the fine for killing a free man can be twice that for killing a free woman, while the fine for killing a slave (whether male or female) is generally half of that for killing a free person.[38]

Another approach to the question of class, going beyond the terms used by the ancients to identify them, is to distinguish between primarily two economic and political sectors—the state sector and the communal/private sector.[39] Although this distinction is in a sense too simplistic and does not adequately indicate the intermingling and even interdependence of the two sectors, such as the model of the agrarian society provides,[40] it provides the basis for refracting the class structure in more detail. Each sector then has laborers, slaves, persons with varying degrees of rank and influence, a system of economic as well as social stratification, and some form of self-governance. Furthermore, substantial variation appears among different countries and during different time periods even within a given country, especially with respect to the relative strength of the state sector vis-à-vis the communal/private sector.[41] The point—obvious at one level, though

37. As Roth indicates (Martha T. Roth, with a contribution by Harry A. Hoffner Jr., *Law Collections from Mesopotamia and Asia Minor*, ed. Piotr Michalowski, 2nd ed., SBLWAW 6 [Atlanta: Society of Biblical Literature and Scholars Press, 1997], 192 n. 1), there is not, as some have argued, a third class identified as an "Assyrian man" or "Assyrian woman"; instead, the MAL texts using these terms are primarily addressing questions of the person's worth, not classifying the individual.

38. Harry A. Hoffner Jr., "Hittite Laws," in Roth, *Law Collections*, 215–16.

39. This distinction is proposed by Igor M. Diakonoff, "Socio-Economic Classes in Babylonia and the Babylonian Concept of Social Stratification," in *Gesellschaftsklassen im Alten Zweistromland und in den angrenzenden Gebieten—XVIII: Rencontre assyriologique internationale, München, 29. Juni bis 3. Juli 1970*, ed. D. O. Edzard (Munich: Verlag der Bayerischen Akademie der Wissenschaften, 1972), 41–52.

40. See discussions above, chap. 3, The Social Structure of Power in Ancient Israel.

41. Diakonoff, "Socio-Economic Classes," describes some of these differences in Agade, Ur III, Old Babylonia, and Old Assyria. In the same volume, also see discussions by Paul Garelli,

generally difficult to discern in detail because of the inadequate sources available to us—is that rank and standing exist as social characteristics and thus also as factors in the area of legal rights, protections, and liabilities.

Biblical laws also give indication of rank and standing—not always transparently or consistently, but in general along these lines: males over females, the monarch over others in the kingdom, certain priests over other cultic functionaries, the household head over others in the family, the eldest son over other siblings, free persons over slaves, Israelites over foreigners and resident aliens. Whether among those outside royal and priestly circles and outside the context of the family there also existed a noticeable distinction between various groups of "free" persons is harder to detect, yet it is reasonable to assume so, just as such social stratification existed in neighboring cultures. Actually, using the word "free" in the context of ancient cultures—at least in Southwest Asia, including of course Israel—may strike one as anomalous and anachronistic. It could simply denote anyone who is not a slave; the term חָפְשִׁי, *hopšî*, commonly translated as "free," occurs most frequently in biblical texts in opposition to "enslaved."[42] Nonetheless, sharp distinctions also existed among the "free" population, with unequal access to economic resources and privileges separating the wealthy and powerful few from the many commoners.[43] Numerous prophetic texts in the Hebrew Bible (e.g., Isa 10:2; Jer 22:16; Amos 5:11) attack the disparities under the monarchy that consigned citizens to a life of poverty and indebtedness. The cities, as noted above, constituted havens for the upper classes. They created for themselves the legal structures governing the nation, privileging themselves with legal protections and advantages to the detriment of the majority of the population.

"Problèmes de stratification sociale dans l'Empire assyrien," 73–79; Friedrich Cornelius, "Das Hethiterreich als Feudalstaat," 31–34; and Viktor Korošec, "Einige Beiträge zur gesellschaftlichen Struktur nach hethitischen Rechtsquellen," 105–11. For wide-ranging discussions of ancient Southwest Asian social systems, see *CANE* 1:273–648. Barry J. Kemp (*Ancient Egypt: Anatomy of a Civilization*, 2nd ed. [London and New York: Routledge, 2006]) provides a detailed description of classes and power structures in ancient Egypt.

42. E.g., Exod 21:2, 5; Deut 15:12–13. A distinctive use of the term is found in 1 Sam 17:25, where the reward expected from the king for someone who can manage to slay Goliath and remove the threat to Israel is that the king will declare that person's household "free," apparently meaning released from taxes and other obligations to the throne.

43. While attention has often been paid to the poor in biblical studies, socioeconomic class has generally escaped scrutiny, as indicated by Gottwald, "Social Class as an Analytic and Hermeneutical Category." Several recent studies have sought to reverse this trend: Green, "Class Differentiation and Power(lessness)"; Jamieson-Drake, *Scribes and Schools*; Rainer Kessler, *The Social History of Ancient Israel: An Introduction*, trans. Linda M. Maloney (Minneapolis: Fortress Press, 2008; German original, 2006), 103–17; Gershon Galil, *The Lower Stratum Families in the New-Assyrian Period*, CHANE 27 (Leiden and Boston: E. J. Brill, 2007); and, earlier, Edzard, *Gesellschaftsklassen im Alten Zweistromland*.

Marriage. Marriage and family law in the cities approximated their counterparts in the villages, though with some significant differences in light
of the social makeup of these two basic kinds of settlements. Of the four
collections of biblical laws, the Deuteronomic laws, commonly associated
with urban living and the monarchic period, include significantly more
regulations on marriage than do the other legal collections, which are usually attributed to the villages or the cult. The reason lies less in the relative
importance of the institution of marriage in these different settings, and
more in the heightened need to regulate affairs among those who have
substantial power and wealth at stake.

   Endogamy among related families probably prevailed as the ideal
among all population groups in the country, but in all likelihood marriage
into unrelated families also proved appealing to those for whom commercial or political alliances offered advantages outweighing the benefits accru-
ing from marriage according to strict blood ties. With regard to the political
realm, the Hebrew Bible frequently tells us about marriage between royal
houses of the region: David's wife Maacah, daughter of the king of Geshur
(2 Sam 3:3); Solomon's wife, daughter of the Egyptian pharaoh (1 Kgs
3:1), as well as seven hundred[44] other princesses taken into his harem
from various neighboring kingdoms (11:3); the Edomite king Hadad's
wife, sister-in-law of the Egyptian pharaoh (11:19); and King Ahab's wife,
Jezebel, daughter of King Ethbaal of Sidon (16:31). We even read in Ps
45:9–10 (45:10–11 MT), often considered to be a song for a royal wedding,
a statement to the king that "daughters of kings are among your precious
women," while his new bride is told to "forget your people and your
father's house." Diplomatic or interdynastic marriages often appear in the
records of other cultures from the third to the first millennia BCE in Egypt,
in the Levant, and throughout Mesopotamia.[45] What was strategic for the
kings was also useful for the elites of Israel, whose interests lay more in
the realm of financial and aristocratic relations.[46] Marriage between two
wealthy families could lead to a merger of their holdings if the daughter/
bride, having no male sibling or other plausible person to inherit from

   44. Such an inflated number, using the symbolism of completeness represented by the
numeral "seven," glorifies the power and influence of this legendary king.
   45. See, e.g., Westbrook, *History*, 232–33, 250, 768, 746–47, 785. For an example of the
detailed process involved in suing for a bride when international relations are at stake,
see Jack M. Sasson, "The Servant's Tale: How Rebekah Found a Spouse," *JNES* 65 (2006):
241–65.
   46. "Distinguished families the world over make it their honor to admit only their peers
for courting their daughters while the sons are left to their devices in satisfying their sexual
needs." Max Weber, *The Religion of India: The Sociology of Hinduism and Buddhism* (Glencoe,
IL: Free Press, 1958), 125–26 (cited by Kautsky, *Politics*, 207).

her father, brought her family's estate into the marriage. Even without the inheritance at stake in this manner, though, a marital alliance led to closer connections between the two families, favorable to each party though also susceptible to exploitation by the stronger of the two.

In light of the wealth and power typical of urban inhabitants, especially during the Iron II period, it is likely that *polygyny* and *concubinage* were practiced to a greater extent by them than villagers could have afforded. Not coincidentally, the men in biblical narratives who are depicted as having more than one wife are all among the wealthy or distinguished personages in tradition: Abraham, Jacob, Esau, Gideon, Elkanah (father of Samuel), David, Solomon, and others including most if not all of the kings. Such practices of the past legitimated similar customs of the present; or rather, prevailing interests in the later cities and states were justified by writing them into the descriptions of the past. Concomitantly, the general *patriarchal* structure of society prevailed in the organized urban and state cultures as well, in one sense more sharply so than in the countryside, where a subsistence economy required the villagers to maximize labor productiveness by drawing as much as possible on the contributions from both genders. Yet even with this patriarchal undergirding of urban marriage practices, women of wealth, power, and class enjoyed more options, leisure, and luxuries than did their counterparts in the rural regions.

To ensure the terms of the marriage, a *marriage contract* of some sort needed to be negotiated between the parties—not just between the bride and groom but also, even especially, between their families. Marital contracts, which carried binding legal weight, are well attested in various cultures of ancient Southwest Asia.[47] In many cases the couple's relationship seems less important than the question of property, which can affect both the inheritance and the question of ownership of the dowry and brideprice. The Hittite laws, for example, display some of the legal nuances, though not all societies followed these same principles. In a brief series of laws (HL 26–30) we can discern some of the elements of the process of marriage. A woman's parents make the first promissory commitment to the groom-to-be, who gives some unspecified amount or commodity to the parents. If the woman then should run off with another man, that man is to compensate the would-be groom for his gift to the parents. If, though, the parents give the daughter in marriage to another party, the parents are to compensate the first man for what he had bestowed on them. If, however, the agreement has gone beyond a promise to constitute a betrothal, with

47. See Westbrook, *History*, passim.

the fiancé paying the parents a bride-price, but the parents subsequently renege on the contract, then the parents are to compensate the fiancé double the amount of the bride-price. On the other hand, if the fiancé refuses to marry the daughter, he forfeits his bride-price.

Provisions such as these are entirely plausible in most Israelite contexts; the distinctive features in cities are that larger sums and more extensive property can be at stake, and written contracts rather than merely oral agreements emerged to guarantee the terms. The best examples from the early Jewish context stem from Persian-period Elephantine, the Jewish colony located in Upper Egypt, near modern-day Aswan.[48] These marriage contracts, called "documents of wifehood," typically include stipulations about the bride-price (מֹהַר, mōhar), the dowry (שִׁלּוּחִים, šillûḥîm), divorce, and protections for the bride regarding any additional wives the man might take. Although ancient Israel apparently possessed no centrally issued marital laws, contracts such as these carried legal weight and could be invoked for determining penalties or compensation if either party violated their terms. Probably a local gathering of household heads who were peers according to class enforced these agreements, but in special instances they could be adjudicated directly by the king or his judges.

The economic contexts of city life in ancient Israel appear most clearly in regard to *divorce*, and we can see in the stipulations the varying interests at play, interests of each married partner as well as of their respective families of origin. The many Akkadian and Assyrian laws that seek to ensure some security for the divorced or widowed woman suggest that they were especially vulnerable without it. As a basic principle, the woman deserves to receive back her dowry, or an amount equal to it, unless she was particularly at fault in the divorce, as through engaging in an extramarital affair. The Laws of Hammurabi record several variables that could render the divorced wife of an upper-class man at economic risk: if she is divorced with children yet to be raised or then again after she has raised them (HL 137); if she is a man's first-ranking wife and is divorced with no children (HL 138); if the dowry is absent, whether spent or nonexistent from the outset (HL 139); if the wife contracts a disease (perhaps a contagious skin disease;[49] HL 148–149). Apparently it was common practice for the hus-

---

48. For texts and discussions, see B. Porten, *The Elephantine Papyri in English: Three Millennia of Cross-Cultural Continuity and Change* (Leiden and New York: E. J. Brill, 1996); and Bezalel Porten and Ada Yardeni, *Textbook of Aramaic Documents from Ancient Egypt, Newly Copied, Edited, and Translated into Hebrew and English*, 4 vols. (Jerusalem: Academon Press, 1986–99).

49. Roth, *Law Collections*, 141 n. 25, with reference for further discussion.

band to have usufruct over his wife's dowry, being able to invest it and reap the profit from it; but if they divorced, he was obliged to return the dowry or its equivalence to his wife.[50] If the dowry included any parcels of land, those would also revert to her or to her parental family. A Middle Assyrian law (A 37), however, distinguishes between whether the husband or the wife initiates the divorce; in the former case the husband is to give the wife something, but not so if she initiates the divorce. Whatever the terms, marriage contracts, especially when written, were legally binding, and failure to fulfill their terms constituted grounds for judicial action. Even if a written tablet or document could not be presented, it probably sufficed to call witnesses who could attest to its stipulations.

Although the Hebrew Bible does not preserve any marriage contracts as such, the Deuteronomic laws do refer to a "writ of divorce" (ספר כריתת, sēper kĕrîtut) which a husband delivers to the wife he is divorcing (Deut 24:1). The context of this passage is the issue of remarriage after divorce, which is permitted except that the woman is forbidden then to remarry her first husband if in the interim she has married and divorced (or survived) a second man.[51] This same text alludes to a vague reason available to a man to divorce a woman: if he finds "something objectionable" (ערות דבר, 'erwat dābār, literally, "nakedness of a thing") about her.[52] Whatever the stimulus for the divorce, biblical laws give only the husband the right to initiate it, although he is not allowed to do so if he has wrongly claimed that she was not a virgin at their marriage (22:13–19) or if he was required to marry her because he had seduced her while she was a virgin and not engaged (22:28–29). Probably customary law in the cities provided more latitude to both the husband and wife who sought a divorce as a means of terminating a marriage. With considerable property and holdings potentially at stake for urban dwellers, issues of inheritance, multiple wives, and social mobility could play decisive roles in marriages. Furthermore, women who had their own means as a result of their inheritance or their parents'

50. Several examples from Babylonian sources give evidence of this practice, as do talmudic texts as well. There are also cases, especially at Elephantine, specifying that the married woman retains the rights to sell her dowry property or dispose of it as she will. See Baruch A. Levine, "mulūgu/melûg: The Origins of a Talmudic Legal Institution," JAOS 88 (1968): 271–85.

51. Jer 3:1 refers to this same situation, using it to indict unfaithful Israel.

52. The phrase probably does not refer to adultery, for which a stronger penalty than a legitimate divorce was expected—either execution or a divorce with shame and loss of dowry and bride-price. Yet having excluded adultery, we are still left to speculate regarding the meaning of 'erwat dābār. Jewish law in the Talmud and the commentaries explored the terms of divorce in considerable detail, adding much more specificity than can be found in the Hebrew Bible but probably not far removed from the range of customary laws in Israel.

position had more chance to initiate a divorce than could the poorer women in the villages.

Reproduction. In all likelihood the legal norms regarding reproductive practices in the cities did not vary much from those prevalent in the villages of ancient Israel, although the circumstances and aims could have differed. While the villagers' needs were heavily affected by their labor demands in a subsistence agrarian context, the urban dwellers tended to be oriented more toward the preservation and continuation of their status and holdings. This principle appears in various forms for the distinct urban groups: For royals, new offspring were essential to maintain a dynastic line and to populate the court with other leaders and advisers loyal to the king. The elites expected their next generation to maintain if not enhance the status quo, to learn to manage the family's affairs and holdings and not jeopardize them, and to acquire the necessary skills for dealing with royalty, elite peers, subordinates, and the agrarian masses. The nonelite privileged class (retainers, merchants, priests, military officers, bureaucrats) had need of progeny toward comparable ends, assuming that they had the approbation of the royals and the elites.

Contraception may not have been appreciably different in practice or in law in the cities of ancient Israel than it was in the village culture. While those living on the land had the most direct familiarity with plants, herbs, and other natural products of potential contraceptive use, this knowledge certainly filtered into the urban community as well. If an upper-class woman of the city desired to prevent conception, she possessed the means and connections to discover what was available, and then to obtain it. There are no known laws or contractual proscriptions from ancient Southwest Asia or Egypt against the practice of contraception. The absence of even the slightest narrative reference to contraception in the Hebrew Bible suggests either that it was not practiced or that it was not much of an issue. We hear nothing similar to the ideal among aristocratic Romans in antiquity for smaller families, often no more than three children; Augustus and other emperors sought to reverse this trend through legislation and exhortation.[53] While we find nothing explicit in the Hebrew Bible along these lines, we may wonder whether the glorification of large families[54] and the remorse, even

53. On Roman practices of contraception, see Keith Hopkins, "Contraception in the Roman Empire," *Comparative Studies in Society and History* 8 (1965): 124–51; and Pierre Salmon, *La limitation des naissances dans la société romaine*, Collection Latomus 250 (Brussels: Latomus Revue d'études latines, 1999), 27–50.

54. Best exhibited in the ancestral legend of Jacob, his two wives, and their two slave women, with twelve sons and an unknown number of daughters (Gen 46:7) altogether; or Job and his wife, with seven sons and three daughters—twice.

shame, over female "barrenness"[55] express a male point of view—a desire for numerous offspring, especially boys. Quite plausibly an upper-class wife had other preferences than to become repeatedly pregnant and face the accompanying health dangers as well as the high likelihood of infant mortality. While this speculation reflects a modern perspective, we can note that queens in ancient Southwest Asia often possessed considerable power and influence apart from their role as mothers, and there is good reason to suspect the same of other women of wealth and prestige. Furthermore, the near impossibility of policing laws against contraception must have been evident to men as well as to women. As long as there was at least one male heir in the royal household and in each wealthy family, the crucial issues of succession and inheritance were resolved. Large families among the upper class did not function to increase production in the same way as they did in the villages.

The situation regarding *abortion* may have been quite different, even though it is very rarely addressed in available texts from the region. A Middle Assyrian law (MAL A53) is most specific and most brutal:

> If a woman aborts her fetus by her own action and they then prove the charges against her and find her guilty, they shall impale her, they shall not bury her. If she dies as a result of aborting her fetus, they shall impale her, they shall not bury her. If any persons should hide that woman because she aborted her fetus [. . .][56]

The woman in question here is referred to in Akkadian as a *sinniltu*, one of either the free or inferior class.[57] The nature of the punishment, which in its severity is not unusual among other Middle Assyrian laws, suggests that she has committed a high crime, probably against her husband but perhaps even against the community since no option is given for the husband to reduce the sentence if he should so wish. No direct counterpart to this law appears in other Southwest Asian collections, including the Hebrew Bible. The closest biblical example to an abortion—though it is notably not willed by the woman herself—may be Num 5:11–31, another harsh text. In this case a jealous husband suspects his wife of infidelity and brings the charge against her, as a result of which a priest gives her a potion to drink. If she is guilty, it will make "her womb discharge and her uterus drop," perhaps a euphemism for an abortion and a collapsed or prolapsed uterus. The presence in the text of both a priest and a cultic setting makes an urban context

55. Again, both Leah and Rachel, as well as Sarah.
56. Roth, *Law Collections*, 174.
57. *CAD*, s.v. *sinništu*.

likely. While the legal problem involves a charge or suspicion of infidelity and perhaps a question of paternity, the penalty has severe consequences for the woman's reproductive health, including perhaps the abortion of a fetus as well as permanent damage to her uterus.

Infanticide, practiced in some societies (such as Greco-Roman) to control family size and perhaps responsible there for some 10 percent of the overall death rate,[58] is difficult but not impossible to imagine for ancient Israel.[59] The exposure of unwanted infants, especially baby girls or infants with severe birth defects, strikes us in the modern world as an unthinkable, abhorrent act. Yet even if the Israelites abstained from exposing infants at birth, *child sacrifice* is not foreign to the Hebrew Bible. Abraham was willing to kill his son Isaac as a religious act (Gen 22); some scholars have regarded this story as an etiology for the prohibition of the practice. Sacrificing children in the worship of the god Molech is explicitly forbidden in Lev 20:2–5,[60] although 2 Kgs 23:10 and Jer 32:35 indicate that it was at times practiced under the monarchy. Other texts refer to cannibalism of children during a period of siege and starvation.[61] The enigmatic text of Ezek 20:25–26 ("I gave them statutes that were not good and laws by which they could not live") seems to use child sacrifice to deconstruct the legal tradition and horrify the people if they followed it: while the Israelites were directed to "give" (נתן, *nātan*) their firstborn sons to YHWH (Exod 22:29b [22:28b MT]), they would be committing an abhorrent act if they interpreted it as a command to sacrifice rather than to dedicate their firstborn sons. All such examples of killing one's own children are not necessary outgrowths of urban living, but they have been attested enough in human history for us to realize that they could have appeared in a culture such as ancient Israel as well.

Sexual Relations, Offenses, and Illicit Sexual Behavior. It is impossible to reconstruct with much certainty the sexual mores of the ancient Israelites, let alone their legal norms and conflicts. At one level we can speculate on the basis of the laws presented in the Hebrew Bible, as we have done in other cases: if there is a prohibition of some act or a description of some conflict needing resolution, we can generally assume that in fact that type of act or conflict occurred or threatened to occur in ancient Israel. At the same time, though, we must also keep in mind the ideological character of

58. Lelis, Percy, and Verstraete, *Age of Marriage*, 26.
59. See above, chap.5, Children and the Elderly.
60. See also Deut 12:31 and 18:10a, without explicit mention of Molech.
61. Deut 28:53–57; 2 Kings 6:26–29; Jer 19:9; Lam 4:10.

these written proscriptions, for special interests may lie behind them and render them different from what they purport to regulate.

The ordering of sexual behavior demanded as much attention in cities as in villages. However, several differences distinguished the two contexts from each other, and it would be intriguing to know which of them left the greater mark on the biblical laws. The hamlets reflect a social context characterized by generally close, interdependent, clan-oriented relations; but more social diversity and hence more chance for sexual expression and potential conflict existed in urban society. As indicated above, several social constellations persisted in the Israelite cities: the royal house, the moneyed elite with their commercial interests, the priestly establishment, the bureaucracy charged with administering affairs in the kingdom, often the military contingent represented especially by its high-ranking officers, and the retainer and slave class attendant on each of these groups. Such a range of personnel, in most cases with spouses and family housed within the city walls or in nearby residential communities, presents a much more volatile complex of interaction and temptation than we might at first think. Though we cannot determine it with certainty, a desire for public propriety may also have played a greater role in determining norms in the cities than in the countryside in order to preserve boundaries important in urban society.

As was observed in our previous discussion of village laws, *adultery* constituted a legal offense limited only to cases in which a married or engaged woman had a sexual affair with a man other than her husband or fiancé, and the judicial consequences could be severe. It bore tremendous weight, so much so that it was termed "the great sin" in ancient Egyptian and Ugaritic sources, as well as in Gen 20:9 (חַטָּאָה גְדֹלָה, *ḥăṭā'â gĕdōlâ*).[62] Of the few dozen Neo-Babylonian (late-7th and 6th c. BCE) marriage contracts that have come to light, several include a curious stipulation of this order: "Should [wife's name] be found with another man, she will die by the iron dagger."[63]

62. The same phrase "great sin" occurs elsewhere in the Hebrew Bible (in Exod 32:21, 30–31; 2 Kgs 17:21) to refer to idolatry or religious disobedience, often depicted metaphorically as adultery. For Egyptian and Ugaritic occurrences of this phrase for adultery, see Jacob J. Rabinowitz, "The 'Great Sin' in Ancient Egyptian Marriage Contracts," *JNES* 18 (1959): 73; and William L. Moran, "The Scandal of the 'Great Sin' at Ugarit," *JNES* 18 (1959): 280–81.

63. Martha T. Roth, "'She Will Die by the Iron Dagger': Adultery and Neo-Babylonian Marriage," *JESHO* 31 (1988): 186–206; the text quoted here is BM 65149; idem, *Babylonian Marriage Agreements, 7th–3rd Centuries B.C.*, AOAT 222 (Kevelaer: Butzon & Bercker; Neukirchen-Vluyn: Neukirchener Verlag, 1989), 15 and passim; and Cornelia Wunsch, *Urkunden zum Ehe-, Vermögens- und Erbrecht aus verschiedenen neubabylonischen Archiven*, Babylonische Archive 2 (Dresden: ISLET, 2003), 3–15. According to Roth ("'She Will Die by the Iron Dagger,'" 189 n. 10), there are no extant cuneiform marriage contracts containing an adultery clause other than these from the Neo-Babylonian period.

It is curious because one might not expect such an offense and capital punishment to be named in a brief marital contract. As has been noted,[64] however, the explanation may derive from the juxtaposition of this clause with
another directed at the groom—not a description of a capital offense but a
strict obligation for him to pay his wife a substantial sum and give her freedom if he should ever take a second wife. The patriarchal structure is still in
place, but it appears that, at least in these contracts and probably much more
broadly as well, both requirements are ingredients for marriage: the wife's
fidelity and the husband's support of her (not only during marriage but also
if she leaves him because he has married another woman). Too many questions are left open,[65] though, for us to know the precise legal significance of
the iron-dagger clause, other than its basic bias against the wife.

Males and females in ancient Israel were treated according to different
standards and expectations; there can be little doubt about this situation,
which has been addressed in innumerable studies by scholars over the last
several decades. The man had considerably wider freedom in choosing
sexual partners than did the woman, who was limited by custom and law
to only her husband. Strictures against the man came only in cases of rape,
sexual contact with an unmarried virgin (who was the charge, if not the
property, of her father or, if deceased, of her brother or another close male
relative), or sexual contact with a married woman (who was the charge or
property of her husband). Only in these instances did a legal consequence
result from his philandering. Several of the biblical laws in Deuteronomy
depict such circumstances, all of them conceivable in Israel's cities.

The context of city versus countryside is explicitly named as a crucial
factor in the case of an *engaged* young woman (identified as a virgin) and
a man (presumably not her fiancé): if their sexual act occurs in the countryside (literally, in an open field), then only the man is executed while the
woman is not punished; but if it happens in the city, then both are to be
stoned to death on the rationale that the woman could have cried for help
and been heard in the city, though not in the country (Deut 22:23–27). She
could have been threatened in the city and not been able to cry out, but
that consideration is not an ameliorating factor in the case.

If the young woman (again identified as a virgin) is *not engaged*, then

64. Roth, "'She Will Die by the Iron Dagger,'" 205.
65. Note Roth's enumeration of the complicated issues (*Babylonian Marriage Agreements*,
15): "Who must discover the adulterous couple? Is the wife's death demanded, or a permis-
sible option? How is the wife executed? Who performs the execution? What would be the
disposition of her dowry? Were the bride's agents, in agreeing to the inclusion of this clause,
abrogating their right to protect her person after her marriage? And did the adultery clause
establish a consequence of adultery for certain brides that was not applicable for all brides?"

the man who has had intercourse with her is obliged to pay her father fifty shekels (presumably in place of the bride-price), marry her, and never divorce her (22:28–29). A payment of this amount of shekels suggests a context of relatively prosperous families, as would be found in the cities.

If a *married* woman and another man are caught *flagrante delicto,* then both suffer capital punishment (22:22). If a husband either *charges* (Deut 22:13–21) or *suspects* (Num 5:11–31) his wife of infidelity, a procedure is outlined for disproving or testing the charge—if not conclusively to our tastes, nonetheless probably sufficient in that legal environment.

In the first two cases mentioned above, the means of discovery (by admission? by charge of rape? by third-party report? by later pregnancy?) remain unstated and are, at any rate, secondary in importance to the clear prohibition of violating the marital agreement. Capital punishment for adultery, which pertains to the first, third, and fourth of these cases, occurs frequently though not uniformly in other Southwest Asian law collections,[66] and often it is the husband who decides the extent of the penalty. The economic dimension of adultery appears not merely in the social subservience of the wife to the husband but also in the issues of paternity and inheritance: the husband may want assurance that he fathered the child or children who will inherit his estate.

While the recorded laws in the Hebrew Bible and ancient Southwest Asia seem impersonal and general—as would only be expected of stipulations intended to apply to many cases that might arise—we must remember that real people produced and applied them—if they were in fact ever applied. For the laws dealing with marriage, divorce, and sexual relations involving persons not married to each other, the circumstances in the cities were decidedly different from those in the rural villages. In urban contexts the social facts (Durkheim's "faits sociaux") of class and status, professional specialization, and state interests dominated the scene. Consequently none of these laws can be regarded as merely "private,"[67] even though individual persons were very much involved, often outside public view. Thus if a man's wife had an affair with another man, it certainly affected them as individuals and may have been resolved away from public oversight, but the very definition of the circumstance and its resolution involved social mores and expectations. Such is the nature of customary law: often community arbiters—elders, judges, and the public as executioners—will be called into the case. Thus these issues of marital and sexual relations,

66. See Roth, "'She Will Die by the Iron Dagger,'" 191–92, for an overview.
67. *Pace* Roth, ibid., 204.

touching on some of the most private matters of human behavior, are to be handled according to acceptable or even prescribed norms of that urban society, differing as they may from the norms of rural society.

Actions crossing class lines presumably demanded special attention in the cities. If, for example, the son of a wealthy merchant family should want to marry a woman from the bureaucrats' neighborhood, his parents might object on the grounds that his family would have little to gain, even if their bride-price paid to the bride's parents was lower than that due a family of their own class. But if that same family had a daughter who was enamored with the son of a lower-class family, her parents probably objected because the union had little chance of increasing their own or their daughter's standing. Of course, the perspectives of the lower-class family were quite the reverse. Consequently the parents of the upper-class family must have acted, through a negotiated marriage, to better their standing as much as possible, whether their marrying child was male or female. Hence also the need for written marriage contracts that spelled out the terms of exchange of bride-price and dowry and the consequences in the event of divorce. The parents of the marrying couple had an interest also in the terms of divorce, if that should happen, since the elder generation's estate could hinge on whether the divorce of their son or daughter led to payment or receipt of substantial sums—notably of the inheritance, if their son was involved. Even the circumstances of adultery—whether the parents' child was the husband or the wife—bore heavily on the parents' standing; the social effect of shame in an upper-class context impacts the family's prestige and influence.

All of these issues were heightened if the royal family was involved. In such cases the interests of the monarchy were zealously defended, and those persons of lesser standing, even if wealthy, confronted an institution of duration and power. Priestly families, for their part, had to rely on the subtle and often-effective influence of religious authority, which generally competed with the economic and political powers in the city and state. In a word, the various laws depicted in the biblical texts about marriage, family, divorce, and sexuality may well have had some anchoring in reality, but the status and power of the individuals in a given situation determined the terms and the outcomes. Legal norms gave a greater level of both protection and latitude to those of higher social standing, and any conflicts ensuing from proscribed behavior such as adultery were generally resolved in favor of status. In this arena of behavior as well as in others, the Hebrew Bible advocates justice due to the weak, but in its repetition this very theme reveals that those with less power all too frequently did not receive the fair treatment that the text purports to promote.

The laws pertaining to *incest* in the cities were not much different from the prohibitions common in the villages.[68] In both contexts, close proximity to other relatives, resulting from the living patterns of extended and compound families, meant that sexual encounters between two closely related persons could easily occur. Incest may have been less frequent in the cities since, unlike the situation in villages, families did not tend to live within larger kinship groups as was the case in villages. Thus of the sexual liaisons identified in Lev 18 and 20, the ones most likely in urban contexts were those within the nuclear or extended family—between parent and child, parent and an in-law, sibling and sibling, uncle or aunt and a child. A case involving a man and his kinsman's wife (Lev 18:20) would have been forbidden but less likely to occur if they did not live in the same city. On the other hand, the types of acts in Lev 18:17–18; 20:14 in which a man has a sexual encounter with multiple related parties (e.g., with a woman and her daughter, with a woman and her granddaughter, with two sisters, with a woman and her mother) seems more plausible in cities than in villages because of the larger, more socially complex urban environment. One other intriguing detail is that several of the sexual connections explicitly forbidden in Lev 18 and 20 are treated as legitimate in the lore about the people's early history: marriage between a brother and a half sister—Abraham and Sarah (Gen 20:12) and potentially Amnon and Tamar (2 Sam 13:1, 13), but prohibited in Lev 18:11 and 20:17; marriage between a man and two sisters—Jacob with Leah and Rachel (Gen 29), but proscribed in Lev 18:18; marriage between a man and his paternal aunt—the parents of Aaron and Moses (as well as Miriam, according to LXX and the Samaritan Pentateuch) (Exod 6:20; Num 26:59), but barred in Lev 18:12 and 20:19. So some of the incest boundaries in Lev 18 and 20 may differ from actual practices of the period; or stated otherwise, the incest laws actually applied in ancient Israel may not be preserved in the book of Leviticus.

The extent to which *homosexuality* was practiced or prohibited in Israel is also extremely difficult to measure. Only two biblical laws seem to refer to it, using the odd phrasing "with a male you shall not lie the lying down of a woman; it is an abomination" (Lev 18:22; similarly in 20:13).[69] Two other biblical narratives—Lot and his two guests at Sodom (Gen 19:1–11) and the Levite and his concubine at Gibeah (Judg 19:22–30)—allude to

68. For a detailed discussion of incest laws in light of Lev 18 and 20, see chap. 5, Sexual Relations, Offenses, and Illicit Sexual Behavior.

69. For a detailed discussion of this formulation, see Saul M. Olyan, "'And with a Male You Shall Not Lie the Lying Down of a Woman': On the Meaning and Significance of Leviticus 18:22 and 20:13," *Journal of the History of Sexuality* 5 (1994): 179–206.

homosexual rape. Both cases, which are pointedly set in cities, are also complicated with three other narrative issues: a potential homosexual gang rape; a potential (Sodom) or actual (Gibeah) gang rape of a female substitute for the males; and violation of hospitality customs. A Middle Assyrian law (MAL A 20) also seems to be dealing with homosexual rape, and the guilty party in this case is to be punished according to principles of retaliation—by sodomizing and then castrating him. The question of consensual homosexuality between two persons is thus not present in most of these texts, although it may be intended in the two Leviticus laws. The word תועבה, *tôʿēbâ* ("abomination"), suggests a religious tone for these two laws, a priestly effort to control social practices. It remains an open question whether such injunctions had a significant effect on the behavior of the people, especially of the powerful upper class, among whom a wide variety of activities could have been condoned and not regulated.

Bestiality was less likely, though not impossible, in the cities. Obviously the number and variety of animals were significantly lower in the urban environment than was the case in the villages,[70] but availability in itself did not pose an obstacle. The "feeder" villages located not far from the cities engaged generally in livestock production as well as agriculture. In addition, a city could even specialize in animal husbandry and training, such as Iron II Megiddo with its substantial trade in horses.[71] The Hittite laws (16th c. BCE) explicitly name several of the animals with which humans are not permitted to have sexual relations: cows, sheep, pigs, dogs, horses, or mules (HL 187, 188, 199, 200a). In all cases except for the final two, capital punishment is prescribed for any violation. The reason for excepting horses and mules, apparently, was that the others were sacrificial animals, which meant that approaching them sexually counted as a religious offense.[72] The biblical laws forbidding bestiality (Exod 22:19 [22:18 MT]; Lev 18:23; 20:15–16; also Deut 27:21) do not identify species of animals, and the punishment in all cases is death—not just for the man or woman involved but also for the animal (so Lev 20:15–16). Consequently, the offense may have been less related to sacrifice and more to the prohibition against mixing types[73] or to the close association of human sexuality with procreation. At any rate, it is difficult to imagine bestiality arising frequently as a legal conflict between two parties in the city, so any strictures against it must have been based primarily in a notion of illicit sexual behavior, especially

---

70. See above chap. 5, for discussion of the situation in villages.
71. Cantrell and I. Finkelstein, "A Kingdom for a Horse."
72. Richard Haase, "The Hittite Kingdom," in Westbrook, *History*, 1:648–49.
73. See below, chap. 7, Mandating Behavior.

from the religious point of view. It is even possible that the biblical laws in Exodus and Leviticus represent mainly a projection of urbanites who imagined a practice occurring in the rural areas and wanted to limit it.

Prostitution, on the other hand, was primarily an urban phenomenon, and it is doubtful that there were any laws prohibiting or restricting it. Even biblical laws stop short of outright prohibiting prostitution as such, although it seems to be viewed negatively in several instances: a father should not turn his daughter into a prostitute (Lev 19:29)—although no punishment is provided, perhaps because such cases occurred mainly among families under financial distress; cultic prostitution is condemned for Israelites (e.g., Deut 23:17 [23:18 MT]), although not necessarily for foreigners living in Israel, who could thus be sexual partners with Israelites; and there are certain limitations for priests, their wives, and their daughters (Lev 21:7, 9, 14).[74] In an especially dramatic commentary from the nonlegal sphere, the prophets often use prostitution metaphorically to describe religious apostasy (e.g., Hos 1–3; Jer 3:1–13; Ezek 16 and 23). However, several legendary accounts about the people's early history exhibit a level of tolerance that probably existed among the people: Tamar and Judah (Gen 38), Rahab at Jericho (Josh 2), Samson and the prostitute in Gaza (Judg 16:1–3). The cities, with their larger populations and greater wealth, served as the natural context for prostitutes to live and work. Rahab, who becomes the protector of Joshua's spies and is ultimately spared along with her family, lives in Jericho's city wall (probably a casemate wall containing rooms for dwelling or storage). Metaphorically, Ezekiel depicts a prostitute as "building [her] platform at the head of every street and making a mound in every square" for her debauchery, for which she does not even take pay (16:30–34). However it may have been regarded by some in the society, it is likely that prostitutes lived and worked in the cities without jeopardy from the legal establishment.

Other ancient Southwest Asian cultures practiced similar leniency with regard to prostitution; one Middle Assyrian law (MAL A 40), for example, does not outlaw prostitutes, only their veiling themselves so they would appear to be married women. Perhaps more to the point in Mesopotamian contexts, if a case involves an unmarried woman—not a prostitute but another unmarried woman, whether preengagement, divorced, or widowed—the situation becomes complicated primarily if property or inheritance is at stake for someone other than herself, such as her father

74. See also Phyllis A. Bird, "Prostitution in the Social World and Religious Rhetoric of Ancient Israel," in *Prostitutes and Courtesans in the Ancient World*, ed. Christopher A. Faraone and Laura K. McClure (Madison: University of Wisconsin Press, 2006), 40–58.

or her clan.[75] Prostitutes can generally hold rights to their own property, or their family members (e.g., a brother) could have secondary interest in the property. While sexual relations are thus normally not prohibited between a man and a prostitute, some Old Babylonian (18th c. BCE) and Neo-Babylonian (6th c. BCE) documents have emerged showing that, for whatever social reasons, a man and a woman, whether a prostitute or not, could be constrained by a legal document or legal authority to cease all sexual contact with each other, and usually it is the woman who is threatened with punishment if it should continue.[76] While a comparable legal restraint is thinkable in ancient Israelite urban settings, prostitution itself was not prohibited in general.

Children and the Elderly. In the previous chapter, we noted the high value placed on *children* in village society, and the same pertains in cities, although probably for quite different reasons. Certainly their status as dependents on their parents, to whom they owed full obedience, remained the same in both contexts. Though from early age children's roles as labor in helping secure the family's subsistence dominated in the countryside, their urban counterparts had much less to contribute to the politics and economy of the city and state. Surely they were groomed to take over their parents' roles when they became old enough, whether that might be in commerce, landholding, the royal house, administration, the affairs of the temple, or slavery. As minors they did not have the same level of legal culpability as did adults, nor did they even appear in court—at least according to extant records from ancient Southwest Asia.[77] They were, however, the subject of law in two primary areas: adoption and inheritance. While no adoption contracts are extant from ancient Israel, they have been found in many cultures and periods of time in the region, and Israel certainly knew the custom as well.[78] Obtaining an heir constituted the dominant purpose for a childless couple to adopt someone. Often the adoptee was not a minor but an adult, and records exist to show that not only males but also females were adopted—and could adopt.

75. Martha T. Roth, "Marriage, Divorce, and the Prostitute in Ancient Mesopotamia," in Faraone and McClure, *Prostitutes and Courtesans in the Ancient World*, 21–39.

76. Ibid., 29–32.

77. Raymond Westbrook, "The Character of Ancient Near Eastern Law," in Westbrook, *History*, 31.

78. The bibliography on adoption in ancient Southwest Asia is extensive. See, e.g., Westbrook, *History*, passim; Elizabeth C. Stone and David I. Owen, *Adoption in Old Babylonian Nippur and the Archive of Mannum-mesu-lissur*, Mesopotamian Civilizations 3 (Winona Lake, IN: Eisenbrauns, 1991); and the earlier study by Martin David, *Die Adoption im altbabylonischen Recht*, Leipziger rechtswissenschaftliche Studien 23 (Leipzig: Theodor Weicher, 1927).

Children, when they attained adult age, had social and legal responsibilities toward their parents. Care and burial of the *elderly* resided in the hands of their offspring, above all the sons, who in most instances were the ones who inherited the familial home and whatever business or hereditary office the earlier generation had.[79] In the absence of a son or daughter, the older couple could adopt an adult, even a slave, to fulfill the role of caretaker, as well as to become the heir. This need for care continued to apply for a widow or widower. The consequences of a child's neglect of duty in this regard could be severe, not just for the parents but also for the son or daughter. The text in Deut 21:18–21 provides for punishment by stoning of a "stubborn and rebellious son." It is inconceivable that the son in question would have been a child since he is charged with gluttony and drunkenness; rather, the offense is that the adult son is not providing adequately for his aged parents. We have no way of knowing whether such a punishment was ever carried out, but the harshness of this text points to the crucial importance attached to this circumstance of elders depending on their children, above all in the cities. In the villages the aged generally had their larger clan around them in the event they lost the support of their own children; such a safety net was less likely to exist in the cities, with neighborhoods defined more by occupation and class than by familial lines.

Personal Injury and Death. Our discussion of personal injury law in the previous chapter dealt with issues of intention, consequence, liability, and penalty, much of it pertinent to both village and city contexts. What is peculiar in urban settings is the effect of class on determining the crime as well as the penalty. The clearest indication of the role of class in personal injury cases comes from the Code of Hammurabi (esp. §§196–223). There we see that the standing of both the injurer and the injured plays the key role in setting the punishment. In a word, if an upper-class person causes injury to another upper-class person, the penalty generally follows the talionic principle, while if an upper-class individual injures someone from the lower class or a slave, then the penalty is less severe and usually monetary in form. For example, if an upper-class man (*awīlum*) blinds the eye of another *awīlum*, then the injurer is to have his own eye blinded. However, if the victim is a commoner (*muškēnum*), then he pays 60 silver shekels; or if a slave, then he pays half of the slave's value in silver (LH 196–199). Even in the case of a medical procedure, the physician—whose standing

79. Circumstances in several ancient Southwest Asian cultures are described in Marten Stol and Sven P. Vleeming, eds., *The Care of the Elderly in the Ancient Near East*, SHCANE 14 (Leiden: E. J. Brill, 1998).

was obviously below that of the elite and of the royal house—is liable for
injury or death, with penalties ranging from amputation of the physician's
hand if the patient was upper class to payment of compensation for a commoner or slave (LH 218–220). Given the importance of class division in
Israel's urban and national society, a comparable pattern is likely to have
prevailed in Israel's cities as well.

Also a factor is the specific body part that is injured, perhaps permanently. One of the earliest known lists is the Old Babylonian Laws of
Eshnunna (§§42–47; 18th c. BCE). In all of these cases each party, the injurer
as well as the injured, is an *awīlum*, a member of the free class, and the
value of the wounded part is assessed in terms of silver shekels[80]:

Nose bitten off	60 shekels
Loss of an eye	60 shekels
Loss of a tooth	30 shekels
Loss of an ear	30 shekels
Breaking a hand	30 shekels
Breaking a foot	30 shekels
Breaking a collarbone	20 shekels
Loss of a finger	20 shekels
Slap to the cheek	10 shekels
Any other injury	10 shekels

The list concludes with the stipulation (LE 47A) that if an *awīlum* causes
the death of another *awīlum* during a brawl, the penalty is 40 shekels—less
than the value attached to a nose or an eye. Other law collections have
somewhat similar though not identical provisions regarding the monetary
value of body parts.[81]

Two cases specifically involving women, with reproductive issues at play,
also occur in various collections, with some differences. In one, a pregnant
woman is struck, resulting in a miscarriage or death. While the loss of the
fetus is treated as a relatively minor injury to a body part (a payment of
usually a lesser sum of silver shekels as compensation[82]), the woman's

80. A silver shekel weighs slightly more than 8 grams.
81. The Sumerian list in LU 18–22, while shorter and fragmentary, dates from an even
earlier period, near 2100 BCE. Other texts listing the value of injured body parts are LH 196–201
and 206–8 and HL 7–16.
82. LL d; SLEx 1'–2'; LH 209, 211, 213; HL 17–18; MAL A 21, A 51–52. See also above, chap.
5, Personal Injury and Death.

death is much more serious, punished with someone's execution,[83] such as the assailant (LL e; MAL A 50) or the assailant's daughter if the deceased woman was of the *awīlum*-class (LH 210), or with a monetary payment if the woman was a commoner or slave (LH 212 and 214). The other case specifically involving women has a woman crushing or seizing a man's testicle in the midst of a quarrel, in which case her finger or hand is to be cut off (MAL A 8; Deut 25:11–12)[84] or, for two testicles, both of her eyes should be gouged out (MAL A 8).

While not necessarily injury as such, slapping the cheek of another represented a form of insult or shaming and was to be punished. Clearest in terms of class distinctions are LH 202–5: an *awīlum* striking the cheek of a higher-class *awīlum* is to be flogged with 60 stripes in public, or for striking the cheek of an *awīlum* of equal status must recompense him 60 silver shekels. Similarly, a commoner (*muškēnum*) must pay another commoner 10 silver shekels for striking that person's cheek. If a slave strikes the cheek of an *awīlum*, the slave's ear is to be cut off. The punishment of amputating the hand of a child who strikes his father, though not necessarily his cheek (LH 195), stems partly from the shame associated with the act and partly from the affront to the patriarchal power.

While some of these stipulations, or variants of them, are conceivable in the context of village life, all of them could have functioned in urban societies. Here is where slavery, monetary compensation, public flogging, physicians, and clear class differentiation are to be found—not only in ancient Israel but also in the cities of ancient Southwest Asia. Written transmission of legal and penal provisions from one generation to another, or from one country to another, occurred among the literate institutions, and laws such as these detailing injuries and penalties may well have been used as exercise texts in urban schools.[85] Yet even if they served only as scribal exercises and not as functioning laws, the need for some procedure for adjudicating damages was not purely academic. Laws such as these existed and circulated because conflicts over intentional and unintentional personal injuries happened only too often.

83. In Exod 21:23–25 the person to suffer the punishment is unidentified, and the penalty follows the law of talion ("eye for an eye").

84. Another interpretation of this penalty associates it with shaming the woman by requiring that her genital hair be shaved; see Johanna Stiebert, *The Construction of Shame in the Hebrew Bible: The Prophetic Contribution*, JSOTSup 346 (London and New York: Sheffield Academic Press, 2002), 25–26 n. 1.

85. See the discussion on this point by Eckart Otto, *Körperverletzungen in den Keilschriftrechten und im Alten Testament: Studien zum Rechtstransfer im Alten Testament*, AOAT 226 (Kevelaer: Verlag Butzon & Bercker; Neukirchen-Vluyn: Neukirchener Verlag, 1991).

Economic Life

For all the intricacies of economic life in Israel's villages as discussed in the preceding chapter, the economy at the urban, national, and indeed international levels took on even more complex structures and dynamics. Israel had a thoroughly agrarian society, but the state levels introduced differences in both scale and substance. The fundamental characteristic in agrarian societies of sharp inequalities, both economic and political, becomes most evident when the powers and capabilities represented in the cities are juxtaposed with those of the rural settlements. Despite the inadequacies we have noted about the urban/rural dichotomy, the contrast between a remote village of 75 and an organized, dominating, well-appointed city— whether of the capital, royal, or administrative type—with its monumental architecture, wealthy residences, city walls, economic center, ceremonial spaces, and military support was immediately apparent, and felt, by anyone who compared the two. Even with their relatively small population, these "containers of power"[86] enjoyed a reach far in excess of their numbers, well able to affect the lives and livelihood of everyone in the distant hamlets.

In the following we consider the loci of economic power in the cities— the royal family, the wealthy landowners and merchants, and less so the bureaucrats and military. The temple and priesthood were also deeply involved in the economic strength of the cities and nations, but we will delay that discussion until the next chapter, which is devoted to the cult, its trappings, and its professional personnel. As with the social issues treated above, we focus here on what is distinctive to the urban and state legal systems in contrast to those of the villages.

Contracts. One of the more-noticeable differences between urban and rural legal systems in ancient Southwest Asia is the proliferation of written contracts in the cities. This dissimilarity runs parallel to the division between the upper and lower classes, or between those among the ruling elite and those not—largely because of the increased level of assets, property, and commercial activities at stake among the powerful and wealthy. Babylonian and Assyrian tablets by the thousands illustrate the widespread practice of securing agreements in contractual form: sales of both real and movable property, loans, rentals, marriages, divorces, adoptions, inheritance terms, manumission of slaves, and other transactions. No counterparts in Hebrew from the Iron II period have yet emerged, but a good number have been

86. Giddens, cited above in chap. 6, note 1.

found from the Persian period, especially in the Aramaic language and above all in Egypt.[87] Nonetheless, the kinds of social and economic systems present in Israelite cities suggest that such contracts were routine there as well, especially with the people's exposure to the Neo-Assyrians, Neo-Babylonians, and Persians.

Though not the same as positive laws, contracts function successfully if the existing legal system recognizes them and allows for their enforcement, if necessary through court intervention. Obligatory in nature, contracts vary in type but generally contain certain elements:

- Identification of the parties (e.g., the seller and buyer, or the predecessor and the heir, or the lessor and the lessee).
- Content of the contract (e.g., if it involves land, there will normally be a description of the land [e.g., cultivated, orchard, pasture], its boundaries, and any houses on it).
- If applicable, specification of the value being exchanged, usually in silver, gold, lead, or kind.
- Provision for damages in the event that the agreement is broken, not fulfilled, or altered. Alternatively, a formulaic curse may call divine punishment on whoever does not comply with the terms of the contract.
- Names of witnesses, typically two or three or more, and the name of the scribe who has written the contract.
- Date and place of the contract, often with reference to the ruling monarch or governor.

From the innumerable extant contracts, one will suffice to illustrate the nature and legal weight attached to them. While other contracts contain much more detail than does this example, its significance for our purposes derives from its status as one of only a few contracts found in the Israelite territory and period. In 1904 archaeologists uncovered two inscriptions at Tell al-Jazari, identified as biblical Gezer (e.g., 1 Kgs 9:15–17) and located some 25 kilometers (15 mi.) southeast of modern Tel Aviv-Yafo. Written in Neo-Assyrian cuneiform, it is dated to the year 651 BCE, when the city was held by the Assyrian Empire and was populated with Israelites, Assyrians,

87. See the compilation and analyses by Porten and Yardeni, *Textbook of Aramaic Documents from Ancient Egypt*, esp. vol. 2, *Contracts*. The collection shows a wide variety of contracts from the 6th–4th c. BCE dealing with deeds of obligation, conveyances, marriage documents, judicial oaths, and court records.

and various deportees from other imperial provinces.[88] The text of this sale contract, to the extent it is legible, reads:

> [1]Seal of Marduk-erība, son of . . .
> [2]Seal of Aba-erība, son of . . .
> [3]Totally: two men, owners of houses (and) field(s).
> [4]The estate of Lu-aḫḫū in (its) enti(rety)
> [5][four seal-impressions]
> [6]The slaves: Ṭuri-Aja; his two wives; his son;
> [7]3 people [. . .]s
> [8]2 wooden [   ]
> [9][   ]-*a-a*
> [10][   ]-*ia-qar*
> . . . .
> [1']The money (x-fold to the owner)
> [2']he shall return. (In his case he may plead)
> [3']but he will not receive. (Guarantee against) an attack of epilepsy
> [4']for 100 days, (against) crime forever.
> [5']Siwan, the 17th of the year after that of
> [6']Aššur-dura-uṣur, governor of Bar-ḫalsi
> _____
> [7']Witness: Zakkî; witness: Ṭebeṭaja;
> [8']Witness: Bēl-apla-iddina; witness: Marduk-nāṣir (from the) ci(ty . . .);
> [9']Witness: Ḫar-Uaṣi, the mayor;
> [10']Witness: Bur-rapi', the estate-(agent);
> [11']Witness: Zēr-ūkin, son of Ṭebeṭaja;
> [12']Witness: Ṭābta-uballiṭ; witness: Si'-(. . .);
> [13']Witness: Mannu-kī-Arbaïl; witness: (. . .);
> [14']Witness: Zēr-ūtu.

The text of the contract, even with its indecipherable and damaged script, contains the bare elements needed in a legal document. The clay tablet is written on both sides: one side with 6 lines, mostly legible, out of a total of 9 or more, and with 4 seal-impressions in the space between lines 4 and 5; and the reverse side with 14 lines and a solid line separating the first 6 lines from the bottom 8. The 2 parties in the contract (lines 1–2) are identified as large landowners ("owners of houses and fields," line 3). The estate being sold is in its entirety (line 4), including slaves and presumably other persons or movable property identified in lines 5–9, only the first line of which is fully legible. The sales price is also not preserved. Lines 1'–2' specify the penalty for breaking the contract,

---

88. Bob Becking, "The Two Neo-Assyrian Documents from Gezer in Their Historical Context," *JEOL* 27 (1981–82): 76–89, with references to previous studies. Most of the following translation and interpretation of the text is based on Becking's article.

which is typically 10 times the original price in Neo-Assyrian contracts. Lines 2'–3' exclude any chance for judicial redress. In lines 3'–4' the buyer is guaranteed against any of the slaves experiencing an epileptic episode within the first one hundred days (cf. LH 278, which specifies a one-month guarantee) or being found guilty of a crime forever (presumably committed prior to the purchase). The colophon in lines 5'–6' provides the date: Siwan is the third month of the year, and the governor named took office in 652 BCE, hence the date of this contract in 651 BCE. The contract concludes by naming twelve witnesses: one is the mayor and another the estate agent. Often the name of the scribe is included and in this case may have been lost.

Such contracts were commonplace in Southwest Asian cultures during the second and first millennia BCE and are only to be expected in ancient Israel and Judah as well, as we see from this Gezer Inscription. The sheer number of witnesses, including the city's mayor, underscores the significance of this transaction, which probably involved a sizeable estate. Though these contracts were considered binding, the inclusion of fines and often of curse formulas suggests that the obligations were at times not met or that someone could tamper with the tablets. Numerous documents recording lawsuits over contested sales, property, inheritances, debts, noncompliance, and more have also been uncovered by archaeologists of these cultures.[89] To our knowledge, it was not a "litigious society" since such legal complaints and conflicts were generally limited to the wealthy few, yet they played a significant role in the urban environment. While these contractual transactions were generally rendered in written form in cities where wealth and literacy were based, in villages an oral agreement sufficed, with witnesses present to attest to its terms.

The Hebrew Bible, "by its nature,"[90] does not preserve any explicit contracts, although they seem to be presupposed in various narratives, reports, wisdom materials, and prophetic critiques, as well as in the literary rendition of laws. We read often of sales, loans, hirings, pledges, and inheritances, just as we do of sureties, deposits, witnesses, debt releases,

89. For example, fifty-two such documents from the Old Babylonian period, together with discussion of various aspects of the judicial process, are presented in Moses Schorr, *Urkunden des altbabylonischen Zivil- und Prozessrechts*, Vorderasiatische Bibliothek (Leipzig: J. C. Hinrichs, 1913), 336–444.

90. Frymer-Kenski ("Israel," 1020) does not comment further on what this "nature" may be that results in the exclusion of contracts. On 1020–27, however, she discusses the types of contracts to which allusions are made in the Hebrew Bible: sale, loan, pledge, debt, hire, as well as the subjects of debt release, suretyship, and deposit.

and more.[91] Narrative descriptions of contracts and contestations are present, for example, in the stories of Abraham and Lot (Gen 13:8–12), Laban and Jacob (Gen 29:15–30), Ruth and Boaz (Ruth 4:1–12), and others. The procedure for conducting a lawsuit when a breach of contract was charged must also have followed traditional patterns.

Real Property. As suggested in the previous chapter, there was a decided difference between *property ownership* in the villages and that in the cities. In a word, that difference lies in the proximity and immediate significance of the property to the owner. Villagers typically lived extremely close to the land they worked for their sustenance and survival. They were clustered in small villages and daily left their modest homes to cultivate their own small plots or to herd their livestock. For each family, their home and their parcel of land—if it had not been sold out of desperation by an earlier generation—generally came to them as inheritance, not acquisition. Since they possessed little more than the bare minimum for raising their own food for the year, the legal system of the village established protections vis-à-vis their peers to guard against loss of their primary means for consumption. Their vulnerability toward others with power and wealth could not so easily be protected.

Real property figured quite differently in the affairs of those residing in the cities, however. Throughout most of the monarchic period (Iron II) and during the colonial rule by Neo-Assyrians, Neo-Babylonians, and Persians, vast portions of the land, probably even the substantial majority of it, were in the hands of the few wealthy and powerful residents of the cities. Large landowners, foreclosing on debts taken out by farmers, had amassed innumerable plots previously owned by villagers. The prophet Isaiah (in 5:8) seems to have such a situation in mind when he poignantly charges:

> Ah, those [of you] who join house with house and field with field,
> Until no room remains but for you to dwell alone in the land!

This practice resulted in the creation of what were known in ancient Rome as latifundia, large estates owned by landholders and worked by peasants on a serf-like basis. The owners might occupy a manor house on the property, or could live in a city elsewhere in the country and have the land managed by an overseer. As the large, well-appointed houses are more frequently found in the Israelite cities than in the countryside, we can

---

91. See further discussions in Raymond Westbrook and Richard Jasnow, eds., *Security for Debt in Ancient Near Eastern Law* CHANE 9 (Leiden and Boston: E. J. Brill, 2001), esp. the chapter by Frymer-Kensky, "Israel," 251–63.

assume that these wealthy landowners tended to prefer urban living to life on their land. The distinction between city and country is also evident in Lev 25:29–31, which exempts a purchaser of an urban dwelling (probably acquired from a poor or indebted person) from having to relinquish it in the Jubilee Year while houses in the unwalled villages are subject to the jubilee release.

The other major landholders, also centered in the cities, were the palace and the temple. The actual extent of crown land is impossible for us now to measure, but it must have been significant. In a sense a strong monarch could in effect lay claim to all the land of the country, and both the royal ideology and the army would enforce it. Only the wealthy elites, not the poor villagers, had any chance of resisting the power of the throne. Knowing their influence and impact, the kings could also offer individual elites a land grant—either outright ownership of an area of property or usufruct rights over certain property, the right to derive benefit and income from the property while its actual ownership remains with the king. Either type of grant creates a patron-client relationship that obligates the recipient (in this case the private individual) to recognize the authority of the sovereign, while the king is expected to offer protection and favor to the client in return.[92]

The temple, likely a major player in the national economy if the model of other ancient Southwest Asian countries is replicated in Israel, also owned substantial land, and not just in the vicinity of the temple. Whether obtained through acquisition, gift, or grant, these properties were exploited for agricultural gain. Peasants and tenant farmers worked these lands, while priests and other cultic officials—somewhat along the lines of ecclesiastical prebendaries in the medieval European church—benefited from the income.[93] As we will see in the following chapter, not just one central temple but actually a number of temples and other cultic installations existed throughout the land and in different periods of time. All of them depended on profits from property and commerce, and generally enjoyed support of the king as well, if their buildings were to be constructed and appointed.

A range of legal issues is plausible in this context of property ownership and management. Though some of the large landowners may have lived on their land, the majority were found in the various cities, along with the state and cultic institutions that owned extensive properties. Some of the potential legal problems paralleled those experienced by the poorer villagers, but

92. Lemche, "Kings and Clients."
93. G. van Driel, *Elusive Silver: In Search of a Role for a Market in an Agrarian Environment: Aspects of Mesopotamia's Society,* Nederlands Instituut voor het Nabije Oosten te Leiden 95 (Leiden: Nederlands Instituut voor het Nabije Oosten, 2002), 31–151.

others stemmed from the distinctive situation of owners, whether persons or institutions, that did not themselves work their land on a daily basis but managed them from afar—with the help of overseers, foremen, hired workers, tenant farmers, or slaves. Following are some of the legal protections and conflicts that such types of property owners needed to have in place in order not to jeopardize their holdings. Laws to address such issues stemmed from those in power, whether from the king, from priests, or from the wealthy landowners, especially those from the latter taking the form of customary laws.

Acquisition of real property occurred through several possible avenues. *Purchase* was the normal means, and numerous contracts from the region indicate the care with which the property was defined and the transaction accomplished, as discussed above. While containing no such explicit contracts, the Hebrew Bible suggests such a practice when the prophet Jeremiah buys a plot of land near his hometown of Anathoth during the Babylonian siege on Jerusalem:

> I wrote in a document, sealed it, called witnesses, and weighed the silver on scales. I took the document of purchase, both the sealed copy and the open copy, according to the rule and regulations. . . . In [the witnesses' presence] I charged Baruch: "Thus says YHWH Sabaoth, God of Israel: 'Take these documents—this deed of purchase, both the sealed one and the open one—and place them in a pottery jar so they will last a long time.'" (Jer 32:10–11, 13–14)

In addition, the Hebrew Bible relates several instances of property exchange through purchase: for example, Abraham bought a burial cave (Gen 23); both King David and King Omri purchased land (2 Sam 24:18–25; 1 Kgs 16:24); Boaz acquired Elimelech's field by purchase (Ruth 4:1–9). Legally at stake was the proper transfer of property according to means that secured it against possible challenge in the future.

Two forms of land acquisition were tied to royal power. By virtue of the absolute or near absolute control that a strong monarch could exercise— limited mainly by the elites—all land of the country could be considered the king's. Whether he could or would actually lay claim to the private property of the rich or of the temple is rather doubtful in most cases because he also depended on their support as well as their commercial enterprises. The king thus had the right, by virtue of the power of *eminent domain*, to lay claim to property at will. In the monarchic context, it was not necessary that the land serve some public purpose or that the previous owner be duly compensated. A classic story from the Hebrew Bible shows, though, how a king's arbitrary desire might at times need a show of legal process: Ahab covets Naboth's vineyard, Jezebel rigs the trial, and "the elders and nobles who lived in the city" convict and execute Naboth (1 Kgs 21).

The other form of royal involvement in land acquisition is evident in the above-mentioned *land grant*. A person, in most cases someone among the elite whom the king sought to obligate to himself, receives from the king a piece of land of any size, often including buildings and people then living on it. Whether granted on a permanent or temporary basis mattered little since the king can easily reclaim it if desired. Numerous examples are present from surrounding cultures.[94] It has been suggested that the biblical text retains this tradition and language of the Neo-Assyrian royal land grant in the accounts of the divine gift of land to Abraham (Gen 15) and of a dynasty to David (2 Sam 7),[95] and by extension perhaps even in the divine gift of the land of Israel to the people, which is pointedly not bestowed in perpetuity (Lev 25:23) or without condition. Other biblical examples include Joshua's designation of land for Caleb (Josh 14:6–15) and the people's doing the same for Joshua himself (Josh 19:49–50). Whether or not the land-grant model was used in these texts, such practices were present in the society and obviously had legal standing.

Illicit alteration of *boundary lines*, in itself a means for acquiring property incrementally, posed special problems, and the allusions to it[96] suggest that it must have happened often enough to warrant the establishment of protections and penalties. Deuteronomy 19:14 reads pointedly:

> You shall not move your neighbor's boundary line, established long ago on the property you will inherit in the land YHWH your God is giving you to possess.

In this verse "boundary line" is often read as "boundary marker" or "boundary stones" (גבול, *gĕbûl*). When I first read this law years ago, I envisioned a tiny plot of arable land with a large stone or a pile of smaller stones at each corner to delimit it vis-à-vis its neighboring plots, and then an adjacent owner surreptitiously, in the dark of night, moving the stack of stones a meter or so to gain that much more property at the expense of the neighbor. As mentioned in the previous chapter, however, it is implausible that villagers, each with a small property inherited from previous generations

---

94. See, e.g., J. N. Postgate, *Neo-Assyrian Royal Grants and Decrees*, Studia Pohl, Series Maior 1 (Rome: Pontifical Biblical Institute, 1969).

95. Among his several studies of the subject, see M. Weinfeld, "The Covenant of Grant in the Old Testament and in the Ancient Near East," *JAOS* 90 (1970): 184–203. Pertinent criticisms of the hypothesis are raised, though, by Gary N. Knoppers, "Ancient Near Eastern Royal Grants and the Davidic Covenant: A Parallel?" *JAOS* 116 (1996): 670–97.

96. For example, Deut 27:17; Prov 15:25; 22:28; 23:10.

and worked meticulously and daily to produce as much foodstuff as possible, would not have noticed it if the boundary markers had been shifted. In other words, the protections in the text of Deut 19:14 must pertain not to poor villagers but to larger landowners who possess extensive estates, which they do not themselves work and cannot personally monitor. The one who shifted boundaries could just as well have been a neighboring estate owner, not a poor farmer who dared not violate the holdings of a powerful neighbor. In addition, despite the reference to a "boundary marker" in the above translation of this verse, the Hebrew text does not mention anything as concrete as a boundary marker or stone; it simply reads, "Do not move your neighbor's boundary," meaning the boundary or border line.[97]

A practice known from Babylonia around 1400–650 BCE may shed light on the social and legal setting of boundaries around private property. Approximately 160 *kudurru* stones, some only fragmentary, have been unearthed from this period in Mesopotamia. Often displaying finely chiseled reliefs of divine, royal, and animal figures, the stones contain texts describing the details of a given estate owned by an individual and, in many cases, granted by the king to this person. *Kudurru*s, too prized and important to be placed in the open on a boundary line, were commonly preserved in a temple if not in the manor house. They describe in detail the layout and borders of the estate, constituting in effect a copy of the property deed (the original was presumably stored elsewhere) and sometimes even an exemption from taxation. Only wealthy landowners, not peasants with small plots of land, could have afforded a *kudurru*.[98] The estates mentioned on these stones during the Iron II period are upward of 320 hectares (800 acres = 1.25 sq. mi.). Reasoning from this analogy of the Babylonian estates and the deeds used to secure them, we can conclude that the law in Deut 19:14 aims to protect the interests of the wealthy landowners above all, even if it could theoretically also be applied to the poorest property holder. Stones erected or piled on the boundary lines may have existed, but most significant and legally binding was the written record describing the estate's extent and preserved elsewhere.

---

97. See also Deut 27:17; Hos 5:10; Job 24:2; Prov 23:10.
98. For analyses of the *kudurru*s, see Kathryn E. Slanski, *The Babylonian Entitlement narûs (kudurrus): A Study in Their Form and Function*, ASOR Books 9 (Boston: American Schools of Oriental Research, 2003); Ursula Seidl, *Die babylonischen Kudurru-Reliefs: Symbole mesopotamischer Gottheiten*, OBO 87 (Freiburg, Switzerland: Universitätsverlag; Göttingen: Vandenhoeck & Ruprecht, 1989); idem, "Kudurru," *RLA* 6 (1980–83): 267–77; and for early compilations of texts, *Babylonian Boundary-Stones and Memorial-Tablets in the British Museum*, ed. L. W. King, 2 vols. (London: British Museum, 1912); and Franz X. Steinmetzer, *Die babylonischen Kudurru (Grenzsteine) als Urkundenform*, Studien zur Geschichte und Kultur des Altertums 11/4–5 (Paderborn: Ferdinand Schöningh, 1922).

Violations of property rights occurred often enough. As we argue in this study, the various law collections from ancient Southwest Asia, including those of the Hebrew Bible, do not record the actual laws functioning throughout all sectors of the respective societies; instead, they typically reflect the bias of the powerful and wealthy—in other words, precisely those individuals and institutions that possessed the largest portions of property in each country, at least during monarchic or imperial times. In the interest of space, I will list only the kinds of laws that would have existed in monarchic Israel to deter or punish violators. Though the Hebrew Bible does not record evidence of all of them, examples are available from other cultures, or the nature of the economic and social systems in Israel makes it likely that such legal conflicts or protections existed. Some of these legal matters include boundary disputes and adjudications; easements; trespass; usufruct; tenancy; leasing; inheritance and succession (see also below); redemption of forfeited land; liability for damages, both to the property owner and to someone on another's land or in the house.[99] One specific example deserves mention, if for no other reason than that it is widely attested in legal history to the present and shows the discriminating legal thinking at work since early times. Both Old Babylonian and biblical law, and probably elsewhere as well, identify burglary or theft according to whether it occurs during the daytime or during nighttime hours. Thus LE 12–13 applies it to both theft from an open field and burglary in a house, while Exod 22:2–3 [22:1–2 MT] envisions only breaking and entering a house. The Eshnunna Laws specify a fine for the daytime infraction and execution if it is done during the night. The Exodus provision excuses a house owner for killing an intruder at night, but the owner incurs bloodguilt if the break-in occurs during the day. The rationale, it would seem, is that the danger of personal injury to the owner and family during the nighttime is considerably higher than it is during the day. The biblical law may imply that the owner should be able to exercise restraint or seek other help during the daytime.

Movable Property. Ownership of movable property can be secured by contract at the time of acquisition, as we have seen, or by the presence of witnesses to attest to a transaction not recorded in writing. Contracts would be most likely for luxury items, furnishings for a house, slaves, animals, and other valuable goods. Undocumented barter and exchange, typically

---

99. For references and discussions of these and other legal issues, see, e.g., Westbrook, ed., *History*, passim; Crüsemann, *The Torah*, passim; and Westbrook, *Property and the Family*.

by means of in-kind produce or goods, prevailed as the method of acquisition not only among the poorer population but often among the elites as well. Payment with silver or money[100] occurred only among the wealthy, while using one's labor as a means of payment prevailed mainly among the peasants. The presence of valuable items in Israel and Judah of Iron II has been established by archaeology and serves as a clear indication of the economic strength of the royal house, the temple, and the elites.[101] Such goods as well as various imported items circulated throughout ancient Southwest Asia, thanks to the substantial network of merchant trade routes.[102] Everyday items, normally self-made or locally produced and not imported, were monetarily less valuable, yet nonetheless essential. Though the homes of the elite and the palace of the king contained goods of fine material and workmanship, the domestic and work buildings of others ranged from moderately furnished to spare.

In their own view, the urban inhabitants, mostly elite, thus had much at stake regarding their movable property, and they assiduously saw to the legal protection of their interests. *Theft* was more likely in cities than in villages, as indicated in the previous chapter. Villagers lived in close social proximity and were well aware of each other's belongings, a circumstance that tended to discourage theft. Cities, on the other hand, even the main power centers with their relatively small size, provided more opportunity and more options for someone inclined to steal. Above all, the absentee landholders dwelling in the cities had to be concerned with the movable goods kept on their rural properties. As a result, Israelite laws distinguished explicitly or indirectly between social classes, both that of the victim and that of the perpetrator, as was the case in other ancient Southwest Asian cultures: if a commoner steals from an upper-class person, the penalty tends to be harsher than if the victim is a fellow commoner. A

100. In Southwest Asia coins were first minted in Asia Minor, in the 7th c. BCE, but they were not much in circulation until after the time of Alexander the Great. They first appear in the Levant during the Persian period, in the 5th c. BCE. See Daniel C. Snell, "Methods of Exchange and Coinage in Ancient Western Asia," *CANE* 3:1487–97.

101. Jamieson-Drake, *Scribes and Schools*, 107–35; see also Wason, *Archaeology of Rank*, 103–26, for a more general and theoretical discussion of the distribution of elite goods and resources as they appear in the archaeological record.

102. See the various discussions, keyed to periods from the third to the first millennia BCE, in Dominique Charpin and Francis Joannès, eds., *La circulation des biens, des personnes et des idées dans le Proche-Orient ancien: Actes de la XXXVIIIe Rencontre assyriologique internationale (Paris, 8–10 juillet 1991)* (Paris: Éditions recherche sur les civilisations, 1992); also J. D. Hawkins, ed., *Trade in the Ancient Near East: Papers Presented to the XXIII Rencontre assyriologique internationale (University of Birmingham, 5–9 July 1976)* (London: British School of Archaeology in Iraq, 1977).

thief, if convicted, can be penalized several times the value of the stolen property, according to biblical law—for example, fourfold for a sheep and fivefold for an ox if the animal has been slaughtered or sold, but only double if the animal is still alive and can be reclaimed (Exod 22:1 and 4 [21:37 and 22:3 MT]). A penalty at this level, substantially outstripping the crime itself, was most likely instituted by the large landowners as a deterrent aimed at those living on or near their estates; poor villagers, who knew the extreme difficulty if not impossibility of paying such a high fee, would hardly have expected their peers to compensate for a theft at such a level, neither to each other nor to a wealthy landowner. A thief who could not pay the fine faced the prospect of being sold into slavery (see, e.g., Exod 22:1 [22:2 MT])—again an expectation more likely originating among the wealthy than among the poor, in whose interest it was to keep their community together. Theft from the temple[103] could lead to an extremely harsh penalty, even execution, if a strong priesthood or major temple was involved; LH 6 and 8 stipulate execution for stolen valuables and a thirtyfold penalty for stealing livestock or a boat—and execution if the thief cannot pay.[104] Similarly, the king's possessions received stricter protection than did those of nonroyals. The punishment for receiving stolen goods could be just as harsh as the remedy for theft itself, normally under the provision that the purchaser knew that the items had been stolen.[105] The general observation regarding theft is that the elites and the powerful handed down stricter controls to curtail and punish it than did the general population.

Slavery. Slavery in ancient Israel is also an institution of far greater economic and legal significance for city dwellers than for villagers—except insofar as the villagers themselves were threatened with the prospect of becoming enslaved, in which case they had little power to affect their legal standing. This topic deserves in-depth treatment because it displays well some of the power dynamics in the legal system, much as did family law in the villages. The law collections from other ancient Southwest Asian cultures contain a wide variety of specific provisions dealing with slaves, making this category one of the more frequently visited topics among the laws of the region. Biblical texts also include many

103. In the Akkadian phrase, the item "belongs to the god."
104. For reference to various other texts and remedies, see Joachim Oelsner, Bruce Wells, and Cornelia Wunsch, "Neo-Babylonian Period," in Westbrook, *History*, 962–65.
105. Several ancient Southwest Asian laws explicitly address these circumstances, as in LH 9–11 and MAL C+G 5.

provisions dealing with slavery, touching on issues of both ownership and treatment.[106]

In all likelihood, Israel's national economy was not as extensively based on slavery as was the case during various periods of Mesopotamian, Egyptian, Greek, and Roman history.[107] Obviously the institution was condoned in Israel and in the biblical laws just as it was in the neighboring countries. Nothing in Israelite or biblical materials[108] suggests that Israel had, in proportion to its overall population, fewer slaves than its neighbors solely because of a conviction that it was fundamentally unjust for one person to own another, nor that the Israelites had a notion of essential or innate human rights. This latter concept of rights did not become prominent until the movements of the eighteenth and nineteenth centuries CE.[109] The closest the Hebrew Bible comes to articulating some degree of identification of a slave owner with a slave occurs in Job 31:15: "Did not the one who made me in my mother's womb also make him? Did not the one make us in one womb?"[110] Yet no effort is made in the Hebrew Bible to advocate general emancipation of the slaves on any grounds, nor should we expect such a movement during the social history of ancient Israel. As has predominated in other societies with slaves in history, the slaves in Israel were basically considered chattel, and any protections they enjoyed derived largely from the pragmatic considerations of their owners.

106. For an effort to set the biblical laws in chronological order, see Innocenzo Cardellini, *Die biblischen "Sklaven"-Gesetze im Lichte des keilschriftlichen Sklavenrechts: Ein Beitrag zur Tradition, Überlieferung und Redaktion der alttestamentlichen Rechtstexte*, BBB 55 (Bonn: Peter Hanstein, 1981).

107. Among the numerous treatments of slavery in antiquity, the series Forschungen zur antiken Sklaverei (Mainz) is especially noteworthy for its breadth and depth of coverage. Focusing primarily on Greece and Rome rather than on ancient Southwest Asia, its numerous volumes are devoted to such topics as the master-slave relationship in economic and political contexts, slaves used in warfare and in mining, fugitive slaves, homeborn slaves, mass enslavements of conquered populations, royal slaves, and more.

108. The New Testament statement in Gal 3:28 does not represent a repudiation of slavery as such but only asserts that such distinctions should not obtain within the Christian community. The slave and the free person continue to exist in the larger society, just as do male and female or Jew and Greek.

109. See the discussion in my "Political Rights and Powers," esp. 93–94.

110. The meaning of this text is anything but clear. The second half could read "Did not the one make both of us in the same womb" (as suggested by the LXX text). Furthermore, the "womb" (רחם [*reḥem*] . . . בטן [*beṭen*]), if intended as one and the same womb in which both Job and his slave were formed, plausibly refers not to a human womb but to some notion of Mother Earth. This idea of the *terra mater* has rarely been studied for the Hebrew Bible, though see Sigmund Mowinckel, "'Moder jord' i Det gamle testamentet," in *Religionshistoriska studier tillägnade Edvard Lehmann den 19 augusti 1927* (Lund: C. W. K. Gleerup, 1927), 131–41; and Terje Stordalen, "Moder jord—etisk impuls i Det gamle testament," in *Makt, eiendom, rettferdighet: Bibelske moraltradisjoner i møte med vår tid*, ed. Jan-Olav Henriksen (Oslo: Gyldendal akademisk, 2000), 115–38.

Issues of ownership, manumission, privileges, and treatment were matters of law parallel to the terms governing the ownership of other real and movable property. As mentioned above in the discussion of class differences, a person could became a slave either through capture in warfare, kidnapping, birth to a slave, sale as a child, self-sale due to indebtedness, or punishment (usually if not able to pay the restitution for a tort or the penalty for a crime).[111] *Indentured servitude* or *debt slavery*[112] may at one level appear to be little more than a contractual means for a debtor to work off a loan, but the power imbalance within a society that grants legal protections only at the discretion of the powerful generally results in a dismal state of subservience and slavery for the many who had no other recourse than to borrow funds to survive. The text in Deut 15:18 concedes that the labor of the slave is valued at twice that of a paid laborer (as translated in NJPS, but not in NRSV); even more harshly, LL 14 expects that the slave's compensation in labor must equal twice the amount originally owed. And if the borrower resorts to selling his children or his wife to pay the debt, the low legal status of women and children may even mean that they disappeared into the mass of slaves. Perhaps the biblical provision that a free man should not sell his wife into slavery but that both should enter debt slavery at the same time actually reflects not an impulse toward gender equality, as some might be tempted to interpret it, but rather the perception of slave owners that it is better to have a married couple as slaves than to have the couple separated and less functional as a result. Many slaves remained in servitude for the entirety of their lives, as implied in Exod 21:5–6 and Deut 15:17—both texts suggesting that it was a personal choice of an enslaved husband in order to remain with his family, even though the options for him must have been bleak if he could not obtain freedom for his family as well. Others received their freedom by working off their debt, by their owners' freeing them for some special reason, by their owners' adopting them in order to support the owner in old age, or by being a concubine of a master who then dies. Just as ownership of a slave required some form of documentation or witnesses, similarly the freeing of a slave should be legally attested as well—not only for the benefit of the slave, but also to keep ownership issues clear in general.

---

111. See Isaac Mendelsohn, *Slavery in the Ancient Near East: A Comparative Study of Slavery in Babylonia, Assyria, Syria, and Palestine from the Middle of the Third Millennium to the End of the First Millennium* (New York: Oxford University Press, 1949), 1–33.

112. A detailed treatment, including a discussion of issues and developments in Mesopotamia and Israel, is available in Gregory C. Chirichigno, *Debt-Slavery in Israel and the Ancient Near East*, JSOTSup 141 (Sheffield: JSOT, 1993).

The potential for poor *treatment* of slaves accounts for the efforts to minimize it. While slave owners had free rein to exploit or punish their slaves at will, it was in neither party's interest for the abuse to be taken to extremes. Beating of slaves certainly occurred, and serious injury could easily follow, as is acknowledged in Exod 21:26–27: if the slave loses an eye or a tooth because of the owner's beating, the slave is to be set free. If the slave dies, the owner is to be punished, but not if the slave does not die immediately (21:20–21).[113] Job 31:13–14 counts it as a virtue that the wealthy Job was responsive to his slaves' complaints, based on the logic that he would otherwise be held accountable if God had to intervene. Nevertheless, slaves had few if any rights. The Laws of Hammurabi include several provisions regarding injuries sustained by slaves due to a third party's action (blinding the slave, breaking a bone, causing a miscarriage, a physician's surgery causing injury to the slave, or the slave being gored by another's ox): in every case the restitution is to be paid to the owner, not to the slave.[114] Such laws, entirely plausible in cultural environments including ancient Israel, obviously reflect the interests of the elites—the slave owners—not the poor and often-enslaved populations.

A variety of other issues and circumstances gave rise to additional legal practices. Any person of whatever *ethnic or national origin*, including a fellow Israelite, could become a slave. Although biblical laws offer special considerations for Hebrew slaves by ordaining that they are to be set free after six years without exacting further repayment of debts from them (Exod 21:2; Deut 15:12–15), it is highly unlikely that this practice was followed in society. Indeed, there would have been little reason for the text even to offer such a provision unless Israelites faced the very real prospect of interminable slavery, as did a foreigner who became enslaved in Israel.[115] Some type of *marking*—whether in clothing, hairstyle, pierced ear (Exod 21:6; Deut 15:17), or other branding—was typically mandated to keep the enslaved populations recognizable and distinct from free persons, and punishment ensued for disobedient slaves and others who abet-

---

113. The text actually uses the word "avenge" (נָקֹם יִנָּקֵם, *nāqōm yinnāqēm*) instead of the more generic "punish," and the meaning of "avenge" in this instance is less than clear, unless it simply indicates some unspecified kind of restitution to be paid or suffered. Another notable feature of Exod 21:20–21 is the time factor regarding the injury: the slave owner is to be punished only if the slave dies immediately after the blow, but not if the slave survives one or two days—presumably on the principle that in the latter case something other than the owner's blow might have caused the death or contributed to it.

114. LH 199, 213–214, 217, 219–220, 223.

115. The only other plausible reason for such a provision will be described shortly—that its inclusion in the literature aimed to curry favor with the powerless.

ted them.[116] A *runaway slave* posed legal problems at several levels—loss of property to the owner, possible charge of complicity against any free person who assists in the escape or gives the slave harbor (LL 12–13; LE 50), remuneration for someone who returns the slave (LU 17; LH 17), and strategy for dealing with a fugitive slave who is apprehended. The provision in Deut 23:15–16 (23:16–17 мт) specifying that a runaway slave is not to be returned to the owner represents a radical departure from LH 15–16 and 19, which prescribe death for anyone who harbors a runaway or assists a slave in escaping.

Gender relations, sexuality, marriage, and family pose a network of complicating factors generally based on custom, but also subject to both legal enforcement and revision.[117] The power of the slave owners, whether male or female, over their own slaves was, if not absolute, then virtually so, extending to the personal realms of sexuality and family. A master could take sexual advantage of his slave, and any offspring would also belong to the master.[118] Whether the master's wife had similar sexual access to their slaves is in theory possible on property grounds, but the larger patriarchal custom of a husband's exclusive rights sexually to his wife renders liaisons between the mistress and her slave less likely. A female slave with whom the master has sexual relations could attain the status of concubine, although she remained subservient to any other wives the master had. The story in Gen 29:31–30:24 of Leah and Rachel, along with the concubines Zilpah and Bilhah, dramatizes the intricacies possible in these circumstances, except that Jacob is depicted as decidedly more passive than what might typically have been expected of a master exploiting his slaves sexually. A concubine who bore her master a child probably gained special privileges; LH 170–171 stipulate that she and her child shall be freed at the death of her master, and the child will even share in the estate along with the other children if the master legally recognizes the child as his offspring,

116. LH 146 and 226–227 refer to a hair lock worn by a slave. MAL A 40 forbids a slave woman from wearing a veil, which is reserved only for free women. For discussion, see Muhammad A. Dandamaev, *Slavery in Babylonia: From Nabopolassar to Alexander the Great (626–331 BC)*, rev. ed., ed. Marvin A. Powell and David B. Weisberg, trans. Victoria A. Powell (DeKalb: Northern Illinois University Press, 1984), 229–34; and Mendelsohn, *Slavery*, 42–50.

117. Westbrook ("The Character of Ancient Near Eastern Law," in Westbrook, *History*, 43–44) argues that the problem is fundamental to the legal system: "A natural conflict existed between family law, which applied to slaves as persons, and property law, which applied to slaves as chattels." While there is good reason for seeing the problem in this manner, the role of the elites—the slave owners—in determining the laws must not be underestimated. While their interests may have been oriented more toward maintaining their property rights, they may nonetheless have felt obliged to make some concessions in the face of personal pressures from their slaves.

118. See Westbrook, "Character," 43–44; and Frymer-Kenski, "Israel," 1004–5.

a threat implied in Sarah's desire to have Abraham drive out the concubine Hagar and her son, Ishmael (Gen 21:9–14). A male slave could, presumably with his master's consent, marry a free woman, and any resulting children as well as part of their combined property will remain with the woman if her husband dies (LH 175–176). If, however, two slaves belonging to one slave owner become married while slaves, their children become the master's slaves also, and the wife and children remain with the master if the enslaved husband becomes free (Exod 21:2–6). And finally there is the matter of the unwed but betrothed female slave, reflected in Lev 19:20: if a man (presumably not her owner) has sexual relations with her, he must pay restitution, but—notably—he and she are not to be executed since she was not free.[119]

The king, as plenipotentiary in the country, could consider and treat all subjects as slaves, in a sense. With an army at his behest, a royal ideology that linked him with the deity, and no constitutional check on his power, little could be done to resist or countermand the monarch's orders. To be sure, a weak king, personally ineffectual or distracted by other concerns, did not pose much of a threat to the lives of the land's inhabitants, but a strong despot's might knew no bounds. The male population could be drawn from the towns and villages to serve in the corvée, forced labor (מס, mas) for constructing the royal palaces, temples, other monumental structures, city walls, roads, water systems, or whatever the king decided to build. The power to amass significant groups of laborers to construct edifices not for their own use is a sure sign of inequality within the society.[120] There was no obligation to pay wages to these workers, who in many instances were drawn away from their own lands during periods crucial to agricultural production. They needed sustenance and shelter during their forced work for the king, but they received nothing more than the minimal to keep them physically effective. They were not slaves in the sense of

---

119. There are more ambiguities in this text than one expects in a law: Is the male sexual partner her owner or a third party? Is she committed/betrothed (נחרפת, neḥĕrepet) to a fellow slave or to a freeman? To whom is the restitution to be paid—to the slave owner or to the fiancé? Since the usual punishment for adultery (involving a married or engaged woman) may well have meant death to both parties (as in Deut 22:22–29), how severe is the penalty in this case if it is short of execution? On the whole, however, one can well concur with Erhard Gerstenberger in his assessment of this text: "Male arrogance and bourgeois presumption toward female slaves are triumphant here" (Leviticus: A Commentary, OTL [Louisville, KY: Westminster John Knox Press, 1996], 274). Most commentators, unfortunately, have tended to minimize this text's significance by simply appealing to the legal status of a slave, or even by considering the greater issue to be that the seducer "offended God by desecrating the Sinaitic oath" (so Jacob Milgrom, Leviticus, a Book of Ritual and Ethics: A Continental Commentary [Minneapolis: Fortress Press, 2004], 238).

120. Wason, Archaeology of Rank, 145–52.

being deprived of their free status forever or until a debt was paid off, but for the season in the corvée they were for all practical purposes enslaved. Others, male and female of whatever age, could be drawn into servitude within the palace. Not only construction work but also military service awaited males in their prime, pawns to be moved around in peacetime and war at the will of the military officers. First Kings 5:13–18 (5:27–32 MT) describes Solomon's massive levy (מַס, *mas*) to build the temple: 30,000 Israelites, in addition to 150,000 other laborers and quarriers plus 3,300 supervisors. Even if these numbers are inflated, as is so much else about the legendary Solomon, they effectively indicate the extent of a king's power to amass workers for his projects.

In addition to the conscription of subjects for corvée and military purposes, the king also owned servants of his own. Many *chattel-slaves* stemmed from foreign populations conquered in warfare and permanently held by the king for hard labor on crown land or in mines and quarries; their numbers were augmented by the corvée from the Israelite population as needed. Beyond these groups, certain persons could also become *palace slaves*, trusted servants of the royal family with somewhat higher status, better provisions, and often skilled professions such as builders or artisans, as evident in Babylonian sources.[121] On the whole, the picture conforms quite well to the image in the *ex eventu* speech of Samuel regarding the legal, limitless powers of Israel's kings:

> This will be the law [מִשְׁפָּט, *mišpāṭ*] of the king who rules over you:
> He will take your sons and assign them to his chariots and horses and
> as runners before his chariots. He will appoint them as commanders of
> thousands and commanders of fifties. They will plow his land and reap
> his harvest, and make his weapons and chariot gear. He will take your
> daughters to serve as perfumers, cooks, and bakers. (1 Sam 8:11–13)

Even the elites were subject to the king's decisions, though they generally were able to avoid conscription into menial labor because of their status and their importance in the country's economy. Furthermore, the wealthy themselves had slaves whom they could send in their stead into the king's service.

Liability. With considerable holdings as well as their elite status at stake, the urbanites of the upper class saw to it that they were protected from loss caused by others. Liability issues occurred also in village contexts, as described in the previous chapter, but the stakes were noticeably different.

---

121. Dandamaev, *Slavery*, 561–84.

For a poor family the loss of what was perhaps their only work animal or one of their few sheep, or negligent destruction of their meager crops, or damage to their tools or household objects—such events had potentially devastating effects on their well-being, if not even their survival. On the other hand, for the wealthy who possessed extensive lands, buildings, livestock, slaves, or other commercial businesses, such losses had much less impact on their livelihood—yet were probably as zealously remedied and punished as possible. These elites also had the power to exact restitution for their loss, even if it had to be taken by force from the one charged with causing it. This difference between the elites and the poor can be expressed in the following manner, even if it represents a simplification: liability and restitution were matters of need and necessity for poor villagers, who could scarcely handle any loss, while the wealthier city dwellers demanded such accountability as a matter of power and wealth security. Two texts in Amos, without specifically mentioning liability and restitution, indicate this prophet's view of the elites' low esteem of the poor: they are willing to buy or sell the needy for a pair of sandals (2:6; 8:6).

Liability pertained to both movable and immovable property. *Leasing* or *borrowing* entailed an expectation that the lessee or borrower accepted full responsibility for damages to or loss of the property or item. In most instances, the land being leased belonged not to the poor but to someone who owned more houses or more lands than one family could utilize, and the lessee was expected to work the land and maintain buildings and equipment in good condition. Herds of sheep or goats, again belonging to someone with many livestock, could also be leased, with new animals born to the herd divided between the owner and the lessee.[122] As described in Exod 22:10–15 (22:9–14 MT), the hirer must normally compensate the owner for the death or loss of any animal, although certain mitigating circumstances may be considered, such as evidence that it was killed by a wild animal or died of an illness or injury; the hirer may also be allowed to swear an oath of innocence and be freed from the obligation to compensate the owner if the remains of the animal could not be delivered.

Similarly, anyone who agrees to hold silver, tools, or other goods for another is also liable for their safekeeping and could be required to repay the owner for their loss (LE 36–37; Exod 22:7–9 [22:6–8 MT]). Moreover, damage to a landowner's crops or animals meant recompense in kind or other assessment (Exod 22:5–6 [22:4–5 MT]). While such provisions prevailed among villagers as well, the involvement of a member of the elite, perhaps

122. Westbrook, *History*, 408–11, 956–58, 1025–26.

an absentee landholder, as the party suffering the loss probably led to a more inflexible application of the principle of restitution than occurred between neighbors of the same class.[123] On the other hand, though the villagers needed ways to remedy cases of injury caused by oxen, dogs, and other domesticated or work animals,[124] such provisions were less urgent for the city dwellers who owned and operated agricultural lands but were less likely to be found in harm's way.

Construction liability, though, was of immediate concern for the urban elite, more so than for the villagers, who as a rule built their own very modest dwellings. For wealthier homes, the owners held their contractors responsible for the work to the extent that the builder might have to pay on a life-for-life basis for damages resulting from failed construction; according to LH 229–231, for example, the contractor, his own child, or his slave, respectively, is to be executed if the collapsed house kills the householder, his child, or his slave. Liability for safe construction extends even to punishing the house owner who has been warned of a dangerous wall but neglects to repair it before it falls and kills an upper-class person (LE 58; LH gap e). Even if these specific provisions from law collections predating Iron II Israel by a millennium did not carry over into monarchic Israel, something of similar effect must have seemed appropriate to the elites in Israel's cities as a deterrent to shoddy workmanship. Other issues of liability and negligence occurred in the various areas of life where a person of the upper and powerful class could suffer loss, and we can be certain that legal provisions were in place to ensure their compensation or retribution.

Responsibilities toward the Vulnerable. As we have seen in this chapter and the preceding discussion of village life, ancient Israel—like so many other cultures in ancient Southwest Asia and elsewhere—was characterized by an asymmetrical distribution of wealth and power, which directly determined their laws and protective provisions. Villages were typically characterized by subsistence living standards; a relative absence of goods with significant market value; a direct dependence on the vagaries of weather, pests, and other natural circumstances affecting food production; and vulnerability to the elites who hired them, lent them resources, and enslaved them when they defaulted on their loans. Those elites, on the other hand, lived at some remove from the locales where their food and other goods were produced. Some occupied rural manor houses, but most resided in the nation's cities,

123. Note the detail into which LH 42–65 goes to adjudicate responsibility and compensation, generally to the benefit of the landowner.
124. See above, chap. 5, Liability.

sites dedicated to the well-being and security of the upper class, including royalty. There they could luxuriate in relative comfort and ease, exercising their power and influence, enjoying their acquisitions, and being served by slaves and laborers. The closest the villagers could come to this lifestyle occurred when, as slaves or laborers, they observed it and were granted some of the bounty. The royal family's distance from, and exploitation of, the rural poor was even greater. Urban and national laws aimed to secure the privileges of wealth and power.

Kings in ancient Southwest Asia could respond unilaterally to this inequity by proclaiming an *andurāru*, an edict forgiving debts and granting freedom to slaves. Another Akkadian term, *mīšaru*, expresses justice in general, in some cases with this same sense of redressing economic wrongs.[125] We cannot know how often and how widespread it was practiced since our evidence is fragmentary. Three edicts from early Babylonia have come to light: King Samsu-iluna (1749–1712 BCE) and King Ammi-ṣaduqa (1646–1626 BCE), both of them successors to Hammurabi; and one other such edict from an unidentified king.[126] There are frequent other references, after the fact, to remissions of debt and manumission of slaves ordered by other kings from the time of Sargon of Akkad (ca. 2200 BCE) to the Neo-Babylonian period. Although all of them target some form of release, their objects vary: commercial debts, slaves (usually only selected ones, esp. debt slaves), pledged persons, tax obligations, illegal impositions on persons. Apparently the succession of a new king to the throne represented an auspicious time to enact such a release since the king could thereby win favor with those who were oppressed and signal that he fulfilled the royal ideology as an advocate of justice. However, far from inaugurating a substantial reform, the *andurāru* was generally followed shortly thereafter by a return to the conditions of debts and slavery. Such is only to be expected since the king depended on the support of the elites, precisely those who benefited from lending and enslaving.

This tradition has often been viewed as the background for the *release laws* found in the Hebrew Bible, even with the differences existing

125. *CAD* A/II 115–17; M/II 116–19.
126. Analyses of the Babylonian evidence are available in Fritz Rudolf Kraus, *Ein Edikt des Königs Ammi-ṣaduqa von Babylon*, Studia et documenta ad iura orientis antiqui pertinentia 5 (Leiden: E. J. Brill, 1958); idem, "Ein Edikt des Königs Samsu-Iluna von Babylon," in *Studies in Honor of Benno Landsberger on His Seventy-fifth Birthday, April 21, 1965*, AS 16 (Chicago: University of Chicago Press, 1965), 225–31; idem, *Königliche Verfügungen in altbabylonischer Zeit*, Studia et documenta 11 (Leiden: E. J. Brill, 1984); Dominique Charpin, "Les édits de 'restauration' des rois babyloniens et leur application," in *Du pouvoir dans l'antiquité: Mots et réalités*, ed. Claude Nicolet, Hautes études du monde gréco-romain 16 (Geneva: Librairie Droz, 1990), 13–24.

between the two contexts and laws.[127] One example is the narrative in Jer 34:8–22 describing an agreement (בְּרִית, bĕrît, "covenant") between King Zedekiah and the residents of Jerusalem (i.e., the elites living there) to proclaim a דְּרוֹר, dĕrôr ("release"), Hebrew cognate of the Akkadian *andurāru*. This *dĕrôr* affects not all slaves but only the Hebrew slaves, both male and female. The story then relates that the people (presumably also King Zedekiah) subsequently reversed the release, subjecting their former slaves once again to slavery, for which divine judgment is proclaimed against them.

The pentateuchal laws contain several provisions regarding release, restoration, as well as other humanitarian considerations to benefit the vulnerable, and we list many of them here in order to discuss them as a whole:

- Remission of debts every seventh year for fellow Israelites only, not for foreigners: Deut 15:1–3.
- Manumission of Hebrew slaves, male and female, after six years of service: Exod 21:2–3; Deut 15:12–18.
- Manumission of Hebrew slaves in the fiftieth (Jubilee) Year: Lev 25:10, 40, 47–55.
- Restoration of ancestral land every (Jubilee) Year: Lev 25:8–17, 25–34.
- Guarantee of loans to needy neighbors, even if the seventh-year remission is near: Deut 15:7–11.
- Protection of Israelites from becoming enslaved: Lev 25:39–46.
- Protection of fugitive slaves (probably only those who escaped from countries outside Israel?) from being returned to their owners: Deut 23:15–16 (23:16–17 MT).
- Provision for fallowing the land every seventh year and letting the poor eat from it that year: Exod 23:10–11; also Lev 25:3–7, though without mention of the poor as beneficiaries.
- Designation of the harvest gleanings for the widows, orphans, and resident aliens: Lev 19:9–10; Deut 24:19–22.
- Contribution of a tithe to the Levites, widows, orphans, and resident aliens every third year: Deut 14:28–29.

127. See, e.g., the discussion in Moshe Weinfeld, "Sabbatical Year and Jubilee in the Pentateuchal Laws and Their Ancient Near Eastern Background," in *The Law in the Bible and in Its Environment*, ed. Timo Veijola, Publications of the Finnish Exegetical Society 51 (Helsinki: Finnish Exegetical Society; Göttingen: Vandenhoeck & Ruprecht, 1990), 39–62.

- Loans without interest to fellow Israelites: Exod 22:25 (22:24 MT); Lev 25:35–37; Deut 23:19–20 (23:20–21 MT).
- Considerate treatment of borrowers for items given as collateral for loans: Exod 22:26–27 (22:25–26 MT); Deut 24:6, 10–13, 17b.
- Payment of wages daily to poor laborers: Deut 24:14–15.
- Prohibition against oppressing resident aliens, widows, and orphans: Exod 22:21–24 (22:20–23 MT); 23:9; Lev 19:33–34.

Primarily the first four in the above list converge to some extent with practices in neighboring cultures: remission of debts, release of slaves, and restoration of land. They represent the kinds of actions that could be unilaterally mandated by the monarch, though the biblical laws differ in placing them on a recurring cycle of seven or fifty years. The remainder of the above provisions envision various considerations or concessions that seem to be expected on a continual basis in Israel.

But to what extent were any of these biblical stipulations actually practiced during Israel's history? Do they point to genuine efforts to redress inequities, or were they, rather, crass attempts to curry favor with the masses while effecting no significant improvement in the economic livelihood of the vulnerable populations? These various humanitarian pronouncements constitute some of the most dramatic, memorable, reform-oriented provisions, reinforced by expressions of divine sanction, in the history of social and economic ethics. Yet though these "laws" exist on the pages of the Hebrew Bible and were surely the products of real persons living in one or the other period of Israel's history, we are left with spare if any evidence that they were ever practiced or enforced. The story from Jer 34:8–22, during the time of King Zedekiah, strikes one as last-ditch bartering for divine favor in the threatening geopolitical environment leading up to the Babylonian sack of Jerusalem: the release may have actually occurred, but it was promptly undone when the slave owners calculated their losses. The slight references in other texts do not indicate a regular practicing of the release laws. According to Neh 5:1–13, the people protested their exploitation at the hands of their compatriots, and Nehemiah effected a sabbatical restoration of land and an elimination of interest on loans. This incident, however, does not reveal a continual, regular practice, even despite the people's pledge in Neh 10:31. First Maccabees 6:49, 53 also refer to the seventh-year fallowing, which resulted in reduced provisions of food. The book of Jubilees employs the jubilee notion only to measure time, not to institute economic reform. Finally, Josephus mentions the fallow year and the jubilee a few times when treating the Hellenistic and Roman periods, but generally only in vague terms.[128]

Frankly, such radical reforms would have had enormous consequences for the economy and society of ancient Israel. The elites, congregating above all in the cities, depended on the production of the lands they had acquired and on the comfort provided by slaves and hired workers. To be required to release their slaves—at least the Israelite slaves—would have deprived the prosperous of labor in both field and home. Forgiving debts would have meant that they had lent resources with little return, perhaps even with significant loss. The provision to lend at no interest to Israelites meant that their capital was being used but to no profit to them. To return land parcels to the families who had previously inherited them from their ancestors would have broken up, if not even dissolved, the estates held by the large landowners. Incentives to accumulate wealth would thus have declined while the risks of investments increased. The allusion in Deut 15:7–11 to creditors' reluctance to lend money as the Sabbatical Year approached points to a very plausible scenario. Equity in wealth distribution is a utopian ideal, which the economic realities of Israel's society—or for that matter, potentially any society—would generally resist. Archaeological evidence of urban sites from ancient Israel clearly indicates that wealth and power, with the trappings of monumental architecture, fine homes, and luxury items, centered there. If a king proclaimed a release on the order of the *andurāru* edicts of Babylonia and Assyria, the nonroyal elites soon pressed for its reversal. In agrarian states, as discussed above,[129] the governing class among the nonroyal elites exercised considerable influence vis-à-vis the monarchy since the king depended on their collaboration in order to manage the country's economy and populace. Whatever form their reciprocal maneuvering for advantage may have taken, we can be assured that the upper class fought any steps by the monarchy to lessen their standing and resources or to reform the economic system on which they depended.

Such considerations cast a different light on the *humanitarian laws* of the Hebrew Bible than is usually perceived. The roots for their empathetic concern run deeply into the subsistence living in the villages. Here were to be found the persons endangered most by the vicissitudes of weather, the overwhelming force of passing armies and raiders, the threat of poverty and enslavement, and alienation from the land. As potential victims

128. For references and discussion, see Fager, *Land Tenure*, 34–36.
129. See chap. 3, The Social Structure of Power in Ancient Israel.

themselves, they knew the importance of mutual support, especially among members of the same clan. The biblical laws of release from indebtedness and servitude were thus consistent with experiences in the village population: they were the ones who most desired to be released periodically from debts and slavery. The drafting of the biblical laws in written form occurred, however, in the cities and at the direction of the elites. The latter generally inflicted rather than suffered from the hardships of lost resources, land, and freedom. Yet they also knew the value of persuasion and rhetoric, and they saw in the release traditions a means for manipulating the poor in the country. By holding out the promise of remission of debts, manumission, and other humanitarian gestures, they tried to convince the masses that relief was imminent if they fell on hard times. The poor certainly recognized when their anticipated release did not occur, and perhaps sporadic remissions ordered by the king, even if limited to only select groups or individuals, gave the vulnerable enough hope that they, too, would someday be restored to independent life in their villages. In this manipulation, the royal and nonroyal elites were complicit since they both stood to gain from the ongoing exploitation and subjugation. It was a cynical, devious practice, yet also probably effective in light of the contrast between the presence of these biblical laws and the near absence of evidence that release and restoration occurred. The poor had no recourse but to cry out to YHWH and to turn to advocates such as the prophets. The powerful and wealthy in the country, however, could continue their oppression undeterred.[130]

CONCLUSION

Life in the Israelite cities proceeded along lines sharply different from those found elsewhere in the country. The urban inhabitants comprised primarily the wealthy and the powerful, and others of a lower class mainly filled positions of service to the elites. The upper class included the royalty and

130. For elaboration of this ideological-critical approach to the "humanitarian laws," see my article "Whose Agony? Whose Ecstasy?" In addition, several of my former doctoral students have developed this approach further with respect to specific legal topics: Harold V. Bennett, *Injustice Made Legal: Deuteronomic Law and the Plight of Widows, Strangers, and Orphans in Ancient Israel* (Grand Rapids, MI, and Cambridge, UK: William B. Eerdmans, 2002); Cheryl B. Anderson, *Women, Ideology, and Violence: Critical Theory and the Construction of Gender in the Book of the Covenant and the Deuteronomic Law*, JSOTSup 394 (London and New York: T&T Clark International, 2004); and Zipporah G. Glass, "Land, Labor, and Law: Viewing Persian Yehud's Economy through Socio-Economic Modeling" (Ph.D. diss., Vanderbilt University, 2010, http://etd.library.vanderbilt.edu/available/etd-07192010-195213/unrestricted/Dissertation_of_Z_Glass_July_19_2010.pdf).

other powerful leaders, among them the priests, high military officers, administrative officials, and wealthy landowners and merchants. The cities were not populous, but they represented a concentration of power. During the period of the monarchies in the northern and southern halves of the country, substantial portions of land were owned by the crown, the temples, and large landowners. As a result, they also could control the well-being and livelihood of the vast majority of the population residing in the countryside, many of whom were hired or indebted to work on the estates. The city dwellers and government officials could avail themselves of the military, the bureaucracy, and hired overseers to enforce their demands and extract taxes, rents, and labor. The cities depended on the villages for their food and their workforce, but they also possessed the means to impose their will.

Those living in the urban centers experienced legal conflicts of their own. As was the case in the villages, they developed certain social conventions in the areas of marriage and sexual behavior. Clan-oriented endogamy was probably also practiced in the cities, but it was likely supplemented with a type of class-oriented endogamy, a preference to marry those considered socially equal, thereby forming alliances among powerful and wealthy families. Marriage contracts and inheritance arrangements required legal documentation to ensure against conflict and confusion in the event of divorce of a spouse or death of a property owner. Sexual behavior deemed unacceptable, whether among equals or across classes, could also threaten relations and needed a mechanism for resolving tensions. Personal injury and wrongful death may well have resulted in stiffer penalties when the victim belonged to the upper class, as was the case in neighboring cultures. Economic loss, especially through theft, negligence, nonpayment, dishonesty, or other cause, also called for a legal response. The poor possessed much fewer resources than did the wealthy and would have suffered more greatly from a loss, and the penalties also weighed more heavily on those with less means to pay them. Nonetheless, the laws from the cities aimed especially to protect the interests of the haves rather than the have-nots, even if it meant that a poor family had to sell themselves into slavery to pay a debt or penalty. Given such circumstances, it is difficult to imagine much charity toward the powerless and defenseless, even while those in need hoped for it and their advocates, such as the prophets, fought for it.

While the urban residents with means had their own interests to protect through legal provisions and procedures, they had much less concern for the internal affairs among the rural population. So long as the villagers paid their taxes and rents, could be conscripted for construction projects and military needs, and did not offer concerted resistance, the city dwellers let them develop and adjudicate their own laws. Only if a dispute could not be resolved at a local level or if it in some way threatened special interests of the elites would it have come to the attention of the upper class or the monarch. The powerful could interfere at will in the lives of the villagers, but they probably chose not to do so as a matter of course.

Consequently, the laws that were remembered and recorded in ancient Israel were primarily those of the cities, the states, and the elites. A high level of literacy was available only in those contexts, and any laws that became written expressed urban standards or urban conceptions of legal practices among the rural populace. To the extent that the legal texts of the Hebrew Bible reflect actually functioning laws, they are thus primarily consonant with those of the cities and the interests they advance.

CHAPTER 7

Law in the Cult

It does seem to me that the influence of religion on people is often exaggerated, while the influence of people on religion is neglected.

—*Amin Maalouf*[1]

Religiosity is not easy to measure, especially not for a society that can no longer be observed and interviewed. It has often been treated as a truism that the people of ancient Israel, just as those of many other ancient societies in that region and beyond, made no distinction between the religious and the secular; many assume that the secular scarcely even existed for them, so imbued were their thoughts and actions by the aspect of divinity. Such a notion can be neither proved nor disproved, but personally I doubt that it is correct. The previous two chapters have displayed many specific legal conflicts and interests that likely occurred in Israel independent of religious impetus or interpretation. Whether it was a property issue, a sexual liaison outside marriage, a personal injury, a matter of class status, or treatment of the poor or the slaves—all such cases involved actionable or conflictual situations that required a judicial response, regardless of any religious dimension. To be sure, a religious interpretation may often have been given to it, as is more than evident in the legal texts of the Hebrew Bible. In some cases a religious or moral impulse may even have affected the outcome; one thinks of efforts to protect the vulnerable, despite the self-interests of the powerful. All the cases treated above in chapters 5 and 6 have social, economic, and political dimensions, without which they would not have arisen or been resolved. Conflating them with the religious dimension only confuses all aspects.

Yet the religious does carry weight in its own right as well. Many, if not most or even all, of the ancient Israelites must have looked to a divine

---

1. Amin Maalouf, *In the Name of Identity: Violence and the Need to Belong*, trans. Barbara Bray (New York: Penguin, 2003), 60.

sphere for aid in coping with their terms of life, which too often could seem beyond their own control. The number of worship sites and religious objects found throughout the land underscores the role that rituals, veneration of the gods, sacrifices and offerings, and religious interpretation apparently played for the people. Beyond such religiosity is the institutionalization of religion, which occurred at both the local and the national levels. Religious professionals in the form of priests and other functionaries developed and maintained a national structure of remarkable reach and tenacity. These institutions provided a context for the expression of public religiosity, while also pursuing their own interests and survival. Both aspects of religion—the worshiper's piety and the worship institution— must be held in view.

The *cult* designates the formal processes of worship, including the site, the objects and furnishings, the rituals and ceremonies, the personnel, and the myths or beliefs expressed through the rituals.[2] It can refer to both the overall outward structure of religious expression and to an individual occasion of it. In our effort to assess the role of law in ancient Israel, we need to think not philosophically about religion but practically about the formal place of religion in the society, to which the term "cult" refers. Inasmuch as cultic aspects and personnel have an influence outside the formal settings of worship, for example, in regulating or adjudicating behavior, we are dealing with cultic law. As will be described, this influence could assume enormous proportions, not only in ancient Israel but also in the wider region of Southwest Asia during that time.

THE CULT

Rather than start, as is often done, with rituals and beliefs, we begin by surveying the material forms of Israelite religion evident in the archaeological record. We also continue our focus on the Iron II period, the time of the monarchies in the northern and southern parts of the land of Israel. This focus stems not from a notion that the premonarchic period of Iron I should be downplayed, for those centuries witnessed the initial stages in the formation of the Israelites' identity and ethos. Nor should we diminish the importance of the Neo-Babylonian, Persian, and Hellenistic periods, when the majority if not the entirety of the Hebrew Bible tradition was composed and committed to writing; in places we will attend to these later developments when they reflect an enhanced or different role played by the cult

---

2. For more on the definition of "cult," see above, chap. 3, The Cult.

and the priests. My choice to concentrate on the monarchic period derives from my interest in understanding the systems of laws that existed during a time when a king or queen was in power, the government and other institutions (priesthood, military, construction, commerce) were centralized, political sovereignty or vassalage indicated some measure of self-determination, social and economic inequality was evident, habitation was spread throughout rural and urban contexts, and the country experienced some degree of geopolitical importance. All such characteristics foster the development of laws and customs in the diverse contexts where power and special interests converged. The domain of religion is one such context.[3]

Cultic Sites

The most immediate and ubiquitous setting for religious expression occurred in the *domestic cult*, which most frequently involved a single family but could at times include a clan (מִשְׁפָּחָה, *mišpāḥâ*) living in close proximity within a village or in nearby villages. In all likelihood, many if not most houses possessed a small shrine, a niche in a wall or some other type of fixture used for religious purposes. Unfortunately, we can rarely attest to their presence since house structures generally have little more than their foundation stones in place—to the extent that their material remains are present at all, which is rarely the case for the mud-brick homes typical of the villages. Gatherings of several members of one clan for certain rituals probably transpired in or near the residence of a household head, the senior member of the clan. Known in the Hebrew Bible as a *bāmâ* (בָּמָה), or "high place," an open-air site, designated by tradition perhaps outside a village, also served the community for rites in common. A substantial number of small cultic objects have been found in domestic settings, as will be discussed below. Various texts in the Hebrew Bible—in Genesis, the Deuteronomistic History, prophetic materials, and Wisdom literature—also

---

3. As in the preceding two chapters, the ideological-critical interpretation of the evidence, both archaeological and textual, is largely my own. For detailed presentations of the evidence, see such resources as the following, along with their references to other specific discussions: Miller, *Religion*; Ziony Zevit, *The Religions of Ancient Israel: A Synthesis of Parallactic Approaches* (London and New York: Continuum, 2001); Richard S. Hess, *Israelite Religions: An Archaeological and Biblical Survey* (Grand Rapids: Baker Academic, 2007); Helga Weippert, *Palästina in vorhellenistischer Zeit* (Munich: Verlag C. H. Beck, 1988), 447–49, 461–74, 620–31; Beth Alpert Nakhai, *Archaeology and the Religions of Canaan and Israel*, ASOR Books 7 (Boston: American Schools of Oriental Research, 2001), 176–200; Albertz, *History of Israelite Religion*; Karel van der Toorn, *Family Religion in Babylonia, Syria, and Israel: Continuity and Change in the Forms of Religious Life*, SHCANE 7 (Leiden: E. J. Brill, 1996); Magnus Ottosson, *Temples and Cult Places in Palestine*, Acta universitatis upsaliensis: Boreas 12 (Uppsala: Almqvist & Wiksell, 1980); and John Bodel and Saul M. Olyan, ed., *Household and Family Religion in Antiquity* (Oxford: Basil Blackwell Publishing, 2008).

describe cultic activities of a domestic nature, though such texts present us with the usual problems with regard to dating, determining social and ideological influences on them, and interpreting them in light of other texts. At a minimum, we can assume that religiosity was expressed widely and variously in these disparate, private settings. Tribal religious functions were less likely to occur during the monarchic period than in premonarchic times since regional sanctuaries, under the control of the king and the national priesthood, would not have tolerated tribal competition.

The *regional cult* represented the next level in terms of range of power and importance. In most cases during the monarchic period, it could be considered an urban cult since it generally occurred within cities; probably few if any cities lacked a cultic installation of some type. However, archaeologists have yet to verify a dedicated cultic building in Megiddo, Hazor, and Gezer from the Iron II period, though Dan and later Lachish have it. Megiddo has revealed numerous cultic items, but it is unclear if they reflect a more-domestic or a centralized worship. In most local administrative cities and residential cities, it would not be surprising to find cultic sites that served public interests and usually also state interests. With the possible exception of the residential cities, which were populated primarily with peasants, artisans, and other laborers, all urban cults functioned as arms of the state cult in their respective regions. The small installation in the Arad fortress in the Negev is an especially distinctive exemplar of an Iron II cultic site, complete with main hall, holy of holies chamber (דביר, *děbîr*), altar, and incense stands. Sites in other cities may also belong to a type of *bāmâ*, or "high place."

The *state cult* was headquartered in the capital cities of the northern and southern kingdoms, where impressive and lavishly appointed cultic sites could function as political and ideological symbols for the whole country. The state cult legitimated the royal house and the kingdom by serving as the earthly dwelling for the national deity. In Samaria of the eighth century BCE, the Omride dynasty constructed monumental buildings on the rocky hilltop above the lower part of the city, and a temple or other cultic installation may well have been included although it has not yet been discovered. Jerusalem has also yielded no material evidence of an Iron II temple, neither the edifice attributed to Solomon in biblical traditions nor any other preexilic predecessor to the Second Temple erected in the early Persian period. At the present time, archaeological exploration of the Temple Mount is generally prohibited. While the absence of material evidence does not mean evidence of the absence of a temple during Iron II, the presence of innumerable modern reconstructions and drawings according to the biblical descriptions also does not confirm its historical existence, though such models give the "Solomonic temple" some verisimilitude. Nonetheless, we can assume that the national religions of the northern and southern kingdoms enjoyed not only royal patronage but also monumental accommodations befitting an essential, influential expression of state power. Other forms of cultic sites, in addition to temples, existed within and without the cities, including "gate shrines," smaller buildings containing cultic objects, and open-air sanctuaries such as that found at Dan. Together they formed a support structure to enhance the national agenda.

Cultic Paraphernalia

The types of artifacts discovered in settlements or other sites generally indicate more about the nature of the cult than do the buildings or sites themselves. As with the structures, the quality of their materials and the level of their artisanship reveal information about the socioeconomic standing of their producers or, as the case may be, of those who commissioned their production. Ranging from crudely formed by hand, to finely crafted by artisans, to mass-produced with molds; from shaped out of local clay, to fashioned with imported metals or precious stones; from heavily used, to carefully preserved—all such features yield details about the character of the society as well as the nature of the religious practices.

Over the years, archaeologists have uncovered a considerable number of cultic objects in sites throughout the land. The details about them and their provenances are less important for our purposes than simply the fact that they were plentiful, varied, and widely distributed in both rural and urban contexts. The following list of items gives an impression of their diversity: figurines—male and female, animal and human; cult vessels, some with anthropomorphic or zoomorphic designs; scarabs and various amulets; seals and bullae; cult stands and incense holders; models of shrines; altars of various types and sizes, often with traces of animal or grain remains on them; iconographic pieces; a מַצֵּבָה (maṣṣēbâ, "sacred pillar") erected at numerous cultic sites either to represent a deity or to mark a place of special religious significance.[4] The clay figurines and plaques, especially those depicting a female with her hands under her breasts or covering her genitalia, have been found by the hundreds throughout seventh-century

---

4. Surveys and illustrations of these objects are readily available in such publications as Miller, *Religion*; Zevit, *Religions*; Hess, *Israelite Religions*; Ephraim Stern, *Archaeology of the Land of the Bible*, vol. 2, *The Assyrian, Babylonian, and Persian Periods (732–332 BCE)* (New York: Doubleday, 2001). References to more specialized studies are also present in these sources.

BCE Judah, including some 2,000 in Iron II Jerusalem alone.[5] Some of the male figurines are displayed riding a horse. All such objects point to variety in cultic practices and loyalties in ancient Israel. Especially noteworthy is the marked increase in these objects in the years leading to the fall of the North and, later, the capture of Jerusalem[6]—as if the population intensified its piety and worship of other gods in the face of imminent destruction. Even without such intensification during these periods, the finds suggest substantial use of figurines and other cultic paraphernalia at potentially any period, which numerous prophetic texts critical of idol worship reinforce. The story in Jer 44:15–19, for example, describes Judean women in Egypt, who cite their earlier worship of the Queen of Heaven as the reason for their prosperity and good fortune during monarchic times in Judah, which Jeremiah in turn reverses by interpreting such practices as the very reason for Jerusalem's ultimate fall (44:20–30).

Cultic Personnel

The types and number of cultic personnel varied according to type and size of the cultic installation. At the most basic and widespread level, the domestic and local religious entities had *nonprofessional officiants* to celebrate rituals and maintain the site and paraphernalia. By "nonprofessional" I mean that they earned their livelihood not through their role as cultic officiants but as farmers, herders, potters, or whatever other means they had in the villages spread across the land. When the time came to venerate the gods within the home or in community gatherings, they were recognized by consensus to be the appropriate ones to take the lead. Calling them "lay priests" confuses their status: they were not trained and legitimated by some priestly body that retained for itself alone certain functions and prerogatives. Rather, these local officiants derived their authority from their own social contexts, and they learned their roles from their predecessors, the previous generation. In a given household the mother or father ensured that the family's gods were properly honored, and in a village some individual probably had the leadership role, perhaps inherited by tradition along a family line. It is a fair guess, though certainly hypothetical, that in light of the basic patriarchal orientation of social life, the mother may have had the leadership role within the household while some male held it in

5. The details are surveyed in Zevit, *Religions*, 266–74.
6. John S. Holladay Jr., "Religion in Israel and Judah under the Monarchy: An Explicitly Archaeological Approach," in *Ancient Israelite Religion: Essays in Honor of Frank Moore Cross*, ed. Patrick D. Miller Jr., Paul D. Hanson, and S. Dean McBride (Philadelphia: Fortress Press, 1987), 275–80.

the public context of communal worship. We can at least be quite certain that cultic activities at this local level proceeded at local directive, independently of the state cult, and that this situation remained largely constant throughout Israel's history.

At the greatest distance from the village cult was the *central priesthood and related functionaries*, located most likely in Samaria and Jerusalem. Here we find, in a sense, the established religion, sanctioned by the kings, visited by the elites, and supported by taxes and income from its own commercial dealings. The priests serving these interests were as plentiful as their support would allow, and they kept the temple in the public eye through celebrating high festival days, relaying divine blessings on the royal house, responding with divine oracles when approached by individuals, appointing the temple with treasures, and generally maintaining a conspicuous place for religion in as many affairs of the kingdom and society as possible. A hierarchical order surely gave structure to the central priesthood, with a chief priest at the head and other priests situated according to roles, seniority, and abilities. A plethora of other cultic functionaries are suggested in biblical texts and probably proliferated during the successful times of the First Temple and even more so during the Second Temple period: Levites, prophets, temple singers, servants, gatekeepers, scribes, and more. Especially vital were the personnel needed to manage the estates, herds, and other commercial interests of the temple, as we will see shortly. According to the model of the agrarian society, the high priest belonged to the governing elite of the nation, while most of the other temple functionaries fit in the privileged but dependent class, those who served the interests of the elites while remaining in a position only tenuously separated from the common people. The actual presence and roles of a high priest in Israel's history have been matters of discussion, with most scholars envisioning a difference between the Iron II and the Persian periods: during the former the king was superior to the high priest, while during the latter, when the monarchy had disappeared, the high priest assumed both cultic and civil leadership roles. Such a division, however, is quite questionable.[7] It is more likely that other emerging elites, when sanctioned by the Persian powers, controlled the civil affairs of the country while the high priest's standing remained primarily in the cult, including the Second Temple's economic interests. Although some scholars have interpreted biblical references to Zadok and Abiathar as indications either of

---

7. Deborah W. Rooke, *Zadok's Heirs: The Role and Development of the High Priesthood in Ancient Israel* (Oxford and New York: Oxford University Press, 2000).

rival groups or of dynastic lines among the priests throughout history,[8] the evidence is not firm, and it is just as possible that these representations in the text result from much-later retrojections of tensions during the Persian or Hellenistic periods.[9]

The third group of cultic officiants are the most difficult to reconstruct— the *regional priesthood and related functionaries*. As indicated above, archaeological evidence points to the existence of shrines or even small temples in the royal cities and the regional administrative cities, and it stands to reason that these cultic sites would also have had their own cultic functionaries. They must have been subordinate to the state cult centered in the capital cities, just as these second- and third-level cities themselves served the administrative, military, and tax-collecting needs of the capitals. We cannot know how tightly the high priest and his cohort held control over these regional cults, but at a minimum we can expect that their religious practices would not have deviated much from what was acceptable in the central cult. The primary factor that could have introduced some variation among the regional cults stemmed, in all likelihood, from their proximity to the populace in the respective regions. If a given region favored a certain god over others or celebrated some religious festival not common in the capital cities, that regional cult may well have accommodated the people by including these practices. But again, it would not have compromised or diverted the interests of the state cult, to which their dominant loyalty was owed. In addition to their priests, these regional cults included other aides and functionaries such as servants and managers of temple lands and holdings.

Orthodoxy, Heterodoxy, and Popular Religion

Religious practices were thus diffused and varied throughout the country. The Israelites, like their counterparts elsewhere in ancient Southwest Asia, believed in the world of the divine. Their problem was not the existence or nonexistence of the deity, but rather the absence of God or the gods: Where is divine help when one needs it? What can one do to ensure the continual presence and support of God or the gods?[10] We can assume that their religiosity expressed sentiments steeped in tradition and attuned to their own circumstances. Their practices, rituals, cultic sites, religious objects, leadership structures, and regulations emerged over time and

8. Miller, *Religion*, 171–74.
9. Hunt, *Missing Priests*.
10. See my "Revelation through Tradition," in *Tradition and Theology in the Old Testament*, ed. Douglas A. Knight (Philadelphia: Fortress Press; London: SPCK, 1977), 147.

formed the venerated heritage that provided them with the means for expression and performance. From this distance it is impossible for us to know of their religious sentiments—whether they longed for order in this world, whether they sought meaning and sense in their existence, or how they reconciled the notion of transcendence with their this-worldly rootedness. It is probably even more difficult for us, situated as we are in our own socioeconomic location and in this modern world, to comprehend the religiosity of an ancient people struggling to survive in a subsistence economy and under the thumb of a powerful monarch and elite class.

Of one thing, however, we can be quite certain: political and economic interests played a role in cultic life in ancient Israel, as is widely the case elsewhere. A state cult prevailed in both kingdoms throughout their histories. It helped to legitimize the kings by proclaiming divine favor over the royal house and participating in a king's acts of going to war, building cities, erecting monuments, and taking other actions of significance for the country. The king also enjoyed special access to the cult and participation in key rituals. In turn, the high priests in service at the main temples presumably frequented the royal court as well, serving as advisers or consultants in matters of state. Even in the domestic and local cults, the role of the household head in certain religious rituals and of the mother in other rituals reinforced their preeminent standing in the household and in the community. The traditions regulating these roles were, to be sure, developed and transmitted by these same persons who benefited most from them.

The relationship among the cultic levels—the domestic, the regional, and the national—needs further comment. According to one proposal, cultic sites, objects, officiants, and practices can be classed either as "established" (or "conformist") or as "nonconformist."[11] In this view, the "established" forms of religion comprise the above-mentioned state cult and the regional cult, with both under the control of the monarchy and normally located in or near cities; the material expressions of their cults generally display similar architectural features, larger scale, finer artisanship, and concentration in specific sites. The "nonconformist" cults, in contrast, tend to be located in domestic settings, with modest physical structures devoted to them; their objects are distributed more widely and often share features in common with other cultures (e.g., the female figurines). Though this description of the differences is helpful in terms of its content, the label "nonconformist" is misleading since it suggests the normativity of the "established" forms. The difference, however, is perspectival. The same problem besets the

11. Holladay, "Religion in Israel and Judah," 266–82.

terms "center" and "periphery," as we noted above in the discussion of village life: villagers will consider their own hamlets, or at least the rural life, as the center and the cities as the periphery, while urbanites reverse the categories.[12] In the case of the cults, the priests in the cities may regard the village cults as nonconforming, but that viewpoint is not shared by those who engage in the religious practices common to the villages. We should recognize that in general the biblical text is a product of the cities and shows a similar bias toward the national rather than the local norms. For these reasons it is fairer to both perspectives for us to use such categories as local (for the villages), regional/urban (for the residential, administrative, and royal cities), and national (for the state). Such terms also situate these "norms" in light of their social and political bases.

This distinction leads us then to another of particular importance for religion. "Orthodoxy" is generally associated with the cultic practices and norms at home in the state temples and regional shrines. The traditions that run counter to it become regarded, then, as "heterodoxy" or "paganism" or "popular religion." Again, a decisive difference in perspective underlies these categories. For example, the poor rural family that beseeches a fertility deity to make their field and their animals fruitful is in their eyes practicing orthodox, traditional rituals that have the best chance of success. That same family would probably be willing to perform rites promoted by the state priesthood, but only in addition to what their ancestors and their neighbors have considered to be efficacious. In fact, it may well be that the vast majority of Israelites, living apart from the cities, deliberately deviated from the norms of the urban priests because they did not make sense to them in their own social and economic milieu. Or more likely, the practices regarded as popular religion[13] continued centuries if not millennia of religious traditions circulating in the cultures of ancient Southwest Asia, and the state religions of Israel and Judah sought to gain control over their adherents by introducing regulations and rites that demanded strict compliance, with severe threats of penalty and even death to those who did not conform. The determiners of "orthodoxy" had the power of the state to bolster their demands. This circle of power served the interests of both parties: the temple priesthood relied on the state for its establishment standing, and the state in turn benefited from the priests' approbation, which lent divine legitimacy to the monarchy.

12. See above, chap. 6, Urban Life.
13. See Rainer Albertz, *Persönliche Frömmigkeit und offizielle Religion: Religionsinterner Pluralismus in Israel und Babylon* (Stuttgart: Calwer Verlag, 1978); and Jacques Berlinerblau, "The 'Popular Religion' Paradigm in Old Testament Research: A Sociological Critique," *JSOT* 60 (1993): 3–26.

Yet cultic dominance, in the form of the state cult, did not emerge easily and contemporaneously with the monarchic state itself. The domestic cults were not inclined to cede authority to the state cult, and probably the regional cults tried to maintain some measure of distinctiveness as well because of tradition and regional differences. Ironically, the priestly class may even have enjoyed more power after the exile than they did before it since under the monarchy they had to share national eminence with the reigning king, whereas during the Persian Empire and later they had the chance of becoming the most influential indigenous group. In this period of the Second Temple, their greatest threat appears to have been the repeated dissonance and division within the priestly ranks as various groups sought to gain preeminence for their own religious viewpoints and cultic practices, especially in the face of the rise of a scriptural corpus.[14]

Quite correctly, several recent studies have departed from the traditional practice of referring to Israelite religion in the singular, as if only one religious tradition, identity, or form existed throughout the centuries of ancient Israel's history.[15] It could be claimed that "Israelite religion" is a collective or generic term, but even that usage obscures the diversity of beliefs and practices across the land. Admittedly, most studies do in fact recognize this diversity and pluralism. Thus a better course is to refer explicitly to the *religions* of ancient Israel, thereby acknowledging that various persons and groups adhered to different religious systems that cannot all be simply identified with each other. Many may have overlapped, and all were at one level syncretistic. If any one religious form claimed to be dominant or orthodox, many if not most Israelites probably did not concur. For example, the Deuteronomistic theology has sometimes been described as affirming one God for one people in one land. In reality, however, the situation was quite the opposite at each of these points: many gods must have been worshiped by diverse groups in a land with strong regional and demographic differences. The repeated insistence of the Deuteronomistic message throughout its books should be indication enough that the people resisted it or at least were not inclined to accept it, preferring instead their own ways of worshiping. My emphasis here on diverse cultic sites and rituals, rather than on "orthodox" conventions, aims to reflect this pluralism of beliefs and practices.

14. See Paul Heger, *Cult as the Catalyst for Division: Cult Disputes as the Motive for Schism in the Pre–70 Pluralistic Environment*, STDJ 65 (Leiden and Boston: E. J. Brill, 2007); and David J. Chalcraft, ed., *Sectarianism in Early Judaism: Sociological Advances* (London and Oakville: Equinox Publishing, 2007).

15. See, e.g., Zevit, *Religions*; and Hess, *Israelite Religions*. Until quite recently the plural form "religions" occurred only in reference to the multiple religions of the general Southwest Asian region, not to multiple religions within ancient Israel alone.

Temple Economy

The biblical descriptions of Jerusalem's first temple and its furnishings suggest an edifice of impressive architectural design and artisanship.[16] Lavishly appointed with gold and other precious materials, it conveys a sense of immense importance, both institutionally and symbolically. Although no archaeological evidence from the Iron II period exists currently to confirm any of the details of the First Temple and its contents, we can at a minimum presume that these literary descriptions fit the kinds of ideal expectations for a state temple in the period when these texts were written, probably during the time of the Persian Empire at the earliest.[17] Even discounting the exaggeration and idealism expressed in these texts, where did the notion originate that temples could be so magnificent, opulent, and powerful?

From Sumerian and Old Babylonian times forward, temples in Southwest Asia typically commanded a substantial place not only in the religion but also in the economy and the politics of their countries.[18] Countless written records uncovered by archaeologists—land sales and deeds, inventories, tax documents, transactions, loan contracts and payments, labor records—depict the temples as central players in the economic welfare of the nations. One calculation, based on various texts from the Sumerian city of Girsu around 3000 BCE, estimates that of the about 100,000 inhabitants of the city, some 35,000 were in the employ of the temples.[19] These workers ranged from menial laborers and slaves to elite members of the high priesthood. Since a temple was considered the house of the god worshiped there, all the details of normal human life had to be produced not only for the people attached to the temple but also for the god: food, textiles, pottery, tools, habitat, and much more.

16. The Hebrew Bible contains numerous descriptions or allusions to features of the temple, esp. in 1 Kgs 6 and Ezek 40–43. The tabernacle, presented as a precursor to the Jerusalem temple and made portable to suit the wanderings of the Israelites of the exodus, is described in Exod 35–40.

17. Comparisons with temple designs found elsewhere in Southwest Asia are instructive but not conclusive. For an example of this combination of literary and comparative studies (together with discussions of later Jerusalem temples), see T. A. Busink, *Der Tempel von Jerusalem von Salomo bis Herodes: Eine archäologisch-historische Studie unter Berücksichtigung des westsemitischen Tempelbaus*, 2 vols. (Leiden: E. J. Brill, 1970–80).

18. Among the wide variety of studies to this very point, see esp. several articles in *State and Temple Economy in the Ancient Near East*, ed. Edward Lipiński, 2 vols., OLA 5–6 (Leuven: Departement Oriëntalistiek, 1979). For a specific example, in this case from Old Babylonian Ur, see Marc Van De Mieroop, *Society and Enterprise in Old Babylonian Ur*, Berliner Beiträge zum Vorderen Orient 12 (Berlin: Dietrich Reimer Verlag, 1992).

19. John F. Robertson, "The Social and Economic Organization of Ancient Mesopotamian Temples," *CANE* 1:450–51.

The temple estates were extensive. From Old Babylonia at the time of Hammurabi (ca. 1750 BCE) have come texts referring to more than 1,000 hectares (2,500 acres) belonging to certain temples. Cultivating the land and controlling the substantial herds of livestock fell to the laborers and tenant farmers contracted by the temple, and the income went into the temple's coffers. Land, animals, and slaves were bought and sold, as attested by numerous sales contracts. In addition, such assets were often donated to the temple by wealthy families as well as the king. Sacrificial animals stemmed either from the temple's own herds or from private individuals, often totaling remarkable numbers. Archives at the temples of Ur during the Old Babylonian period, for example, indicate that they had herds exceeding 16,800 animals.[20] Megiddo, a site in the southern Levant revealing repeated construction of cultic buildings and structures from the Early Bronze Age onward, yields evidence of a massive temple from EB IB (ca. 3000–2900 BCE) that was 40 meters (131 ft.) long and 15 meters (49 ft.) wide—substantially larger than the "Solomonic temple" described in 1 Kgs 6:2 and the visionary temple of Ezekiel (Ezek 40). Within it were the remains of some 20,000 bones, mostly from sheep, goats, and cattle sacrificed at the temple.[21]

In light of the wealth controlled by the temples in major cities, it should come as no surprise that they in effect functioned also as "banks," with the temple's god typically named as creditor, sometimes along with a merchant (Akkadian *tamkāru*). Evidence of such loans stems from Old Babylonian as well as Neo-Assyrian times.[22] Private individuals borrowed money for business purposes, and others used the loans to purchase freedom for slaves and for those who had pledged themselves. Especially significant are the large numbers of small loans, presumably to the poor, in the form of seed or a few shekels of silver, and the interest rate charged by temples in this microfinancing was 20 percent, well below the 33.3 percent charged

20. Robertson, "Social and Economic Organization," *CANE* 1:446.
21. Found at Level J–4, the building is described in Israel Finkelstein and David Ussishkin, "Area J," in Finkelstein, Ussishkin, and Halpern, *Megiddo III: The 1992–1996 Seasons*, 1:38–65; and Israel Finkelstein, David Ussishkin, and Jennifer Peersmann, "Area J (the 1998–2000 Seasons)," in *Megiddo IV: The 1998–2000 Seasons*, ed. Israel Finkelstein, David Ussishkin, and Baruch Halpern (Tel Aviv: Tel Aviv University, 2006), 1:29–53. For the archaeological report on the bones, see Paula Wapnish and Brian Hesse, "Mammal Remains from the Early Bronze Sacred Compound," in *Megiddo III*, ed. I. Finkelstein, Ussishkin, and Halpern, 2:429–62. In contrast to the EB evidence, Megiddo's cultic buildings during Iron II, to the extent that they even existed, are certainly much smaller.
22. Rivkah Harris, "Old Babylonian Temple Loans," *JCS* 14 (1960): 126–37; and Raymond Bogaert, *Les origines antiques de la banque de dépôt: Une mise au point accompagnée d'une esquisse des opérations de banque en Mésopotamie* (Leyden: A. W. Sijthoff, 1966).

privately.[23] In the Neo-Assyrian and Neo-Babylonian periods, which overlap with Iron II in Israel, considerable evidence again exists that temples
issued loans to citizens, both in kind (e.g., barley seeds) and in silver.
Interest rates could be 20 percent or even lower per annum, but increase
to 50 percent in the event of a late payment. Surety, whether in the form
of property or person, was often expected in order to obtain the loan.[24]
An additional bank-like function of the temples, as noted above,[25] can be
observed in their role as depositories for *kudurru* stones, the formal records
of ownership of landed estates during the Neo-Assyrian period.

The wealth and influence of the state cult were tied closely to the power
of the reigning monarch. The depiction of King Solomon as the chief
patron in building the temple is consistent with the image of the state cult,
even if the story in 1 Kgs 6 stems from a much-later period than the 10th
c. BCE commonly projected for his reign. To be sure, the line between the
royal house and the temple shifted depending on the strength of the two
sides. Even when a monarch desired control over the regional and state
cults, religious leaders could frustrate a weak king's efforts by maneuvering political and economic affairs as well as by invoking divine will. In
other circumstances, the king became the foremost contributor to the
temple with gifts of precious objects, designation of slaves taken in war,
and transfer of crown land for temple space. Insofar as the cult served the
interests of the state, a strong king could exploit the temple's holdings for
state—or personal—benefit, and probably did so frequently by appropriating agricultural income, seizing temple land and moveable properties, and
generally interfering with the economic activities of the priesthood. The
Hebrew Bible describes two instances in which King Asa and later King
Ahaz, both of Judah, seize silver and gold from the temple and send them
as a gift to foreign monarchs to plead with them—successfully—for military assistance (1 Kgs 15:18–20; 2 Kgs 16:8–9). King Josiah's much-touted
religious reform, aiming to eliminate non-Yahwistic worship and destroy
cultic sites elsewhere in the country, thereby centralizing the Yahwistic cult
in Jerusalem (2 Kgs 23:1–25), may actually have concealed a clever, deliberate economic and political strategy for consolidating his power after the
Assyrian decline.[26]

It has recently been proposed that a type of "sacred economy" best
describes the economic system of ancient Israel and other countries in the

23. Harris, "Old Babylonian Temple Loans," 132.
24. Bogaert, *Les origines antiques de la banque de dépôt*, 60–63, 104–29.
25. See above, chap. 6, Real Property.
26. W. Eugene Claburn, "The Fiscal Basis of Josiah's Reforms," *JBL* 92 (1973): 12–22.

region.[27] Characterizing the "temple-city" as one of the key nodes alongside the "village-commune" and the "despotic state," this proposal is one of few efforts to call attention to the major if not all-important economic role of the temple in ancient Israel. It is offered, however, primarily as an economic model with a synchronic, not diachronic, purview,[28] focusing above all on the tension between the village-commune and the temple-city due to the latter's extraction of goods and services from the former. In my view, this picture downplays the role of the state: not only did the king and the state derive income from taxing the villagers (thus producing a tension with them as well), but the monarchy and the temple also operated with some strain between them, the king needing the divine legitimacy that the temple could offer, and the priests dependent on royal favor and support. The economic system of the country must, it is true, be taken into consideration in both historical and textual studies, yet the chief players are the palace and the temple as well as the wealthy elite and, at farther remove, the rural agrarians.

All evidence thus points to a tradition of strong and active involvement by temples in the economies of ancient Southwest Asia, stretching from Sumerian (i.e., the Early Bronze Age) and Old Babylonian to Neo-Assyrian, Neo-Babylonian, and Persian periods.[29] Iron II, the time of the Israelite monarchies, fits squarely in the latter part of this millennia-long pattern. We lack the epigraphic records from Israelite and Judean cultic centers about the lands and slaves they owned, the financial transactions they conducted, the valuables they held for citizens, and the loans they gave to rich and poor. The Hebrew Bible alludes to donations from private individuals to the cult: persons pledged to the temple, with specific values assigned to them depending on their age and gender (Lev 27:1–8); animals, houses, land, and other votive offerings consecrated to the deity, which can be redeemed at prices set by the priests—plus one-fifth (Lev 27:9–33); substantial gifts in silver from the leaders of clans and tribes (Num 7); and a steady stream

27. Roland Boer, "The Sacred Economy of Ancient 'Israel,'" *SJOT* 21 (2007): 29–48; idem, *Political Myth: On the Use and Abuse of Biblical Themes* (Durham and London: Duke University Press, 2009), 89–115.

28. Boer, "Sacred Economy," 44; idem, *Political Myth*, 112–13.

29. J. N. Postgate has drawn attention to this dominant role of the temple in the economies of the region: "The Role of the Temple in the Mesopotamian Secular Community," in *Man, Settlement, and Urbanism*, ed. Peter J. Ucko, Ruth Tringham, and G. W. Dimbleby (Cambridge, MA: Schenkman, 1972), 811–25; idem, *Early Mesopotamia: Society and Economy at the Dawn of History* (London and New York: Routledge, 1992), 109–36. John M. Lundquist even proposes its central role in society as one of the defining characteristics of what constitutes a temple; "What Is a Temple? A Preliminary Typology," in *The Quest for the Kingdom of God: Studies in Honor of George E. Mendenhall*, ed. H. B. Huffmon, F. A. Spina, and A. R. W. Green (Winona Lake, IN: Eisenbrauns, 1983), 205–20.

of sacrifices brought to the temple. That the text states they were given to YHWH does little to obscure the reality that the priests were the ones who received them and determined how they were to be used. Further, the coin most frequently mentioned in the Hebrew Bible is the "sacred shekel," or "shekel of the sanctuary" (שֶׁקֶל הַקֹּדֶשׁ, šeqel haqqōdeš), probably a standard measurement in weight of silver established by the temple. Even without the contemporaneous temple records from the Iron II period, we thus can safely assume that the temples in Israel and Judah functioned as major economic players in the two kingdoms. A comparable situation emerged in the Persian period, when the emperor Darius I sponsored the building of the Second Temple around 515 BCE and, most likely, endowed it with tax-free land grants to support itself.[30]

THE LAWS

In one sense, the subject matter and jurisdiction of cultic laws in ancient Israel possessed a much more limited focus than could be said of the laws in villages and cities. While the latter two contexts touched potentially on every aspect of social, economic, and political life, the laws of the cult concentrated on matters directly affecting religious rituals, festivals, practices, paraphernalia, and sites. In another sense, however, this focus was not at all confined to the cultic sphere alone since potentially everyone in the country participated in the local, regional, or national cult, and the kinds of obligations to which they then submitted themselves affected aspects of their lives and behavior away from the cultic sites and the religious leaders. Furthermore, as noted above, the economic reach of the temples extended well beyond the confines of the cult itself—into landownership, commerce, banking, slavery, taxation, contributions, and more. Even the domestic cult sought to order life for the village communities and residential areas, offering people the means for trying to ensure fertility, safety, health, and survival. Thus the reach of the cult was not at all restricted, even if it purported to be limited to religion.

Identifying Cultic Laws

A number of criteria can aid us in reconstructing the legal systems of the cults. As in the previous two chapters, we are not interested here in the formulation of specific laws but are more concerned with the kinds of areas

30. Cf. Joel Weinberg, however, who proposes a different model in which the "citizen-temple community" in Persian Yehud involved a coalition of the indigenous community members and the priesthood; *The Citizen-Temple Community*, trans. Daniel L. Smith-Christopher, JSOTSup 151 (Sheffield: JSOT Press, 1992), 24–33.

that cultic officials sought to control among the people. Again, the two avenues to follow in this reconstructive task are, first, to identify the types of interests at stake among those who have the power or standing to exercise control through the cult and, second, to specify the areas over which conflicts could arise that needed to be adjudicated by cultic officials. The criteria in the following list do not all need to be present in each individual case, but usually several will be at work:[31]

1. Cultic laws are expressed in an absolutistic manner, with no equivocation about their validity and no exceptions allowed.

2. Cultic laws generally seek to uphold the social, political, and institutional status quo. At the local or domestic levels, religion reinforces the structures and values of the household, clan, and tribe or region. At the national level, however, cultic laws protect the current political and economic systems of the state.

3. Cultic laws attend to economic welfare: at the local level the subsistence of the villagers is at stake, whereas at the national level the state and temple economies are protected and advanced.

4. Cultic laws reserve a significant role for the priests in the adjudication of disputes affecting the practice and property of the religious institutions.

5. Cultic laws define the terms of proper worship and ritual.

6. Cultic laws stipulate the terms for admission to the cult and membership in the cultic community.

7. Cultic laws may include a motive clause, referring to divine powers as enforcers or instigators of the given requirement.

8. Cultic laws often include sanctions, which generally take an extreme form (execution, banishment, or other strict punishment).

9. Cultic laws ensure the standing and prerogatives of the cultic officiants, from the father or mother's overseeing rituals in the home to the central priesthood and other religious personnel at the temple in the nation's capital.

10. Cultic laws regulate the use and significance of cultic buildings and paraphernalia.

31. See the appendix for a comparison with the criteria used in identifying village laws and urban/national laws.

These elements form what we are calling cultic laws. But are they really "laws"? Why not simply consider them religious ordinances internal to the cultic institutions? When considered in light of the attributes of law described in chapter 2 above, they do seem to qualify as components of the legal systems of ancient Israel. Both authority and social legitimacy attach to them, though in different ways depending on the context. The central and regional cults derive their authority from the state and from the elites who attend their rituals, while the local and domestic cults found their legitimacy in the villages that organize them. For example, the laws of purity issued by the central priests may be more authoritative in the urban than in the rural areas, and the village cults probably have no ambition to influence life in the cities. Rulings by cultic officials in both contexts have the potential of setting precedent for subsequent similar cases. A reciprocal relationship also exists, both at the human-human and at the human-divine levels. Compliance with the laws issued by the cult, whether central or local, implies that benefits will accrue to that person from others in the community as well as from the deity. And finally, sanctions generally attach to the laws of the cult, often quite dire consequences if the violation is regarded as a rebuke to the god. In all of these respects, the cultic commands and proscriptions function as laws, and their association with the world of divinity does not lessen but actually enhances their potential for controlling behavior among humans. For their own part, the prophets of Israel certainly seek to draw a connection between justice and morality.

Whether or not the laws now presented in the Hebrew Bible actually functioned during either the First or the Second Temple periods is difficult to know. In all likelihood, they did not have any more or any less application than did the other biblical laws, which is to say that their actual relevance during most of these periods was minimal. They, just as the other biblical laws, exist as literature, created in time and space but without having necessarily functioned as applied law. Nonetheless, it is reasonable to assume that the cults—local, regional, and national—did operate with legal prescriptions of their own, even though they were not necessarily preserved in the final biblical text. Some of the legal principles, if not their details, from the Iron II period could have lived on into the Second Temple period and influenced the written texts that later emerged. At the most, we should regard biblical laws relating to the cult as reflecting Second Temple ideals and, perhaps, realities. If any are thought to be reminiscent of Iron II practices, they must be in keeping with the plausible political, economic, and religious terms of the monarchies of that time.

Substantive Law in the Cult

Applying these criteria to the cultic situations in ancient Israel yields a range of legal provisions and controls. As with the previous two chapters, our goal here is not to articulate the actual wording of specific laws. Rather, we will try to envision the kinds of legal issues that the cults sought to control, the nature of the conflicts that needed to be adjudicated or prevented, and the interests that needed protection. At all points, the discussions above regarding the legal systems in the villages, the cities, and the states set the contexts in which these cultic laws functioned. The biblical laws, as already mentioned, possess value in the reconstruction of Israel's cultic laws, but primarily in expressing the points of view of the state cult and, by inference then, the related or alternative practices of the local cults. The special interests of the cult are affected as much by internal cultic matters as they are by socioeconomic concerns external to the cult, and these special interests are often revealed in the biblical laws.

Access to the Cult and Membership in the Cultic Community

There was little sense in establishing regulations for *admission to the cult* if it were not a valuable or desirable place to which to come—or if the cultic functionaries did not want to limit access for reasons of their own. In both instances a marked difference appeared between the local and the national cults.

The local cults likely functioned as a much more inclusive context for worshipers than did the national cult. Socialization of the young, a primary task within the settings of families and villages, meant that their elders saw to their upbringing so they would conform properly to the family and the larger community, and religious practices and understandings belonged to the set of social knowledge the children needed to acquire. Religiosity itself, the inclination to venerate powers or principles greater than one's own existence and generally outside human control, is to a great extent an acquired or at least a cultivated trait, highly valued in a village society that depends on the beneficence believed to come from the gods. Without beseeching their higher powers, those eking out an existence in the hinterlands feared that their lives and livelihood could be imperiled. The cult was their conduit to the powers that sent rain, ensured fertility, healed sickness, and protected from danger. All members of the family and village needed to contribute to the ongoing process of petitioning, appeasing, and attending to the deities. Excluding or exempting community members diminished the cult's efficacy. Those from outside the given community or region, the "strangers" and "resident aliens," may have been less welcome in the Israelite cultic activities, but they did not lack for other gods of their own to venerate and other rituals to perform.

The national cult, on the other hand, characterized itself to a great extent in terms of its association with established power in the country, thereby holding a lofty position apart from the masses. While it valued the respect—and to be sure also the donations, meager as they must have been—of those living at a subsistence level throughout the countryside, it engaged itself predominantly with the wealthy and the powerful. The temple economy alone meant that the peers of the upper-level urban priests were the other large landowners and merchants, as well as those overseeing such affairs for the royal house. Peasants—and the vast major- ity across the land may never have visited the temple's precincts in their lives because of the cost and the distance—hardly enjoyed the privileges accorded the elites. Access to the national cult, at least in part, followed lines of class and status. In addition, though, were the more-subtle forms of control available to cultic functionaries through the exclusionary system of clean/unclean. While this system receives further discussion below, at this juncture we need to consider its relevance in excluding certain persons from the worship context.

Biblical laws detail various types of conditions, whether willed or unwilled, that render a person "unclean" (טָמֵא, ṭāmēʾ). This category is interpreted theologically in terms of the notion of holiness: "uncleanness" is not fit for association with the holy, whether it be the cultic setting, the objects and persons dedicated to holy functions, or the divine world itself. By extension, though, anyone or anything considered "unclean" is also unfit for association or contact with others in social settings, especially due to the contagion factor: an "unclean" person or object renders another object or person also "unclean" by contact and sometimes by mere proximity.[32]

While the *purity laws* usually do not explicitly bar an "unclean" person from access to the cult, the prohibitions have this net effect.[33] One text that addresses cultic access directly is Lev 12:4, concerning a woman who has just given birth: "For thirty-three days she shall remain in a condition of

---

32. For example, merely being in the tent where someone has recently died is enough to render a person unclean, according to Num 19:14.

33. Saul M. Olyan extends this point further in arguing that the Hebrew Bible's main binary oppositions—holy/common, clean/unclean, Israelite/alien, and whole/blemished—function to establish hierarchical social relations and restrict access to the cult; *Rites and Rank: Hierarchy in Biblical Representations of Cult* (Princeton, NJ: Princeton University Press, 2000). Others have highlighted a sense of gradations in holiness prevailing in the biblical literature with respect to priests and other officiants, cultic spaces, rituals, cultic festivals, and purity laws; see, e.g., Philip Peter Jenson, *Graded Holiness: A Key to the Priestly Conception of the World*, JSOTSup 106 (Sheffield: JSOT Press, 1992); and Miller, *Religion*, 144–48.

blood purification. She shall not touch any holy object nor enter the sanctuary until her period of purification is completed." The next verse doubles the time if a baby girl is born. Beyond this case, someone who tends to the death of a family member or touches anything declared unclean seems also to be excluded for fear of "defiling YHWH's tabernacle."[34] It is possible that all purity standards were motivated, at least in part, by a similar concern. Though we have no way of knowing whether these prohibitions were actually enforced during ancient Israel's history, we can, however, infer a difference between the local and the national levels in several regards.

First, the diversity of religious practices and beliefs at the local level of villages makes it unlikely that uniform standards for cultic access existed across the country during most of Israel's history, especially in the Iron II period of the monarchy. A variety of taboos such as those described in the purity laws may well have existed among the people, but it is hardly plausible that they were the same everywhere, nor that they were systematized and promulgated until much later, probably late in the Persian period if not in the Hellenistic period. Individual cultic settings, whether in homes or in local cultic sites, determined their own terms for who could participate. If anything was common in these domestic and local cults, it was probably the exclusion of outsiders who were, as a rule, not crucial to the veneration of the deities necessary for the ongoing well-being of the given community or household. The frequent biblical injunctions regarding aliens or strangers (e.g., Lev 17:12; 18:26; 24:22; Num 15:14–15) suggests that they were, in reality, not treated equally, neither in the cult nor elsewhere.

Second, the difference in types of cultic officiants would also have affected the decisions about access. Cultic activities in the households and at the village "high places" depended on the involvement of nonprofessional religious individuals, those whose everyday roles normally found them as fathers and mothers, farmers and herders, potters and food preparers, and much more. All who lived at a subsistence level had to take care of their own cultic needs since they lacked the means to support a professional priest. The story in Judg 17–18 portrays what must be a wealthy family since they can hire their own Levitical priest, an unimaginable option for the vast majority of rural families. The cultic officials in cities, on the other hand, constituted the central priesthood, with their primary base in Samaria

---

34. Num 19:13 reads: "All who touch a corpse, the body of someone who has died, and do not purify themselves, defile YHWH's tabernacle and are to be cut off from Israel. Since the water of purification has not been sprinkled on them, they remain unclean; their uncleanness is still on them." While this text does not explicitly prohibit entrance to the cultic site, it indicates the intended consequence of such a violation.

or Jerusalem and their outlying contingents in the royal and administrative cities. Though they could claim religious jurisdiction over the whole population, it is unlikely that their immediate influence extended much beyond the cities that housed their temples and the urban "high places." Thus they had little direct power over the cultic activities in the multitudinous villages, much as they may have desired that dominance. The Deuteronomistic conception of a Yahwistic religion centralized in Jerusalem and King Josiah's reported campaign to stamp out the local cults—both literary themes stemming from the Persian period at the earliest—represent more an ideal than a reality. Similarly, the so-called Songs of Ascents (Pss 120–134) stemmed ultimately from the central priesthood in Persian Yehud in an effort to draw pilgrims to the Jerusalem temple, where these priests controlled cultic access, rituals, and offerings.[35]

Finally, the larger question is the connection between social and ritual exclusion. Barring someone considered "unclean" from the cult had significance, but prohibiting that person from social interaction represented a potentially serious loss for the unclean person's family. In other contexts we have indicated that all members of a lower-class household needed to contribute as fully as possible to food production and other domestic needs if the household hoped to survive the rigors of their harsh terms of life. As is evident in the list in the next section below, various purity laws included in the Pentateuch require the temporary or even permanent removal of individuals from contact with others, a severe sacrifice for a family at the subsistence level. To be sure, in some of the cases the "unclean" person could have functioned without the risk of touching another person, but it would have been harder to avoid "contagion" through everyday household objects and food with which the "unclean" individual came into contact. The sheer practicalities of life thus inhibit the development of taboos and restrictions that threaten the very survival of the group. For example, women, who are especially targeted in the biblical purity laws to regulate their actions at times of birth and menstruation, were essential for all the daily affairs of life, including the functioning of the local cult. A full-blown, rigidly enforced system of purity laws is thinkable as a product more of the central cult, dominated by male priests, than of the agriculturalists of Israel, and these biblical laws were directed more toward urban dwellers

---

35. Loren D. Crow (*The Songs of Ascents (Psalms 120–134): Their Place in Israelite History and Religion*, SBLDS 148 [Atlanta: Scholars Press, 1996]) argues that Pss 120–134 are probably based on folk songs from the rural areas that were redacted by priests in the Persian period to emphasize that Jerusalem, as the place that YHWH has especially blessed, should be the center of Jewish religious life and the destination of pilgrims.

than toward the poor in the countryside. The local cult was more inclusive than was the national cult.

Mandating Behavior

Inasmuch as cultic access can be related to behavior or conditions apart from the cult, we should consider in more depth the types of behavior that are affirmed or rejected by cultic officials or the cultic communities—thus the very prerogative of the cult to regulate both access and behavior. The majority of priestly laws presented in the Hebrew Bible occupy themselves with affairs within the cult—sacrifices and offerings, rituals, festivals, building and ornament, priestly duties, and the like. However, others address a range of behavior by the people outside the formal cult. There are regulations regarding, for example, illicit sexual actions (Lev 18), vows made by women (Num 30), deference owed to the elderly (Lev 19:32), adjudication of an adultery charge against a wife (Num 5:11–31), some capital cases (Lev 20), provision for cities of refuge for cases of unintentional killing (Num 35), several miscellaneous noncultic regulations (esp. in Lev 19), the humanitarian laws about the Sabbatical and Jubilee Years of release (Lev 25), wearing fringes and a blue cord on clothing (Num 15:37–41), blasphemy (Lev 24:10–16, 23), honoring the Sabbath (Num 15:32–36), and the various taboos (to be discussed shortly). The last three or perhaps four seem, while religious in nature, to be behavior fulfilled outside the cult.

Frankly, it is puzzling that the long collection of priestly texts with explicit directives for the people (Exod 25–31; Lev 1–27; Num 5–6; 15; 18–19; 28–30; 35–36) addresses so few noncultic matters, and the ones present are far from exhaustive in covering the broad expanse of possible legal issues and conflicts in the society, the kinds of behaviors surveyed in this book. This sporadic, even idiosyncratic inclusion of "secular" law suggests either that the priests were out of touch with the everyday lives of the wider population or that they were preoccupied with their own agendas and interests. For example, the demand for honest weights and measures (Lev 19:35–36) may have arisen to protect the temple's economic transactions, not those of the poor. Or again, the requirement that a given field not be planted with more than one kind of seed (Lev 19:19; also Deut 22:9) does not reflect the exigencies of subsistence farming but rather the demands of a command economy for specialized agriculture, such as existed under the monarchy or in colonial times. It is also possible that these few noncultic laws stemmed from the regional priests in administrative cities, at a remove from the central temple and somewhat closer to the general populace. Alternatively, these references to noncultic legal matters may have been added to the text by a later redactor, perhaps in the Hellenistic period, as we will be arguing below for the texts about some of the taboos.[36] The laws in the book of Deuteronomy also reveal priestly interests (note esp. the theme of the centralization of the cult) in addition to the "humanitarian" laws, which may reflect more of a prophetic or even popular influence, perhaps manipulated by the elites behind this literature.[37] But both the Deuteronomic collection and the Covenant Code incorporate more noncultic topics than does the priestly collection, even though they also are very limited in their range of legal subjects.

The biblical laws dealing with *purity and impurity* constitute the most extensive and detailed set of regulations stemming from the cult and applying to behavior outside of the cult, as well as within the cult. We begin with a closer look at this system of clean/unclean, which can be divided between temporary and long-lasting (or permanent) conditions:

Temporary conditions, including recurring conditions, caused by

- Skin disorder, such as discoloration, boils, burns; unclean usually for seven days; remedy: examined and absolved by priest (Lev 13–14).
- Unnatural bodily discharge by either male or female; unclean until healed, plus seven days; remedy: bathing and sacrifice (Lev 15:2–15, 25–30).
- Menstruation; unclean for at least seven days including the menstrual period; remedy: unspecified purification ritual (Lev 15:19–24, 33; 2 Sam 11:4).
- Emission of semen; unclean until evening, both the man and also any woman lying with him; remedy: bathing (Lev 15:16–18).
- Intercourse between a man and a woman during her menstrual period; unclean for seven days; remedy: unspecified purification ritual (Lev 15:24, 33).
- Childbirth; unclean 33 days for the mother of a male child, 66 days for the mother of a female child; remedy: sacrifice (Lev 12).
- Touching a corpse, a human bone, or a grave or being in a

36. Most of these specific texts (Lev 1–7; 11–15; 17–27; Num 5–6; 15; 19; 28–30; 35–36) belong to those that Martin Noth considers to be additions to the Priestly narrative source; see Noth, *Überlieferungsgeschichte des Pentateuch*, 7–8 = *History of Pentateuchal Traditions*, 8–9.

37. See chap. 6, Responsibilities toward the Vulnerable; also my article "Whose Agony? Whose Ecstasy?"

tent where someone has died; unclean for seven days; remedy: bathing and purification ritual on third and seventh days (Num 19:11–20).

- Touching an unclean person; unclean until evening; remedy: bathing (Lev 15).
- Touching an unclean object or another's purification water; unclean until evening; remedy: bathing (Lev 15; Num 19:21–22).
- Eating any food (animal, bird, aquatic life, insect, reptile) explicitly designated as unclean; unclean for a usually indeterminate time; remedy: unspecified (Lev 11; also Deut 14:3–21).
- Touching the carcass of any unclean animal or any object with which it has had contact; unclean until evening; remedy: washing one's clothes (Lev 11:24–40).
- Eating or touching the carcass of a clean animal that died of natural causes; unclean until evening; remedy: washing one's clothes (Lev 11:39–40; Deut 14:21).
- Sacrificing the red heifer, which affects both the priest and the ones doing the burning or gathering the ashes; unclean until evening; remedy: bathing (Num 19:2–10).

Long-lasting or permanent conditions caused by

- Chronic skin disease (צרעת, ṣāraʿat), which was previously thought to be leprosy (Hansen's disease) but must for now remain an unidentified disease;[38] unclean as long as condition remains; remedy: examination by priest, bathing, shaving, and sacrifice (Lev 13–14; Num 5:2–3).
- Failure to undergo the purification ritual; remedy: banishment (Num 19:13, 20).

These purity laws form an enormous topic, both in the history of religions and in the scholarly literature analyzing and interpreting them. They belong to the larger phenomenon of *taboos*, present in most if not all human societies throughout history. Taboos have been associated with an extremely wide range of objects, persons, actions, relations, words, divine

---

38. Jacob Milgrom, *Leviticus 1–16: A New Translation with Introduction and Commentary*, AB 3 (New York: Doubleday, 1991), 816–26; and David P. Wright, *The Disposal of Impurity: Elimination Rites in the Bible and in Hittite and Mesopotamian Literature*, SBLDS 101 (Atlanta: Scholars Press, 1987), passim. Note that it is apparently a disease from which one can recover and thus be declared "clean" for both cultic and general social association.

and quasi-divine forces, and more. They identify what is to be avoided and often provide for the means to recover from any violation committed against them.[39] Though historians and anthropologists of religions have cataloged and compared a wide assortment of taboos,[40] some of their early notions proceeded from now-outdated assumptions about primitivism, mechanistic dangers, and sympathetic magic, ideas that played a role even in some early twentieth-century biblical studies. Any number of explanations have sought to account for the origins and proliferation of taboos—for example, that they reflect a concern for real or imagined natural dangers, or a sense of the anomalous in nature (or "matter out of place"[41]), or a respect for or fear of the sacred (the "numinous" or $mana$[42]), or phobic reactions to perceived threats, or behavioral counterparts to a group's rites and myths. Although our present project does not depend on a specific etiological theory, the apparent ubiquity of taboos gives us grounds to assume that they were present among both the rural and the urban populations of ancient Israel. We cannot know which specific taboos occurred in those contexts, but we can be assured that the taboos reflected or fit the people's worldviews, religious practices, everyday lives, and threats to survival.

Concerns regarding purity and impurity represent a subset of taboos, providing a language and rhetoric with which to describe special aspects of the world or of life that present perceived dangers, whether to the cult or to the community apart from the formal cult. To call something "unclean" is to associate it with undesirable, even repugnant matter or behavior, although it does not in most cases imply banishment. If it is only a temporary condition, some ritual act can overcome the impurity and lead to cleanness and restoration of full participation in the community and the cult. An inevitable question then arises: who determines what is clean or unclean, and who sets the terms for purification? Again, a distinct difference on these questions must have prevailed between groups within ancient Israel, just as must be the case in other cultural settings similar to Israel's.

In my view, none of the purity laws listed above from the Hebrew Bible

39. For overviews and bibliographies, see Lynn Holden, *Encyclopedia of Taboos* (Oxford, UK; Santa Barbara, CA; and Denver, CO: ABC-CLIO, 2000). On the term and concept of "taboo," see also Jenson, *Graded Holiness*, 72–74.

40. One of the most notable early compilations is James George Frazer, *Taboo and the Perils of the Soul*, part 2 of *The Golden Bough: A Study in Magic and Religion*, 12 vols., 3rd ed. (New York: Macmillan, 1935). See the critique by Douglas (*Purity and Danger*, 1–40), including references to biblical studies.

41. This is the well-known understanding advanced by Mary Douglas in *Purity and Danger*.

42. See the classic work of Rudolf Otto, *The Idea of the Holy*, trans. John W. Harvey (London: Oxford University Press, 1923; German original, 1917).

was necessarily at home among the rural, poor people, by far the largest demographic group in the country. Too many other pressures, particularly those associated with domestic needs in a subsistence economy, counter-vailed against condemning actions or quarantining objects and personnel essential to everyday life. Taboos in general were likely, but not necessarily the ones enumerated in the Hebrew Bible. *Skin disorders* and *other visible bodily ailments* were of concern, but they were more likely to be treated with natural medicines that allowed the ill person to continue working than for the person to be shunned from association with others.

Concerns with *sexual and reproductive processes* were certainly com-monplace—but not in the form of taboos denigrating them, except perhaps to limit them to marital relationships. As mentioned above in the discus-sion of village laws,[43] reproduction was as much a familial as an economic imperative for married couples. Menstruation was not understood accord-ing to modern biomedical knowledge, and it is difficult to know the extent to which the taboos regarding it, widely observable throughout human societies, reflect ambivalence, mystery, or gender attitudes.[44] In all likeli-hood, women regarded menstruation as natural and routine and, aware of their own essential contributions to a subsistence economy, resisted any suggestion that they be barred from contributing to the welfare of the fam-ily for seven days or longer every month of the year. Similarly, a man who had a seminal emission could not easily forgo a day of work simply on those grounds. And considering a woman unclean for 33 or 66 days after giving birth is, quite in addition to its patriarchal bias, potentially paralyz-ing for a poor, rural community that depends on the full involvement of adult women as soon as they have physically recovered from childbirth. In all of these cases, the biblical laws do not explicitly forbid work or social interactions while unclean, but some level of restriction is implied if the "unclean" person is to be kept from contaminating and rendering unclean anything or anyone she or he touches.

If practiced, the rules regarding the touching of a *human corpse or ani-mal carcass* must have been extremely burdensome in an agrarian context. Death was no stranger in that world, and it would not surprise to find a mystery, if not a sanctity, associated with it. With a life expectancy of forty years or lower and an infant-mortality rate probably in excess of 50 percent, the death of family and community members occurred all too frequently.

43. See above, chap. 5, Reproduction.
44. Note the various discussions in *Wholly Woman, Holy Blood: A Feminist Critique of Purity and Impurity*, ed. Kristin De Troyer, Judith A. Herbert, Judith Ann Johnson, and Anne-Marie Korte, SAC (Harrisburg, PA: Trinity Press International, 2003).

In the well-to-do urban settings, as was practiced in Egypt, slaves or funer-
ary professionals could tend to the corpses, leaving the elites "clean." Such
an option was unavailable among the rural poor, who had no slaves or
other lower-status persons to take care of the deceased. Instead, these
families presumably prepared and buried their own dead—and probably
lovingly so. To add a stigma of impurity would only increase their burden.
It is more likely that a community would have embraced a family for their
loss, especially if kinship ties connected them to the others. Disposing of
the body of an animal, whether bred or wild, was also an essential and
not uncommon task for those making their living off the land, unlike the
options of the urban elite.

Food taboos are arbitrarily set in a given culture, and rarely can one
determine their origins and initial reasons, as opposed to their later ratio-
nales. While the evidence would be impossible to gather, it is imaginable
that virtually all available species of animals, reptiles, insects, sea life, and
birds have been or could be part of the accepted diet of people in some
culture in history—with the exception of species known to be poisonous
or harmful. Sensitivities or scruples limiting the consumption of certain
food types are therefore socially constructed, sometimes with influence
from the religious establishment. Individuals and groups whose economic
or social circumstances dictate that they eat whatever is available, whether
wild or raised, cannot afford the luxury of a selective menu. Though it is
difficult to ascertain food taboos among the population of ancient Israel,
we know more about their actual diet because of textual allusions as well
as material remains and agricultural studies.[45] Agricultural crops included
grains (wheat, millet, barley), legumes (various types of beans and peas),
fruits (grapes, olives, figs, pomegranates, various berries), vegetables
(cucumbers, various melons, onions, leeks), and spices. Their sources
for meat included goats, sheep, cattle, and chickens. Not all parts of the
country were equally conducive for raising all of these food types. While
this list may give the impression of an expansive diet, only royalty and the
elites could really afford to draw on such a menu. The vast majority of the
Israelite population had to survive on meager fare, raised on their own
small plot of land if they were fortunate enough to retain it through hard
times. We can assume, therefore, that they would not have been inclined
to think first of food prohibitions.

The food taboos listed in biblical laws include species from the major

---

45. See, e.g., D. Hopkins, *Highlands of Canaan*; and idem, "The Subsistence Struggles of
Early Israel," *BA* 50 (1987): 178–91.

groups, from insects and reptiles to water, land, and air creatures. In contrast to the reasons later exegetes have attributed to their exclusion, the biblical text does not explain why they are taboo—for example, that they are unhealthy or dangerous to eat or abnormal in some manner or linked to polytheistic powers. Rather, the biblical laws simply and unequivocally dismiss them as "unclean" or "abominable," connecting the taboo with divine will and holiness. The rhetoric most likely stems from the priests, that is, from the central priests attached to the state cult and not from the regional priests, much less from villagers who performed rituals in their own local cults. These temple priests were in a position to systematize all of the taboos, whether food or other, into categories according to type, and the stipulations they included are at times remarkable in their detail. Note, for example, the descriptions in Lev 13–14 about skin disorders and mold in houses, including details about the color of the spots, their spread, the color of hair on an afflicted person's spots, the possible judgments and consequences, and the purification rituals. Or again, in Lev 11 the priests do not simply declare the camel, rock badger, rabbit, and pig to be unclean but attribute to them a common trait—that they do not have both but only one of the taxonomic features of being cleft-footed and ruminant (chewing the cud).[46]

The case of the forbidden *pig* in biblical law may show the history of a taboo while also providing a key to the relation of biblical law to practiced law. According to archaeological and textual evidence, pigs figured substantially in the life of Southwest Asian cultures during the Middle Bronze Age—in the economy, in the crown's animal husbandry, in religious sacrifices (esp. for Hittites), and in the dietary and utilitarian needs (e.g., use of the pigskin) of some of the population.[47] After that period, the number of both domesticated pigs and perhaps even wild boars appears to have declined significantly in the Late Bronze Age and early Iron Age and remained low through the rest of the Iron Age and the Persian period.

46. As has often been noted, the text errs in classifying the rabbit as a ruminant: while its constant jaw movement makes it look like it is chewing the cud, it actually is not.

47. See various essays in Brigitte Lion and Cécile Michel, ed., *De la domestication au tabou: Le cas des suidés dans le Proche-Orient ancien* (Paris: De Boccard, 2006); also Brigitte Lion, "Les porcs à Nuzi," in *General Studies and Excavations at Nuzi 11/2: In Honor of David I. Owen on the Occasion of His 65th Birthday, October 28, 2005*, ed. Gernot Wilhelm, Studies on the Civilization and Culture of Nuzi and the Hurrians 18 (Bethesda, MD: CDL Press, 2009), 259–86. In Egypt there was a similar shift, although the decline began some four centuries earlier, in the Middle and New Kingdoms; Richard W. Redding, "The Role of the Pig in the Subsistence System of Ancient Egypt: A Parable on the Potential of Faunal Data," in *Animal Use and Culture Change*, ed. Pam J. Crabtree and Kathleen Ryan, MASCA Research Papers in Science and Archaeology, Supplement to vol. 8 (Philadelphia: University of Pennsylvania Press, 1991), 20–30.

Only in rare places and for relatively short time spans during this period has evidence of pig bones been found; these primary exceptions are the Philistine cities of Ashkelon, Tel Miqne (commonly identified with biblical Ekron), and Tel Batash (thought to be the site of biblical Timnah), all three with pig remains from Iron I but not later. In contrast, in Hellenistic and Roman times the urban demand for pork was high, and rural production shifted to meet this demand, or at least it did so in designated places conducive to swine husbandry.[48]

While this near absence of pigs during the Iron and Persian periods is often attributed to the biblical prohibition against pork consumption, quite a different explanation is more likely, in my view. Ecological or other grounds may account for the decline following the Late Bronze Age, especially since this paucity of pig bones occurs over the wider Levantine region during that period, not just within the Israelite area. There is also some evidence from Egypt that swine were associated with the lower class, disdained by the elites in the cities,[49] and the urban upper class in Israel might also have found swine and swineherds repugnant. Moreover, economic and political motives were involved if the upper class in the cities saw in the pig a potential threat to their taxation system.[50] The omnivorous pig is exceptionally efficient in converting its feed into meat, much more so than is the case for sheep or cattle, and there are numerous other benefits from raising swine. If the urban elites during the monarchic period desired other food products from the rural areas, then pig husbandry would have diverted the farmers' energy from raising what was preferred in the cities— even though pigs would have been more highly beneficial to villagers on a subsistence diet.

While declaring pigs to be taboo is one way to stigmatize pig husbandry, it is more likely that there was no need to do so if pigs were already largely absent in Israel from the Iron Age through most if not all of the Persian period.[51] However, circumstances changed when the Hellenists introduced

48. Brian Hesse and Paula Wapnish, "Can Pig Remains Be Used for Ethnic Diagnosis in the Ancient Near East?" in *The Archaeology of Israel: Constructing the Past, Interpreting the Present*, ed. Neil Asher Silberman and David Small, JSOTSup 237 (Sheffield: Sheffield Academic Press, 1997), 238–70. See also Marvin Harris, "The Abominable Pig," in *Good to Eat: Riddles of Food and Culture* (New York: Simon & Schuster, 1985), 67–87.

49. Hesse and Wapnish, "Can Pig Remains Be Used for Ethnic Diagnosis?" 252–53.

50. Paul Diener and Eugene E. Robkin, "Ecology, Evolution, and the Search for Cultural Origins: The Question of Islamic Pig Prohibition," *Current Anthropology* 19 (1978): 493–540, esp. 501–3; see also the sometimes heated discussion with sixteen respondents on 509–35.

51. Faust (*Israel's Ethnogenesis*, 35–40) concurs largely with the above depiction of the data, but he speculates that the taboo originated in the Iron I period, when the Israelites sought to distinguish themselves ethnically from the Philistines. His notion does not explain the region-

substantial consumption of pork to the region. The indigenous population, drawing perhaps on their earlier traditions about diet and animal
husbandry, may have turned pork into a food taboo, with the result that
a difference between Jewish dietary laws and cult on the one hand and
the cultural practices of the Hellenistic colonizers on the other took shape,
encouraged by the Jewish priests. Also stemming from the late period,
the vague references in Isa 65:4 and 66:3, 17 to eating or sacrificing pork
are part of a diatribe against perfidy, and the didactic stories in 2 Macc
6:18–7:42 (see also 1 Macc 1:47) underscore further cultural and religious
differences during the late Second Temple period.

Additional support, albeit *e silentio*, for this late dating of the priestly
taboo system comes also from archaeology. While a common, if not the
most common, purification ritual for the unclean is bathing, the *bathing
pool* (מִקְוֶה, *miqweh*), well known from Jewish religious practice, does not
appear in the archaeological record in Israel until the second century BCE,
and from then until the fall of the Second Temple they are attested by the
hundreds.[52] The purpose, whether religious or not, cannot be definitively
deduced from the material evidence, but this proliferation of pools suitable
for purification rites coincides well with our postulated time frame for the
recording of the priests' purity system.

Taboos can thus be expected in ancient Israel, both among the farmers
and herders and among the elites in the cities. But what is shunned by
custom does not normally rise to the level of being legally actionable. Late
in Israel's history the priests found in taboos a convenient means to control
access to the cult and to exert standards for behavior even outside the formal
cult. While drawing on some taboos already current in the population and
introducing others, they developed a system, complete with many details,
to promulgate as religious "laws." Since priestly jurisdiction rarely reached
beyond the cult except by dint of the effectiveness of certain priests or the
sanction of the king, it is unlikely that this system of purity was widespread
among the populace or the various sects during the periods down through
Hellenistic times. Later rabbinic discussions in the Mishnah elaborate on

wide decline of pig consumption during Iron II and then its resurgence in the Hellenistic
period.

52. Shaye J. D. Cohen, "The Judaean Legal Tradition and the *Halakhah* of the Mishnah,"
in *The Cambridge Companion to the Talmud and Rabbinic Literature*, ed. Charlotte Elisheva
Fonrobert and Martin S. Jaffee (Cambridge and New York: Cambridge University Press, 2007),
132. See also Benjamin G. Wright III, "Jewish Ritual Baths—Interpreting the Digs and the
Texts: Some Issues in the Social History of Second Temple Judaism," in *The Archaeology of
Israel: Constructing the Past, Interpreting the Present*, ed. Neil Asher Silberman and David
Small, JSOTSup 237 (Sheffield: Sheffield Academic Press, 1997), 190–214.

these laws in extended detail, applying them to circumstances known in their times and revealing the ambiguities and unaddressed conditions in the biblical laws themselves. Reading through these Mishnaic chapters provides one with a sense of how substantially the biblical prohibitions can affect everyday life—and also how much they depend on religious and judicial professionals to explicate them and enforce their application. As significant as the rabbinic interpretations are in their own right, however, they constitute the views of later communities and not necessarily the practices in the Hellenistic and Persian periods or earlier.

Requirements and Prerogatives of Religious Professionals

The *responsibilities and duties* of the priests, Levites, and other cultic functionaries are enumerated in various biblical texts (e.g., Num 3–4; 8:5–26; 18). While these duties are sometimes related in the narratives about the tabernacle tent during the wilderness period, they point to a division of labor in the later temple cult. The details are less important for our purposes than is the mere presence of a hierarchical, male-dominated structure in the central and regional cults, with presumably a looser system of responsibilities in the household and local cults.

A fee-for-service arrangement appears to be the acceptable means for *remunerating* the religious professionals. A legend about Saul and Samuel features such a payment as the expected means for securing a prophetic oracle: Saul is prepared to pay Samuel a quarter of a silver shekel for information that can lead to finding his lost donkeys (1 Sam 9:3–10). The most common means is for the priest to take a portion of certain offerings and sacrifices (e.g., Lev 2:2–3, 10; 6:16–18, 26, 29; 7:10, 31–36; 10:12–20; Deut 18:1–8), and the story in 1 Sam 2:12–17 relates an offense committed by Eli's priestly sons in taking more than their allotted portions. Sacrificing elsewhere than in the temple was probably commonplace throughout the land as families or communities sought favor with their gods, most frequently without the means to pay a religious professional. The biblical regulations represent an effort to draw all such cultic activity to the central and regional cults, which would have the effect of supporting the professional priests there.

It is difficult to know the extent of the *priests' judicial role* in Israelite society. They may well have aspired to more than they actually enjoyed, and we need to remember that they are the authors of the biblical laws that recognize their authority. For example, they have set themselves as the ultimate arbiters to decide on the status of "clean" or "unclean": using their own criteria, described in intriguing detail in Lev 13–14, they inspect a skin disease or comparable eruption (mold?) in a house and declare whether or not the condition is virulent. Yet any number of such cases among the rural population may have existed that never came to the attention of the central or regional priests, and the cultic officiants in the villages would not necessarily have had the adjudicatory powers attributed to the priests in the biblical texts. According to Deut 17:8–13, priests (here Levitical priests) are also given a key judicial role in the appeals process for homicide, personal injury, or other legal conflict (probably involving property): if local courts fail to resolve a case, it should be brought to the central (or regional?) priests and judge for a decision, which is binding and final. In my view, few if any such cases would not be settled at the local level among the rural population since they would have been loath to yield authority to others outside their community, especially when they had their own elders to adjudicate the matter and when the lives and property of their own community members were at stake. The only type of case that may have reached a higher level is one involving regional or national interests, such as harm against a royal representative or encroachment on crown or temple lands. For such instances the priests may have insinuated themselves into the judicial process, securing for themselves standing in the eyes of the king and the elites. To be sure, the text in Deut 17:8–13 implies a pre-monarchical setting, yet its wording does everything but name Jerusalem explicitly: "go up" (וְעָלִיתָ, wěʿālîtā), typically used as a shortened form for "going up to Jerusalem," and "the place that YHWH your God shall choose," the conventional circumlocution in Deuteronomy for Jerusalem. In addition, the section immediately following in Deut 17:14–18 names the king and the royal authority directly, which in turn provides the general political context for the judicial actions of the central priests.

Apart from the priestly laws in the Pentateuch, the biblical text is at times very critical of the priests and other religious leaders, charging them with *inappropriate behavior* or finding in them elements of discord and corruption. The story in 1 Sam 22 shows the priests taking sides politically with David, as a result of which Saul orders the slaughtering of eighty-five of them as well as the inhabitants of their hometown, with only Abiathar escaping. Later, following another incident of partisanship by the priest Abiathar, Solomon deposes him from his high position and banishes him from the court (1 Kgs 1:7–8; 2:26–27). The prophets are particularly critical of what they regard as evil acts by the religious professionals, whether priests or prophets: inebriation (Isa 28:7, both priests and prophets), abominable acts (Jer 6:15, using the same word found in cultic laws, תּוֹעֵבָה, tôʿēbâ, "abomination," to describe the behavior of prophets and priests), profiteering (Jer 6:13 and 8:10—both prophets and priests), committing adultery (prophets in Jer 23:14, and priests in 1 Sam 2:22–25), neglecting their duties (again both prophets and priests in Jer 2:8; Ezek 22:26, 28; Hos 4:4–6). They occupied positions of power and influence, and they could exploit these positions as easily as they could fulfill them properly. Compared to their urban counterparts, the nonprofessional cultic leaders among the rural population were less likely to capitalize on their roles at the expense of their neighbors since villagers lived in close proximity with each other and would have observed and sought to halt actions that did not serve the common good.

CONCLUSION

The world of the cult in ancient Israel is multilayered and intricate. To consider all forms as parts of a unified whole both overestimates its capacity to speak with one voice and underestimates its reach into the everyday lives of the people. Religiosity among the rural population was a natural and vital expression for those who lived on the edge of survival from year to year. Individual families faced constant threats from disease and death, lack of sufficient food, labor-intensive means of production, and demands from central authorities. Warding off the ominous powers, whether otherworldly or this-worldly, required regular, even daily attention. The small village communities, often with clan ties to other nearby villages, helped to lessen some of these burdens, and rituals at the "high places" shared by these peasants offered the means to petition in concert for support and to appease the deities. At the regional level, whether in some type of tribal setting or in the administrative and royal cities, the cult served larger purposes, involving persons not necessarily related to each other (or only remotely so) but with political and economic interests in common. Here the deity or deities were invoked for the advantage of the group as much as for individual benefit. In the state cult, finally, religious expressions and actions tied the reigning monarch and the governing class to the divine world, imperative for the success as well as the justice of the kingdom.

This description is supported by the material evidence. From the domestic cult to the state cult, shrines, figurines, altars, and other cultic paraphernalia have been uncovered in sufficient numbers and distribution to suggest that religious activities figured into the lives of the people, from small families to large groups, although how often they were used is impossible to know. At the same time, however, the evidence suggests diversity in religiosity, not uniformity. Monotheism was not widespread until late in

Israel's history; until it became established, the people worshiped whichever god and through whatever rituals seemed most efficacious to them. As
indicated above, we need to think of the *religions* of ancient Israel, not a
single, monolithic, commonly shared religious doctrine or set of practices.
In this respect the religious diversity paralleled the multiplicity of legal
systems across the country.

From the religious authorities stemmed ordinances governing ritual procedures and maintenance of the cult, often expressed in legal form but generally not classified as actionable offenses in the manner of crimes and torts.
Other directives set conditions for participation in the cultic community as
well as requirements for noncultic behavior, and these provisions rose to the
level of laws according to the above four defining characteristics of law.[53]
Some distinction should be made between laws developed by the domestic
and local cults on the one hand, and those issuing from the regional and
central cults on the other. Only in the latter contexts could there have been
a realistic interest in controlling religious behavior among worshipers on a
national scale, at cultic sites other than their own settings. Those who oversaw the domestic and local cults, however, focused on the immediate needs
of their participants to have the means for religious expression and solici-
tation of divine support. Another difference lies in the economic interests,
which loomed far larger in the case of the central temples than they did for
the local and domestic cults. Following the traditions of state cults in other
Southwest Asian countries, the temples presumably possessed extensive
holdings in land, livestock, goods, and slaves, as well as a substantial staff of
religious professionals. All of them needed attention and protection, which
we can expect to be reflected in the laws from the central cults.

The most distinctive area of cultic laws deals with purity and impurity.
The system of taboos encompasses a wide range: food (animals, birds,
insects, reptiles, aquatic life), diseases, reproduction, sexual activity, death.
In strictly forbidding whatever was deemed to be unclean, the priests not
only set terms for access to the cult but also sought to affect everyday
actions outside the cult. Their primary audience seems to have been the
urban populations that could visit the temples: we have no evidence that
they actively solicited adherence among the majority of the population, living in villages. In those local and domestic settings cultic taboos are likely
as well, but only specific types must have evolved that would not further
worsen the chances of survival in the subsistence economy prevailing
among villagers.

53. See above, chap. 2, The Nature and Sources of Law.

The origin of the cultic laws remains an open question. I have no doubt that both local and central cults existed throughout monarchic times and that local and especially domestic cults were ubiquitous even before the founding of the nation-state. It is inconceivable that the worshipers would not have developed traditions involving rituals, regular festivals, and expectations for the officiants. How widely any given practice or belief was shared is as difficult to determine as is the point at which they became described in writing. They could have persisted, in all their diversity across the land, without the aid of a written text. The same can be said of the laws controlling access to the cult and defining acceptable behavior outside the cultic setting. The Persian period is plausible as the context of this written process, especially during periods when the Persian emperors encouraged the temple in Yehud to function in an organized manner. Such a situation seems more conceivable, at least to me, than does a period when the community was in a weakened state because of dislocation and physical duress, as occurred during the exile. While some scholars have attributed a certain ossification to religious developments during the Persian period,[54] these centuries from the sixth through the fourth BCE actually experienced a restoration of the cult and a determination to develop a foundation for its ongoing survival.

54. See, e.g., Wellhausen, *Prolegomena*, 419–25.

Epilogue

Working with written texts can give literary critics and historians a sense of assuredness not readily available to social historians. Yet if their meanings are to be elucidated, texts also require interpretations at every turn, as do human actions and material products. And when these interpretations acquire a level of certainty among their proponents, they have a way of closing off inquiry. They may be "accepted" or "valid," but they always deserve new scrutiny and augmentation.

Biblical scholarship is no stranger to "assured results." For many readers of the Bible, both past and present, there is no question that Moses mediated all of the laws directly from the Israelites' God, as claimed in the directives preserved in the Pentateuch. If readers were to think that this literal interpretation is a straightforward, self-evident, unassailable truth, then they need to be reminded that a literal reading is itself an interpretation based on a certain hypothesis about the nature of the text. Why can that same text not be taken, for example, poetically, allegorically, fictionally, dramatically, or psychologically—rather than literally? Or for the present topic, why must the laws be considered inspired, realistic, or normative—rather than arbitrary, idealistic, or exploitative? Could it be that there is little direct relation between the laws reported in the Pentateuch and the wide variety of laws functioning among the ancient Israelites in settings ranging from the tiniest hamlet to the largest city?

Biblical critics of the past three centuries have produced hypotheses based on their understandings of comparative data, developmental schemes, political and social backgrounds, religious history, and literary characteristics. These proposals have resulted in the identification of specific legal collections, arranged in historical sequence and related both to political happenings and to other parts of the Hebrew Bible. With few exceptions, most scholars find their starting points in a tenth- or ninth-century BCE dating of the Covenant Code, a late seventh-century attribution for the Deuteronomic Code, a setting for the Holiness Code usually in the exilic or postexilic periods, a postexilic provenance for the Priestly Code, and the Ten Commandments almost anywhere between Moses and Ezra. Even with some disagreements over the fine points in this scheme, the general order seems so assured that it often becomes the measuring stick to determine when much other biblical literature and even the history of Israelite religion should be reckoned. At one time the exilic period was generally thought to be the time of greatest literary activity, but now many prefer either to set it earlier to coincide with the Deuteronomic movement or to situate it considerably later, in the Persian or Hellenistic periods. Whatever the details, my point is that much of this dating and identifying of legal collections is taken for granted. When so much scholarly work has been invested in refining these proposals, it is easy to forget the speculative and hypothetical nature of it all—including even the old, traditional notion of the Mosaic authorship of the Pentateuch.

This book aims to sidestep this whole debate, even though I have occasionally expressed an opinion about one aspect or another of it. Instead, I suggest that we expand our field of vision both horizontally and vertically, to use spatial metaphors. Horizontally, much else in the way of legal activity was occurring in ancient Israel than just that which became captured in the pentateuchal texts. The vast majority of Israel's population, ranging between 80 percent and 95 percent, lived outside the urban centers, in villages averaging only 0.3–0.6 hectares (0.75–1.5 acres) in size and containing only 75–150 inhabitants or even fewer. Scattered throughout the entire land, these hamlets constituted social microcosms that are not writ large in the biblical literature. They produced their own legal traditions to keep their affairs running smoothly, and these customary laws were remembered and applied orally throughout the generations, adjusting as circumstances required. On individual legal issues there was no more likelihood of consistency among all the villages than there was between the villages on the one hand and the cities on the other. However, the urban legal traditions are largely the only ones preserved in the Hebrew Bible, I have argued. Israel's cities, quite small in population, housed primarily the powerful and the wealthy, along with their retainers, administrators, and slaves. They depended on the resources of the villages for food, taxes, rents, and labor, and to this end they needed to control access to these resources. Yet we know of no effort by the cities or the state to construct detailed systems of civil and religious laws and press them on the whole country, at least not during monarchic times. The villagers were able to maintain their own customs and legal traditions so long as the interests of the powerful were not compromised. Considered from the perspective of our analytical methods, a sociohistorical study of *biblical* laws (as opposed to *Israelite* laws) will not alone uncover the villagers' laws but will mainly stay within the social world of the cities. To go beyond the urban world requires a second step.

The vertical expansion of our perspective is possible through the means of ideological criticism. The question "Whose text is it?" leads to the realization that special interests and agendas undergird the laws recorded in the Hebrew Bible. Expressing urban rather than rural concerns, they also advance the causes of their authors. Even those provisions that seem on the surface to represent humanitarian concerns for the poor and powerless have a way of benefiting the powerful, and evidence that they were ever actually practiced as economic correctives is spotty at best. The modern fields of legal theory known as legal realism and Critical Legal Studies are based on the premise that laws cannot help but have political and economic dimensions, even (and perhaps especially) when they claim to be objective and unbiased. Consequently, justice often does not reach those who deserve and need it most. Following such lines of reasoning, we can put ourselves in a position not only to understand the biblical law collections in a deeper manner but also to seek to recover the hidden laws of the villages of ancient Israel.

Archaeological research provides essential information for such an effort. For this reason I began each of the three main substantive chapters with a review of the material findings from villages, cities, and cults. The results accentuate the power resident in cities, the vulnerability of villages, and the diversity of cultic practices. Based on this understanding of social realities in each setting, it was then possible to envision some of the kinds of legal conflicts that could occur, which in turn issued in customary laws. I readily admit the hypothetical nature of these three constructs—the legal systems of villages, cities, and cults—yet also contend that it is no more hypothetical than are other historical reconstructions and literary interpretations. For me, shifting both the starting point and the goal is critical: beginning not with texts but with the economic and political worlds of ancient Israel, and ending not with a theological interpretation of texts and history but with an empathetic understanding of power imbalances and the ideologies of laws.

My aim has been to draw attention to the largely uncharted world of "living laws" in ancient Israel, the customary laws that developed in the course of everyday life to guide behavior and handle adjudication in the many social, political, economic, and religious settings across the land. For the urban and much of the cultic settings, the focus fell on the monarchic period of Iron II, when powerful leaders, elites, and institutions steered political and economic systems of nationwide significance. For the much more populous world of the villages, scattered throughout the land, the whole period from the beginning of the Iron Age and well into Hellenistic times (ca. 1200–150 BCE) served as the time frame. Here local laws responded variously, not uniformly, to the particular needs and conflicts that arose in those settings. Over this much-longer period, the social and economic conditions within villages probably experienced less change than did the circumstances within the cities and the monarchic institutions, where power and self-interest invited competition and exploitation.

These real worlds produced laws and legal processes that the biblical literature did not usually capture, and our only way forward is to make the effort to reconstruct those worlds and their legal traditions. Considering the complexity of the task, it has been possible in this study to treat only selected legal topics from the social, political, economic, and religious domains, and many others await investigation. In each and every case, law and power interact in ways often inimical to equity or fairness, and realizing justice was as elusive a problem in ancient times as it can be for us today.

Appendix

Criteria for Identifying Laws

Villages	Cities and States	Cult
1. Village laws reflect and promote the social customs and traditions of the community. Representing what is often called customary laws, they are developed and transmitted in oral form.	1. Urban laws will rarely assume written form during the periods in which they are functioning as living law, except insofar as they are reflected in contracts and other legal documents. On the other hand, state laws, while quite minimal and general, may be written in the form of proclamations and administrative procedures.	1. Cultic laws are expressed in an absolutistic manner, with no equivocation about their validity and no exceptions allowed.
2. Village laws recognize the social and political hierarchy basic to village life and kinship groups, especially the patriarchal structure and local leadership.	2. The patriarchal structure prevails also within urban families, perhaps ameliorated somewhat by the increased status and wealth of the whole family, including the wife.	2. Cultic laws generally seek to uphold the social, political, and institutional status quo. At the local or domestic levels, religion reinforces the structures and values of the household, clan, and tribe or region. At the national level, however, cultic laws protect the current political and economic systems of the state.
3. Village laws seek to ensure cooperation and eliminate discord among members of the community. They attempt, as needed, to resolve conflicts, to remedy losses and injuries, and to clarify liability.	3. The composition of the nonroyal urban population is primarily determined not by kinship and clan ties or by long-standing family associations but rather by the power and prestige acquired and held by its inhabitants. Consequently, urban laws are less likely than village laws to seek to secure restitution and restoration for a wronged neighbor whose loss threatens their subsistence and participation in the community.	3. Cultic laws attend to economic welfare: at the local level the subsistence of the villagers is at stake, whereas at the national level the state and temple economies are protected and advanced.
4. Village laws are especially concerned with matters affecting the family, kinship groups, marriage, and sexuality.	4. A variety of the conflicts seen in villages occur also in cities: issues involving marriage, family,	4. Cultic laws reserve a significant role for the priests in the
5. Village laws do not contemplate the more-		

Villages	Cities and States	Cult
complex, layered society found in cities or at the national level. 6. Village laws tend to be oriented toward life on the land, toward agricultural or pastoral existence. 7. Village laws are more likely than urban or national laws to be responsive to conditions of vulnerability among the lower classes, as in the case of persons who suffer from hardships, death of a provider, or natural catastrophe. 8. Village laws foster the interests of the given village and, usually, those of nearby or similar villages as well, especially those with which there may be kinship ties. 9. Village laws rarely involve any formal institutions larger than kinship ties, at most only an ad hoc deliberative gathering of village or regional elders. 10. Village laws do not support the diversion of the community's produce or resources to cities or other parts of the country, except insofar as a direct benefit (e.g., trade or security) can come to the villagers as a result. 11. Village laws are sensitive	sexuality, personal injury, and property loss or damage. 5. Urban laws reflect and reinforce the large-scale institutions based in cities, including the monarchy, the central priesthood, the governmental administration, and the military. 6. Though village laws are oriented toward life on the land—such as agriculture, pastoralism, and supporting functions—urban laws focus heavily on commercial and property issues. The scale of these economics is not merely local—as in the case of peasants, who own at most only their mud-brick dwelling and the small arable plot they have inherited—but extends well beyond the cities to encompass landholdings accumulated in the countryside, often from those same peasants, as well as merchant activity with others in the country or even with traders and suppliers in distant lands. 7. Urban and state laws are less responsive to the vulnerability of the lower classes than are village laws. 8. State laws, which may generally not be overly complex in an ancient agrarian kingdom, are oriented toward two ends: establishing and preserving the preeminent power of the monarch, and securing the crown property and the ongoing revenue desired for the comforts of the royal house. 9. Taxation, military conscription, and labor conscription are determined by the state, effected by the bureaucracy, and enforced by the	adjudication of disputes affecting the practice and property of the religious institutions. 5. Cultic laws define the terms of proper worship and ritual. 6. Cultic laws stipulate the terms for admission to the cult and membership in the cultic community. 7. Cultic laws may include a motive clause, referring to divine powers as enforcers or instigators of the given requirement. 8. Cultic laws often include sanctions, which generally take an extreme form (execution, banishment, or other strict punishment). 9. Cultic laws ensure the standing and prerogatives of the cultic officiants, from the father or mother's overseeing rituals in the home to the central priesthood and other religious personnel at the temple in the nation's capital. 10. Cultic laws regulate the use and significance of cultic buildings and paraphernalia.

Villages	Cities and States	Cult
to the priorities and perils inherent to a subsistence economy. 12. Village laws tend to exclude or give limited protection to outsiders. ##1–11 have counterparts in the city/state laws.	military. 10. State laws normally do not interfere with legal cases at the local levels unless there may be an impingement on state interests. 11. Much more so than is the case in villages, socioeconomic status and political position affect the legal rights and prerogatives of urban dwellers. 12. State laws will seek, where possible, to use legal as well as political means to contain the powers and influence of the nonroyal elites. 13. While absolute power lies in the hands of the monarch, it is potentially curbed by the interventions of the commercial, military, or priestly elites. 14. State laws prescribe hereditary royal succession and yet need to adjust to coups d'état when they prove successful. 15. State laws must yield to imperial laws during periods of colonization. ## 1–11 have counterparts in the village laws.	

Bibliography

Ahlström, Gösta W. *Aspects of Syncretism in Israelite Religion*. Translated by Eric J. Sharpe. Horae Soederblomianae 5. Lund: C. W. K. Gleerup, 1963.

———. *The History of Ancient Palestine*. Minneapolis: Fortress; Sheffield: Sheffield Academic Press, 1993.

Aichele, George, Fred W. Burnett, Elizabeth A. Castelli, Robert M. Fowler, David Jobling, Stephen D. Moore, Gary A. Phillips, Tina Pippin, Regina M. Schwartz, and Wilhelm Wuellner (The Bible and Culture Collective). *The Postmodern Bible*. New Haven: Yale University Press, 1995.

Albertz, Rainer. *A History of Israelite Religion in the Old Testament Period*. 2 vols. OTL. Louisville, KY: Westminster John Knox Press, 1994.

———. *Israel in Exile: The History and Literature of the Sixth Century B.C.E.* Translated by David Green. SBLSBL 3. Atlanta: Society of Biblical Literature, 2003. German original, 2001.

———. *Persönliche Frömmigkeit und offizielle Religion: Religionsinterner Pluralismus in Israel und Babylon*. Stuttgart: Calwer Verlag, 1978.

Alt, Albrecht. "Die Ursprünge des israelitischen Rechts." In *Kleine Schriften zur Geschichte des Volkes Israel*, 1:278–332. Munich: Verlag C. H. Beck, 1953. Original essay in 1934. Translated by R. A. Wilson as "The Origins of Israelite Law." In *Essays on Old Testament History and Religion*, 133–71. Garden City, NY: Doubleday, 1967.

Altman, Andrew. *Critical Legal Studies: A Liberal Critique*. Princeton, NJ: Princeton University Press, 1990.

Anderson, Cheryl B. *Ancient Laws and Contemporary Controversies: The Need for Inclusive Biblical Interpretation*. Oxford: Oxford University Press, 2009.

———. *Women, Ideology, and Violence: Critical Theory and the Construction of Gender in the Book of the Covenant and the Deuteronomic Law*. JSOTSup 394. London and New York: T&T Clark International, 2004.

Assmann, Aleida. "Exkarnation: Gedanken zur Grenze zwischen Körper und Schrift." In *Raum und Verfahren*, edited by Alois Martin Müller and Jörg Huber, 133–55. Interventionen 2. Basel: Stroemfeld/Roter Stern, 1993.

Assmann, Aleida, and Dietrich Harth, eds. *Kultur als Lebenswelt und Monument*. Frankfurt am Main: Fischer Taschenbuch, 1991.

Assmann, Jan. *Das kulturelle Gedächtnis: Schrift, Erinnerung und politische Identität in frühen Hochkulturen*. 2nd ed. Munich: Verlag C. H. Beck, 1999.

———. *Religion and Cultural Memory: Ten Studies*. Translated by Rodney Livingstone. Stanford, CA: Stanford University Press, 2006. German original, 2000.

Assmann, Jan, and Tonio Hölscher, eds. *Kultur und Gedächtnis*. Frankfurt am Main: Suhrkamp, 1988.

Aufrecht, Walter E., Neil A. Mirau, and Steven W. Gauley, eds. *Urbanism in Antiquity: From Mesopotamia to Crete*. JSOTSup 244. Sheffield: Sheffield Academic Press, 1997.

Baines, John. "Literacy and Ancient Egyptian Society." In *Visual and Written Culture in Ancient Egypt*, 33–62. Oxford: Oxford University Press, 2007.

Baines, John, and Christopher Eyre. "Four Notes on Literacy." In *Visual and Written Culture in Ancient Egypt*, by John Baines, 63–94. Oxford: Oxford University Press, 2007.

Bartlett, Katharine T., and Rosanne Kennedy, eds. *Feminist Legal Theory: Readings in Law and Gender*. Boulder, CO: Westview Press, 1991.

Bauman, Richard W. *Critical Legal Studies: A Guide to the Literature*. Boulder, CO: Westview Press, 1996.

Becking, Bob. "The Two Neo-Assyrian Documents from Gezer in Their Historical Context." *JEOL* 27 (1981–82): 76–89.

Belkin, Lawrence A., and Eileen F. Wheeler. "Reconstruction of the Megiddo Stables." In *Megiddo IV: The 1998–2002 Seasons*, edited by Israel Finkelstein, David Ussishkin, and Baruch Halpern, 2:666–87. Tel Aviv: Emery and Claire Yass Publications in Archaeology, 2006.

Bendor, S. *The Social Structure of Ancient Israel: The Institution of the Family (beit ᵓab) from the Settlement to the End of the Monarchy*. Jerusalem Biblical Studies 7. Jerusalem: Simor, 1996.

Bennett, Harold V. *Injustice Made Legal: Deuteronomic Law and the Plight of Widows, Strangers, and Orphans in Ancient Israel*. Grand Rapids, MI, and Cambridge, UK: William B. Eerdmans, 2002.

Berlinerblau, Jacques. "The 'Popular Religion' Paradigm in Old Testament Research: A Sociological Critique." *JSOT* 60 (1993): 3–26.

Berquist, Jon L. *Judaism in Persia's Shadow: A Social and Historical Approach*. Minneapolis: Fortress Press, 1995.

———. "Postcolonialism and Imperial Motives for Canonization." *Semeia* 75 (1996): 15–35.

Berquist, Jon L., and Claudia V. Camp, eds. *Constructions of Space II: The Biblical City and Other Imagined Spaces*. LHBOTS 490. New York and London: T&T Clark, 2008.

Betz, Hans Dieter, et al., eds. *Religion in Geschichte und Gegenwart*. 4th ed. 8 vols. Tübingen: J. C. B. Mohr (Paul Siebeck), 1998–2007.

Bird, Phyllis A. *Missing Persons and Mistaken Identities: Women and Gender in Ancient Israel*. Minneapolis: Fortress Press, 1997.

———. "Prostitution in the Social World and Religious Rhetoric of Ancient Israel." In *Prostitutes and Courtesans in the Ancient World*, edited by Christopher A. Faraone and Laura K. McClure, 40–58. Madison: University of Wisconsin Press, 2006.

Black, Henry Campbell. *Black's Law Dictionary*. 5th ed. St. Paul: West Publishing, 1979.

Blenkinsopp, Joseph. *Sage, Priest, Prophet: Religious and Intellectual Leadership in Ancient Israel*. LAI. Louisville, KY: Westminster John Knox Press, 1995.

Blum, Erhard. *Studien zur Komposition des Pentateuch*. BZAW 189. Berlin: de Gruyter, 1990.

Bodel, John, and Saul M. Olyan, eds. *Household and Family Religion in Antiquity*. Oxford: Basil Blackwell Publishing, 2008.

Boer, Roland. *Political Myth: On the Use and Abuse of Biblical Themes*. Durham, NC, and London, UK: Duke University Press, 2009.

————. "The Sacred Economy of Ancient 'Israel.'" *SJOT* 21 (2007): 29–48.

Bogaert, Raymond. *Les origines antiques de la banque de dépôt: Une mise au point accompagnée d'une esquisse des opérations de banque en Mésopotamie*. Leyden: A. W. Sijthoff, 1966.

Bohannan, Paul. *Justice and Judgment among the Tiv*. London: Oxford University Press, 1957.

Borowski, Oded. *Agriculture in Iron Age Israel*. Winona Lake, IN: Eisenbrauns, 1987.

Botterweck, G. Johannes, Helmer Ringgren, and Heinz-Josef Fabry, eds. *Theologisches Wörterbuch zum Alten Testament*. Stuttgart: W. Kohlhammer, 1970–. Translated by J. T. Willis, G. W. Bromiley, D. E. Green, and D. W. Stott as *Theological Dictionary of the Old Testament*. 15 vols. Grand Rapids: William B. Eerdmans, 1974–.

Boyle, James, ed. *Critical Legal Studies*. Aldershot: Ashgate/Dartmouth, 1992.

Braudel, Ferdinand. *Civilization and Capitalism, 15th–18th Century*. 3 vols. London: Collins; New York: Harper & Row, 1981–84.

————. "La longue durée." *Annales économies, sociétés, civilisations* 13 (1958): 725–53.

————. *The Mediterranean and the Mediterranean World in the Age of Philip II*. Translated by Siân Reynolds. 2 vols. New York: Harper & Row, 1972–76. French original, 2nd ed., 1966.

Bretschneider, J., J. Driessen, and K. van Lerberghe, eds. *Power and Architecture: Monumental Public Architecture in the Bronze Age Near East and Aegean*. OLA 156. Leuven: Uitgeverij Peeters, 2007.

Briant, Pierre. *From Cyrus to Alexander: A History of the Persian Empire*. Translated by Peter T. Daniels. Winona Lake, IN: Eisenbrauns, 2002. French original, 1996.

Broshi, Magen. "The Expansion of Jerusalem in the Reigns of Hezekiah and Manasseh." *IEJ* 24 (1974): 21–26.

Broshi, Magen, and Israel Finkelstein. "The Population of Palestine in Iron Age II." *BASOR* 287 (1992): 47–60.

Buccellati, Giorgio. *Cities and Nations of Ancient Syria: An Essay on Political Institutions with Special Reference to the Israelite Kingdoms*. Studi semitici 26. Rome: Istituto di Studi del Vicino Oriente, Università di Roma, 1967.

Bunimovitz, Shlomo. "On the Edge of Empires—Late Bronze Age (1500–1200 BCE)." In *The Archaeology of Society in the Holy Land*, edited by Thomas E. Levy, 320–31. New York: Facts on File, 1995.

Busink, T. A. *Der Tempel von Jerusalem von Salomo bis Herodes: Eine archäologisch-historische Studie unter Berücksichtigung des westsemitischen Tempelbaus*. 2 vols. Leiden: E. J. Brill, 1970–80.

Cantrell, Deborah O'Daniel. "The Horsemen of Israel: Horses and Chariotry in Monarchic Israel (Ninth–Eighth Centuries B.C.E.)." Ph.D. diss., Vanderbilt University, 2008.

————. "Stable Issues." In *Megiddo IV: The 1998–2002 Seasons*, edited by Israel Finkelstein, David Ussishkin, and Baruch Halpern, 2:630–42. Tel Aviv: Emery and Claire Yass Publications in Archaeology, 2006.

Cantrell, Deborah O., and Israel Finkelstein. "A Kingdom for a Horse: The Megiddo Stables and Eighth Century Israel." In *Megiddo IV: The 1998–2002 Seasons*, edited by Israel Finkelstein, David Ussishkin, and Baruch Halpern, 2:643–65. Tel Aviv: Emery and Claire Yass Publications in Archaeology, 2006.

Cardellini, Innocenzo. *Die biblischen "Sklaven"-Gesetze im Lichte des keilschriftlichen Sklavenrechts: Ein Beitrag zur Tradition, Überlieferung und Redaktion der alttestamentlichen Rechtstexte*. BBB 55. Bonn: Peter Hanstein, 1981.

Carr, David M. *Writing on the Tablet of the Heart: Origins of Scripture and Literature*. Oxford and New York: Oxford University Press, 2005.

Carroll, Robert P. "The Myth of the Empty Land." *Semeia* 59 (1992): 79–93.

Chalcraft, David J., ed. *Sectarianism in Early Judaism: Sociological Advances*. London, UK, and Oakville, CT: Equinox Publishing, 2007.

Charpin, Dominique. "Les édits de 'restauration' des rois babyloniens et leur application." In *Du pouvoir dans l'antiquité: Mots et réalités*, edited by Claude Nicolet, 13–24. Hautes études du monde gréco-romain 16. Geneva: Librairie Droz, 1990.

Charpin, Dominique, and Francis Joannès, eds. *La circulation des biens, des personnes et des idées dans le Proche-Orient ancien: Actes de la XXXVIIIe Rencontre assyriologique internationale (Paris, 8–10 juillet 1991)*. Paris: Éditions recherche sur les civilisations, 1992.

Childs, Brevard. *Introduction to the Old Testament as Scripture*. Philadelphia: Fortress Press, 1979.

Chirichigno, Gregory C. *Debt-Slavery in Israel and the Ancient Near East*. JSOTSup 141. Sheffield: JSOT Press, 1993.

Claburn, W. Eugene. "The Fiscal Basis of Josiah's Reforms." *JBL* 92 (1973): 12–22.

Cohen, Shaye J. D. "The Judaean Legal Tradition and the *Halakhah* of the Mishnah." In *The Cambridge Companion to the Talmud and Rabbinic Literature*, edited by Charlotte Elisheva Fonrobert and Martin S. Jaffee, 121–43. Cambridge and New York: Cambridge University Press, 2007.

Cornelius, Friedrich. "Das Hethiterreich als Feudalstaat." In *Gesellschaftsklassen im Alten Zweistromland und in den angrenzenden Gebieten—XVIII: Rencontre assyriologique internationale, München, 29. Juni bis 3. Juli 1970*, edited by D. O. Edzard, 31–34. Munich: Verlag der Bayerischen Akademie der Wissenschaften, 1972.

Cotterrell, Roger. *The Sociology of Law: An Introduction*. London: Butterworths, 1984.

Cover, Robert M. *Justice Accused: Antislavery and the Judicial Process*. New Haven, CT, and London, UK: Yale University Press, 1975.

Crenshaw, James L. *Prophetic Conflict: Its Effect upon Israelite Religion*. BZAW 124. Berlin: de Gruyter, 1971.

Crow, Loren D. *The Songs of Ascents (Psalms 120–134): Their Place in Israelite History and Religion*. SBLDS 148. Atlanta: Scholars Press, 1996.

Crüsemann, Frank. "Israel in der Perserzeit: Eine Skizze in Auseinandersetzung mit Max Weber." In *Max Webers Sicht des antiken Christentums: Interpretation und Kritik*, edited by Wolfgang Schluchter, 205–32. Frankfurt am Main: Suhrkamp, 1985.

———. *The Torah: Theology and Social History of Old Testament Law*. Translated by Allan W. Mahnke. Minneapolis: Fortress Press, 1996. German original, 1992.

Culley, Robert C. *Oral Formulaic Language in the Biblical Psalms*. Near and Middle East Series 4. Toronto: University of Toronto Press, 1967.

Danby, Herbert. *The Mishnah*. London: Oxford University Press, 1933.

Dandamaev, Muhammad A. *Slavery in Babylonia: From Nabopolassar to Alexander the Great (626–331 BC)*. Rev. ed. Edited by Marvin A. Powell and David B. Weisberg. Translated by Victoria A. Powell. DeKalb: Northern Illinois University Press, 1984.

Daube, David. *The Deed and the Doer in the Bible: David Daube's Gifford Lectures*. Edited and compiled by Calum Carmichael. Vol. 1. West Conshohocken, PA: Templeton Foundation, 2008.

———. *Studies in Biblical Law*. Cambridge: Cambridge University Press, 1947.

David, Martin. *Die Adoption im altbabylonischen Recht*. Leipziger rechtswissenschaftliche Studien 23. Leipzig: Theodor Weicher, 1927.

Davies, Philip R. *In Search of "Ancient Israel."* JSOTSup 148. Sheffield: Sheffield Academic Press, 1992.

———. *Memories of Ancient Israel: An Introduction to Biblical History—Ancient and Modern*. Louisville, KY, and London, UK: Westminster John Knox Press, 2008.

Dégh, Linda. "What Did the Grimm Brothers Give to and Take from the Folk?" In *The Brothers Grimm and Folktale*, edited by James M. McGlathery, 66–90. Urbana and Chicago: University of Illinois Press, 1988.

De Troyer, Kristin, Judith A. Herbert, Judith Ann Johnson, and Anne-Marie Korte, eds. *Wholly Woman, Holy Blood: A Feminist Critique of Purity and Impurity*. SAC. Harrisburg, PA: Trinity Press International, 2003.

Dever, William G. "Syro-Palestinian and Biblical Archaeology." In *The Hebrew Bible and Its Modern Interpreters*, edited by Douglas A. Knight and Gene M. Tucker, 31–74. BMI. Philadelphia: Fortress Press; Chico, CA: Scholars Press, 1985.

Diakonoff, Igor M. "Socio-Economic Classes in Babylonia and the Babylonian Concept of Social Stratification." In *Gesellschaftsklassen im Alten Zweistromland und in den angrenzenden Gebieten—XVIII: Rencontre assyriologique internationale, München, 29. Juni bis 3. Juli 1970*, edited by D. O. Edzard, 41–52. Munich: Verlag der Bayerischen Akademie der Wissenschaften, 1972.

Diener, Paul, and Eugene E. Robkin. "Ecology, Evolution, and the Search for Cultural Origins: The Question of Islamic Pig Prohibition." *Current Anthropology* 19 (1978): 493–540.

Diodorus of Sicily. *Diodorus Siculus*. Vol. 1, *Books 1–2.34*. Translated by C. H. Oldfather. LCL 279. London: William Heinemann; New York: G. P. Putnam's Sons, 1933.

Dobbs-Allsopp, F. W., J. J. M. Roberts, C. L. Seow, and R. E. Whitaker. *Hebrew Inscriptions: Texts from the Biblical Period of the Monarchy, with Concordance*. New Haven, CT, and London, UK: Yale University Press, 2005.

Donovan, James M., and H. Edwin Anderson III. *Anthropology and Law*. New York and Oxford: Berghahn Books, 2003.

Douglas, Mary. *Purity and Danger: An Analysis of Concepts of Pollution and Taboo*. London: Routledge & Kegan Paul, 1966.

Douzinas, Costas, and Adam Gearey. *Critical Jurisprudence: The Political Philosophy of Justice*. Oxford, UK, and Portland, OR: Hart Publishing, 2005.

Douzinas, Costas, Ronnie Warrington, and Shaun McVeigh. *Postmodern Jurisprudence: The Law of Text in the Texts of Law*. London and New York: Routledge, 1993.

Driel, G. van. *Elusive Silver: In Search of a Role for a Market in an Agrarian Environment: Aspects of Mesopotamia's Society.* Nederlands Instituut voor het Nabije Oosten te Leiden 95. Leiden: Nederlands Instituut voor het Nabije Oosten, 2002.

Durkheim, Émile. *The Rules of the Sociological Method.* Edited and introduced by Steven Lukes. Translated by W. D. Halls. New York: Free Press, 1982. Originally published as *Les règles de la méthode sociologique.* Paris: F. Alcan, 1895.

Eagleton, Terry. *Criticism and Ideology: A Study in Marxist Literary Theory.* London: Verso Press, 1976.

Edzard, D. O., ed. *Gesellschaftsklassen im Alten Zweistromland und in den angrenzenden Gebieten—XVIII: Rencontre assyriologique internationale, München, 29. Juni bis 3. Juli 1970.* Munich: Verlag der Bayerischen Akademie der Wissenschaften, 1972.

Ehrlich, Eugen. *Fundamental Principles of the Sociology of Law.* Cambridge, MA: Harvard University Press, 1936. Originally published as *Grundlegung der Soziologie des Rechts.* Munich: Duncker & Humblot, 1913.

Eissfeldt, Otto. *The Old Testament, an Introduction: The History of the Formation of the Old Testament.* Translated by Peter R. Ackroyd. New York and Evanston: Harper & Row, 1965. German original, 3rd ed., 1964.

Erll, Astrid, Ansgar Nünning, and Sara B. Young, eds. *Cultural Memory Studies: An International and Interdisciplinary Handbook.* Media and Cultural Memory 8. Berlin and New York: Walter de Gruyter, 2008.

Fager, Jeffrey A. *Land Tenure and the Biblical Jubilee: Uncovering Hebrew Ethics through the Sociology of Knowledge.* JSOTSup 155. Sheffield: Sheffield Academic Press, 1993.

Faust, Avraham. *Israel's Ethnogenesis: Settlement, Interaction, Expansion, and Resistance.* London, UK, and Oakville, CT: Equinox Publishing, 2006.

Feeley-Harnik, Gillian. "Is Historical Anthropology Possible? The Case of the Runaway Slave." In *Humanizing America's Iconic Book: Society of Biblical Literature Centennial Addresses 1980,* edited by Gene M. Tucker and Douglas A. Knight, 95–126. SBLBSNA 6. Chico: Scholars Press, 1982.

Finkelstein, Israel. "The Archaeology of the Days of Manasseh." In *Scripture and Other Artifacts: Essays on the Bible and Archaeology in Honor of Philip J. King,* edited by Michael D. Coogan, J. Cheryl Exum, and Lawrence E. Stager, 169–87. Louisville, KY: Westminster John Knox Press, 1994.

———. *Archaeology of the Israelite Settlement.* Jerusalem: Israel Exploration Society, 1988.

———. "The Archaeology of the United Monarchy: An Alternative View." *Levant* 28 (1996): 177–87.

———. "The Emergence of Israel: A Phase in the Cyclic History of Canaan in the Third and Second Millennia BCE." In *From Nomadism to Monarchy: Archaeological and Historical Aspects of Early Israel,* edited by Israel Finkelstein and Nadav Na'aman, 150–78. Jerusalem: Israel Exploration Society; Washington: Biblical Archaeology Society, 1994.

———. "A Few Notes on Demographic Data from Recent Generations and Ethnoarchaeology." *PEQ* 122 (1990): 47–52.

———. "Hazor and the North in the Iron Age: A Low Chronology Perspective." *BASOR* 314 (1999): 55–70.

Finkelstein, Israel, Baruch Halpern, Gunnar Lehmann, and Herman Michael Niemann. "The Megiddo Hinterland Project." In *Megiddo IV: The 1998–2002 Seasons*, edited by Israel Finkelstein, David Ussishkin, and Baruch Halpern, 2:705–76. Tel Aviv: Emery and Claire Yass Publications in Archaeology, 2006.

Finkelstein, Israel, and David Ussishkin. "Archaeological and Historical Conclusions." In *Megiddo III: The 1992–1996 Seasons*, edited by Israel Finkelstein, David Ussishkin, and Baruch Halpern, 2:576–605. Tel Aviv: Institute of Archaeology, Tel Aviv University, 2000.

Finkelstein, Israel, and David Ussishkin. "Area J." In *Megiddo III: The 1992–1996 Seasons*, edited by Israel Finkelstein, David Ussishkin, and Baruch Halpern, 1:25–74. Tel Aviv: Institute of Archaeology, Tel Aviv University, 2000.

Finkelstein, Israel, and Neil Asher Silberman. *The Bible Unearthed: Archaeology's New Vision of Ancient Israel and the Origin of Its Sacred Texts*. New York and London: Simon & Schuster, 2001.

Finkelstein, Israel, David Ussishkin, and Jennifer Peersmann, "Area J (the 1998–2000 Seasons)." In *Megiddo IV: The 1998–2002 Seasons*, edited by Israel Finkelstein, David Ussishkin, and Baruch Halpern, 1:29–53. Tel Aviv: Emery and Claire Yass Publications in Archaeology, 2006.

Finkelstein, Israel, Zvi Lederman, and Shlomo Bunimovitz. *Highlands of Many Cultures: The Southern Samaria Survey; The Sites*. 2 vols. Tel Aviv: Tel Aviv University, 1997.

Finkelstein, Jacob J. *The Ox That Gored*. Transactions of the American Philosophical Society, new series, 71/2. Philadelphia: American Philosophical Society, 1981.

———. "Sex Offenses in Sumerian Laws." *JAOS* 86 (1966): 355–72.

Fishbane, Michael A. *Biblical Interpretation in Ancient Israel*. Oxford: Clarendon; New York: Oxford University Press, 1985.

Flanagan, James W. "Chiefs in Israel." *JSOT* 20 (1981): 47–73.

———. *David's Social Drama: A Hologram of Israel's Early Iron Age*. SWBA 7. Sheffield: Almond Press, 1988.

Frazer, James George. *Taboo and the Perils of the Soul*. Part 2 of *The Golden Bough: A Study in Magic and Religion*. 3rd ed. 12 vols. New York: Macmillan, 1935.

Freedman, David Noel, ed. *The Anchor Bible Dictionary*. 6 vols. New York: Doubleday, 1992.

Frei, Peter. "Persian Imperial Authorization: A Summary." In *Persia and Torah: The Theory of Imperial Authorization of the Pentateuch*, edited by James W. Watts, 5–40. SBLSymS 17. Atlanta: Society of Biblical Literature, 2001.

———. "Zentralgewalt und Lokalautonomie im Achämenidenreich." In Peter Frei and Klaus Koch, *Reichsidee und Reichsorganisation im Perserreich*, 5–131. 2nd ed. OBO 55. Freiburg, Switzerland: Universitätsverlag Freiburg; Göttingen: Vandenhoeck & Ruprecht, 1996.

Freire, Paulo. *Pedagogy of the Oppressed*. Translated by Myra Bergman Ramos. New York: Seabury Press, 1970; Portuguese original, 1968.

Frick, Frank S. *The City in Ancient Israel*. SBLDS 36. Missoula, MT: Scholars Press, 1977.

Fritz, Volkmar. *The City in Ancient Israel*. Sheffield: Sheffield Academic Press, 1995.

Frymer-Kenski, Tikva. "Israel." In *A History of Ancient Near Eastern Law*, edited by Raymond Westbrook, 2:975–1046. Leiden and Boston: E. J. Brill, 2003.

Gagarin, Michael. *Writing Greek Law*. Cambridge: Cambridge University Press, 2008.

Galil, Gershon. *The Lower Stratum Families in the New-Assyrian Period*. CHANE 27. Leiden and Boston: E. J. Brill, 2007.

Garelli, Paul. "Problèmes de stratification sociale dans l'Empire assyrien." In *Gesellschaftsklassen im Alten Zweistromland und in den angrenzenden Gebieten—XVIII: Rencontre assyriologique internationale, München, 29. Juni bis 3. Juli 1970*, edited by D. O. Edzard, 73–79. Munich: Verlag der Bayerischen Akademie der Wissenschaften, 1972.

Gelb, Ignace J., et al., eds. *The Assyrian Dictionary of the Oriental Institute of the University of Chicago*. Chicago: The Oriental Institute; Glückstadt: J. J. Augustin Verlagsbuchhandlung, 1956–

Genovés, Santiago. "Estimation of Age and Mortality." In *Science in Archaeology: A Survey of Progress and Research*, edited by Don Brothwell and Eric Higgs, 440–52. Rev. ed. New York and Washington, DC: Praeger, 1969.

Gerstenberger, Erhard. *Leviticus: A Commentary*. Old Testament Library. Louisville, KY: Westminster John Knox Press, 1996.

———. *Wesen und Herkunft des "apodiktischen Rechts."* WMANT 20. Neukirchen: Neukirchener Verlag, 1965.

Geus, C. H. J. de. *Towns in Ancient Israel and in the Southern Levant*. Palaestina antiqua 10. Leuven: Peeters, 2003.

Giddens, Anthony. *The Constitution of Society: Outline of the Theory of Structuration*. Berkeley and Los Angeles: University of California Press, 1984.

Glass, Zipporah G. "Land, Labor, and Law: Viewing Persian Yehud's Economy through Socio-Economic Modeling." Ph.D. diss., Vanderbilt University, 2010. http://etd.library.vanderbilt.edu/available/etd-07192010-195213/unrestricted/Dissertation_of_Z_Glass_July_19_2010.pdf.

Gluckman, Max. *The Ideas in Barotse Jurisprudence*. New Haven, CT: Yale University Press, 1965.

———. *The Judicial Process among the Barotse of Northern Rhodesia*. Glencoe, IL: Free Press, 1955.

———. *Politics, Law and Ritual in Tribal Society*. Oxford: Basil Blackwell Publishing, 1965.

Gonen, Rivka. "Urban Canaan in the Late Bronze Period." *BASOR* 253 (1984): 61–73.

Gottwald, Norman K. "Early Israel and 'the Asiatic Mode of Production' in Canaan." *SBLSP* 10 (1976): 145–54.

———. "Social Class and Ideology in Isaiah 40–55: An Eagletonian Reading." *Semeia* 59 (1992): 43–57.

———. "Social Class as an Analytic and Hermeneutical Category in Biblical Studies." *JBL* 112 (1993): 3–22.

———. *The Tribes of Yahweh: A Sociology of the Religion of Liberated Israel, 1250–1050 B.C.E.* Maryknoll, NY: Orbis Books, 1979.

Grabbe, Lester L. *Judaism from Cyrus to Hadrian.* Vol. 1, *The Persian and Greek Periods*; Vol. 2, *The Roman Period.* Minneapolis: Fortress Press, 1992.

Graf, Karl Heinrich. *Die geschichtlichen Bücher des Alten Testaments: Zwei historisch-kritische Untersuchungen.* Leipzig: T. O. Weigel, 1866.

———."Die sogenannte Grundschrift des Pentateuchs." *Archiv für wissenschaftliche Erforschung des Alten Testaments* 1 (1869): 466–77.

Green, Timothy Mark. "Class Differentiation and Power(lessness) in Eighth-Century-BCE Israel and Judah." Ph.D. diss., Vanderbilt University, 1997.

Grimm, Jacob, and Wilhelm Grimm. *The Complete Fairy Tales.* With an Introduction by Padraic Colum and a Folkloristic Commentary by Joseph Campbell. London and New York: Routledge, 2002. German original in 1812–1815.

Gulliver, P. H. *Social Control in an African Society: A Study of the Arusha.* Boston: Boston University Press, 1963.

Haase, Richard. "The Hittite Kingdom." In *A History of Ancient Near Eastern Law.* 2 vols., edited by Raymond Westbrook, 2:619–56. Leiden and Boston: E. J. Brill, 2003.

Halbwachs, Maurice. *The Collective Memory.* Translated by Francis J. Ditter Jr. and Vida Yazdi Ditter. New York: Harper & Row, 1980. French original, 1950.

Hallo, William W., ed. *The Context of Scripture.* 3 vols. Leiden and Boston: E. J. Brill, 1997–2002.

Harrelson, Walter. *The Ten Commandments and Human Rights.* Rev. ed. Macon, GA: Mercer University Press, 1997.

Harris, Marvin. "The Abominable Pig." In *Good to Eat: Riddles of Food and Culture*, 67–87. New York: Simon & Schuster, 1985.

Harris, Rivkah. "Old Babylonian Temple Loans." *JCS* 14 (1960): 126–37.

Hart, H. L. A. *The Concept of Law.* 2nd ed. Oxford: Clarendon Press, 1994.

Hawkins, J. D., ed. *Trade in the Ancient Near East: Papers Presented to the XXIII Rencontre assyriologique internationale (University of Birmingham, 5–9 July 1976).* London: British School of Archaeology in Iraq, 1977.

Heger, Paul. *Cult as the Catalyst for Division: Cult Disputes as the Motive for Schism in the Pre-70 Pluralistic Environment.* STDJ 65. Leiden and Boston: E. J. Brill, 2007.

Hendry, Joy. *Understanding Japanese Society.* 2nd ed. London and New York: Routledge, 1995.

Herzog, Ze'ev. "Administrative Structures in the Iron Age." In *The Architecture of Ancient Israel from the Prehistoric to the Persian Periods: In Memory of Immanuel (Munya) Dunayevsky*, edited by Aharon Kempinski and Ronny Reich, 223–30. Jerusalem: Israel Exploration Society, 1992.

———. *Archaeology of the City: Urban Planning in Ancient Israel and Its Social Implications.* Tel Aviv University, Sonia and Marco Nadler Institute of Archaeology Monograph Series 13. Tel Aviv: Emery and Claire Yass Archaeology Press, 1997.

———. "Cities." *ABD* (1992), 1:1031–43.

———. "Settlement and Fortification Planning in the Iron Age." In *The Architecture of Ancient Israel from the Prehistoric to the Persian Periods: In Memory of Immanuel (Munya) Dunayevsky*, edited by Aharon Kempinski and Ronny Reich, 231–74. Jerusalem: Israel Exploration Society, 1992.

Hess, Richard S. *Israelite Religions: An Archaeological and Biblical Survey*. Grand Rapids: Baker Academic, 2007.

Hesse, Brian, and Paula Wapnish. "Can Pig Remains Be Used for Ethnic Diagnosis in the Ancient Near East?" In *The Archaeology of Israel: Constructing the Past, Interpreting the Present*, edited by Neil Asher Silberman and David Small, 238–70. JSOTSup 237. Sheffield: Sheffield Academic Press, 1997.

Hobbes, Thomas. *Leviathan*. London: Andrew Crooke, 1651.

Hoebel, E. Adamson. *The Law of Primitive Man: A Study in Comparative Legal Dynamics*. Cambridge, MA: Harvard University Press, 1954.

Hoffner, Harry A., Jr. "Hittite Laws." In Martha T. Roth, *Law Collections from Mesopotamia and Asia Minor*, edited by Piotr Michalowski, 213–45. 2nd ed. SBLWAW 6. Atlanta: Society of Biblical Literature and Scholars Press, 1997.

Hoglund, Kenneth. "The Achaemenid Context." In *Second Temple Studies*, vol. 1, *The Persian Period*, edited by Philip R. Davies, 54–72. JSOTSup 117. Sheffield: Sheffield Academic Press, 1991.

Holden, Lynn. *Encyclopedia of Taboos*. Oxford, UK; Santa Barbara, CA; and Denver, CO: ABC-CLIO, 2000.

Holladay, John S., Jr. "Religion in Israel and Judah under the Monarchy: An Explicitly Archaeological Approach." In *Ancient Israelite Religion: Essays in Honor of Frank Moore Cross*, edited by Patrick D. Miller Jr., Paul D. Hanson, and S. Dean McBride, 249–99. Philadelphia: Fortress Press, 1987.

Hopkins, David C. *The Highlands of Canaan: Agricultural Life in the Early Iron Age*. SWBA 3. Sheffield: Almond Press, 1985.

————. "The Subsistence Struggles of Early Israel." *BA* 50 (1987): 178–91.

Hopkins, Keith. "Contraception in the Roman Empire." *Comparative Studies in Society and History* 8 (1965): 124–51.

Hunt, Alice. *Missing Priests: The Zadokites in Tradition and History*. LHBOTS 452. New York and London: T&T Clark, 2006.

Jamieson-Drake, David W. *Scribes and Schools in Monarchic Judah: A Socio-Archeological Approach*. JSOTSup 109. Sheffield: Almond Press, 1991.

Jenni, Ernst, ed., with assistance from Claus Westermann. *Theologischer Handwörterbuch zum Alten Testament*. 2 vols. Munich: Chr. Kaiser Verlag; Zurich: Theologischer Verlag, 1971–76. Translated by Mark E. Biddle as *Theological Lexicon of the Old Testament*. 3 vols. Peabody, MA: Hendrickson Publishers, 1997.

Jenson, Philip Peter. *Graded Holiness: A Key to the Priestly Conception of the World*. JSOTSup 106. Sheffield: JSOT Press, 1992.

Jobling, David. "Feminism and 'Mode of Production' in Ancient Israel: Search for a Method." In *The Bible and the Politics of Exegesis: Essays in Honor of Norman K. Gottwald on His Sixty-fifth Birthday*, edited by David Jobling, Peggy L. Day, and Gerald T. Sheppard, 239–51. Cleveland: Pilgrim Press, 1991.

Jütte, Robert. *Lust ohne Last: Geschichte der Empfängnisverhütung von der Antike bis zur Gegenwart*. Munich: Verlag C. H. Beck, 2003.

Kairys, David, ed. *The Politics of Law: A Progressive Critique*. Rev. ed. New York: Pantheon Books, 1990.

Kautsky, John H. *The Politics of Aristocratic Empires*. Chapel Hill: University of North Carolina Press, 1982.

Kemp, Barry J. *Ancient Egypt: Anatomy of a Civilization*. 2nd ed. London and New York: Routledge, 2006.

Kessler, Rainer. *The Social History of Ancient Israel: An Introduction*. Translated by Linda M. Maloney. Minneapolis: Fortress Press, 2008. German original, 2006.

King, L. W., ed. *Babylonian Boundary-Stones and Memorial-Tablets in the British Museum*. 2 vols. London: British Museum, 1912.

King, Philip J., and Lawrence E. Stager. *Life in Biblical Israel*. LAI. Louisville, KY, and London, UK: Westminster John Knox Press, 2001.

Knight, Douglas A. "Cosmogony and Order in the Hebrew Tradition." In *Cosmogony and Ethical Order: New Studies in Comparative Ethics*, edited by Robin W. Lovin and Frank E. Reynolds, 133–57. Chicago and London: University of Chicago Press, 1985.

———. "Deuteronomy and the Deuteronomists." In *Old Testament Interpretation: Past, Present, and Future; Essays in Honor of Gene M. Tucker*, edited by James Luther Mays, David L. Petersen, and Kent Harold Richards, 61–79. Nashville: Abingdon Press, 1995.

———. "Herrens bud—elitens interesser? Lov, makt, og rettferdighet i Det gamle testamente." *NTT* 97 (1996): 235–45.

———. "Jeremiah and the Dimensions of the Moral Life." In *The Divine Helmsman: Studies on God's Control of Human Events; Presented to Lou H. Silberman*, edited by James L. Crenshaw and Samuel Sandmel, 87–105. New York: Ktav, 1980.

———. "Political Rights and Powers in Monarchic Israel." *Semeia* 66 (1994): 93–117.

———. *Rediscovering the Traditions of Israel*. 3rd ed. SBLSBL 16. Atlanta: Society of Biblical Literature; Leiden: E. J. Brill, 2006.

———. "Revelation through Tradition." In *Tradition and Theology in the Old Testament*, edited by Douglas A. Knight, 143–80. Philadelphia: Fortress Press; London: SPCK, 1977.

———. "The Social Basis of Morality and Religion in Ancient Israel." In *Language, Theology, and the Bible: Essays in Honour of James Barr*, edited by Samuel E. Balentine and John Barton, 151–69. Oxford: Clarendon Press, 1994.

———. "Village Law and the Book of the Covenant." In *"A Wise and Discerning Mind": Essays in Honor of Burke O. Long*, edited by Saul M. Olyan and Robert C. Culley, 163–79. BJS 325. Providence, RI: Brown Judaic Studies, 2000.

———. "Whose Agony? Whose Ecstasy? The Politics of Deuteronomic Law." In *Shall Not the Judge of All the Earth Do What Is Right? Studies on the Nature of God in Tribute to James L. Crenshaw*, edited by David Penchansky and Paul L. Redditt, 97–112. Winona Lake, IN: Eisenbrauns, 2000.

Knoppers, Gary N. "Ancient Near Eastern Royal Grants and the Davidic Covenant: A Parallel?" *JAOS* 116 (1996): 670–97.

Korošec, Viktor. "Einige Beiträge zur gesellschaftlichen Struktur nach hethitischen Rechtsquellen." In *Gesellschaftsklassen im Alten Zweistromland und in den angrenzenden Gebieten—XVIII: Rencontre assyriologique internationale, München, 29. Juni bis 3. Juli 1970*, edited by D. O. Edzard, 105–11. Munich: Verlag der Bayerischen Akademie der Wissenschaften, 1972.

Kraus, Fritz Rudolf. *Ein Edikt des Königs Ammi-ṣaduqa von Babylon*. Studia et documenta ad iura orientis antiqui pertinentia 5. Leiden: E. J. Brill, 1958.

————."Ein Edikt des Königs Samsu-Iluna von Babylon." In *Studies in Honor of Benno Landsberger on His Seventy-fifth Birthday, April 21, 1965*, 225–31. AS 16. Chicago: University of Chicago Press, 1965.

————. *Königliche Verfügungen in altbabylonischer Zeit*. Studia et documenta 11. Leiden: E. J. Brill, 1984.

Kuhrt, Amélie. *The Persian Empire*. 2 vols. London and New York: Routledge, 2007.

Lelis, Arnold A., William A. Percy, and Beert C. Verstraete. *The Age of Marriage in Ancient Rome*. Studies in Classics 26. Lewiston, NY; Queenston, ON; and Lampeter, UK: Edwin Mellen Press, 2003.

Lemche, Niels Peter. *Ancient Israel: A New History of Israelite Society*. Translated by Fred Cryer. Biblical Seminar 5. Sheffield: Sheffield Academic Press, 1988. Danish original, 1984.

————. "Justice in Western Asia in Antiquity, or: Why No Laws Were Needed!" *Chicago-Kent Law Review* 70 (1995): 1695–1716.

————. "Kings and Clients: On Loyalty between the Ruler and the Ruled in Ancient 'Israel.'" *Semeia* 66 (1994): 119–32.

————. "On the Use of 'System Theory,' 'Macro Theories,' and 'Evolutionistic Thinking' in Modern OT Research and Biblical Archaeology." *SJOT* 2 (1990): 73–88.

————. *Prelude to Israel's Past: Background and Beginnings of Israelite History and Identity*. Translated by E. F. Maniscalco. Peabody, MA: Hendrickson Publishers, 1998. German original, 1996.

Lenski, Gerhard. *Power and Privilege: A Theory of Social Stratification*. New York: McGraw-Hill, 1966; reprint, Chapel Hill: University of North Carolina Press, 1984.

Leonard, Jerry, ed. *Legal Studies as Cultural Studies: A Reader in (Post)modern Critical Theory*. Albany: State University of New York Press, 1995.

Lerner, Gerda. *The Creation of Patriarchy*. New York and Oxford: Oxford University Press, 1986.

Levine, Baruch A. "*mulūgu/melûg*: The Origins of a Talmudic Legal Institution." *JAOS* 88 (1968): 271–85.

Levinson, Bernard M. *Deuteronomy and the Hermeneutics of Legal Innovation*. New York and Oxford: Oxford University Press, 1997.

————. *Legal Revision and Religious Renewal in Ancient Israel*. Cambridge: Cambridge University Press, 2008.

Levy, Thomas E., ed. *The Archaeology of Society in the Holy Land*. New York: Facts on File, 1995.

Lion, Brigitte. "Les porcs à Nuzi." In *General Studies and Excavations at Nuzi 11/2: In Honor of David I. Owen on the Occasion of His 65th Birthday, October 28, 2005*, edited by Gernot Wilhelm, 259–86. Studies on the Civilization and Culture of Nuzi and the Hurrians 18. Bethesda, MD: CDL Press, 2009.

Lion, Brigitte, and Cécile Michel, ed. *De la domestication au tabou: Le cas des suidés dans le Proche-Orient ancien*. Paris: De Boccard, 2006.

Lipiński, Edward, ed. *State and Temple Economy in the Ancient Near East*. 2 vols. OLA 5–6. Leuven: Departement Oriëntalistiek, 1979.

Lipschits, Oded. "Demographic Changes in Judah between the Seventh and the Fifth Centuries B.C.E." In *Judah and the Judeans in the Neo-Babylonian Period*, edited by Oded Lipschits and Joseph Blenkinsopp, 323–76. Winona Lake, IN: Eisenbrauns, 2003.

———. *The Fall and Rise of Jerusalem: Judah under Babylonian Rule.* Winona Lake, IN: Eisenbrauns, 2005.

Lipschits, Oded, and Manfred Oeming, eds. *Judah and the Judeans in the Persian Period.* Winona Lake, IN: Eisenbrauns, 2006.

Llewellyn, K. N., and E. Adamson Hoebel. *The Cheyenne Way: Conflict and Case Law in Primitive Jurisprudence.* Norman: University of Oklahoma Press, 1941.

Long, Burke O. "Recent Field Studies in Oral Literature and the Question of *Sitz im Leben.*" *Semeia* 5 (1976): 35–49.

———. "Recent Field Studies in Oral Literature and Their Bearing on OT Criticism." *VT* 26 (1976): 187–98.

Lord, Albert B. *The Singer of Tales.* Harvard Studies in Comparative Literature 24. Cambridge, MA: Harvard University Press, 1960; 2nd ed. with CD, edited by Stephen Mitchell and Gregory Nagy, 2000.

Lovin, Robin W., and Frank E. Reynolds, eds. *Cosmogony and Ethical Order: New Studies in Comparative Ethics.* Chicago and London: University of Chicago Press, 1985.

Lundquist, John M. "What Is a Temple? A Preliminary Typology." In *The Quest for the Kingdom of God: Studies in Honor of George E. Mendenhall,* edited by H. B. Huffmon, F. A. Spina, and A. R. W. Green, 205–20. Winona Lake, IN: Eisenbrauns, 1983.

Maalouf, Amin. *In the Name of Identity: Violence and the Need to Belong.* Translated by Barbara Bray. New York: Penguin, 2003.

Maine, Henry Sumner. *Ancient Law: Its Connection with the Early History of Society and Its Relation to Modern Ideas.* 1861. Reprinted with foreword by Lawrence Rosen. Tucson: University of Arizona Press, 1986.

Malinowski, Bronislaw. *Crime and Custom in Savage Society.* New York: Humanities Press; London: Routledge & Kegan Paul, 1926.

Matthews, Victor H., and Don C. Benjamin. *Social World of Ancient Israel, 1250–587 BCE.* Peabody, MA: Hendrickson Publishers, 1993.

McNutt, Paula M. *Reconstructing the Society of Ancient Israel.* LAI. Louisville, KY: Westminster John Knox; London: SPCK, 1999.

Mendelsohn, Isaac. *Slavery in the Ancient Near East: A Comparative Study of Slavery in Babylonia, Assyria, Syria, and Palestine from the Middle of the Third Millennium to the End of the First Millennium.* New York: Oxford University Press, 1949.

Meyers, Carol. *Discovering Eve: Ancient Israelite Women in Context.* New York and Oxford: Oxford University Press, 1988.

Meyers, Eric M., James F. Strange, and Carol L. Meyers. *Excavations at Ancient Meiron, Upper Galilee, Israel, 1971–72, 1974–75, 1977.* Cambridge, MA: American Schools of Oriental Research, 1981.

Milgrom, Jacob. *Leviticus 1–16: A New Translation with Introduction and Commentary.* AB 3. New York: Doubleday, 1991.

———. *Leviticus, a Book of Ritual and Ethics: A Continental Commentary.* Minneapolis: Fortress Press, 2004.

Miller, Patrick D. *The Religion of Ancient Israel.* LAI. Louisville, KY: Westminster John Knox; London: SPCK, 2000.

Moran, William L. "The Ancient Near Eastern Background of the Love of God in Deuteronomy." *CBQ* 25 (1963): 77–87.

———. "The Scandal of the 'Great Sin' at Ugarit." *JNES* 18 (1959): 280–81.

Mowinckel, Sigmund. "'Moder jord' i Det gamle testamentet." In *Religionshistoriska studier tillägnade Edvard Lehmann den 19 augusti 1927,* 131–41. Lund: C. W. K. Gleerup, 1927.

Na'aman, Nadav. "When and How Did Jerusalem Become a Great City? The Rise of Jerusalem as Judah's Premier City in the Eighth–Seventh Centuries B.C.E." *BASOR* 347 (2007): 21–56.

Nader, Laura, and Harry F. Todd, Jr., eds. *The Disputing Process: Law in Ten Societies.* New York: Columbia University Press, 1978.

Nakhai, Beth Alpert. *Archaeology and the Religions of Canaan and Israel.* ASOR Books 7. Boston: American Schools of Oriental Research, 2001.

Nemet-Nejat, Karen Rhea. *Daily Life in Ancient Mesopotamia.* Westport, CT, and London, UK: Greenwood Press, 1998.

Neusner, Jacob. *The Mishnah: A New Translation.* New Haven, CT: Yale University Press, 1988.

Newman, Katherine S. *Law and Economic Organization: A Comparative Study of Preindustrial Societies.* Cambridge and New York: Cambridge University Press, 1983.

Niditch, Susan. *Oral World and Written Word: Ancient Israelite Literature.* LAI. Louisville, KY: Westminster John Knox Press, 1996; London: SPCK, 1997.

Nieuwenhuijze, C. A. O. van. "The Near Eastern Village: A Profile." *The Middle East Journal* 16 (1961): 295–308.

Noth, Martin. *Das System der zwölf Stamme Israels.* BWANT 4/1. Stuttgart: W. Kohlhammer, 1930. 2nd ed., Darmstadt: Wissenschaftliche Buchgesellschaft, 1966.

———. *Überlieferungsgeschichte des Pentateuch.* Stuttgart: W. Kohlhammer, 1948. 3rd ed., 1966. Translated by Bernhard W. Anderson as *A History of Pentateuchal Traditions.* Englewood Cliffs, NJ: Prentice-Hall, 1972.

Oelsner, Joachim, Bruce Wells, and Cornelia Wunsch. "Neo-Babylonian Period." In *A History of Ancient Near Eastern Law,* 2 vols., edited by Raymond Westbrook, 2:911–74. Leiden and Boston: E. J. Brill, 2003.

Olmstead, A. T. *History of the Persian Empire.* Chicago: University of Chicago Press, 1948.

Olyan, Saul M. "'And with a Male You Shall Not Lie the Lying Down of a Woman': On the Meaning and Significance of Leviticus 18:22 and 20:13." *Journal of the History of Sexuality* 5 (1994): 179–206.

———. *Rites and Rank: Hierarchy in Biblical Representations of Cult.* Princeton, NJ: Princeton University Press, 2000.

———. "What Do We Really Know about Women's Rites in the Israelite Family Context?" *Journal of Ancient Near Eastern Religions* 10 (2010): 55-67.

Otto, Eckart. "Exkarnation ins Recht und Kanonsbildung in der Hebräischen Bibel." *ZABR* 5 (1999): 99–110.

———. *Körperverletzungen in den Keilschriftrechten und im Alten Testament:*

Studien zum Rechtstransfer im Alten Testament. AOAT 226. Kevelaer: Verlag Butzon & Bercker; Neukirchen-Vluyn: Neukirchener Verlag, 1991.

Otto, Rudolf. *The Idea of the Holy.* Translated by John W. Harvey. London: Oxford University Press, 1923. German original, 1917.

Ottosson, Magnus. *Temples and Cult Places in Palestine.* Acta universitatis upsaliensis: Boreas 12. Uppsala: Almqvist & Wiksell, 1980.

Pareto, Vilfredo. *The Mind and Society.* Vol. 4, *The General Form of Society.* Translated by Andrew Bongiorno and Arthur Livingston, with the advice of James Harvey Rogers. New York: Harcourt, Brace & Co., 1935. Original, *Trattato di sociologia generale,* 1916.

Parkin, Robert. *Kinship: An Introduction to Basic Concepts.* Oxford: Basil Blackwell Publishing, 1997.

Petersen, William. "A Demographer's View of Prehistoric Demography." *Current Anthropology* 16, no. 2 (1975): 227–45.

Plato. *Laws.* In *Plato: Laws, Books 1–6.* Translated by R. G. Bury. LCL 187. Cambridge, MA, and London, UK: Harvard University Press, 1926 and 2001.

Polaski, Donald C. "What Mean These Stones? Inscriptions, Textuality, and Power in Persia and Yehud." In *Approaching Yehud: New Approaches to the Study of the Persian Period,* edited by Jon L. Berquist, 37–48. SemeiaSt 50. Atlanta: Society of Biblical Literature, 2007.

Porten, Bezalel. *The Elephantine Papyri in English: Three Millennia of Cross-Cultural Continuity and Change.* Leiden and New York: E. J. Brill, 1996.

Porten, Bezalel, and Ada Yardeni. *Textbook of Aramaic Documents from Ancient Egypt, Newly Copied, Edited, and Translated into Hebrew and English.* 4 vols. Jerusalem: Academon Press, 1986–99.

Pospíšil, Leopold. *Anthropology of Law: A Comparative Theory.* New York: Harper & Row, 1971.

———. *The Ethnology of Law.* Addison-Wesley Module in Anthropology 12. Reading, MA: Addison-Wesley, 1972.

Postgate, J. N. [John Nicholas.] *Early Mesopotamia: Society and Economy at the Dawn of History.* London and New York: Routledge, 1992.

———. *Neo-Assyrian Royal Grants and Decrees.* Studia Pohl, Series Maior 1. Rome: Pontifical Biblical Institute, 1969.

———. "The Role of the Temple in the Mesopotamian Secular Community." In *Man, Settlement, and Urbanism,* edited by Peter J. Ucko, Ruth Tringham, and G. W. Dimbleby, 811–25. Cambridge, MA: Schenkman, 1972.

Potts, Daniel T. *Mesopotamian Civilization: The Material Foundations.* London: Athlone Press, 1997.

Pritchard, James B., ed. *Ancient Near Eastern Texts Relating to the Old Testament.* 3rd ed. Princeton, NJ: Princeton University Press, 1969.

Rabinowitz, Jacob J. "The 'Great Sin' in Ancient Egyptian Marriage Contracts." *JNES* 18 (1959): 73.

Reasons, Charles E., and Robert M. Rich. *The Sociology of Law: A Conflict Perspective.* Toronto: Butterworths, 1978.

Redding, Richard W. "The Role of the Pig in the Subsistence System of Ancient Egypt: A Parable on the Potential of Faunal Data." In *Animal Use and Culture*

Change, edited by Pam J. Crabtree and Kathleen Ryan, 20–30. MASCA Research Papers in Science and Archaeology. Supplement to vol. 8. Philadelphia: University of Pennsylvania Press, 1991.

Redford, Donald B. "The So-Called 'Codification' of Egyptian Law under Darius I." In *Persia and Torah: The Theory of Imperial Authorization of the Pentateuch*, edited by James W. Watts, 135–59. SBLSymS 17. Atlanta: Society of Biblical Literature, 2001.

Reiner, Erica. *Astral Magic in Babylonia*. Transactions of the American Philosophical Society 85/4. Philadelphia: American Philosophical Society, 1995.

Rendsburg, Gary A. "No Stelae, No Queens: Two Issues concerning the Kings of Israel and Judah." In *The Archaeology of Difference: Gender, Ethnicity, Class, and the "Other" in Antiquity: Studies in Honor of Eric M. Meyers*, edited by Douglas R. Edwards and C. Thomas McCollough, 95–107. AASOR 60–61. Boston: American Schools of Oriental Research, 2007.

Richards, Janet, and Mary Van Buren, eds. *Order, Legitimacy, and Wealth in Ancient States*. Cambridge: Cambridge University Press, 2000.

Riddle, John M. *Contraception and Abortion from the Ancient World to the Renaissance*. Cambridge, MA, and London, UK: Harvard University Press, 1992.

Robertson, John F. "The Social and Economic Organization of Ancient Mesopotamian Temples." *CANE* 1:443–54.

Rölleke, Heinz. "New Results of Research on *Grimms' Fairy Tales*." In *The Brothers Grimm and Folktale*, edited by James M. McGlathery, 101–111. Urbana and Chicago: University of Illinois Press, 1988.

Rollston, Christopher A. "Scribal Education in Ancient Israel: The Old Hebrew Epigraphic Evidence." *BASOR* 344 (2006): 47–74.

Rooke, Deborah W. *Zadok's Heirs: The Role and Development of the High Priesthood in Ancient Israel*. Oxford and New York: Oxford University Press, 2000.

Roth, Martha T. *Babylonian Marriage Agreements, 7th–3rd Centuries B.C.* AOAT 222. Kevelaer: Butzon & Bercker; Neukirchen-Vluyn: Neukirchener Verlag, 1989.

———. "Marriage, Divorce, and the Prostitute in Ancient Mesopotamia." In *Prostitutes and Courtesans in the Ancient World*, edited by Christopher A. Faraone and Laura K. McClure, 21–39. Madison: University of Wisconsin Press, 2006.

———. "'She Will Die by the Iron Dagger': Adultery and Neo-Babylonian Marriage." *JESHO* 31 (1988): 186–206.

Roth, Martha T., with a contribution by Harry A. Hoffner Jr. *Law Collections from Mesopotamia and Asia Minor*. Edited by Piotr Michalowski. 2nd ed. SBLWAW 6. Atlanta: Society of Biblical Literature and Scholars Press, 1997.

Salmon, Pierre. *La limitation des naissances dans la société romaine*. Collection Latomus 250. Brussels: Latomus Revue d'études latines, 1999.

Sanders, James A. *Torah and Canon*. Philadelphia: Fortress Press, 1972.

Sasson, Jack M. "Comparative Observations on the Near Eastern Epic Traditions." In *A Companion to Ancient Epic*, edited by John Miles Foley, 215–32. Oxford: Basil Blackwell Publishing, 2005.

———. *Jonah: A New Translation with Introduction, Commentary, and Interpretation*. AB 24B. New York: Doubleday, 1992.

———. "The Servant's Tale: How Rebekah Found a Spouse." *JNES* 65 (2006): 241–65.

Sasson, Jack M., ed. *Civilizations of the Ancient Near East.* 4 vols. New York: Charles Scribner's Sons, 1995.

Sauer, James A. "Transjordan in the Bronze and Iron Ages: A Critique of Glueck's Synthesis." *BASOR* 263 (1986): 1–26.

Schapera, Isaac. "The Sin of Cain." *Journal of the Royal Anthropological Institute* 85 (1955): 33–43. Reprinted in *Anthropological Approaches to the Old Testament,* edited by Bernhard Lang, 26–42. IRT 8. Philadelphia: Fortress Press; London: SPCK, 1985.

Scherf, Walter. "Jacob and Wilhelm Grimm: A Few Small Corrections to a Commonly Held Image." In *The Brothers Grimm and Folktale,* edited by James M. McGlathery, 178–91. Urbana and Chicago: University of Illinois Press, 1988.

Schloen, J. David. *The House of the Father as Fact and Symbol: Patrimonialism in Ugarit and the Ancient Near East.* Studies in the Archaeology and the History of the Levant 2. Winona Lake, IN: Eisenbrauns, 2001.

Schmid, Hans Heinrich. *Gerechtigkeit als Weltordnung: Hintergrund und Geschichte des alttestamentlichen Gerechtigkeitsbegriffes.* BHT 40. Tübingen: Mohr [Siebeck], 1968.

Schorr, Moses. *Urkunden des altbabylonischen Zivil- und Prozessrechts.* Vorderasiatische Bibliothek. Leipzig: J. C. Hinrichs, 1913.

Schwartz, Glenn M., and Steven E. Falconer, eds. *Archaeological Views from the Countryside: Village Communities in Early Complex Societies.* Washington and London: Smithsonian Institution Press, 1994.

Segovia, Fernando F., and Mary Ann Tolbert, eds. *Reading from This Place.* Vol. 1, *Social Location and Biblical Interpretation in the United States.* Minneapolis: Fortress Press, 1995.

Segovia, Fernando F., and Mary Ann Tolbert, eds. *Reading from This Place.* Vol. 2, *Social Location and Biblical Interpretation in Global Perspective.* Minneapolis: Fortress Press, 1995.

Seidl, Ursula. *Die babylonischen Kudurru-Reliefs: Symbole mesopotamischer Gottheiten.* OBO 87. Freiburg, Switzerland: Universitätsverlag; Göttingen: Vandenhoeck & Ruprecht, 1989.

———. "Kudurru." *RLA* 6 (1980–83): 267–77.

Shiloh, Yigal. "The Population of Iron Age Palestine in the Light of a Sample Analysis of Urban Plans, Areas, and Population Density." *BASOR* 239 (1980): 25–35.

Slanski, Kathryn E. *The Babylonian Entitlement narûs (kudurrus): A Study in Their Form and Function.* ASOR Books 9. Boston: American Schools of Oriental Research, 2003.

Smend, Rudolf. "Das Nein des Amos." *EvT* 23 (1963): 404–23.

Smith, Morton. *Palestinian Parties and Politics That Shaped the Old Testament.* New York: Columbia University Press, 1971.

Sneed, Mark R., ed. *Concepts of Class in Ancient Israel.* South Florida Studies in the History of Judaism 201. Atlanta: Scholars Press, 1999.

Snell, Daniel C. *Life in the Ancient Near East, 3100–332 B.C.E.* New Haven and London: Yale University Press, 1997.

———. "Methods of Exchange and Coinage in Ancient Western Asia." *CANE* 3:1487–97.

Solvang, Elna K. *A Woman's Place Is in the House: Royal Women of Judah and*

Their Involvement in the House of David. JSOTSup 349. London and New York: Sheffield Academic Press, 2003.

Spiegelberg, Wilhelm. *Die sogenannte demotische Chronik des Pap. 215 der Bibliothèque nationale zu Paris, nebst den auf der Rückseite des Papyrus stehenden Texten*. Leipzig: J. C. Hinrichs, 1914.

Stacy, Helen M. *Postmodernism and the Law: Jurisprudence in a Fragmenting World*. Aldershot: Ashgate/Dartmouth, 2001.

Stager, Lawrence E. "The Archaeology of the Family in Ancient Israel." *BASOR* 260 (1985): 1–35.

Steinmetzer, Franz X. *Die babylonischen Kudurru (Grenzsteine) als Urkundenform*. Studien zur Geschichte und Kultur des Altertums 11/4–5. Paderborn: Ferdinand Schöningh, 1922.

Stern, Ephraim. *Archaeology of the Land of the Bible*. Vol. 2, *The Assyrian, Babylonian, and Persian Periods (732–332 BCE)*. New York: Doubleday, 2001.

Stiebert, Johanna. *The Construction of Shame in the Hebrew Bible: The Prophetic Contribution*. JSOTSup 346. London and New York: Sheffield Academic Press, 2002.

Stol, Marten. *Birth in Babylonia and the Bible: Its Mediterranean Setting*. Cuneiform Monographs 14. Groningen: Styx, 2000.

Stol, Marten, and Sven P. Vleeming, eds. *The Care of the Elderly in the Ancient Near East*. SHCANE 14. Leiden: E. J. Brill, 1998.

Stone, Elizabeth. "City-States and Their Centers: The Mesopotamian Example." In *The Archaeology of City-States: Cross-Cultural Approaches*, edited by Deborah L. Nichols and Thomas H. Charlton, 15–26. Smithsonian Series in Archaeological Inquiry. Washington and London: Smithsonian Institution Press, 1997.

———. "The Development of Cities in Ancient Mesopotamia." *CANE* 1:235-48.

Stone, Elizabeth C., and David I. Owen. *Adoption in Old Babylonian Nippur and the Archive of Mannum-mesu-lissur*. Mesopotamian Civilizations 3. Winona Lake, IN: Eisenbrauns, 1991.

Stordalen, Terje. "Moder jord—etisk impuls i Det gamle testament." In *Makt, eiendom, rettferdighet: Bibelske moraltradisjoner i møte med vår tid*, edited by Jan-Olav Henriksen, 115–38. Oslo: Gyldendal akademisk, 2000.

Timasheff, N. S. *An Introduction to the Sociology of Law*. Harvard Sociological Studies 3. Cambridge, MA: Harvard University Committee on Research in the Social Sciences, 1939.

Toorn, Karel van der. *Family Religion in Babylonia, Syria, and Israel: Continuity and Change in the Forms of Religious Life*. SHCANE 7. Leiden: E. J. Brill, 1996.

———. *Scribal Culture and the Making of the Hebrew Bible*. Cambridge, MA, and London, UK: Harvard University Press, 2007.

———. *Sin and Sanction in Israel and Mesopotamia: A Comparative Study*. Assen: Van Gorcum, 1985.

Trigger, Bruce G. "The Evolution of Pre-Industrial Cities: A Multilinear Perspective." In *Mélanges offerts à Jean Vercoutter*, edited by Francis Geus and Florence Thill, 343–53. Paris: Éditions recherche sur les civilisations, 1985.

———. *Understanding Early Civilizations: A Comparative Study*. Cambridge and New York: Cambridge University Press, 2003.

Unger, Roberto Mangabeira. *The Critical Legal Studies Movement*. Cambridge, MA, and London, UK: Harvard University Press, 1986.

————. *Knowledge and Politics*. New York: Free Press, 1975.

Ussishkin, David. "Solomon's Jerusalem: The Text and the Facts on the Ground." In *Jerusalem in Bible and Archaeology: The First Temple Period*, edited by Andrew G. Vaughn and Ann E. Killebrew, 103–15. SBLSymS 18. Atlanta: Society of Biblical Literature, 2003.

————. "Was the 'Solomonic' City Gate at Megiddo Built by King Solomon?" *BASOR* 239 (1980): 1–18.

Van De Mieroop, Marc. *The Ancient Mesopotamian City*. Oxford: Clarendon Press; New York: Oxford University Press, 1997.

————. *A History of the Ancient Near East, ca. 3000–323 BC*. 2nd ed. Malden, MA, and Oxford, UK: Basil Blackwell Publishing, 2007.

————. *Society and Enterprise in Old Babylonian Ur*. Berliner Beiträge zum Vorderen Orient 12. Berlin: Dietrich Reimer Verlag, 1992.

Voigtlander, Elizabeth N., trans. *The Bisitun Inscription of Darius the Great: Babylonian Version*. Corpus inscriptionum iranicarum, Part I, Inscriptions of Ancient Iran. Vol. 2, The Babylonian Versions of the Achaemenian Inscriptions, Texts 1. London: Lund Humphries, 1978.

Wapnish, Paula, and Brian Hesse, "Mammal Remains from the Early Bronze Sacred Compound." In *Megiddo III: The 1992–1996 Seasons*, edited by Israel Finkelstein, David Ussishkin, and Baruch Halpern, 2:429–62. Tel Aviv: Institute of Archaeology, Tel Aviv University, 2000.

Wason, Paul K. *The Archaeology of Rank*. Cambridge: Cambridge University Press, 1994.

Weber, Max. *Ancient Judaism*. Translated and edited by Hans H. Gerth and Don Martindale. New York: Free Press, 1952. German original, 1917–19.

————. *The Religion of India: The Sociology of Hinduism and Buddhism*. Glencoe, IL: Free Press, 1958.

————. *The Theory of Social and Economic Organization*. Translated by A. M. Henderson and Talcott Parsons. Edited by Talcott Parsons. New York: Oxford University Press, 1947. German original, 1920.

Weinberg, Joel. *The Citizen-Temple Community*. Translated by Daniel L. Smith-Christopher. JSOTSup 151. Sheffield: JSOT Press, 1992.

Weinfeld, Moshe. "The Covenant of Grant in the Old Testament and in the Ancient Near East." *JAOS* 90 (1970): 184–203.

————. "Sabbatical Year and Jubilee in the Pentateuchal Laws and Their Ancient Near Eastern Background." In *The Law in the Bible and in Its Environment*, edited by Timo Veijola, 39–62. Publications of the Finnish Exegetical Society 51. Helsinki: Finnish Exegetical Society; Göttingen: Vandenhoeck & Ruprecht, 1990.

Weippert, Helga. *Palästina in vorhellenistischer Zeit*. Munich: Verlag C. H. Beck, 1988.

Wellhausen, Julius. *Prolegomena to the History of Israel*. Reprinted with introduction by Douglas A. Knight. SPRTS. Atlanta: Scholars Press, 1994. Originally published as *Prolegomena zur Geschichte Israels*, 2nd ed. of *Geschichte Israels*, vol. 1 (1878). Berlin: G. Reimer, 1883.

Westbrook, Raymond. "The Character of Ancient Near Eastern Law." In *A History of Ancient Near Eastern Law*, 2 vols., edited by Raymond Westbrook, 1:1–90. Leiden and Boston: E. J. Brill, 2003.

———. "Lex talionis and Exodus 21,22–25." *RB* 93 (1986): 52–69.

———. *Property and the Family in Biblical Law*. JSOTSup 113. Sheffield: Sheffield Academic Press, 1991.

———, ed. *A History of Ancient Near Eastern Law*. 2 vols. Leiden and Boston: E. J. Brill, 2003.

Westbrook, Raymond, and Richard Jasnow, eds. *Security for Debt in Ancient Near Eastern Law*. CHANE 9. Leiden and Boston: E. J. Brill, 2001.

Westbrook, Raymond, and Bruce Wells. *Everyday Law in Biblical Israel: An Introduction*. Louisville, KY: Westminster John Knox Press, 2009.

Whitelam, Keith W. *The Just King: Monarchical Judicial Authority in Ancient Israel*. JSOTSup 12. Sheffield: JSOT Press, 1979.

Whitt, William D. "The Story of the Semitic Alphabet." *CANE* 4:2379–97.

Widengren, Geo. *Religionsphänomenologie*. Berlin: de Gruyter, 1969.

Wolff, Edward N. *Recent Trends in Household Wealth in the United States: Rising Debt and the Middle-Class Squeeze—An Update to 2007*. Working Paper No. 589. Annandale-on-Hudson, NY: Levy Economics Institute, Bard College, March 2010. http://www.levyinstitute.org/pubs/wp_589.pdf.

Wright, Benjamin G., III. "Jewish Ritual Baths—Interpreting the Digs and the Texts: Some Issues in the Social History of Second Temple Judaism." In *The Archaeology of Israel: Constructing the Past, Interpreting the Present*, edited by Neil Asher Silberman and David Small, 191–214. JSOTSup 237. Sheffield: Sheffield Academic Press, 1997.

Wright, David P. *The Disposal of Impurity: Elimination Rites in the Bible and in Hittite and Mesopotamian Literature*. SBLDS 101. Atlanta: Scholars Press, 1987.

Wunsch, Cornelia. *Urkunden zum Ehe-, Vermögens- und Erbrecht aus verschiedenen neubabylonischen Archiven*. Babylonische Archive 2. Dresden: ISLET, 2003.

Zertal, Adam. *The Manasseh Hill Country Survey*. 2 vols. CHANE 21. Leiden and Boston: E. J. Brill, 2004–8.

Zevit, Ziony. *The Religions of Ancient Israel: A Synthesis of Parallactic Approaches*. London and New York: Continuum, 2001.

Zimmerli, Walther. "Prophetic Proclamation and Reinterpretation." In *Tradition and Theology in the Old Testament*, edited by Douglas A. Knight, 69–100. Philadelphia: Fortress Press; London: SPCK, 1977; reprint, Atlanta: Society of Biblical Literature, 2007.

Zwingenberger, Uta. *Dorfkultur der frühen Eisenzeit in Mittelpalästina*. OBO 180. Freiburg, Switzerland: Universitätsverlag; and Göttingen: Vandenhoeck & Ruprecht, 2001.

Index of Ancient Sources

Index of Authors

Index of Subjects

Aaron, 191
abortion, 134–35, 185–86
Abraham, 131–32, 181, 186, 191, 202, 204–5, 214
Achan, 14, 55
adoption, 101, 194–95, 198, 211
adultery, 48, 135–36, 183n52, 187–90, 214n119, 247, 258
    See also sexual relations
Agade (or Akkad), 178n41, 218
agrarian state, 13, 27, 63–65, 70, 146, 172–73, 221, 231
agriculture, 21–22, 70, 72n23, 121, 125, 127, 129, 149, 155, 162–65, 176, 192, 247, 252
Ahab, 77, 143, 180, 205
Ahaz, 238
Ahmose II *or* Amasis, 106
Ammi-ṣaduqa, 218
Amnon, 191
amphictyony, 40n14, 73–74
amtu, 178
ancient law, 45–49
andurāru, 218–21
animals, 149–52
    See also under liability
apodictic, 24, 33, 91–93
Arad, 228
archaeology, 3–4, 16, 70, 128, 263
Aristotle, 134
Asa, 238
Ashdod, 160
Ashkelon, 160, 254
Asiatic mode of production, 144
Asshur, 170, 174
Assyria
    Middle Assyria, 43, 136, 178, 183, 185, 192–93, 136, 178, 183, 185
    Neo-Assyria, 17, 22, 25, 78, 80, 94, 100, 102, 108, 158, 161–62, 164, 166–70, 179n43, 198–202, 205, 237–39
    Old Assyria, 178n41
Assyrian language, 106
Augustus, 184
authority, 13, 38, 67–69, 73, 92
awīlu (or *awīlum* or *aʾīlu*), 177–78, 195–97

Babylonia
    Neo-Babylonia, 9n3, 27, 78–81, 102–5, 108, 119, 123n14, 161–62, 167, 169–70, 185n50, 187, 188n65, 194, 198–99, 202, 204, 206, 209n104, 212n111, 213n116, 215, 218, 220–21, 226, 229n4, 238–39
    Old Babylonia, 28, 35, 94, 134n30, 151n72, 174, 178nn39, 41; 194, 196, 201n89, 207, 218, 221, 236–39
banishment, 137–39, 143, 241, 249–50
bathing pool (*miqweh*), 255
Beersheba, 80, 125, 164–65
Behistun *or* Besitun, 105, 105n29
bestiality, 139–40, 192–93
    See also under sexual relations
Bethel, 80
Beth-Shean, 160
Bilhah, 213
Bill of Rights, 13–14
Black's Law Dictionary, 13
blasphemy, 23, 247
blood vengeance, 48, 142–43
Boaz, 202, 204
boundary, property, 35–36, 146–47, 205–7
Brando, Marlon, 2n2
bribe. *See* corruption, judicial
bride-price, 132

299